# TAKING SIDES

Clashing Views in

## World Politics

**SIXTEENTH EDITION**

D0451412

# TAKING SIDES

Clashing Views in

## World Politics

**SIXTEENTH EDITION**

Selected, Edited, and with Introductions by

**John T. Rourke**
*University of Connecticut*

TAKING SIDES: CLASHING VIEWS IN WORLD POLITICS,
SIXTEENTH EDITION

Published by McGraw-Hill, a business unit of The McGraw-Hill Companies, Inc., 1221 Avenue
of the Americas, New York, NY 10020. Copyright © 2014 by The McGraw-Hill Companies, Inc.
Printed in the United States of America. All rights reserved. Previous editions © 2013, 2012, and
2011. No part of this publication may be reproduced or distributed in any form or by any means,
or stored in a database or retrieval system, without the prior written consent of The McGraw-Hill
Companies, Inc., including, but not limited to, in any network or other electronic storage or
transmission, or broadcast for distance learning.

Some ancillaries, including electronic and print components, may not be available to customers
outside the United States.

This book is printed on acid-free paper.

Taking Sides® is a registered trademark of The McGraw-Hill Companies, Inc.
Taking Sides is published by the **Contemporary Learning Series** group within the McGraw-Hill
Higher Education division.

1 2 3 4 5 6 7 8 9 0 DOC/DOC 1 0 9 8 7 6 5 4 3

MHID: 0-07-813954-6
ISBN: 978-0-07-813954-3
ISSN: 1094-754X (print)
ISSN: 2158-1452 (online)

Acquisitions Editor: *Joan McNamara*
Marketing Director: *Adam Kloza*
Marketing Manager: *Nathan Edwards*
Senior Developmental Editor: *Jade Benedict*
Project Manager: *Jessica Portz*
Buyer: *Jennifer Pickel*
Cover Designer: *Studio Montage, St. Louis, MO*
Senior Content Licensing Specialist: *Shirley Lanners*
Media Project Manager: *Sridevi Palani*
Printer: RR Donnelley Crawfordsville

Compositor: MPS Limited
Cover Image: © *F1online digitale Bildagentur GmbH/Alamy RF*
Typeface: ITC Stone Serif Std

www.mhhe.com

# Editors/Academic Advisory Board

Members of the Academic Advisory Board are instrumental in the final selection of articles for each edition of TAKING SIDES. Their review of articles for content, level, and appropriateness provides critical direction to the editors and staff. We think that you will find their careful consideration well reflected in this volume.

## TAKING SIDES: Clashing Views in WORLD POLITICS
Sixteenth Edition

## EDITOR

**John T. Rourke**
*University of Connecticut*

## ACADEMIC ADVISORY BOARD MEMBERS

# Preface

In the first edition of *Taking Sides: Clashing Views in World Politics*, I wrote of my belief in informed argument: [A] book that debates vital issues is valuable and necessary. . . . [It is important] to recognize that world politics is usually not a subject of absolute rights and absolute wrongs and of easy policy choices. We all have a responsibility to study the issues thoughtfully, and we should be careful to understand all sides of the debates.

It is gratifying to discover, as indicated by the success of *Taking Sides* over 15 editions, that so many of my colleagues share this belief in the value of a debate-format text.

The format of this edition follows a formula that has proved successful in acquainting students with the global issues that we face and in generating discussion of those issues and the policy choices that address them. This book addresses 17 issues on a wide range of topics in international relations. Each issue has two readings, one pro and one con. Each is also accompanied by an issue introduction, which sets the stage for the debate, provides some background information on each author, and generally puts the issue into its political context. Each issue concludes with a postscript that summarizes the debate, gives the reader paths for further investigation, and suggests additional readings that might be helpful. I have also provided relevant Internet site addresses (URLs) in each postscript and on the Internet References page that accompanies each part opener. At the back of the book is a listing of all the contributors to this volume, which will give you information on the political scientists and other commentators whose views are debated here.

I have continued to emphasize issues that are currently being debated in the policy sphere. The authors of the selections are a mix of practitioners, scholars, and noted political commentators.

## Changes to This Edition

The dynamic, constantly changing nature of the world political system and the many helpful comments from reviewers have brought about significant changes to this edition. More than 70 percent of the issues are new or contain one or more new readings since the fifteenth edition. They are: Is the European Union's Eurozone in Serious Danger of Collapsing? (Issue 1), Should Russia Be Considered a Hostile Country? (Issue 2); Is China Becoming a Dangerous Superpower? (Issue 3); Are the Palestinians Blocking the Path to Peace in the Middle East? (Issue 4); Should Force Be Used if Necessary to Prevent Iran from Acquiring Nuclear Weapons? (Issue 5); Does the Islamist Movement Threaten the Democracy Gained in the "Arab Spring"? (Issue 7); Does China's Currency Manipulation Warrant International and National Action?

(Issue 9); Should U.S. Forces Continue to Fight in Afghanistan? (Issue 11); Is the Use and Threat of Force Necessary in International Relations? (Issue 13); Is the UN a Worthwhile Organization? (Issue 14); Should the United States Ratify the Convention to Eliminate All Forms of Discrimination Against Women? (Issue 16); and Are International Negotiations to Control Global Warming Useful? (Issue 17).

It is important to note that the changes to this edition from the last should not disguise the fact that most of the issues address enduring human concerns, such as global political organization, arms and arms control, justice, development, and the environment. Also important is the fact that many of the issues have both a specific and a larger topic. For instance, Issue 15 is about the specific topic of the performance of United Nations peacekeeping, but it is also about more general topics. These include the proper role of international organizations in the global system and the degree to which countries should subordinate their sovereignty to them.

## A Word to the Instructor

An *Instructor's Resource Guide with Test Questions* (multiple-choice and essay) is available through the publisher for instructors using Taking Sides in the classroom. A general guidebook, *Using Taking Sides in the Classroom*, which discusses methods and techniques for integrating the pro–con approach into any classroom setting, is also available. An online version of *Using Taking Sides in the Classroom* and a correspondence service for Taking Sides adopters can be found at www.mhhe.com/cls. *Taking Sides: Clashing Views in World Politics* is only one title in the Taking Sides series. If you are interested in seeing the table of contents for any of the other titles, please visit the Taking Sides website at www.mhhe.com/cls.

## A Note Especially for the Student Reader

You will find that the debates in this book are not one-sided. Each author strongly believes in his or her position. And if you read the debates without prejudging them, you will see that each author makes cogent points. An author may not be "right," but the arguments made in an essay should not be dismissed out of hand, and you should work to remain tolerant of those who hold beliefs that are different from your own. There is an additional consideration to keep in mind as you pursue this debate approach to world politics. To consider divergent views objectively does not mean that you have to remain forever neutral. In fact, once you are informed, you ought to form convictions. More important, you should try to influence international policy to conform better with your beliefs. Write letters to policymakers; donate to causes you support; work for candidates who agree with your views; join an activist organization. Do something, whichever side of an issue you are on!

# Acknowledgments

I received many helpful comments and suggestions from colleagues and readers across the United States and Canada. Their suggestions have markedly enhanced the quality of this edition of *Taking Sides*. If as you read this book you are reminded of a selection or an issue that could be included in a future edition, please write to me in care of McGraw-Hill/Contemporary Learning Series with your recommendations or e-mail them to me at john.rourke@uconn.edu.

**John T. Rourke**
*University of Connecticut*

*For my son and friend—John Michael*

# The Educational Experience of Disciplinary Controversy*

BRENT D. SLIFE
*Brigham Young University*

As a long-time user of the Taking Sides books, I have seen first-hand their educational impact on students. A student we will call "Brittany" is a prime example. Until her role in a Taking Sides panel discussion, she had not participated once in class discussions. It is probably fair to say that she was sleepwalking through the course. However, once she was assigned to a "side" of the panel discussion, she vigorously pitched in "to do battle," as she put it, with the opposing team. She described a "kind of energy" as she and the rest of her team prepared for the upcoming debate. In fact, she found herself and her teammates "talking trash" good-naturedly with the opposing team before the actual discussion, despite her usual reserve. Because she wanted to win, she "drilled down" and even did extra research.

The panel discussion itself, she reported, was exhilarating, but what I noticed afterward was probably the most intriguing. Not only did she participate in class more frequently, taking more risks in class discussions because she knew her teammates would support her, she also found herself having a position from which to see other positions in the discipline. Somehow, as she explained, her advocating a particular position on the panel, even though she knew I had arbitrarily assigned it, gave her a stake in other discussions and a perspective from which to contribute to them. Brittany's experience nicely illustrates the unique educational impact of the Taking Sides series.

Taking Sides is designed quite intentionally to shore up some of the weaknesses of many contemporary educational settings. The unique energy that Brittany experienced is a result of Taking Sides specific focus on the controversial side of academic disciplines. For several good reasons instructors and textbooks have traditionally focused almost exclusively on the more factual or settled aspects of their disciplines. This focus has led, in turn, to educational strategies that can rob the subject matter of its vitality.

Taking Sides, on the other hand, is uniquely structured to highlight the more issue-oriented aspects of a discipline, allowing students to care about and even invest in the subject matter as did Brittany. Involvement can spur a deeper understanding of the topic and help students to appreciate how knowledge advancement is sometimes driven by passionate positions.

*The full text of this essay and references are available online at: http://highered.mcgraw-hill .com/sites/0076667771/information_center_view0/

# Including the Controversial

A case could be made that a complete understanding of any discipline includes its controversies. Controversies may not be considered "knowledge" per se, depending on the discipline, but there is surely no doubt that they are part of the process of advancing knowledge. The conflicts generated among disciplinary leaders often produce problem-solving energy, if not disciplinary passions. In fact, they can drive entire disciplinary conferences and whole programs of investigation. In this sense, disciplinary controversies are not just "error" or an indication of the absence of knowledge; they can be viewed as a positive part of the discipline, a generator of disciplinary vigor if not purpose.

If this is true, then de-emphasizing the controversial elements of a discipline is de-emphasizing a vital part of the discipline itself. Students may learn accepted aspects of the discipline, but they may not learn, at least directly, the disputed aspects. This de-emphasis may not only produce an incomplete or inaccurate sense of the discipline, but it may also mislead the student to understand the field as more sterile, less emotional, and less "messy" than it truly is. The more rational, factual side is clearly important, perhaps even the more important. The question, however, is: do these more settled and perhaps rational aspects of the discipline have to monopolize courses for beginning students?

Another way to put the question might be: couldn't some portion of the course be devoted to the more controversial, thus allowing the student to engage the field in a more emotional manner? In some sense, the more settled and accepted the information is, the less students can feel they are truly participating in the disciplinary enterprise. After all, this information is already decided; there is no room for involvement in developing and "owning" the information. Students may even assume they will be punished for challenging the disciplinary status quo.

# Specific Educational Benefits

*Engaging the Discipline.* When controversy is placed in the foreground of an educational experience, it gives disciplinary novices (students) permission to participate in and perhaps even form their own positions on some of the issues in the field. After all, some issues have not been addressed; some problems have not been solved. As Brittany put it, she was ready to "do battle" with the alternative position, even though she was quite aware of the arbitrariness of her own positional assignment. She was aware that something was at stake; something was to be decided.

In other words, it is the very *lack* of resolution in a controversy that invites students to make sense of the issues themselves and perhaps even venture their own thoughts. Obviously, students should be encouraged to be humble about these positions, understanding that their perspective is fledgling, but even novice positions can facilitate greater engagement with the materials. In a sense, the controversy, and thus a vital part of the discipline, becomes their own, as the example of Brittany illustrates. She not only "owned" a disciplinary position, she used it as a conceptual bridge to engage other settled and unsettled aspects of the discipline.

*Appreciating the Messy.* Students can also experience the messiness of disciplines using Taking Sides. I use the term "messiness" because conventional texts are notorious for representing the field too neatly and too logically, as if there were no human involvement. If disciplines are more than their settled aspects, there are also unsettled elements, including poorly defined terms and inadequately understood concepts, which also need to be appreciated. This messiness is what led Brittany to "drill down" and do "extra research" in her preparation for her panel discussion. She knew that some of the basic terms and understandings were at play.

Good conventional texts may attempt to include these unsettled aspects, but they typically do so in a deceptively logical fashion, as though the controversy is solely rational. This presentation may not only distort these aspects of the discipline but also deliver merely a secondhand report. By contrast, Taking Sides books—in pitting two authors against one another—facilitate an *experience* with actual published authorities, who are struggling with the issues from completely different perspectives. In reading both articles, students cannot help but struggle *with* the authors. They do not need to be *told* that the terms of the debate are problematic; the students *experience* these terms as problematic when they attempt to understand what is at stake in the authors' positions.

*Preventing Premature Closure.* The Taking Sides structure also serves to prevent students from prematurely closing controversies. Premature closure can occur by underestimating the controversy's depth or deciding it without a proper appreciation for the issues involved. Taking Sides prevents this prematurity by helping the student to experience how two reasonable and highly educated people can so thoroughly disagree. In other words, premature closure is discouraged because real experts are countering each other, sometimes point by point.

A student would almost have to ignore one side of the controversy, one of the experts, to prematurely close the issue. Brittany, for example, reported that she became "absolutely convinced" of the validity of the first authors' position, only to have the second reading put this position into question! Obviously, if the issue could be closed or settled so easily, presumably the experts or leaders of the discipline would have done so already. Controversies are controversies because they are *deeply* problematic, so it is important for the student to appreciate this, and thus have a more profound understanding of the disciplinary meanings involved.

*Rehabilitating the Dialectic.* One of the truly unique benefits of the Taking Sides experience is its rehabilitation of the age-old educational tradition of the dialectic. Since at least the time of Socrates, educators have understood that a *full* understanding of any disciplinary meaning, explanation, or bit of information requires not only knowing what this meaning or information is but also knowing what it isn't. The dialectic, in this sense, is the educational relation of a concept to its alternative (see Rychlak, 2003). As dialectician Joseph Rychlak (1991) explains, all meanings "reach beyond themselves" and are thus clarified and have implications beyond their synonyms. It may be trivial to note, for example, that one cannot fully comprehend what "up" means without understanding what "down" means. However, this dialectic is not trivial when the meanings are disciplinary, such as when the political science student realizes that justice is incomprehensible without some apprehension of the meaning of injustice.

One of the more fascinating educational moments, when using Taking Sides books, occurs when students recognize that they cannot properly understand even one side of the controversy without taking into account another side. Brittany described learning very quickly that she clarified and even became aware of important aspects of her own position only *after* she understood the alternative to her position. This dialectical awareness is also pivotal to truly critical thinking.

*Facilitating Critical Thinking.* I say "truly" critical thinking because critical thinking has sometimes been confused with rigorous thinking (see Slife et al., 2005). Rigorous thinking is the application of rigorous reasoning or analytical thinking to a particular problem, which is surely an important skill in most any field. Still, it is not truly *critical* thinking until one has an alternative perspective from which to criticize a perspective. Recall that Brittany did not participate in class until she developed a perspective to view other perspectives. In other words, one must have a (critical) perspective "outside of" or alternative to the perspective being critiqued. Otherwise, one is "inside" the perspective being critiqued and cannot "see" it as a whole.

As many recent educational formulations of critical thinking attest, this approach means that critical thinkers should develop at least a dialectic of perspectives (one plus an alternative). That is to say, they should have an awareness of their own perspective as *facilitated* by an understanding of at least one alternative perspective. Without an alternative, students assume either they have no position or their position is the *only* one possible. A point of comparison, on the other hand, prevents the reification of one's perspective and allows students to have a perspective on their perspectives. A clear strength of the Taking Sides' juxtaposition of alternative perspectives is that it facilitates this kind of critical thinking.

These five benefits—engaging the discipline, appreciating the messy, preventing premature closure, rehabilitating the dialectic, and facilitating critical thinking—are probably not exclusive to controversy. However, they are, I would contend, a relatively unique *package* of educational advantages that students can gain with the inclusion of a Taking Sides approach in the classroom. Controversy, of course, is rarely helpful on its own; settled information and sound reasoning must buttress and perhaps even ground controversy. Otherwise, it is more heat than light. Even so, an *exclusive* focus on the settled and more cognitive aspects can deprive students of the vitality of a discipline and prevent the ownership of information that is so important to real learning.

# Contents In Brief

**UNIT 1    Regional and Country Issues    1**

Issue 1.    Is the European Union's Eurozone in Serious Danger of Collapsing?  2

Issue 2.    Should Russia Be Considered a Hostile Country?  21

Issue 3.    Is China Becoming a Dangerous Superpower?  41

Issue 4.    Are the Palestinians Blocking the Path to Peace in the Middle East?  58

Issue 5.    Should Force Be Used if Necessary to Prevent Iran from Acquiring Nuclear Weapons?  78

Issue 6.    Is U.S. Policy Toward Latin America on the Right Track?  104

Issue 7.    Does the Islamist Movement Threaten the Democracy Gained in the "Arab Spring"?  123

**UNIT 2    Economic Issues    141**

Issue 8.    Is Economic Globalization Good for Both Rich and Poor?  142

Issue 9.    Does China's Currency Manipulation Warrant International and National Action?  158

**UNIT 3    Armaments and Violence Issues    171**

Issue 10.   Should the United States Ratify the Comprehensive Nuclear Test Ban Treaty?  172

Issue 11.   Should U.S. Forces Continue to Fight in Afghanistan?  184

Issue 12.   Does Using Drones to Attack Terrorists Globally Violate International Law?  201

Issue 13.   Is the Use and Threat of Force Necessary in International Relations?  216

**UNIT 4    International Law and Organization Issues    231**

Issue 14.   Is the UN a Worthwhile Organization?  232

Issue 15.   Is U.S. Refusal to Join the International Criminal Court Wise?  246

Issue 16.   Should the United States Ratify the Convention to Eliminate All Forms of Discrimination Against Women?  269

**UNIT 5    Environmental Issues    285**

Issue 17.   Are International Negotiations to Control Global Warming Useful?  286

# Contents

Preface   vii

The Educational Experience of Disciplinary Controversy   xi

Topic Guide   xxv

Introduction   xxvii


## UNIT 1   REGIONAL AND COUNTRY ISSUES   1

Issue 1.   **Is the European Union's Eurozone in Serious Danger of Collapsing?**   2

YES:   **Simon Johnson,** from "The Troubled Eurozone," Testimony during Hearings on "Outlook for the Eurozone" before the Committee on the Budget, U.S. Senate (February 1, 2012)   5

NO:   **Guido Westerwelle,** from "The Euro and the Future of Europe," address delivered at the Brookings Institution, Washington, DC (January 20, 2012)   13

Simon Johnson, the Ronald Kurtz Professor of Entrepreneurship at the Sloan School of Management, Massachusetts Institute of Technology, Senior Fellow at the Peterson Institute for International Economics, member of the Congressional Budget Office's Panel of Economic Advisers, and member of the Federal Deposit Insurance Corporation's Systemic Resolution Advisory Committee, tells Congress that although for over two years Europe's political leaders have promised to do whatever it takes to save the euro, the currency of the European Union, they have failed to change the dangerous trends in Europe's economies or markets, and, as a result, the euro crisis is continuing to get deeper, broader, and more dangerous. Guido Westerwelle, the foreign minister of Germany, a member of the Bundestag (one house of Parliament) since 1996, the chairman of the Free Democratic Party, and the former vice chancellor, is much more optimistic about the future of the euro, arguing that the European Union and its countries have both the capacity and the will to stabilize the short-term financial difficulties that have caused problems and to institute long-term reforms that will prevent a reoccurrence of the current difficulties.

Issue 2.   **Should Russia Be Considered a Hostile Country?**   21

YES:   **Ariel Cohen,** from Testimony during Hearings on "Rethinking Reset: Re-Examining the Obama Administration Russia Policy," before the Committee on Foreign Affairs, U.S. House of Representatives (July 7, 2011)   23

NO:   **Steven Pifer,** from Testimony during Hearings on "The Future Course of the U.S.-Russia Relationship," before the Committee on Foreign Affairs, U.S. House of Representatives (March 21, 2012)   31

Ariel Cohen, the senior research fellow for Russian and Eurasian Studies and International Energy Policy at the Heritage Foundation, testifies that

Russia's increasingly authoritarian government is pursuing polices that are antithetical to U.S. national interests. Steven Pifer, the director of the Brookings Arms Control Initiative and a senior fellow in the Center on the United States and Europe, concedes that there are some conflict points in U.S.–Russia relations, but argues that it would be an error to treat Russia as implacably hostile rather than work with it to manage differences.

### Issue 3.    Is China Becoming a Dangerous Superpower?    41

YES:  **Dean Cheng**, from Testimony during Hearings on "Investigating the Chinese Threat, Part I: Military and Economic Aggression" before the Committee on Foreign Affairs, U.S. House of Representatives (March 28, 2012)    *43*

NO:   **Hu Jintao**, from "Building a China-U.S. Cooperative Partnership Based on Mutual Respect and Mutual Benefit," address to a welcome banquet, Marriott Wardman Park Hotel, Washington, DC (January 2, 2011)    *51*

Dean Cheng, the research fellow for Chinese political and security affairs at the Heritage Foundation, argues that China's increasing military and economic power and its comprehensive policy of harnessing all aspects of its military, economic, and diplomatic assets to assert its power are creating a powerful rival to U.S. power and interests in Asia and the Pacific region. Hu Jintao, the president of China and Communist Party chairman, tells an American audience that his country and theirs share an ultimate goal of creating a stable and prosperous international order and that both countries can and should cooperate and work with people across the world to share opportunities, meet challenges, and build a better future for mankind.

### Issue 4.    Are the Palestinians Blocking the Path to Peace in the Middle East?    58

YES:  **Benjamin Netanyahu**, from *Address to the 66th session of the General Assembly of United Nations at Its Headquarters in New York City* (September 23, 2011)    *61*

NO:   **Mahmoud Abbas**, from *Address to the 66th Session of the General Assembly of United Nations at Its Headquarters in New York City* (September 23, 2011)    *69*

Benjamin Netanyahu, prime minister of Israel, tells the UN General Assembly that on behalf of the people of Israel, "I extend my hand to the Palestinian people, with whom we seek a just and lasting peace," and claims this has always been Israel's position but that the Palestinians have not reciprocated. Mahmoud Abbas, president of the Palestinian National Authority, tells the UN General Assembly that the Palestinian people want to "achieve a just and comprehensive peace in our region that ensures the inalienable, legitimate national rights of the Palestinian people as defined by the resolutions of international legitimacy of the United Nations," but that, "The Israeli government refuses to commit to . . . negotiations that are based on international law and United Nations resolutions."

### Issue 5.    Should Force Be Used if Necessary to Prevent Iran from Acquiring Nuclear Weapons?    78

YES:  **Norman Podhoretz**, from "Stopping Iran: Why the Case for Military Action Still Stands," *Commentary* (February 2008)    *80*

NO:    Paul R. Pillar, from "We Can Live with a Nuclear Iran,"
    *Washington Monthly* (April 2012)    *92*

Norman Podhoretz, editor-at-large of the opinion journal *Commentary*, argues that the consequences of Iran acquiring nuclear weapons will be disastrous and that there is far less risk using whatever measures are necessary, including military force, to prevent the consequences than there is in dealing with a nuclear-armed Iran. Paul R. Pillar, who teaches in the Security Studies Program at Georgetown University, maintains that a nuclear-armed Iran with a bomb would be much less dangerous than many people contend it would be and that war with Iran would be much more costly than many people contend it would be.

## Issue 6.    Is U.S. Policy Toward Latin America on the Right Track?    104

YES:    Arturo A. Valenzuela, from Testimony during Hearings on "U.S. Policy Toward the Americas in 2010 and Beyond" before the Subcommittee on the Western Hemisphere, Committee on Foreign Affairs, U.S. House of Representatives (March 10, 2010)    *106*

NO:    Otto J. Reich, from Testimony during Hearings on "U.S. Policy Toward the Americas in 2010 and Beyond" before the Subcommittee on the Western Hemisphere, Committee on Foreign Affairs, U.S. House of Representatives (March 10, 2010)    *116*

Arturo A. Valenzuela, the U.S. assistant secretary of state for Western Hemisphere affairs, describes the views and policies of the Obama administration regarding the Western Hemisphere, as focused on three priorities critical to everyone in the region: promoting social and economic opportunity, ensuring safety, and strengthening effective institutions of democratic governance. Otto J. Reich, the U.S. assistant secretary of state for Western Hemisphere affairs during the administration of President George H. W. Bush, tells Congress that he believes the U.S. government today is underestimating the security threats in the Western Hemisphere.

## Issue 7.    Does the Islamist Movement Threaten the Democracy Gained in the "Arab Spring"?    123

YES:    Andrew C. McCarthy, from "Islam Is Islam, and That's It," *National Review* (no. 1, January 23, 2012)    *125*

NO:    Hillary Rodham Clinton, from *Keynote Address at the National Democratic Institute's 2011 Democracy Awards Dinner* (U.S. Department of State, November 7, 2011)    *130*

Andrew C. McCarthy, a columnist for the *National Review*, argues that it is dangerously misleading to portray the Arab/Muslim world as a separate civilization that has values and goals that are fundamentally at odds with those of the United States and the rest of the West. U.S. Secretary of State Hillary Rodham Clinton welcomes the Arab democratization movement and contends that it is a positive development for the national interest of the United States.

# UNIT 2 ECONOMIC ISSUES 141

## Issue 8. Is Economic Globalization Good for Both Rich and Poor? 142

YES: **International Monetary Fund Staff,** from "Globalization: A Brief Overview," *Issues Brief* (May 2008) *144*

NO: **Ravinder Rena,** from "Globalization Still Hurting Poor Nations," *Africa Economic Analysis* (January 2008) *152*

Staff members of the International Monetary Fund conclude on the basis of experiences across the world that unhindered international economic interchange, the core principle of globalization, seems to underpin greater prosperity. Ravinder Rena, an associate professor of economics at the Eritrea Institute of Technology, contends that globalization creates losers as well as winners and the losers are disproportionately found among the world's poorer countries.

## Issue 9. Does China's Currency Manipulation Warrant International and National Action? 158

YES: **Gordon G. Chang,** from Testimony during Hearings on "China and U.S. Interests" before the Committee on Foreign Affairs, U.S. House of Representatives (January 19, 2011) *161*

NO: **Pieter Bottelier and Uri Dadush,** from "The RMB: Myths and Tougher-To-Deal-With Realities," Testimony during Hearings on "China's Exchange Rate Policy" before the Committee on Ways and Means, U.S. House of Representatives (March 24, 2010) *164*

Gordon Chang, a columnist at *Forbes,* the financial magazine, argues that China is manipulating the value of its currency in a way that is harming the U.S. international economic position and that it is time to use international and, if necessary, national pressure to remedy the situation. Pieter Bottelier, the senior adjunct professor of China studies at the School of Advanced International Studies at Johns Hopkins University and the former chief of the World Bank's resident mission in Beijing, and Uri Dadush, the director of the International Economics Program at the Carnegie Endowment for International Peace and former (2002–2008) World Bank's director of international trade, contend that dangerous myths about China's currency may unwisely touch off a strong U.S. reaction while more effective solutions will be overlooked.

# UNIT 3 ARMAMENTS AND VIOLENCE ISSUES 171

## Issue 10. Should the United States Ratify the Comprehensive Nuclear Test Ban Treaty? 172

YES: **Ellen Tauscher,** from "The Case for the Comprehensive Nuclear Test Ban Treaty," Remarks at the Arms Control Association Annual Meeting at the Carnegie Endowment for International Peace, U.S. Department of State (May 10, 2011) *174*

NO:   **Baker Spring**, from "U.S. Should Reject Ratification of the Comprehensive Test Ban Treaty," *The Heritage Foundation Web Memo* #3272 (May 26, 2011)   *179*

U.S. Under Secretary of State for Arms Control and International Security Ellen Tauscher expresses the view that the United States will lose nothing and gains much by ratifying the Comprehensive Test Ban Treaty. Baker Spring, the F. M. Kirby Research Fellow in National Security Policy at The Heritage Foundation, asserts that the problems with the Comprehensive Test Ban Treaty that led the U.S. Senate to reject it in 1999 have, if anything, worsened in the intervening years.

## Issue 11.   Should U.S. Forces Continue to Fight in Afghanistan?   184

YES:   **Ileana Ros-Lehtinen, Howard Berman, Adam Smith, and Buck McKeon**, from "Continue to Fight," remarks on the floor of the U.S. House of Representatives on House Concurrent Resolution 28, *Directing the President . . . to Remove the United States Armed Forces from Afghanistan* (March 17, 2011)   *186*

NO:   **Dennis Kucinich, Barbara Lee, Walter B. Jones, Jason Chaffetz, and Ron Paul**, from "Withdraw Immediately," remarks on the floor of the U.S. House of Representatives on House Concurrent Resolution 28, *Directing the President . . . to Remove the United States Armed Forces from Afghanistan* (March 17, 2011)   *192*

Representatives Ileana Ros-Lehtinen (R-FL), Howard Berman (D-CA), Adam Smith (D-WA), and Buck McKeon (D-CA) oppose a resolution before the U.S. House of Representatives calling for the immediate withdrawal of U.S. military forces from Afghanistan, arguing that it is important that American troops remain until the U.S. goal of providing Afghanistan with the ability to defend itself against being once again taken over by the Taliban and al Qaeda is complete. Representatives Dennis Kucinich (D-OH), Barbara Lee (D-CA), Walter Jones (D-NC), Jason Chaffez (R-UT), and Ron Paul (R-TX) support a resolution before the U.S. House of Representatives calling for the withdrawal of all U.S. troops from Afghanistan no later than December 31, 2011, and argue that there is no good reason to continue the loss of American lives and the expense that the war entails.

## Issue 12.   Does Using Drones to Attack Terrorists Globally Violate International Law?   201

YES:   **Mary Ellen O'Connell**, from "Lawful Use of Combat Drones," Testimony during Hearings on "Rise of the Drones II: Examining the Legality of Unmanned Targeting," before the Subcommittee on National Security and Foreign Affairs, Committee on Oversight and Government Reform, U.S. House of Representatives (April 28, 2010)   *203*

NO:   **Michael W. Lewis**, from "Examining the Legality of Unmanned Targeting," Testimony during Hearings on "Rise of the Drones II: Examining the Legality of Unmanned Targeting," before the Subcommittee on National Security and Foreign Affairs, Committee on Oversight and Government Reform, U.S. House of Representatives (April 28, 2010)   *208*

Mary Ellen O'Connell, a research professor at the Kroc Institute, University of Notre Dame, and the Robert and Marion Short Professor of Law at the School of Law, University of Notre Dame, tells a congressional committee that the United States is failing more often than not to follow the most important single rule governing drones: restricting their use to the battlefield. Michael W. Lewis, a professor of law at Ohio Northern University's Pettit College of Law, disagrees, contending that there is nothing inherently illegal about using drones to target specific terrorists or groups of terrorists on or away from the battlefield.

### Issue 13.   Is the Use and Threat of Force Necessary in International Relations?   216

**YES:   Peter Van Uhm**, from "Why I Chose a Gun," address delivered at TEDxAmerstam, Amsterdam, The Netherlands (November 25, 2011)   *218*

**NO:   Peace Pledge Union**, from *What Is Pacifism?* www.ppu.org.uk/   *221*

Peter Van Uhm, a general in the Royal Netherlands Army and chief of the Netherlands Defense Staff (the equivalent of the U.S. Joint Chiefs of Staff), explains that he became a soldier because sometimes only the gun stands between good and evil. The Peace Pledge Union, a pacifist organization in Great Britain that has been campaigning for a warless world since 1934, argues on its website that war is indefensible, that it is wrong for people to kill each other in large numbers.

## UNIT 4   INTERNATIONAL LAW AND ORGANIZATION ISSUES   231

### Issue 14.   Is the UN a Worthwhile Organization?   232

**YES:   Susan E. Rice**, from "Six Reasons the United Nations Is Indispensable," address delivered at the World Affairs Council of Oregon, Portland, Oregon (February 11, 2011)   *234*

**NO:   Bruce S. Thornton**, from "The U.N.: So Bad It's Almost Beautiful," *Hoover Digest* (January 2012)   *240*

Susan E. Rice, U.S. ambassador to the United Nations, tells an audience that the United States is much better off—much stronger, much safer, and more secure—in a world with the United Nations than the United States would be in a world without the UN. Bruce S. Thornton, a research fellow at the Hoover Institution at Stanford University in California, writes that the United Nations is fatally flawed by not having consistent, unifying moral and political principles shared by member nations that can justify UN policies or legitimize the use of force to deter and punish aggression.

### Issue 15.   Is U.S. Refusal to Join the International Criminal Court Wise?   246

**YES:   Brett Schaefer and Steven Groves**, from "The U.S. Should Not Join the International Criminal Court," Backgrounder on International Organization, The Heritage Foundation (August 18, 2009)   *248*

NO:   **Jonathan F. Fanton,** from "The Challenge of International Justice," Remarks to the U.S. Military Academy at West Point, New York (May 5, 2008)   *262*

Brett Schaefer, the Jay Kingham fellow in international regulatory affairs at the Heritage Foundation, and Steven Groves, the Bernard and Barbara Lomas fellow in the Margaret Thatcher Center for Freedom, a division of the Kathryn and Shelby Cullom Davis Institute for International Studies at the Heritage Foundation, contend that although the court's supporters have a noble purpose, there are a number of reasons to be cautious and concerned about how ratification of the Rome Statute would affect U.S. sovereignty and how ICC action could affect politically precarious situations around the world. Jonathan F. Fanton, president of the John D. and Catherine T. MacArthur Foundation, which is headquartered in Chicago, Illinois, and is among the world's largest independent foundations, maintains that creation of the International Court of Justice is an important step toward creating a more just world, and that the fear that many Americans have expressed about the court has not materialized.

**Issue 16.   Should the United States Ratify the Convention to Eliminate All Forms of Discrimination Against Women?   269**

YES:   **Melanne Verveer,** from Testimony during Hearings on "Ratify the CEDAW," before the Subcommittee on Human Rights and the Law, the Committee on the Judiciary, U.S. Senate (November 18, 2010)   *271*

NO:   **Steven Groves,** from Testimony during Hearings on "Reject CEDAW," before the Subcommittee on Human Rights and the Law, the Committee on the Judiciary, U.S. Senate (November 18, 2010)   *276*

Melanne Verveer, ambassador-at-large, Office of Global Women's Issues, U.S. Department of State, tells a congressional committee that the U.S. Senate should ratify the Convention on the Elimination of All Forms of Discrimination Against Women (CEDAW) because doing so would send a powerful message about the U.S. commitment to equality for women across the globe. Steven Groves, the Bernard and Barbara Lomas Fellow in the Margaret Thatcher Center for Freedom, a division of the Kathryn and Shelby Cullom Davis Institute for International Studies at the Heritage Foundation, headquartered in Washington, DC, contends that ratifying CEDAW would neither advance U.S. international interests nor enhance the rights of women in the United States.

# UNIT 5   ENVIRONMENTAL ISSUES   285

**Issue 17.   Are International Negotiations to Control Global Warming Useful?   286**

YES:   **Elliot Diringer,** from "The Threats of Climate Change," Testimony during Hearings on "UN Climate Talks and Power Politics—It's Not about the Temperature" before the Subcommittee on Oversight and Investigations, Committee on Foreign Affairs, U.S. House of Representatives (May 25, 2011)   *289*

NO:    **Steven F. Hayward**, from "Climate Change Negotiations: Implausible and Unpromising," Testimony during Hearings on "UN Climate Talks and Power Politics—It's Not about the Temperature" before the Subcommittee on Oversight and Investigations, Committee on Foreign Affairs, U.S. House of Representatives (May 25, 2011)    *297*

Elliot Diringer, the vice president for international strategies at the Pew Center on Global Climate Change (now renamed the Center for Climate and Energy Solutions, located in Arlington, VA) contends that global warming seriously threatens U.S. prosperity and national security and that it is imperative to seek a global solution to climate change. Steven F. Hayward, the F. K. Weyerhaeuser Fellow at the American Enterprise Institute in Washington, DC, says that the current diplomatic effort to curb global warming has failed so far and is unlikely to improve, and that the best way to address global warming is through a revised national energy policy.

**Contributors    302**

# Topic Guide

This topic guide suggests how the selections in this book relate to the subjects covered in your course. You may want to use the topics listed on these pages to search the web more easily. On the following pages a number of websites have been gathered specifically for this book. They are arranged to reflect the units of this *Taking Sides* reader. You can link to these sites by going to www.mhhe.com/cls.

**All issues and their articles that relate to each topic are listed below the bold-faced term.**

## Afghanistan

11. Should U.S. Forces Continue to Fight in Afghanistan?

## Arab Spring

7. Does the Islamist Movement Threaten the Democracy Gained in the "Arab Spring"?

## China

3. Is China Becoming a Dangerous Superpower?
9. Does China's Currency Manipulation Warrant International and National Action?

## Culture

13. Is the Use and Threat of Force Necessary in International Relations?

## Currency

1. Is the European Union's Eurozone in Serious Danger of Collapsing?

## Democracy

7. Does the Islamist Movement Threaten the Democracy Gained in the "Arab Spring"?

## Economic Issues

1. Is the European Union's Eurozone in Serious Danger of Collapsing?
3. Is China Becoming a Dangerous Superpower?
8. Is Economic Globalization Good for Both Rich and Poor?

## Foreign Policy

6. Is U.S. Policy Toward Latin America on the Right Track?
12. Does Using Drones to Attack Terrorists Globally Violate International Law?

## Globalization

3. Is China Becoming a Dangerous Superpower?
8. Is Economic Globalization Good for Both Rich and Poor?
9. Is Capitalism a Failed Model for a Globalized Economy?

## Global Warming

17. Are International Negotiations to Control Global Warming Useful?

## Human Rights

3. Is China Becoming a Dangerous Superpower?

## International Court

15. Is U.S. Refusal to Join the International Criminal Court Wise?

## International Law

9. Does China's Currency Manipulation Warrant International and National Action?
12. Does Using Drones to Attack Terrorists Globally Violate International Law?
16. Should the United States Ratify the Convention to Eliminate All Forms of Discrimination Against Women?

## International Relations

2. Should Russia Be Considered a Hostile Country?
3. Is China Becoming a Dangerous Superpower?
12. Does Using Drones to Attack Terrorists Globally Violate International Law?
13. Is the Use and Threat of Force Necessary in International Relations?

## Iran

5. Should Force Be Used if Necessary to Prevent Iran from Acquiring Nuclear Weapons?

## Israel

4. Are the Palestinians Blocking the Path to Peace in the Middle East?

## Latin America

6. Is U.S. Policy Toward Latin America on the Right Track?

## Middle East

4. Are the Palestinians Blocking the Path to Peace in the Middle East?
7. Does the Islamist Movement Threaten the Democracy Gained in the "Arab Spring"?
11. Should U.S. Forces Continue to Fight in Afghanistan?

## Nuclear Weapons

5. Should Force Be Used if Necessary to Prevent Iran from Acquiring Nuclear Weapons?
10. Should the United States Ratify the Comprehensive Nuclear Test Ban Treaty?

## Palestine

4. Are the Palestinians Blocking the Path to Peace in the Middle East?

## Peace

4. Are the Palestinians Blocking the Path to Peace in the Middle East?

## Policy

5. Should Force Be Used if Necessary to Prevent Iran from Acquiring Nuclear Weapons?
6. Is U.S. Policy Toward Latin America on the Right Track?
10. Should the United States Ratify the Comprehensive Nuclear Test Ban Treaty?
13. Is the Use and Threat of Force Necessary in International Relations?
15. Is U.S. Refusal to Join the International Criminal Court Wise?

## Regional Issues

1. Is the European Union's Eurozone in Serious Danger of Collapsing?

## Russia

2. Should Russia Be Considered a Hostile Country?

## Security, Global

5. Should Force Be Used if Necessary to Prevent Iran from Acquiring Nuclear Weapons?
10. Should the United States Ratify the Comprehensive Nuclear Test Ban Treaty?
12. Does Using Drones to Attack Terrorists Globally Violate International Law?
13. Is the Use and Threat of Force Necessary in International Relations?

## Security, National

5. Should Force Be Used if Necessary to Prevent Iran from Acquiring Nuclear Weapons?

## Technology

12. Does Using Drones to Attack Terrorists Globally Violate International Law?

## Terrorism

12. Does Using Drones to Attack Terrorists Globally Violate International Law?

## Trade

3. Is China Becoming a Dangerous Superpower?
8. Is Economic Globalization Good for Both Rich and Poor?
9. Does China's Currency Manipulation Warrant International and National Action?

## United Nations

10. Should the United States Ratify the Comprehensive Nuclear Test Ban Treaty?
14. Is the UN a Worthwhile Organization?

## War

11. Should U.S. Forces Continue to Fight in Afghanistan?
12. Does Using Drones to Attack Terrorists Globally Violate International Law?

## Western Hemisphere

1. Is the European Union's Eurozone in Serious Danger of Collapsing?
6. Is U.S. Policy Toward Latin America on the Right Track?

# Introduction

## World Politics

John T. Rourke

**S**ome years ago, the Rolling Stones recorded "Sympathy with the Devil." If you have never heard it, go find a copy. It is worth listening to. The theme of the song is echoed in a wonderful essay by Marshall Berman, "Have Sympathy for the Devil" (*New American Review*, 1973). The common theme of the Stones' and Berman's works is based on Johann Goethe's *Faust*. In that classic drama, the protagonist, Dr. Faust, trades his soul to gain great power. He attempts to do good, but in the end he commits evil by, in contemporary paraphrase, "doing the wrong things for the right reasons." Does that make Faust evil, the personification of the devil Mephistopheles among us? Or is the good doctor merely misguided in his effort to make the world better as he saw it and imagined it might be? The point that the Stones and Berman make is that it is important to avoid falling prey to the trap of many zealots who are so convinced of the truth of their own views that they feel righteously at liberty to condemn those who disagree with them as stupid or even diabolical.

It is to the principle of rational discourse, of tolerant debate, that this reader is dedicated. There are many issues in this volume that appropriately excite passion—for example, Issue 7 on whether or not Israel should agree to an independent Palestinian state.

As you will see, each of the authors in all the debates strongly believes in his or her position. If you read these debates objectively, you will find that each side makes cogent points. They may or may not be right, but they should not be dismissed out of hand. It is important to repeat that the debate format does not imply that you should remain forever neutral. In fact, once you are informed, you ought to form convictions, and you should try to act on those convictions and try to influence international policy to conform better with your beliefs. Ponder the similarities in the views of two very different leaders, a very young president in a relatively young democracy and a very old emperor in a very old country: In 1963 President John F. Kennedy, in recalling the words of the author of the epic poem *The Divine Comedy* (1321), told a West German audience, "Dante once said that the hottest places in hell are reserved for those who in a period of moral crisis maintain their neutrality." That very same year, while speaking to the United Nations, Ethiopia's emperor Haile Selassie (1892–1975) said, "Throughout history it has been the inaction of those who could have acted, the indifference of those who should have known better, the silence of the voice of justice when it mattered most that made it possible for evil to triumph."

The point is: Become Informed. Then do something! Write letters to poli-cymakers, donate money to causes you support, work for candidates with whom you agree, join an activist organization, or any of the many other things that you can do to make a difference. What you do is less important than that you do it.

# Approaches to Studying International Politics

As will become evident as you read this volume, there are many approaches to the study of international politics. Some political scientists and most practi-tioners specialize in substantive topics, and this reader is organized along top-ical lines.

Unit 1 (Issues 1 through 7) focuses on regional and country-specific issues, including the U.S. positions in the world trends in Russian domestic and foreign policy, whether China should be considered a growing threat, who is responsible for the lack of peace between Israelis and Palestinians, whether diplomacy or force is the best way to address Iran's alleged nuclear weapons program, the pros and cons of U.S. policy toward Latin America, and the impli-cations of the Arab Spring.

Unit 2 (Issues 8 and 9) deals with economic issues. Issue 8 debates the question of whether economic globalization has been good for both rich and poor. Whether China's currency manipulation warrants international and national action is taken up in Issue 9. Gordon G. Chang, a research fellow at the Heritage Foundation, argues that China is manipulating the value of its currency in a way that is harming the U.S. international economic position and it is time to use international and, if necessary, national pressure to rem-edy the situation. Pieter Bottelier, former chief of the World Bank's resident mission in Beijing, and Uri Dadush, former director of international trade at the World Bank, contend that dangerous myths about China's currency may unwisely touch off a strong U.S. reaction while more effective solutions will be overlooked.

Unit 3 (Issues 10 through 13) deals with arms and violence. Issue 10 examines whether the U.S. Senate should ratify the Comprehensive Nuclear Test Ban Treaty. Issue 11 focuses toward the other end of the arms spectrum by asking whether U.S. troops should soon exit Afghanistan. On a related topic, Issue 12 explores whether the use of drones to attack terrorists outside Afghan-istan in Pakistan and elsewhere around the world violates international law. Perhaps the most fundamental question of all about the use of force is the subject of Issue 13, which asks whether human need to use force at all.

Unit 4 (Issues 14 through 16) addresses controversies related to interna-tional law and organizations. The ability of the United Nations to meet its goals is severely constrained by a number of factors, and in Issue 14, U.S. Ambassador to the UN Susan Rice and Bruce Thornton of the Hoover Institu-tion debate whether the UN is fundamentally flawed or is a vital if flawed, actor on the world stage. Issue 15 evaluates the wisdom of establishing a per-manent international criminal court to punish those who violate the law of war. It is easy to advocate such a court as long as it is trying and sometimes punishing alleged war criminals from other countries. But one has to understand that one day a citizen of one's own country could be put on trial. The third debate in Unit 4, Issue 16, takes up the convention to eliminate all forms of discrimination against women. The United States is nearly the only country that has not ratified the treaty and this issue inquires whether that is a laudable U.S. stand.

Unit 5, which consists of Issue 17, addresses the environment. Over the past few decades there has been an effort to reach an international agreement to reduce or reverse global warming. There has been little progress, and the debate centers on whether it is worthwhile to continue to seek solutions through global diplomacy or whether it would be better for the United States and other countries to concentrate on domestic changes to increase energy sources that emit no or fewer greenhouse gases.

Political scientists also approach their subject from differing methodological perspectives. You will see, for example, that world politics can be studied from different levels of analysis. The question is, What is the basic source of the forces that shape the conduct of politics? Possible answers are world forces, the individual political processes of the specific countries, or the personal attributes of a country's leaders and decision makers. Various readings will illustrate all three levels.

Another way for students and practitioners of world politics to approach their subject is to focus on what is called the realist versus the idealist (or liberal) debate. Realists tend to assume that the world is permanently flawed and therefore advocate following policies in their country's narrow self-interests. Idealists take the approach that the world condition can be improved substantially by following policies that, at least in the short term, call for some risk or self-sacrifice. This divergence is an element of many of the debates in this book. Issue 15 is one example. In the first reading, Brett Schaefer and Steven Groves from the Heritage Foundation, a conservative think tank, write that there are a number of reasons to be wary about how ratification of the Rome Statute would affect U.S. sovereignty and how ICC action could affect politically precarious situations around the world. Jonathan F. Fanton, head of one of the world's largest foundations promoting world peace, disagrees, arguing that the ICC is a major step toward a more just world and does not pose any threat to the United States.

# Dynamics of World Politics

The action on the global stage today is vastly different from what it was a few decades ago, or even a few years ago. Technology is one of the causes of this change. Technology has changed communications, manufacturing, health care, and many other aspects of the human condition. Technology has given humans the ability to create biological, chemical, and nuclear compounds and other materials that in relatively small amounts have the ability to kill and injure huge numbers of people. Another negative by-product of technology may be the vastly increased consumption of petroleum and other natural resources and the global environmental degradation that has been caused by discharges of waste products, deforestation, and a host of other technology enhanced human activities. Technology has also changed warfare in many ways. Some of these, like the use of drones to attack enemies away from the immediate battlefield, covered in Issue 12, raise new matters of law and morality that need to be addressed. Technology is also a key element of Issue 10, which deals with the ability to ensure the stability of the current U.S. nuclear arms arsenal and the ability to verify that other countries are not secretly testing nuclear weapons as well as whether the United States should agree to never again test nuclear weapons.

Technological changes also highlight the increased role of economics in world politics. Economics has always played a role, but traditionally the main focus has been on strategic-political questions—especially military power. This concern still strongly exists, but now it shares the international spotlight with economic issues. One important change in recent decades has been the rapid growth of regional and global markets and the promotion of free trade and other forms of international economic interchange. Issue 1 is about the world's most advanced regional effort at governance, the European Union, and the threat that the ongoing economic crisis in several countries that use the common currency, the euro, pose not only to that currency but to the very future of the EU. In part because of the dominance of the United States, capitalism is the prevailing economic globalization model for domestic economic systems, and Issue 3 debates whether that will and should continue.

Another change in the world system has to do with the main international actors. At one time states (countries) were practically the only international actors on the world stage. Now, and increasingly so, there are other actors. Some actors are regional. Others, such as the United Nations, are global actors. Turning to the most notable international organization, Issue 14 examines the UN, the role of that world organization, and the proper approach of member countries to it and to global cooperation. Issue 15 focuses on whether or not a supranational criminal court should be established to take over the prosecution and punishment of war criminals from the domestic courts and ad hoc tribunals that have sometimes dealt with such cases in the past.

## Perceptions Versus Reality

In addition to addressing the general changes in the world system outlined above, the debates in this reader explore the controversies that exist over many of the fundamental issues that face the world. One key to these debates is the differing perceptions that protagonists bring to them. There may be a reality in world politics, but very often that reality is obscured. Many observers, for example, are alarmed by the seeming rise in radical actions by Islamic fundamentalists. However, the image of Islamic radicalism is not a fact but a perception, perhaps correct, perhaps not. In cases such as this, though, it is often the perception, not the reality, that is more important because policy is formulated on what decision makers think, not necessarily on what is. Thus, perception becomes the operating guide, or operational reality, whether it is true or not. Perceptions result from many factors. One factor is the information that decision makers receive. For a variety of reasons, the facts and analyses that are given to leaders are often inaccurate or represent only part of the picture. The conflicting perceptions of Israelis and Palestinians, for example, make the achievement of peace in Israel very difficult. Many Israelis and Palestinians fervently believe that the conflict that has occurred in the region over the past 50 years is the responsibility of the other. Both sides also believe in the righteousness of their own policies. Even if both sides are well-meaning, the perceptions of hostility that each holds mean that the operational reality often has to be violence. These differing perceptions are a key element in the debate in Issue 3 about whether China is becoming a dangerous superpower.

A related aspect of perception is the tendency to see oneself differently than some others do. Specifically, the tendency is to see oneself as benevolent and to perceive rivals as sinister. This reverse image is part of Issue 5, the debate over Iran's nuclear program. Many Americans and others see Iran as a rogue nation intent on developing nuclear weapons to use to threaten or attack other countries. But Iran claims that its intentions are only to develop nuclear energy plants, as many other countries have, and that even if it does choose to develop nuclear weapons, they would only be for defense against such hostile nuclear powers as the United States and Israel. Which view is the reality and which is the perception? Perceptions, then, are crucial to understanding international politics. It is important to understand objective reality, but it is also necessary to comprehend subjective reality in order to be able to predict and analyze another country's actions.

# Levels of Analysis

Political scientists approach the study of international politics from different levels of analysis. The most macroscopic view is system-level analysis. This is a top-down approach that maintains that world factors virtually compel countries to follow certain foreign policies. Governing factors include the number of powerful actors, geographic relationships, economic needs, and technology. System analysts hold that a country's internal political system and its leaders do not have a major impact on policy. As such, political scientists who work from this perspective are interested in exploring the governing factors, how they cause policy, and how and why systems change.

After the end of World War II, the world was structured as a bipolar system, dominated by the United States and the Soviet Union. Furthermore, each superpower was supported by a tightly organized and dependent group of allies. For a variety of reasons, including changing economics and the nuclear standoff, the bipolar system has faded. Some political scientists argue that the bipolar system is being replaced by a multipolar system. In such a configuration, those who favor balance-of-power politics maintain that it is unwise to ignore power considerations. Is it possible that the future holds a tripolar system, as Issue 2 on Russia's policy and Issue 3 on China's capabilities and intensions suggest might be possible? State-level analysis is the middle and most common level of analysis. Social scientists who study world politics from this perspective focus on how countries, singly or comparatively, make foreign policy. In other words, this perspective is concerned with internal political dynamics, such as the roles of and interactions between the executive and legislative branches of government, the impact of bureaucracy, the role of interest groups, and the effect of public opinion. This level of analysis is very much in evidence in Issue 16, about whether the United States like almost every other country in the world should ratify the Convention to Eliminate All Forms of Discrimination Against Women. Whatever the international ramifications, whether U.S. troops in Afghanistan should or should not be immediately withdrawn, as Issue 11 debates, the decision will be heavily rooted in public opinion and other domestic political factors in the United States. The dangers to the global environment, which are debated in Issue 17, extend beyond rarified scientific controversy to important issues of public policy. For example, should the United States and other industrialized countries adopt policies that are costly in terms of economics and lifestyle to significantly reduce the emission of carbon dioxide and other harmful gases? This debate pits interest groups against one another as they try to get the governments of their respective countries to support or reject the steps necessary to reduce the consumption of resources and the emission of waste products. Yet another state-level issue, the nature of governance in the Middle East and North Africa, is at issue in Issue 7. Beginning with the popular overthrow of Tunisia's long-time authoritarian president in December 2010, the democracy movement has also led to the downfall of authoritarian regimes in Egypt and Libya, and strong protests against nondemocratic regimes in Syria, Yemen, and several other countries in the region. The issue is what types of political regimes will succeed the fallen dictators and what the U.S. attitude should be toward democratization in these largely Muslim countries.

A third level of analysis, which is the most microscopic, is human-level analysis. This approach focuses, in part, on the role of individual decision makers. This technique is applied under the assumption that individuals make decisions and that the nature of those decisions is determined by the decision makers' perceptions, predilections, and strengths and weaknesses. A great deal of Issue 6 on U.S. Latin America policy is based on the question of who had wiser foreign policy views: President George W. Bush or Barack Obama.

# The Political and Ecological Future

Future world alternatives are discussed in many of the issues in this volume. Abraham Lincoln once said, "A house divided against itself cannot stand." One suspects that the sixteenth president might say something similar about the world today if he were with us. Issue 1, for example, debates whether growing globalization is a positive or negative trend. The world has responded to globalization by creating and strengthening the UN, the IMF, the World Bank, the World Trade Organization, and many other international organizations to try to regulate the increasing number of international interactions. There can be little doubt that the role of global governance is growing, and this reality is the spark behind specific debates about the future that are taken up in many of the selections. Far-reaching alternatives to a state-centric system based on sovereign countries include international organizations (Issue 14) taking over some (or all) of the sovereign responsibilities of national governments, such as the prosecution of international war criminals (Issue 15). The global future also involves the ability of the world to prosper economically while not denuding itself of its natural resources or destroying the environment. This is the focus of Issue 17, on the environment.

## Increased Role of Economics

Economics has always played a part in international relations, but the traditional focus has been on strategic political affairs, especially questions of military power. Now, however, political scientists are increasingly focusing on the international political economy or the economic dimensions of world politics. International trade, for instance, has increased dramatically, expanding from an annual world export total of $20 billion in 1933 to $18 trillion in 2011. The impact has been profound. The domestic economic health of most countries is heavily affected by trade and other aspects of international economics. Since World War II there has been an emphasis on expanding free trade by decreasing tariffs and other barriers to international commerce. In recent years, however, a downturn in the economies of many of the industrialized countries has increased calls for more protectionism. Yet restrictions on trade and other economic activity can also be used as diplomatic weapons. The intertwining of economies and the creation of organizations to regulate them, such as the World Trade Organization, is raising issues of sovereignty and other concerns. International political economy is the subject of all of Unit 2 and its two issues (8 and 9).

## Conclusion

Having discussed many of the various dimensions and approaches to the study of world politics, it is incumbent on this editor to advise against your becoming too structured by them. Issues of focus and methodology are important both to studying international relations and to understanding how others are analyzing global conduct. However, they are also partially pedagogical. In the final analysis, world politics is a highly interrelated, perhaps seamless, subject. No one level of analysis, for instance, can fully explain the events on the world stage. Instead, using each of the levels to analyze events and trends will bring the greatest understanding.

Similarly, the realist–idealist division is less precise in practice than it may appear. As some of the debates indicate, each side often stresses its own standards of morality. Which is more moral: defeating a dictatorship or sparing the sword and saving lives that would almost inevitably be lost in the dictator's overthrow? Furthermore, realists usually do not reject moral considerations. Rather, they contend that morality is but one of the factors that a country's decision makers must consider. Realists are also apt to argue that standards of morality differ when dealing with a country as opposed to an individual. By the same token, most idealists do not completely ignore the often dangerous nature of the world. Nor do they argue that a country must totally sacrifice its short-term interests to promote the betterment of the current and future world. Thus, realism and idealism can be seen most accurately as the ends of a continuum—with most political scientists and practitioners falling somewhere between, rather than at, the extremes. The best advice, then, is this: think broadly about international politics. The subject is very complex, and the more creative and expansive you are in selecting your foci and methodologies, the more insight you will gain. To end where we began, with Dr. Faust, I offer his last words in Goethe's drama, *"Mehr licht,"* . . . More light! That is the goal of this book.

# Internet References . . .

## WWW Virtual Library: International Affairs Resources

Maintained by Wayne A. Selcher, the professor of international studies at Elizabethtown College in Elizabethtown, Pennsylvania, this site contains approximately 2,000 annotated links relating to a broad spectrum of international affairs. The sites listed are those that the Webmaster believes have long-term value and that are cost-free, and many have further links to help in extended research.

**www.etown.edu/vl/**

## Country Indicators for Foreign Policy

Hosted by Carlton University in Canada, the Country Indicators for Foreign Policy (CIFP) project represents an ongoing effort to identify and assemble statistical information conveying the key features of the economic, political, social, and cultural environments of countries around the world.

**www.carleton.ca/cifp/**

## U.S. Department of State

The information on this site is organized into categories based on countries, topics, and other criteria. "Background Notes," which provide information on regions and specific countries, can be accessed through this site.

**www.state.gov/countries/**

## worldatlas.com

The world may be "getting smaller," but geography is still important. This organization's site contains a wide variety of maps and a range of other useful information.

**www.worldatlas.com/aatlas/world.htm**

# Regional and Country Issues

*T*he issues in this section deal with countries that are major regional powers. In this era of interdependence among nations, it is important to understand the concerns that these issues address and the actors involved because they will shape the world and will affect the lives of all people.

- Is the European Union's Eurozone in Serious Danger of Collapsing?
- Should Russia Be Considered a Hostile Country?
- Is China Becoming a Dangerous Superpower?
- Are the Palestinians Blocking the Path to Peace in the Middle East?
- Should Force Be Used if Necessary to Prevent Iran from Acquiring Nuclear Weapons?
- Is U.S. Policy Toward Latin America on the Right Track?
- Does the Islamist Movement Threaten the Democracy Gained in the "Arab Spring"?

# ISSUE 1

# Is the European Union's Eurozone in Serious Danger of Collapsing?

**YES: Simon Johnson,** from "The Troubled Eurozone," Testimony during Hearings on "Outlook for the Eurozone" before the Committee on the Budget, U.S. Senate (February 1, 2012)

**NO: Guido Westerwelle,** from "The Euro and the Future of Europe," address delivered at the Brookings Institution, Washington, DC (January 20, 2012)

## ISSUE SUMMARY

**YES:** Simon Johnson, the Ronald Kurtz Professor of Entrepreneurship at the Sloan School of Management, Massachusetts Institute of Technology, Senior Fellow at the Peterson Institute for International Economics, member of the Congressional Budget Office's Panel of Economic Advisers, and member of the Federal Deposit Insurance Corporation's Systemic Resolution Advisory Committee, tells Congress that although for over two years Europe's political leaders have promised to do whatever it takes to save the euro, the currency of the European Union, they have failed to change the dangerous trends in Europe's economies or markets, and, as a result, the euro crisis is continuing to get deeper, broader, and more dangerous.

**NO:** Guido Westerwelle, the foreign minister of Germany, a member of the Bundestag (one house of Parliament) since 1996, the chairman of the Free Democratic Party, and the former vice chancellor, is much more optimistic about the future of the euro, arguing that the European Union and its countries have both the capacity and the will to stabilize the short-term financial difficulties that have caused problems and to institute long-term reforms that will prevent a reoccurrence of the current difficulties.

In the aftermath of World War II (1939–1945), the shattered countries of Europe sought to diminish the importance of national borders and build common institutions as a way to ensure future peace and prosperity. The first step in doing that came in 1952 when Belgium, France, (West) Germany, Italy, Luxembourg, and the Netherlands created the European Coal and Steel Community, a common market for coal, iron, and steel products. From this genesis, the European community has increased in membership, has expanded its functions, and has undergone a series of name changes. The current name, the European Union (EU), was adopted in 1993 by the then 12 members of the organization to symbolize the EU's goal of becoming a single economic entity. The EU now includes 27 countries with a combined population of over 500 million and a gross domestic product (2011 GDP) of over $17.5 trillion, somewhat larger than that of the United States ($15.0 trillion) for that year. In addition to very advanced economic integration, the EU has also achieved significant political integration. It has its own executive branch, Parliament, and courts, and its annual budget in 2011 was approximately $142 billion.

Another key step toward economic integration of the EU was taken in 1993 when the EU countries agree to eventually give up their national currencies and adopt a single common currency, the euro. Not all countries had to adopt the euro, and some such as Great Britain have not. Those countries that chose to adopt the euro had to commit to meeting certain standards for prudent government finance such as keeping their budget deficits to a low level. The countries that use the euro are referred to as the eurozone. As of 2012, there were 17 countries in the eurozone. They included Germany, France, and all the other major economies in the EU other than Great Britain. The euro began to be used for transactions between eurozone countries in 1999 and went into general circulation for all transactions within and between eurozone countries in 2002.

For a number of years, the euro worked well. A single currency made economic transactions between the eurozone countries much easier, and the currency maintained its strength on the international monetary exchange markets. But there were problems. A key one was that some eurozone countries did not abide by criteria for eurozone membership. Just as was occurring in the United States, budget deficits soared. The eurozone's problems were made markedly worse, as the U.S. economy was, by the global recession that took hold in late 2008 and that continues to plague government finance around the world. Doubts about the stability of the euro began to erode its value on international markets and worries that some countries would default on their national debt made it hard for them to borrow to pay for their deficits and led investors to increasingly withdraw money from those countries. Greece was the most embattled country and teetered on the edge of not being able to pay its debts and thereby being legally bankrupt. The EU financial institutions moved to aid Greece, but there was heavy pressure on Greece to drastically cut its spending or raise its taxes to reduce its deficit spending, but efforts to do so were met with strong, sometimes violent, opposition by Greek citizens faced with losing their jobs with the Greek government, having their government benefits cut, having their taxes raised, or otherwise being adversely affected by the economic reform efforts. While Greece was the "poster child" of the euro crisis, other, even larger economies, such as Spain and Italy, are also in precarious budget positions. Further complicating matters, the stronger eurozone

3

countries that need to provide the financial aid to assist the weaker countries have faced substantial opposition from their citizens, many of whom are angry about having to support what they see as the profligate economic practices of the weaker countries.

Most Americans have paid little attention to the crisis, but because the EU is such an important U.S. trading partner and because of the massive U.S. investment in Europe, a collapse of the euro and the ensuing economic instability of Europe in general would negatively impact the American economy. In the following two readings, Simon Johnson, a professor of economics at MIT, and German Foreign Minister Guido Westerwelle give differing views of the severity of the eurozone's problems and their potential impact on the United States. Simon warns that a rapid shift from low-level crisis to collapse is very plausible, contends that so far there is little political will to take the necessary measures to avoid a collapse, and concludes that Europe's economy remains in a precarious position. Westerwelle says that the image of Europe as a continent mired in gloom and self-absorption is mostly a misleading caricature and that the EU is well on its way to solving its economic difficulties.

# The Troubled Eurozone

## The Euro Area's Last Stand

For over two years Europe's political leaders have promised to do whatever it takes to save the euro area. Yet problems are growing and solutions still seem far off. The October 27 and December 9, 2011 agreements of European leaders failed to change the dangerous trends in Europe's economies or markets. The implicit risk of default priced in sovereign bond markets reached all-time highs in the last three months. The trend is similar with bank default risk. The crisis is continuing to get deeper, broader, and more dangerous.

A combination of misdiagnosis, lack of political will, and dysfunctional politics across 17 nations have all contributed to the failure so far to stem Europe's growing crisis. Yet problems are growing and solutions still seem far off. The October 27 and December 9, 2011 agreements of European leaders failed to change the dangerous trends in Europe's economies or markets. The implicit risk of default priced in sovereign bond markets reached all-time highs in the last three months. The trend is similar with bank default risk. The crisis is continuing to get deeper, broader, and more dangerous.

## Key Systemic Problems in the Euro Area

Within the complex sphere of Europe's crisis, if we had to pick one issue that turns this crisis from a tough economic adjustment into a potentially calamitous collapse, we would argue it is the transformation of Europe's sovereign debt market.

## European Sovereign Bonds Are Now Deeply Subordinated Claims on Recessionary Economies

The euro area's immediate problems, in large part, reflect transition from a regime where sovereign debts were perceived to be sacrosanct ("risk-free") to one in which investors perceived that sovereign defaults were possible. Neither investors nor Europe's politicians understood the full ramifications of no bailout clauses in the Maastricht Treaty [a basic EU treaty] until recently. With the new risk premium needed to compensate for default risk, some European nations will need to radically reduce their debt levels and change its maturity structure.

U.S. Senate, February 1, 2012.

The treatment of private investors in the upcoming Greek debt restructuring has made it ever clearer that Europe's sovereign bonds bear substantial risk. On July 27, 2011, the EU Council of Ministers finally admitted that a Greek default was needed—although to date they prefer to describe this default as voluntary, referring to it as private sector involvement (PSI).

Soon after this announcement it was apparent Greece could not afford the proposed deal, and more funds would be needed. At the summit on October 27, 2011, Europe's leaders announced that for Greek debt the PSI "haircut" would rise from 21 to 50 percent in order to provide these funds, while the official creditors promised no additional funds specifically for Greece.

Those nonofficial creditors holding Greek bonds learned a new lesson: They are the residual financiers to European issuers when the troika's programs fail. The Greek press reported that the government was prepared to change laws governing its bonds in order to force nonofficial creditors to bear these losses. . . .

*We* should not underestimate the damage these steps have inflicted on Europe's €8.4 trillion sovereign bond markets. For example, the Italian government has issued bonds with a face value of over €1.8 trillion. The groups holding these bonds are banks, pension funds, insurance companies, and Italian households. These investors bought them as safe, low-return instruments that could be used to hedge liabilities and provide for future income needs. It was once hard to imagine these could ever be restructured or default.

Now, however, it is clear they are not safe. They have default risk, and their ultimate value is subject to the political constraint and subjective decisions by a collective of individuals in the Italian government and society, the ECB, the European Union, and the International Monetary Fund (IMF). An investor buying an Italian bond today needs to forecast an immediate, complex process that has been evolving in unpredictable ways. Investors naturally want a high return in order to bear these risks. . . . [However,] once risk premiums are incorporated in debt, Greece, Ireland, Portugal, and Italy do not appear solvent. For example, with a debt/GDP ratio of 120 percent and a 500-basis-point risk premium, Italy would need to maintain a 6 percent of GDP larger primary surplus to keep its debt stock stable relative to the size of its economy. This is unlikely to be politically sustainable.

## Crisis Spreads into Europe's Core Banks and Incites Capital Flight from the Periphery

On August 27, 2011, Christine Lagarde, the managing director of the IMF [International Monetary Fund], shocked European officialdom with a speech decrying inadequate capital levels in European banks. She referred to analysis by IMF staff showing that, if European banks were stressed for market-implied sovereign default risks, they were €200 billion to €300 billion short of capital. . . . This was the first time the IMF admitted that sovereign default risk needed to be taken into account for the largest banks in Europe. . . .

# Macroeconomic Programs: Too Timid to Restore Confidence or Growth

While it may already be too late to avoid extensive defaults, we can still consider what needs to be done to reduce the risk of default. To avoid defaults and restructurings, Europe needs to introduce policies that bring market risk premiums on sovereign (and hence bank) debts down. Investors need to feel confident that, with a 2 to 3 percent risk premium, it is worth the risk to hold onto several trillion euros worth of troubled nations' sovereign debts, as well as the much larger non-sovereign debts. . . .

The available evidence from the outcomes of the programs in Portugal, Ireland, and Greece, as well as the recently announced budget plans in Italy and Spain, suggests current policies will fail at this task. These programs all plan for gradual reductions in budget deficits, implying continued buildup of total government debts, while partially substituting private debt for official debt. In Portugal and Ireland the programs rely on external financing until 2013 when it is anticipated the program countries will reenter markets to finance ongoing budget deficits and ever higher debt stocks at modest interest rates. In Italy, optimistic growth assumptions help bring the budget to balance in 2013, but debt stocks remain far too high. Spain announced it would miss its 2011 budget deficit target of 6 percent, raising it to 8 percent. In Greece, budget revenue and GDP growth forecasts are again proving too optimistic.

Any successful program must recognize the fact that appetite for periphery debt amongst investors will not recover to "pre-crisis" levels, because default risk is now a reality that was not foreseen prior to 2009 and because debt stocks are now higher in the periphery. For example, Ireland is currently running a budget deficit measured at 12.5 percent of GNP. The troika program calls for that budget deficit to fall to 10.6 percent of GNP in 2012. Ireland's stock of official debt will reach 145 percent of GNP in 2013, while it also has contingent liabilities to its banking sector that amount to over 100 percent of GNP. An investor looking at these numbers must recognize there is serious risk of default. Since market access is highly unlikely, who will finance Ireland from 2013 onwards?

With sovereign risk premiums rising, and capital flowing out of the periphery from banks while deficits and competiveness improve little, it is not surprising that peripheral economies are in trouble. The Purchasing Managers' Index (PMI) indicates a bleak picture. It is no coincidence that a new major "downturn" started soon after German politicians made clear they were planning to let Greece default. It is also clear that the programs are failing to restore growth.

The stark contrast between unemployment in Germany and the periphery reflects the dynamics of the crisis. The strong core is becoming stronger— German unemployment is lower than it was in 2008—while Greece, Ireland, Portugal, and Spain have high unemployment that continues to rise. Italy's troubles are recent, so with a sharp recession beginning, we anticipate Italian unemployment will soon rise sharply also.

# Solutions

Europe may continue to veer towards a major financial collapse. European economies are in decline due to capital outflows from fear of sovereign and bank defaults. Recessions and continued budget deficits only raise the risk of default. Macroeconomic adjustment programs are not strong enough and do not reflect the large measures needed given the lack of exchange rate devaluation. As the GIIPS decline, there is serious risk that other indebted and heavily banked nations in the euro area, such as France, Belgium, and Austria, could be pulled into trouble themselves. [Johnson then outlines a range of possible solutions. The details are not pivotal to the question here].

# Playing with Fire: Ways the Euro Area Could Come to an End

Policymakers often have trouble grasping the danger that small tail risks pose to leveraged systems. As we discussed above, a mere 10 percent annual risk of an Italian crisis is already inconsistent with Italian long-term solvency. If Italy has a disorderly crisis, how safe are French banks? And if those banks aren't safe, how safe is France's sovereign debt? Low-probability bad events can very quickly generate a wave of collapse through leveraged systems. Our concern is that, when compared with financial crises elsewhere, the potential triggers for a euro area collapse are numerous.

## A Unilateral Exit, or the Credible Threat of One

At a midnight press conference on November 2, 2011 in southern France, German Chancellor Angela Merkel and French President Nicolas Sarkozy for the first time entertained the idea that a nation could leave the euro area. Merkel and Sarkozy chose to take a hard line with Greek politicians and their electorate: either complete the existing agreement or leave. The background to this threat was the tough politics in Greece. After 18 months of large budget cuts and some structural reforms, Greece's economy remains in decline. Prime Minister George Papandreou's government was weak, and in a last desperate gesture he attempted to force further reforms through by offering Greek citizens a referendum with an implicit choice of "reform or exit."

An exit from the euro area can be forced in minutes. The Eurosystem only needs to cut off a national central bank from the payments system and prevent that nation from printing new cash euros. Once this is achieved, a bank deposit in Greece would no longer be the same as a deposit in Germany, because one would not be able to get cash for a Greek deposit and one would not be able to transfer it to a non-Greek bank. Of course, the moment people understand such a change could be imminent in their nation, they would run to their banks and attempt to withdraw cash or transfer funds. This is what is now happening in Greece. The country is losing 2.5 percent of GDP monthly in deposits from banks.

There would be enormous, painful ramifications for all of Europe if Greece or another nation made a disorderly exit. Since there is no legal basis for exit, all financial contracts and indebtedness between Greek and non-Greek entities would have uncertain value as the parties could dispute whether these are to be paid in drachmas or euros. Trade between the exiting nation and the rest of the euro area would dry up. The mere fact that a country did exit would have ramifications for the other troubled nations, most likely inciting further capital flight from Europe's core banks and some of the core sovereigns. The euro itself would probably weaken sharply, and "currency risk" would be added into the euro.

## The Weak Periphery Lashes Out Against Germany, While Germany Fights Back

The political dynamics of crisis invariably pit creditors against debtors, potentially leading to flare-ups that cause creditors to give up. In Ireland, against strong popular opposition, the ECB is forcing Irish citizens to take on further debt in order to bail out creditors of bankrupt banks. In Greece, Prime Minister Papandreou was essentially ordered to revoke his planned referendum, while Greece's opposition leader was ordered to write a letter promising he supported Greece's troika program, despite the fact that he clearly did not support it nor did he participate actively in any negotiations to agree to it. French and German politicians are also playing an instrumental role in supporting Italy's new technocratic prime minister, while they eschewed former prime minister Silvio Berlusconi towards the end of his term. Meanwhile in Germany, "bailout fatigue" has set in as electorates and politicians turn against more funds to nations that, they perceive, are failing to reform sufficiently quickly.

While there are many outcomes of such discord, one possibility is that it leads to a messy grab for power. The troubled nations already have the power to take over decision making at the ECB. They may well usurp control in order to provide much larger ECB bailouts. This would raise concerns in financial markets and could lead to rising long-term yields on all euro-denominated debts. Germany would be forced to pay more to finance itself, and German savers would ultimately be paying for the periphery bailouts through inflation and a weak euro. In Germany this would lead to rising calls to leave the euro area.

Once there is a small risk that Germany could leave, market prices for euro-denominated assets would again change sharply. New risk premiums would need to be added to national debts where nations are expected to have weak currencies, while Germany and other strong nations might see their risk premiums fall even further. Such changes would reinforce the recent trends in which the core nations continue to strengthen relative to the periphery, but those changes would also be highly destabilizing for financial markets.

## Economics of Austerity May Fail

The third risk for the euro area is that economic, political, and social realities eventually prove that the system simply cannot work. After all, the euro area is a dream of political leaders that has been imposed on disparate economies.

Few nations sought popular support to create the euro. The German leadership avoided a referendum, and in France the Maastricht treaty was passed with a thin majority of 51 percent. Marine Le Pen, who is third in opinion polls for the spring 2012 French presidential election, is calling for France to leave the euro area and reintroduce the franc. Even though most European leaders are highly committed to maintaining this dream, no one can be sure what the costs are in order to keep it.

A plausible negative scenario is that those costs, in the eyes of the electorate, eventually appear too high. The evidence to date suggests Europe's periphery, even in a fairly benign outcome, will be condemned to many years or even a decade of tough austerity, high unemployment, and little hope for future growth. A good comparison is the "lost decade" of the 1980s in Latin America when nations hardly grew due to the large debt overhangs from unaffordable debts. However, those nations had the benefit of flexible exchange rates, while Europe's periphery faces a more difficult period with uncompetitive economies. Latin America's problems ended only when the creditor nations accepted large writedowns and debt restructuring.

Another comparison would be the heavily indebted United Kingdom during the 1920s when the government managed policies to restore currency convertibility after the war. Britain suffered with a weak economy for a decade, before ending in the Great Depression, despite a booming global economy throughout the 1920s. However, this too is not a good comparison since Britain had far more flexible wages and prices than Europe's periphery, with nominal wages falling 28 percent during the 1920–21 recession.

## Markets Lose Patience

Our final scenario is the most likely. Faced with the reality of failing adjustment programs, difficult politics, and rising risks that one or more peripheral nations may rebel, or Germany may rescind its support, investors may simply decide that the cumulative risks mean the euro area has a moderate risk of failing.

If investors decide there is a low but significant probability that the euro area might fail, we would encounter another version of Rudi Dornbusch's astute observation: "The crisis takes a much longer time coming than you think, and then it happens much faster than you would have thought." Here's why: The failure of the euro area will be a calamitous financial event. As Dornbusch famously remarked of the Mexican 1994–95 crisis, "It took forever and then it took a night."

If one believes the euro might fail, one should avoid being invested in European financial institutions, and in euro-denominated assets, until the outcome of the new pattern of currencies is clearer. As a result, a large swathe of euro-denominated assets would quickly fall in value. The euro itself would cheapen sharply, but so would the value of European bank debt and European shares, and most sovereigns would see their bonds trade off sharply. This in turn would make it expensive for even the Germans to raise finance in euros. Despite their impeccable credit record, they would be attempting to issue bonds in what is perceived as a flawed currency.

A small risk of the euro "breaking up" would have great importance for the euro swap market. This market is used by Europe's insurance companies, banks, and pension funds to hedge their interest rate risk. A swap contract allows, for example, a pension fund to lock in a long-term interest rate for their investments, in return for promising to pay short-term interest rates to their contract counterparty. It is an important market that underlies the ability of insurance companies, pension funds, and others to make long-term commitments to provide society with annuities, pensions, and savings from insurance policies. The notional value of these swaps is many times euro area GDP.

The euro swap market could quickly collapse if markets begin to question the survival of the euro. Euro swap rates are calculated as the average interest rate paid on euro-denominated interbank loans for 44 of Europe's banks. Approximately half of these banks are in "troubled nations." So the interest rate will reflect both inflation risk and credit risk of the participating banks. If investors decided that the euro may not exist in several years' time, swap interest rates would naturally rise because people would be concerned that banks could fail and that the "euro" interest rate could turn into something else—for example, the average of a basket of new currencies with some, such as the Greek drachma, likely to be highly inflationary. . . .

## Dreams Versus Reality

There is no doubt that European political leaders are highly committed to keeping the euro area together, and so far, there is widespread support from business leaders and the population to maintain it. There is also, rightly, great fear that disorderly collapse of the euro area would impose untold costs on the global economy. All these factors suggest the euro area will hold together.

However, many financial collapses started this way. A far more dramatic creation and collapse was the downfall of the ruble zone when the Soviet Union collapsed in 1991. Argentina's attempt to peg its currency to the dollar in the 1990s was initially highly successful but ended when its politicians and society could not make the adjustments needed to hold the structure together. The Baltic nations—Estonia, Latvia, and Lithuania—have managed to maintain their pegs but only after dramatic wage adjustments and recessions.

More relevant, the various exchange rate arrangements that Europe created prior to the euro all failed. With the creation of the euro, Europe's leaders raised the stakes by ensuring the costs of a new round of failures would be far greater than those of the past, but otherwise arguably little has changed to make this attempt more likely to succeed than the previous one. Small probabilities of very negative events can be destabilizing. A lot of things can go wrong at the level of individual countries within the euro area—and one country's debacle can easily spill over to affect default risk and interest rates in the other 16 countries. The euro swap market is based, in part, on interest rates charged by 44 banks in a range of countries; about half of these banks may be considered to be located in troubled or potentially troubled countries. If the euro swap market comes under pressure or ceases to function, this would have major implications for the funding of all European sovereigns—including those that are a relatively good credit risk.

At the least, we expect several more sovereign defaults and multiple further crises to plague Europe in the next several years. There is simply too much debt, and adjustment programs are too slow to prevent it. But this prediction implies that the long-term social costs, including unemployment and recessions rather than growth, attributable to this currency union are serious. Sometimes it is easier to make these adjustments through flexible exchange rates, and we certainly would have seen more rapid recovery if peripheral nations had the leeway to use exchange rates.

When we combine multiple years of stagnation with leveraged financial institutions and nervous financial markets, a rapid shift from low-level crisis to collapse is very plausible. European leaders could take measures to reduce this risk (through further actions on sovereign debt restructurings, more aggressive economic adjustment, and increased bailout funds). However, so far, there is little political will to take these necessary measures. Europe's economy remains, therefore, in a dangerous state.

**Guido Westerwelle**  →  **NO**

# The Euro and the Future of Europe

The famous line from Mark Twain's memoirs about Wagner is also true for Europe: "The music is better than it sounds." And I say that as a great fan of both Richard Wagner and of European integration.

I know that there are many questions and concerns about Europe these days. Questions about the current crisis and what it means for Europeans, Americans and others around the globe. Questions also about Germany's approach to the crisis, about the place it sees for itself in Europe.

I have come here to answer four fundamental questions as openly and directly as possible:

- What is the nature of the crisis we are facing?
- What are we trying to achieve?
- What is Germany's role in all of this?

And, of course:

- What's in it for the United States?

## First, the Nature of the Crisis

The term "Euro-crisis" is convenient but misleading. In its first ten years, the common currency has been remarkably successful by any standard. Its exchange rate and inflation rate are as stable as that of the Deutsche Mark.

The Euro has assumed the role of a second global reserve currency. In times of globalization the Euro was the right thing to do. If we did not have it, we would have to invent it now—as a lesson learnt from this financial crisis that would have had worse effects without a common currency. But it is also obvious that a number of European countries are no longer enjoying sufficient trust in the financial markets.

The reasons are slightly different in each case. But three things are at the root of the crisis. To begin with, the world financial crisis as the trigger; secondly, excessive public and private debt; and [thirdly] growing macroeconomic imbalances as a result of lacking competitiveness and flaws in Eurozone governance. All of these factors are interlinked.

In the aftermath of the financial crisis of 2008 the state had to rescue an over-leveraged and ill-invested banking sector. At the same time it had to

Westerwelle, Guido. From speech delivered at the Brookings Institution, January 20, 2012. Reprinted by permission of the Embassy of the Federal Republic of Germany.

provide a huge fiscal stimulus for the economy. The German fiscal stimulus, by the way, was comparable in relative size to US efforts at the time.

As a result, financial markets started questioning the ability of some Eurozone members to repay their debt or to grow their way out of the debt burden—first in Greece, then in Ireland, then in Portugal. The debt crisis morphed into a crisis of confidence, questioning the political will and determination of Eurozone members to fix the flaws in the construction of the monetary union.

## What Are We Trying to Achieve?

There are those who argue that an early and massive rescue operation would somehow have prevented the crisis from developing. As if some sort of unlimited guarantee of Greek sovereign debt by all other Eurozone members in the spring of 2010 could have put everything on hold. I frankly don't think that this argument holds up. It focuses exclusively on the contagion issue but completely ignores the deeper origins of the crisis.

The same is true, in my view, for the argument that Germany, Europe's anchor of stability, somehow misreads the nature of the crisis. That we are trying to amend the rule-book instead of putting out the fire. From the very beginning we have focused on a double-track strategy: Linking solidarity with partners under pressure with a firm commitment to fix the Eurozone and put all members on a path of fiscal responsibility.

Let me emphasize this point again because it represents the core of our approach: There are those who argue that we underestimate the severity of the crisis. That we mistakenly focus on long-term remedies for what is in reality a short-term problem. My answer is: It is actually this argument itself that underestimates the nature and the scope of the crisis. Yes, we need short-term crisis management. But we should not opt for measures that would lay the ground for an even bigger crisis in years to come. And most importantly: our short-term measures will only be credible and effective if we address the root causes at the same time.

Solidarity with countries having liquidity problems is an indispensable part of our effort. We are now in the final stages of setting up a permanent European Stability Mechanism to deal with liquidity problems. Germany's share of these financial guarantees is more than a quarter of the total. The German parliament has approved financial guarantees of more than 200 billion Euros. Translated into the size of the US economy this would be the equivalent of far more than one trillion US dollars in guarantees by the US Treasury. Can you imagine members of Congress approving such a sum to help out non-Americans? The theory that Germany is not demonstrating solidarity with its fellow Eurozone partners in trouble is an urban legend and simply not accurate.

The European Central Bank also has a very important role in managing the crisis. It will do what it considers necessary and appropriate within its mandate. It is not for me to comment or to give advice. The core of the problem, however, goes even deeper than providing liquidity. The crisis of confidence requires decisive action on two fronts.

First, we have to fix the flaws in the Eurozone's construction. When setting it up shortly after the fall of the Berlin Wall we were not able to go all the way and create a Political Union, side by side with the Economic and Monetary Union. It took a while for the consequences of this failure to become apparent because we enjoyed a decade of low interest rates and strong economic growth especially in Southern Eurozone members. This made it so tempting and easy to neglect the dangerous productivity and competitiveness gap within the Eurozone.

We thought we were doing well even without stronger coordination of fiscal and economic policies. This was a mistake. We also allowed the hallmark of our monetary union, the Stability and Growth Pact, to be hollowed out and violated numerous times without real consequences. This was another mistake. And we did not reduce public and private debt in good times. This was our third mistake. We are now addressing and correcting all three of them.

This is why we have pushed for changes to the European Treaties. This is why we hope to conclude a new Fiscal Compact by the end of this month. With this compact, we will firmly establish the principles of future fiscal responsibility. We will introduce strong "debt-brake" provisions in member states' legal frameworks. And we will significantly strengthen policy coordination within the Eurozone and its prospective members. I am confident that most non-Euro members of the EU will join in this effort. Our door will also remain open to Great Britain.

Yet in my view, tighter rules and better coordination cannot be the end of the story. We have to recognize that we need nothing less than a paradigm change for our countries and our societies. The debt economy itself has reached its limits. Fiscal responsibility and sustainability are not arcane concepts for experts. Nor are they awkward hobbies of Germans still traumatized by memories of hyper-inflation three generations ago. They are the imperative of our time.

The policies of debt, combined with the shortcomings of the Eurozone construction, and compounded by the effects of the financial crisis, have led us into the danger zone. We have taken it too far. Beyond the point of credibility. And—allow me the question—can we really be sure that this is only a problem of the Eurozone?

It is this triple origin of the crisis that defies all the easy answers, all the "big-bazooka"-remedies put forward by economists and pundits on both sides of the Atlantic—and on the island in-between. That is why we are focusing our efforts on creating a Union for Stability in Europe and on moving towards fiscal sustainability and growth here and now. We cannot postpone this fundamental change of direction to a distant future.

Rescue packages and short-term liquidity are not a solution to the crisis. They are buying us time in which to address the root causes—no less, but also no more. The key is therefore to strike the right balance between easing the short-term pain and laying the foundations for long-term gain.

Europe has decided to no longer ease the symptoms of the crisis by fighting debt with more debt. This is an enormous challenge. It will be neither easy nor quick. But it is the only viable path to a stronger Europe in the future. Our partners in Greece, in Ireland and Portugal, and many other countries, deserve our respect and our support for the efforts and sacrifices they have made.

When we discuss the merits of this argument let us not overlook the different demographic realities of our societies. In Germany and many parts of Europe every Euro of debt will have to be shouldered by fewer and fewer taxpayers in the future.

By no means do I advocate austerity only. Apart from the debt issue the widening gap in competitiveness between Eurozone members is the most important cause of the crisis. Budget cuts alone will not do the trick. Structural reforms are essential for the creation of new growth. They are also essential for the long-term cohesion of the Eurozone.

It is simply not acceptable that one out of five Europeans under the age of 25 is without a job. In some countries we are even talking about one out of three. Here we can and must do better. Reforming labor markets is only one element but a very important one. We know from our own experience ten years ago, when Germany was singled out as the "sick man of Europe," that these reforms are politically difficult but very beneficial for long-term growth and employment. This is the very challenge that some of our partners in Europe are now facing. Others, like the Baltic states, have already success-fully implemented these reforms and have returned to solid growth. And we will do more: We will employ unused EU structural funds to stimulate eco-nomic growth. We will focus the upcoming EU budget for the years 2014 to 2020 on innovation and new technologies and move away from subsidizing the economy of yesterday. A budget, by the way, to which Germany will be the biggest net contributor. And, finally, we should never lose sight of the benefits of free trade. We work hard to expand free access to the emerging markets. Shouldn't we also put the issue of a Trans-Atlantic Free Trade Area high on our agenda? A free-trade area that is not weakening our WTO [World Trade Organization] efforts for global free trade? We are, after all, more deeply integrated through trade and investment ties than any other two economic areas of the world.

## This Brings Me to My Third Question: What Is Germany's Role in All This?

When you look at most of the public commentary you can't help but feel a dilemma: We are either criticised for being too cautious in addressing the crisis or for being too dominant in dictating our own policies to others. We take both views seriously. And we believe both are beside the point.

To be perfectly clear from the outset: There is no good future for Germany without a good future for a united Europe. While there are undoubtedly dif-ferences in opinion among German political parties on the details of crisis management, there is a broad consensus that the answer to the current crisis has to be "more Europe," not "less Europe." Germany is and remains deeply and firmly committed to a united Europe.

The integrated single European market is the basis of our wealth and economic prosperity. The integrated decision-making in Brussels, while often tedious and full of compromises, has been the basis of more than six decades of peace among EU member states. The integrated trade and foreign policies are our best chance to preserve our European way of life and to assert our values and interests in a globalized world with new centers of powers.

"Going it alone" is not an option for Germany, however strong our economy may be. History has taught us, with chapters too dark to forget, that European integration was—and remains—the only convincing and viable answer to the "German question." This fundamental insight continues to guide our policies. I am personally deeply committed to the idea of a European Germany.

However, it would be wrong to deny that there are different visions of what Europe should be. There are those who do not want an open, tolerant and integrated Europe. There are those who stress the differences, be they ethnic or religious, rather than what unites us. They are advocating a "fortress Europe." This is a vision that we need to oppose forcefully. Re-nationalization in a time of globalization is a dangerous concept. The financial, political and human cost of a disintegrating Europe would be crippling. And it would be foolish to believe that Europe could withdraw into some sheltered corner. Yet it is only if we can put our own house in order that we can seriously and credibly establish Europe as a strong political actor on the global stage. I am deeply convinced that Europe has something to offer beyond preserving its wealth and its own security. We are a community of values. We are founded upon the fundamental rights of the individual. Our European model of shared sovereignty can be an inspiration in a globalized world in need of order.

## This Leads Me to My Fourth and Final Point: What's in it for the United States?

I firmly believe in what Vice President Joe Biden said so eloquently in his speech to the Munich Security Conference three years ago: "In sharing ideals and searching for partners in a more complex world, Americans and Europeans still look to one another before they look to anyone else."

This is what we have done in the past. This is what we are doing today. This is what we have to do in the future.

The effects of globalisation confront us with new challenges: from climate change to water and food shortages, from cyber security to the protection of the global commons. New powers are rising faster than we could foresee only a few years ago. Their growing economic weight increasingly translates into political weight. Every government on our two continents is shifting resources towards fast-growing new centers of power in Asia and elsewhere.

And yet, when we confront the pressing issues of today it is above all Americans and Europeans who share the same values, interests, objectives and resources: We continue to fight alongside each other in Afghanistan. At the Bonn Conference in December we pushed forward our joint strategy for a gradual transfer of responsibility to the Afghan authorities. We are working on a political solution to prevent the country from ever again becoming a safe haven for terrorism. We stand firmly together in confronting Iran's increasingly dangerous course. The EU will put into place a new and very substantial round of sanctions this coming Monday to forcefully make the point that Iran's behavior in the nuclear issue is unacceptable and a danger to world peace. We are working closely together and with our partners in the Arab League to address the ongoing bloodshed in Syria where a brutal regime resorts to violence against its own people. We are joining forces to support the transformation underway in the Arab world towards more representative, more participatory political systems. Both America and the EU put a particular emphasis on the empowerment of women as a key to successful transformation. We work closely together to facilitate a negotiated and lasting peace between Israelis and Palestinians. We will re-affirm our close alliance at the NATO Summit in Chicago in May. An alliance of collective defense, an alliance that gives itself the means to be an element of stability in an increasingly fragile world.

Possibly the most important common task of all will be to restore the legitimacy and viability of our economic model. The proper regulation of the global financial system is still unfinished business. We have to continue to work on it together and in the G20-framework. This includes making sure the IMF has what it takes to play its crucial role in the global system.

If we do not address these issues in a convincing fashion we will face a systemic crisis of legitimacy that by far transcends our two economies. It would undermine our own political systems. And it would sharply diminish our ability to successfully promote our values and interests globally.

## When I Look at the American Debate Over the Past Weeks I See Mostly a Caricature of Europe. The Image of a Continent Mired in Gloom and Self-Absorption. I Beg to Differ.

First point: We actually overcame socialism in Europe 20 years ago. And we owe this among others to the firm commitment to the idea of freedom by both Democratic and Republican American administrations.

Secondly, the World Economic Forum's most recent "Global Competitiveness Index" lists seven European countries in its Top Ten list, three of them members of the Eurozone. European companies are among the fastest-growing businesses in America, investing billions of dollars and creating thousands of jobs in this country. Finally, Europe is the largest donor of development assistance and humanitarian aid across the globe. In short: Europe is a strong and vibrant continent and I firmly believe that we will emerge stronger from this crisis.

My vision of our future strategic partnership sees the United States and a united Europe at the core of an "enlarged West." In a world with new centers of power agreement between the US and the EU will no longer be sufficient to shape global solutions. But we can and we should be a motor of progress. We have to engage with new powers and bring on board new partners in order to build a broader consensus. In a world where the idea of freedom continues to gain strength it is imperative that the West, the cradle of freedom, stands together.

# EXPLORING THE ISSUE

## Is the European Union's Eurozone in Serious Danger of Collapsing?

### Questions for Critical Thinking and Reflection

1. Who is right, those who say troubled eurozone countries must accept "pain" through budget cuts and higher taxes to balance their budgets and end the deficits that have cause the eruozone crisis or those who say that raising taxes, cutting services, firing public employees, and similar steps unfairly punish the needy to ensure that the banks and investors in European bonds?
2. Should American taxpayers through U.S. contributions to the IMF get involved in the eurozone crisis? What are the U.S. stakes in the stability of the EU's economy?
3. Some argue that the eurozone crisis foreshadows a similar financial meltdown in the United States if it does not put its financial affairs in order. Do you agree?

## Is There Common Ground?

During the balance of 2012 after the testimony, Professor Johnson's alarmed testimony and Foreign Minister Westerwelle's more optimistic speech, the eurozone crisis continued to roil Europe politically and economically. The crisis created something of a north–south split in the EU. Most of the countries in economic trouble from high budget deficits and soaring public debt are in the south, with Greece, Spain, Italy, and Portugal the most troubled. In the north are Germany and most of the other eurozone countries with the financial resources to assist the troubled countries in avoiding defaulting on their debt and making Europe's shaky economic situation worse. These northern countries have insisted that bailout money to Greece and the other countries in trouble be contingent on those countries agreeing to changes that will reduce their deficits. The troubled countries have resisted these requirements because they included reduced services, higher taxes, and other politically unpopular policies.

The International Monetary Fund also became involved in possibly extending funds to the trouble countries, and that further entwined the eurozone crisis with U.S. politics and the United States' own massive budget problems. The funds needed for Europe would require an infusion of capital into the IMF from its member countries, of which the United States is the largest contributor. But President Barack Obama put off asking Congress for the needed funds until after the November 2012 presidential election. Moreover, funding the IMF will come at the very time the United States is trying to come to grips with in own immense budget deficits and the need to cut them back by taxing more or spending less.

Greece's government fell in early 2012 over public anger at its attempt to introduce austerity measures, and new elections in May did not result in a stable government with a clear mandate. As a result, the Greek economy has continued to stagger, with unemployment reaching 25 percent in the country in October 2012. Spain's unemployment rate was also 25 percent, and the overall rate in the eurozone was 11.4 percent (compared to 8.1 percent in the United States). By contrast, Germany's rate was a relatively enviable 5.4 percent.

## Additional Resources

A book published late in 2012 on the crisis is Costas Lapavitsas, *Crisis in the Eurozone* (Verso, 2012). Also see Congressional Research Service, *The Eurozone Crisis: Overview and Issues for Congress,* a report to Congress (R42377), September 26, 2012. It is available online at www.fas.org/sgp/crs/row/R42377.pdf. For the latest news try the online editions of financially oriented newspapers such as Great Britain's *Financial Times* and its U.S. equivalent, *The Wall Street Journal.*

# ISSUE 2

## Should Russia Be Considered a Hostile Country?

YES: **Ariel Cohen**, from Testimony during Hearings on "Rethinking Reset: Re-Examining the Obama Administration Russia Policy," before the Committee on Foreign Affairs, U.S. House of Representatives (July 7, 2011)

NO: **Steven Pifer,** from Testimony during Hearings on "The Future Course of the U.S.-Russia Relationship," before the Committee on Foreign Affairs, U.S. House of Representatives (March 21, 2012)

### ISSUE SUMMARY

YES: Ariel Cohen, the senior research fellow for Russian and Eurasian Studies and International Energy Policy at the Heritage Foundation, testifies that Russia's increasingly authoritarian government is pursuing polices that are antithetical to U.S. national interests.

NO: Steven Pifer, the director of the Brookings Arms Control Initiative and a senior fellow in the Center on the United States and Europe, concedes that there are some conflict points in U.S.–Russia relations, but argues that it would be an error to treat Russia as implacably hostile rather than work with it to manage differences.

**R**ussia has experienced two momentous revolutions during the twentieth century. The first began in March 1917. After a brief moment of attempted democracy, that revolution descended into totalitarian government, with the takeover of the Bolshevik Communists in November and the establishment of the Union of Soviet Socialist Republics (USSR), with Russia one of its 15 republics.

The second great revolution arguably occurred in 1991 when the USSR collapsed and its 15 republics became independent countries. Of these former Soviet republics (FSRs), Russia is by far the largest, has the largest population, and is in reality and potentially the most powerful. Russia retained the bulk of the Soviet Union's nuclear weapons and their delivery systems. When Russia reemerged as independent, its president, Boris Yeltsin, seemed to offer the hope of strong, democratic leadership that would economically rejuvenate and democratize Russia internally and that, externally, would work to make Russia a peaceful and cooperative neighbor. However, these prospects soon faded amid Russia's vast problems. The country's economy fell more deeply into shambles, leaving 22 percent of all Russians below the poverty level. Russia's economic turmoil also caused a steep decline in Russia's military capabilities. To make matters even worse, the rekindling of an independence movement by the Chechens, a Muslim nation in the Caucuses Mountains region, led to savage fighting.

Yeltsin's ill-fated presidency ended when he resigned on December 31, 1999. His elected successor, Vladimir Putin, had spent most of his professional career in the KGB (*Komitet Gosudarstvennoi Bezopasnosti*/Committee for State Security), the Soviet secret police, and headed its successor, Russia's FSB (*Federal'naya Sluzhba Bezopasnosti*/Federal Security Service).

For good or ill, Putin brought a level of stability to Russia. Slowly, Russia's economy steadied itself. Moreover, with a well-educated populace, vast mineral and energy resources, and a large (if antiquated) industrial base, Russia had a base to grow economically. Similarly, while Russian military forces fell into disarray in the 1990s, the country retained a potent nuclear arsenal. Furthermore, its large population, weapons manufacturing capacity, and huge land mass make it likely that the breakdown of Russia's conventional military capabilities and geostrategic importance will only be temporary.

Putin served two terms as president, but was ineligible to run for a third term. In what most outside observers considered little more than a sham transfer of power, Putin's prime minister, Dmitry Medvedev, was elected president in 2008 and promptly named his former boss, Putin, as prime minister. Then in 2012, with Putin once again eligible under the Russian Constitution to be president, Medvedev stepped aside, and Putin was elected to a third term. Putin returned to the presidency following the 2012 presidential elections, and Medvedev once again became prime minister.

Whether Putin has been serving as president or prime minister, Russia under his leadership has become steadily less democratic. Most of the independent news media is gone, local authorities have lost much of their power, and the opposition movement and leaders are increasingly repressed and individuals are sometimes jailed. There are also numerous issues that divide Russia from the United States. For example, Moscow believes that it is threatened by the U.S. drive to deploy a ballistic missile defense system and by the expansion of the North Atlantic Treaty Organization to even include some FSRs.

When President George W. Bush first came to office in 2001, he felt he could work with at that point President Putin, but U.S.–Russia relations generally deteriorated as the years went on. After meeting with the then-president Medvedev at the White House in June 2010, President Barack Obama declared that he and Medvedev had "succeeded in resetting" the relationship between Washington and Moscow. In the first reading, Ariel Cohen criticizes Obama's reset policy as misguided and naive. In the second reading, Steven Pifer asserts that the United States should continue to explore ways to work with Russia to advance American interests and to build a more positive, sustainable bilateral relationship.

# YES ⤶

Ariel Cohen

# Rethinking Reset: Re-Examining the Obama Administration Russia Policy

In March 2009, Secretary of State Hillary Clinton presented her Russian counterpart, Sergei Lavrov, with a red button symbolizing a new reset policy with the Russian Federation. Symbolically, as the result of incompetent translation, the inscription on the button read overload instead of reset. Ever since, President Obama has spent an inordinate amount of time cultivating Russian President Dmitry Medvedev and making him his principal diplomatic interlocutor—despite the fact that Medvedev is Prime Minister Vladimir Putin's appointed protégé, with no political base of his own.

The grave error made in assessing who was in charge led to a chain of strategic miscalculations in relations with Moscow. While grooming Medvedev, the Administration agreed to cut U.S. strategic nuclear forces under the New START [Strategic Arms Reduction Treaty], abandoned the original program of missile defense deployment in Poland and the Czech Republic, engaged Russia in futile missile defense talks, pursued a policy of geopolitical neglect in the former Soviet Union, and toned down criticism of the violation of political freedom in Russia. However, the reality remains that Medvedev has only limited capacity to deliver and looks increasingly unlikely to continue in office.

Putin still is Russia's national leader and the real power behind—and on—the throne. Even with Medvedev as President, Russia is still willing to use force to achieve its geo-economic goals as well. Control of energy corridors from the Caspian Sea to the Black Sea and beyond was an objective of the Russian military operation against Georgia in August 2008. This year, Gazprom [Russia's national gas company] opens the Nord Stream pipeline from Russia to Germany, with spurs to other European countries, increasing their dependence on Russian energy. This has been clearly confirmed by incidents over the last two decades involving delays in energy supplies to Azerbaijan, as well as the Baltic States, Belarus, Bulgaria, Croatia, Georgia, Serbia, Slovakia, and Ukraine and other countries. From the American perspective, Russia's energy nationalism and continued collusion with anti-American regimes in Iran, Syria and Venezuela are troubling long-term geopolitical trends and should be sources of frustration in Washington.

U.S. House of Representatives, July 7, 2011.

In the last two and a half years of reset, despite the rhetoric about needed improvements in the rule of law, Russian whistleblowers died in jail or were severely beaten; Russian courts continued to sentence political opponents to lengthy prison terms for crimes they had not committed; peaceful demonstrators were beaten and incarcerated; and the state refused registration to democratic political parties. And things are likely to get worse.

Based on the reset record, top White House and State Department officials now privately recognize that they bet on the wrong horse, as it is unlikely that Medvedev will wield any real power beyond the spring of 2012 even if he nominally remains in office. However, the Administration cannot publicly admit its mistake, as this would undermine the very notion of this over-personalized reset policy.

## Obama's "Reset": Neglecting American Values and Interests

The reset announced by the Obama Administration in February 2009 was part of the White House's broader new realism in U.S. foreign policy, a bizarre hybrid that combined a reluctance to defend human rights in Russia, China, and Iran with apologies for alleged crimes caused by American exceptionalism. The Administration revised down the scope of American priorities in Russia and Eurasia, de-facto allowing Russia to build what President Medvedev called a zone of privileged interests in the former Soviet Union, effectively denying these countries a democratic path of development and close relations with the Euro-Atlantic zone. This pseudo-realism has adulterated fundamental American interests and abhors the use of force to protect them. One could argue that that brand of realism had already shown its shortcomings in the 1980s, when it ignored the revolutions that ended the Cold War. The Obama Administration failed to understand that there is no escape from both protecting U.S. interests and pursuing moral imperatives in politics, even in world politics.

Underlying the Obama Administration's reset of relations with Russia was its supposed promotion of democracy and human rights even as it sought engagement on the two countries' common interests. The state of democracy inside Russia is, in fact, being addressed by Washington and Moscow. Michael McFaul, the President's Senior Director for Russia on the National Security Council, who President Obama nominated to be the next U.S. Ambassador in Russia, is the leader of a bilateral working group on civil society for the U.S. side, in partnership with Vladislav Surkov, Putin's and Russian President Dmitry Medvedev's political architect.

Beyond domestic political engagement, the Obama Administration's reset policy has primarily been a series of concessions to a regime in Moscow that is seeking Soviet-like superpower prestige and status through forced nuclear equality with Washington. This approach has far-reaching negative implications for U.S. security and foreign policy as well as for the security of U.S. allies.

# Popular Front on the Offensive: Putin Returns?

Whoever occupies the Oval office is facing a complex system of U.S.–Russian relations. These include nuclear nonproliferation and arms control, the supply of U.S. and NATO troops in Afghanistan via Russian territory, human rights and Islamist extremism in Russia, the energy and sovereignty concerns of U.S. friends and allies, and the Iranian quest for weapons of mass destruction, to name just a few. The Obama Administration cannot address these issues by pretending that Medvedev and his narrow circle of supporters wield the real power. In fact, it is the Putin group—which includes the key energy, military and security services officials, businessmen, and the leadership of the United Russia ruling party—that exercises the ultimate power.

Now Putin, no great friend of America, is likely to move back from the Prime Minister's office to the Kremlin in the spring of 2012, raising tough questions about Obama's Russian policy. Putin has publicly disagreed with Medvedev, his handpicked successor, on a number of key policy issues, many of them vital to U.S. interests. While Medvedev has generally articulated positions which are considered liberal in Russia, Putin has consistently criticized the U.S. and stuck to the statist line. Some of the issues on which the two have apparent differences include the role of freedom in the country, the legacy of [Soviet dictator] Joseph Stalin (Putin called him "an effective manager"), and the collapse of the Soviet Union. Putin called it the greatest geopolitical catastrophe of the twentieth century, while his protégé thinks the Bolshevik October putsch was the greatest geopolitical catastrophe for Russia.

The two have also argued on modernization. Medvedev wants a broad-based rejuvenation of the state, including the political system, while his mentor emphasizes boosting Russia's military capabilities through science and technology (just as the czars and the Soviets did); Libya (Medvedev wants to work with the Allies, while Putin blames the U.S. for destabilization of the Middle East); and persecution of former oil magnate Mikhail Khodorkovsky. Medvedev said that the man does not represent any danger to the public, while Putin intervened in the ongoing trial and demanded that he continue to sit in jail.

Putin also supports friendship with China and Venezuela and good relations with Iran. At various points Putin accused the U.S. of supporting Islamist terrorists in the North Caucasus in order to dismantle Russia, illegally intervening in Iraq, being responsible for the global economic recession, and toppling regimes in the Middle East through promotion of social media. Putin pays lip service to the fight against corruption, and directly intervenes in prominent court cases. Putin formed his worldview in the KGB and by reading Russian nationalist philosophers, including some with fascist sympathies. Pro-Putin elites include the top officers of the security services and the armed forces, the military-industrial complex, state company bosses, and a part of the business class. They are a mix of statists, imperialists, and nationalists. They support a future for Russia that is rooted in its imperial past and Christian Orthodoxy.

Last month, worried about his own and his party's declining popularity and anxious to outmaneuver Medvedev, Putin launched the Popular Front, a political contraption that would consist of United Russia, women's and environmental organizations, sympathetic businessmen, and trade unions. Putin may allow communists and possibly Vladimir Zhirinovsky's ultranationalists in the next Parliament, but no real democratic opposition. This could spell the end of the feeble multi-party system in Russia.

Free from concern about a serious U.S. response, the Kremlin has continued to prosecute Putin's political enemies:

- In June, the Russian Justice Ministry denied registration to the Party of People's Freedom (PARNAS), a new party created by prominent opposition leaders, such as the former Prime Minister Mikhail Kasyanov; former Deputy Prime Minister Boris Nemtsov; former Duma Deputy Chairman Vladimir Ryzhkov, and former Deputy Energy Minister Vladimir Milov—an early indication that December's parliamentary elections will be neither free nor fair.
- In May, prosecutors opened a criminal investigation of anti-corruption whistleblower Aleksey Navalny for what he said was revenge for exposing alleged fraud at Russian state companies.
- In December 2010, former oligarchs Mikhail Khodorkovsky and Platon Lebedev were sentenced, in their second trial, to additional lengthy terms in Siberian prisons on charges of embezzlement and money laundering.
- On May 31, the European Court of Justice ruled that the Russian state had seriously violated Khodorkovsky's rights during his arrest and trial detention. Despite Medvedev's talk about Khodorkovsky not being a threat to the public, the courts continue to reject his appeals for an early release.

## The Cost of U.S.–Russian Relations Is Too High

While the gains from the reset relationship have been exaggerated, the cost in terms of U.S. diminished security, geopolitical losses and moral authority has been high. The Obama Administration has disavowed linkages between its Russia policy components, as it placed punishing Russian misbehavior in one area by withholding concessions in another off limits. There is good reason to believe, moreover, that Russian leaders do not take White House efforts to promote freedom and human rights seriously. They know that the U.S. Administration is chained to the reset and will do little more than verbally object to the Kremlin's abuses of human rights and the rule of law. The talk of democracy is for domestic [U.S.] consumption, said one official Russian visitor to Washington last fall. This perceived American softness is perhaps one reason why Medvedev told the *Financial Times* on June 18, "Let me tell you that no one wishes the re-election of Barack Obama as U.S. president as I do."

## Russia's Nuclear Arms Policy

The Administration may be jeopardizing U.S. and allied missile defenses. The New START treaty is a cornerstone of President Obama's dangerously naive policy of unilateral nuclear disarmament known as "getting to zero," i.e., achieving a world without nuclear weapons. . . .

During the Cold War, the Soviet Union deployed thousands of short-range nuclear weapons capable of being used against military and civilian targets. Russia's current military doctrine focuses on deterring the U.S. while winning regional conflicts. This doctrine allows the use of nuclear weapons in response to large-scale aggression with conventional weapons in situations critical to the national security of the Russian Federation and its allies. It does not exclude preemptive nuclear strikes in situations critical to Russia's national security and state survival. Russia's most recent draft national security strategy imagines possible future military conflicts over energy resources and emphasizes the need to modernize its armed forces. . . .

During the recent wars in Chechnya (1994–1996 and 1999–2004) and Georgia (2008), Russia's conventional military forces were generally unprepared and ineffective. As a result, Russia has come to view its nuclear arsenal, especially its advantage in short-range nuclear weapons, as an important component of its national power in regional conflict along its periphery. The Kremlin realizes the strategic significance of using its short range nuclear weapons to gain political leverage, especially as it pertains to NATO member states. . . .

Recently, Russia's Army General Makhmut Gareyev, President of the Academy of Military Sciences, went so far as to say that "The nuclear weapons of all major nuclear powers are ultimately designed to be used against Russia, whether we want to admit it or not." This statement, regardless of its obvious paranoia, goes a long way toward explaining Russia's insistence on its short-range nuclear weapons overhaul. For Moscow, nuclear arms are the weapon of choice in certain situations. Short-range nuclear weapons are likely to be used when Moscow faces a threat that it cannot counter with conventional weapons. Short-range nuclear weapons are thought to have de-escalation qualities by demonstrating Russia's will to resolve a conflict by using them early.

Russian nuclear policy is characterized by a perceived need to use short-range nuclear weapons in many scenarios. For example, the Russian leadership has stated that if the NATO alliance were to use precision conventional weapons against Russian troops, Russia would be forced to respond with short-range nuclear weapons. Conflicts on its borders, especially in Chechnya and the Northern Caucasus and with China (over the Far East), or conflicts involving strategically important Central Asia, might also prompt Moscow to use short-range nuclear weapons.

Russia's military exercises conclusively demonstrate that Moscow sees nuclear weapons as having both offensive and defensive applications. In September 2009, during the Zapad military exercise, the Russian air force reportedly practiced using short-range nuclear weapons against Poland, a NATO ally. In July 2010, Russia conducted Vostok, a large-scale military exercise in the Far East, and simulated a low-yield nuclear strike consistent with its policy of using short-range nuclear weapons in regional conflicts. The enemy in this exercise was China; the Russians worry about the numerical and potential technological disparity between the two countries.

Finally, the Russian military industrial base is undergoing a radical reform that will significantly reshape its personnel, technology, and organization. The goal of this reform is to reduce the Soviet-era military bureaucracy and develop small but well-equipped rapid deployment forces. Russian military spending is limited at times due to the country's poor economic performance. Especially after the recent global economic crisis, Russia found it challenging to provide the funding to maintain a large and effective conventional army. The ambitious new $640 billion procurement package seeks to overcome these difficulties. In the meantime, Moscow will continue to regard Russia's nuclear weapons as a force equalizer against more technologically advanced or powerful nations.

Russia views its nuclear arsenal generally, and its short-range nuclear arsenal in particular, as a vital and legitimate means to counterbalance conventional superiority by NATO and a variety of plausible threats from China, as well as a powerful deterrent in regional conflicts. In tactical nuclear weapons negotiations, Moscow is all but certain to make far-reaching demands, which will result in another treaty that is lopsided in Russia's favor and leaves the U.S. exposed to threats by other countries and non-state actors.

It is never too early in the arms control treaty process for Senators, individually and in groupings, to exercise their power to advise the President and his Administration. This is the case, in part, because the Administration can make significant concessions even in the course of organizing future negotiations. Senators should make their concerns known even absent a public statement by the President regarding the U.S. negotiating stance. Indeed, this is precisely the path that 41 Senators took on March 22, 2011, in sending President Obama a letter expressing their concerns about what may be contained in a new arms control treaty with Russia.

## Energy Nationalism Threatens Friends and Allies

Russia's energy nationalism should also be a source of frustration in Washington. From an American perspective, growing European dependence on energy imports from monopolistic Russian oil and gas exporters is a negative long-term geopolitical trend.

Energy issues spill over into the realm of the geopolitical balance-of-power. When energy prices skyrocketed in 2007–2008, Russia quickly evolved into an assertive anti-status quo power that challenged the U.S. and its allies on many fronts, especially in the territory of the former Soviet Union, as the 2008 Russian–Georgian Five Day War and continuous pressure on Ukraine demonstrated. There are also ongoing frictions in the Balkans and the Middle East, where Russia has opposed Western policies. This happens both because of the ample funding available to finance a more ambitious foreign policy due to energy revenues and the self-assurance which comes with general economic prosperity, as well as from Moscow's tendency to use energy as a foreign policy tool. As oil prices rise, it is safe to expect Russia's cockiness to return.

Russia's strategic goals include preventing countries around its borders from becoming pro-American as well as increasing control over the transportation of Russia hydrocarbons through the territory of its neighbors. Furthermore, the Kremlin aims to control the export of oil and gas from neighboring countries by directing their flow via the Russian pipeline system. By locating pipelines and gas storage facilities in Austria, Hungary, Bulgaria, Greece and Turkey, Russia connects them to Moscow with ties that bind. Sometimes, these ties also include lucrative personal economic deals, as demonstrated by the employment of Gerhardt Schroeder as Chairman of the North Stream gas pipeline consortium, and similar arrangements for other prominent European politicians.

Russia is willing to use force to achieve its geo-economic goals as well. Control of energy corridors from the Caspian Sea to the Black Sea and beyond was an objective of the Russian military operation against Georgia in August 2008. This has been clearly confirmed over the years by incidents involving delays in energy supplies to Azerbaijan, the Baltic states, Belarus, Croatia, Georgia, Serbia, Slovakia, and Ukraine, to mention a few. Many argue that Moscow's international energy behavior leaves its partners insecure and makes observers doubt that Russia is a responsible player, especially when unconstrained by competition and powerful investment sources.

Despite the fall in energy demand across Europe, Russia raced to secure its natural gas market share and bypass Ukraine, the principal transit country. It is building Nord Stream and South Stream pipeline systems. Europe may diminish its dependence on Russian gas by boosting an alternative pipeline, Nabucco, but in order to do so, it requires U.S. political support for Turkey, Azerbaijan, Turkmenistan, and Kazakhstan to cooperate on this mega-project. However, unlike the Clinton and the George W. Bush Administrations, the Obama Administration has downgraded Eurasian energy on its priority list. Very little political support materialized, which jeopardizes the future of Nabucco. However, it is primarily the European Union members' responsibility to diversify its sources of natural gas. Unfortunately, so far, no necessary leadership from Europe has materialized in this case.

In sum, the developed world economies and energy net importers in general will benefit from greater stability, security, transparency, and the rule of law in energy-exporting states, to ensure that oil and gas remain readily available, ample, affordable, and safe. However, the Kremlin views energy as a tool of assertive foreign policy and uses it broadly, often without much concern for diplomatic niceties. If current trends prevail, this decade may see the Kremlin translating this energy monopoly into increasing foreign and security policy influence in Europe. In particular, Russia is seeking recognition of its zone of privileged interests in the post-Soviet space and Eastern Europe. This has already affected geopolitical issues important to the West, such as NATO expansion, ballistic missile defense, the tension around the status of Kosovo, and Moscow's increasing influence in the post-Soviet space. . . .

# Conclusion

Twenty years after the end of the Cold War and the collapse of communism, Russia's anti-American policies should be over.

In order to reaffirm America's priorities when dealing with Russia, the U.S. should concentrate on its own national interests, as well as the values of freedom and justice. Facing these unchanging political realities and impeding threats to U.S. interests, the U.S. should rethink its strategy for engaging with Russia's leadership.

The Administration needs to stop its policy of pleasing Moscow and instead add pressure on Russia to start a reset of its own policies. In particular, Congress should ensure that missile defenses are developed for the benefit of American troops and allies and prevent the Administration from granting far-reaching concessions to Russia in negotiating short-range nuclear weapons deals.

Congress has an important role to play in changing the relations with Russia in the energy field for the better, for the benefit of the Russian and American peoples and our European allies. It is time to make the Russian oil and gas sector more transparent and open to foreign investment while curbing the use of energy as a geopolitical tool, which endangers Russia's neighbors.

Congress should send a strong signal that it cares about America's friends in the former Soviet Union and Eastern Europe and expand US ties with those who reach out for freedom. Finally Congress should enable the U.S. to deny visas to corrupt Russian businessmen, examine their banking practices and acquisitions, and target Russian police and prosecutors who fabricate evidence, and judges who rubber stamp convictions. . . . Certainly, the Russian people can benefit from its relations with America. Russia, and important emerging market, a large consumer, and a cornucopia of raw materials, should have access to U.S. science—especially health sciences, technology, and investment—if Moscow improves its foreign and domestic policies. However, Congress and the Administration should not tolerate Russian mischief, either domestic or geopolitical. The U.S. should not shy away from articulating its priorities and values to its Russian partners—and play hardball when necessary.

Steven Pifer                                          → **NO**

# The Future Course of the
# U.S.-Russia Relationship

## Introduction

The U.S. relationship with Russia has been and will, for the foreseeable future, remain a mix of issues on which the two countries can cooperate and issues where their positions conflict. The goal for Washington should be to make progress on those issues where U.S. and Russian interests coincide while protecting American positions and managing differences where interests diverge.

The Obama administration's "reset" policy has improved the U.S.-Russian relationship. By any objective measure, the relationship is stronger today than it was in 2008, the low point in U.S.-Russian relations after the collapse of the Soviet Union. This does not mean the relationship is without problems. Washington and Moscow disagree on issues such as missile defense in Europe, Syria, the post-Soviet space, and democracy and human rights within Russia. On May 7, Vladimir Putin will return to the Russian presidency. This should not entail a change in the strategic course of Russian foreign policy, though the tone and style will likely differ from that of Dmitry Medvedev.

Mr. Putin will have to confront domestic political and economic challenges that may affect his foreign policy choices: he could resort to the traditional Russian tactic of depicting a foreign adversary to rally domestic support as during his election campaign, or he could pursue a more accommodating foreign policy so that he can focus on issues at home. We do not yet know. It remains in the U.S. interest to engage Russia where engagement can advance American policy goals. In doing so, the United States will at times have to be prepared to take account of Russian interests if it wishes to secure Moscow's help on questions that matter to Washington. For example, U.S. readiness to accommodate Russian concerns in negotiating the New START Treaty contributed to Moscow's decision to open new supply routes for NATO to Afghanistan and to support a UN Security Council resolution that imposed an arms embargo on Iran.

Looking forward in its relations with Russia, the United States should pursue further reductions of nuclear arms, including non-strategic nuclear weapons; continue to explore a cooperative NATO-Russia missile defense

U.S. House of Representatives, March 21, 2012.

arrangement; seek to work jointly to deal with the proliferation challenges posed by North Korea and Iran; and consult on steps to bolster security and stability in Central Asia as the NATO coalition prepares to withdraw its military forces from Afghanistan. The United States should explore ways to increase trade and investment relations with Russia, which could help build a foundation for a more sustainable relationship. While Moscow's decisions about its business and investment climate—for example, to strengthen rule of law and tackle corruption—are the most important factor in this regard, Congress should now graduate Russia from the provisions of the Jackson-Vanik amendment, an action that is long overdue. On questions where positions diverge, such as Syria, Washington should press its case. Differing views of the post-Soviet space represent the potential flashpoint most likely to trigger a major U.S.-Russia crisis; Washington should consult closely with Moscow in a transparent way to manage differences over that region. With regard to democracy and human rights within Russia, the U.S. government should continue to voice its concerns, consider ways to assist the growth of civil society in Russia, and maintain contact with the full spectrum of Russian society. But Washington should recognize that its ability to affect the internal situation in Russia is limited.

## The Reset

The Obama administration in February 2009 announced its intention to reset the U.S. relationship with Russia. The past three years have witnessed significant progress in U.S.-Russian relations, including:

1. The New START Treaty was signed, ratified and entered into force. Russia is the only country capable of physically destroying the United States. New START strengthens U.S. security by reducing and limiting Russian strategic offensive forces while allowing the United States to maintain a robust and effective nuclear deterrent. The treaty requires data exchanges, notifications and other monitoring measures that provide significant insights into, and predictability about, Russian strategic forces. That allows for better-informed decisions by the Defense Department as to how to equip and operate U.S. strategic forces. The treaty also strengthens the U.S. hand in encouraging other countries to tighten global non-proliferation norms.
2. Russia has permitted a significant expansion of the amount of materiel, including lethal military equipment, and personnel that transit through Russia or Russian airspace to the NATO operation in Afghanistan. Russia today is considering making available an air base in Ulyanovsk to support refueling and the transit of non-lethal military equipment to Afghanistan. This kind of support has resulted in significant cost savings for the U.S. military. Moreover, these supply routes mean that the United States and NATO do not have to depend solely on transit through Pakistan.
3. Russia has supported measures to tighten pressure on Iran, in order to persuade it to abandon its program to acquire a nuclear weapons capability. This includes the Russian vote in June 2010 for UN Security

Council Resolution 1929. Among other things, that resolution provided for an embargo on arms transfers to the Iranian regime. Despite some ambiguity as to whether or not the resolution applied to air defense systems, Moscow subsequently announced the outright cancellation of a previously agreed sale of the S-300 air defense system to Tehran. When I worked on these issues in the U.S. government during the first George W. Bush term, no one would have contemplated Russia taking such action.

4. Russia has, with U.S. support, secured entry into the World Trade Organization. This should benefit American companies, as it will further open the Russian market to U.S. exports and require that Russia play by the rules of a trade regime to which U.S. business is comfortably accustomed.

By any objective measure, the U.S.-Russian relationship is stronger today than it was in 2008. Then, sharp differences over the future of strategic arms limitations, missile defense in Europe, NATO enlargement and Georgia dominated the agenda. Relations between Washington and Moscow plunged to their lowest point since the end of the Soviet Union. The bilateral relationship had become so thin that there are no indications that concern about damaging it affected in any way the Kremlin's decisions regarding military operations against Georgia. The Russian government saw little of value to lose in its relationship with Washington. That was not a good situation from the point of view of U.S. interests. It is different today. There are things in the U.S.-Russian relationship that Moscow cares about, and that translates to leverage and even a restraining influence on Russian actions.

This does not mean that all is going well on the U.S.-Russia agenda. Although the rhetoric is less inflammatory than it was four years ago, missile defense poses a difficult problem on both the bilateral and NATO-Russia agendas. The countries clearly differ over Syria. Moscow's misguided support for Mr. Assad—which stems from the fact that he is one of Russia's few allies and from the Russian desire to pay NATO back for what they consider the misuse of March 2011 UN Security Council Resolution 1973 on Libya—has led the Kremlin to an unwise policy. It is alienating the Arab world and will position Moscow poorly with the Syrian people once Mr. Assad leaves the scene.

The democracy and human rights situation within Russia remains difficult and troubling. The problems are epitomized by the flaws in the recent parliamentary and presidential elections, the appalling treatment of Sergey Magnitsky and others, and the unresolved murders of journalists such as Anna Politkovskaya.

# Mr. Putin's Return

Vladimir Putin will make his formal return to the Russian presidency on May 7. The presidential election process that culminated on March 4 was marked by the absence of a level playing field, process flaws and reports of fraud on election day. The turnout and vote count reported by the Central Electoral Commission in some regions strained credibility. All that said, Mr. Putin remains the most popular political figure in Russia. While ballot box-stuffing and other fraud may have inflated his vote count to the official figure of 63.6 percent, there is no compelling evidence that he did not clear the 50 percent threshold required for victory.

The democratic situation within Russia has regressed since Mr. Putin entered the national scene. But politics in Russia today are different from what they were just six months ago. An opposition has emerged, however disparate it might be, which appears to reflect the concerns of the growing urban middle class. The presidential election returns in Moscow were striking: Mr. Putin fell below 50 percent. His instinct now may well be to repress the opposition, but the old tactics will not work as they did before. One of the biggest question marks about Mr. Putin's next presidential term is how he will respond to and deal with an opposition whose sentiments are likely to spread.

As for foreign policy, Washington has grown comfortably accustomed to dealing with Mr. Medvedev over the past three years. Mr. Putin's return portends a more complicated U.S.-Russian relationship, but there is no reason to expect that relations will plunge over a cliff. There are a number of considerations to bear in mind regarding Mr. Putin and Russia's approach to the United States.

First, Mr. Putin as prime minister was nominally number two to Mr. Medvedev, but no one doubts who held real power in Moscow. As the American Embassy reportedly put it, Mr. Putin played Batman to Mr. Medvedev's Robin—a comparison that Mr. Putin undoubtedly enjoyed in private. He kept a close eye on things. It is inconceivable that the New START Treaty, expanded supply routes through Russia for NATO forces in Afghanistan, and Moscow's support for an arms embargo on Iran would have happened had Mr. Putin opposed them. There is no reason to assume that his return to the presidency will mean a major change in the strategic course of Russian foreign policy. We should expect a significant degree of continuity.

Second, the tone of the bilateral relationship will likely change. Mr. Putin spent his formative years in the 1980s as a KGB officer. As his rhetoric during the election campaign made clear, he holds a wary skepticism about U.S. goals and policies. For example, his comments suggest he does not see the upheavals that swept countries such as Georgia, Ukraine, Tunisia or Egypt as manifestations of popular discontent but instead believes they were inspired, funded and directed by Washington. This may seem like a paranoiac view, but Mr. Putin has made so many allusions to it that it is hard to conclude that he does not believe it. That is a complicating factor for the bilateral relationship.

Mr. Putin's experience as president dealing with the Bush administration, moreover, was not a happy one. In 2001–02, he supported U.S. military action against the Taliban, including overruling his advisors to support the deployment of U.S. military units into Central Asia; shut down the Russian signals intelligence facility in Lourdes, Cuba; agreed to deepen relations with NATO; calmly accepted the administration's decision to withdraw from the Anti-Ballistic Missile Treaty; and agreed to a minimalist arms control agreement that fell far short of Moscow's desires. In his view, he received little in return. His perception is that Washington made no effort to accommodate Moscow's concerns on issues such as the future of strategic arms limits, missile defense deployments in Europe, NATO enlargement, relations with Russia's neighbors in the post-Soviet space or graduating Russia from the Jackson-Vanik amendment. The reset, after all, took place during Mr. Medvedev's presidency.

Third, Mr. Putin faces tough issues at home, both economically and politically. The Russian economy and government revenues remain overly dependent on exports of oil and natural gas. The Russian state budget remains pegged to the price of oil. While Mr. Medvedev called for economic modernization and diversification, there are few signs of progress or of a realistic plan to achieve those aims. Corruption remains rampant. The lack of confidence in the economy is reflected in the fact that Russia experienced capital outflow of $84 billion last year. And Mr. Putin made a striking number of electoral promises, including higher salaries, rising pensions and greater defense spending, that will need to be funded. While sustained high oil prices could allow him to avoid tough calls, economic questions could face him with a major challenge.

Moreover, politics today in Russia have changed. For the first time in his experience, Mr. Putin will have to deal with the outside world without being confident that he has a rock-solid political base at home. It will be interesting to see how that affects his foreign policy choices. Soviet and Russian leaders in the past resorted to the image of a foreign adversary—all too often the United States—to rally domestic support, and one can see aspects of that in Mr. Putin's campaign rhetoric. But the constituency to whom that appeals is already largely on Mr. Putin's side. Will that ploy resonate with an increasingly unhappy urban middle class? He may conclude that he can focus better on his domestic challenges if his foreign policy results in more positive relations with countries such as the United States. We do not yet know.

Fourth, Mr. Putin has shown himself to be realistic, particularly when it comes to money. A major article that he published in the run-up to the election described a large military modernization program designed to reassert parity with the United States. But during his first presidency, when huge energy revenues flowed into the Russian government budget from 2003 to 2007, he chose not to increase defense spending significantly. Instead, the extra money—and there was plenty of it—went to build international currency reserves and a "rainy day" fund on which the government drew heavily during the 2008–09 economic crisis. Having a large arsenal of weapons did not save the Soviet Union. Mr. Putin understands that. If circumstances force him to make tough choices, he may prove pragmatic and not necessarily choose guns over butter.

Fifth, Mr. Putin likely will not fully show his hand regarding the United States until 2013. He expects to be around for another six and possibly twelve years. He may see little harm in waiting six months to learn who will be his opposite number in the White House.

The upshot is that Mr. Putin's return can and probably will mean more bumpiness in the U.S.-Russia relationship. He will pursue his view of Russian interests. On certain issues, those will conflict with U.S. interests, and Washington and Moscow will disagree, perhaps heatedly. His style will differ markedly from Mr. Medvedev's, and Mr. Obama may come to miss his meetings with his friend, Dmitry. But Mr. Putin is not likely to seek to turn the relationship upside down or take it back to the grim days of 2008. For all the rhetoric, Washington should be able to deal with him on a number of issues.

## A Policy Agenda for the U.S. Relationship with Russia

Looking forward, a positive relationship with Russia can advance U.S. interests, even if Washington and Moscow differ on some issues and if the United States is frustrated about corruption and the democracy and human rights situation in Russia. Russian support remains critical to achieving key Washington policy goals such as sustaining pressure on the nuclear rogue states and supporting coalition military operations in Afghanistan. There are a number of issues on which Moscow can play a spoiler role if it believes the United States is not paying due regard to Russian interests.

Improving U.S.-Russian relations further may prove more difficult than it has been in the past three years, as the easier questions have been settled. Nevertheless, Washington should seek to work with Russia on a number of issues.

First, Washington should engage Moscow on a further bilateral round of nuclear arms reductions, this time including strategic and non-strategic nuclear weapons, whether deployed or non-deployed, under a common ceiling in a follow-on agreement to New START. . . .

Second, Washington and NATO should continue to pursue a cooperative missile defense arrangement with Russia. That prospect is currently stalled by Moscow's demand for a legal guarantee that U.S. missile defenses in Europe not be directed against Russian strategic missile forces. While it is reasonable for the Russians to be concerned that missile defenses could affect the offense-defense relationship, that is a concern for the future. It is very difficult to see the U.S. plan for missile defenses in Europe over the next decade posing any serious threat to Russian strategic missiles. . . .

[Pifer presents three other points, including working with Russia to defuse crises with North Korea and Iran over their nuclear weapons programs, to try to stabilize Afghansistan, and to better trade relations.]

## Coping with Problem Issues

While the U.S.-Russian agenda holds issues where cooperation is in the U.S. interest, there are other questions where the policies of Washington and Moscow conflict. That will continue to be the case for the foreseeable future. Where interests diverge, the U.S. government should make its case, seek ways to encourage change in Russian policy, and be prepared to manage differences that persist.

Washington and Moscow, for example, disagree sharply over Syria, where the Russians have unfortunately attached themselves to an autocrat whose days may well be numbered. U.S. diplomacy should seek to persuade Moscow to adopt a different course, one that would be better for the people of Syria and for Russia's interests in the region.

U.S. and Russian interests differ in the post-Soviet space, the region that is most likely to generate a major crisis in bilateral relations. Moscow seeks to gain influence over its neighbors, using mechanisms such as the Customs Union with Kazakhstan and Belarus. The Russians seek deference from other states in the post-Soviet space on issues that they define as affecting critical Russian interests. One example is staunch Russian opposition to the enlargement of NATO or the European Union into the post-Soviet space. Russian policies often seem to have the effect of pushing neighboring states away from Moscow, but the Russians have not changed course.

The United States takes a different approach, rejecting the notion of a sphere of influence and supporting the right of each post-Soviet state to choose its own course. Some tension between the two approaches is inevitable. Washington should expect the kinds of tit-for-tat exchanges that have occurred in the past, such as when a U.S. Navy ship visit to Georgia was followed by a Russian warship calling on Venezuela. Given the difference in approaches, it would be wise for Washington and Moscow to consult closely and be transparent with one another on their policies in the post-Soviet space, so as to avoid surprises and minimize the chances that a clash of interests could escalate.

One other difficult issue is the democracy and human rights situation within Russia. While Russian citizens today enjoy considerably more individual freedoms than they did during the time of the Soviet Union, it is equally true that they enjoy fewer freedoms, are more subject to arbitrary and capricious state action, and have less political influence than during the 1990s, however chaotic that period was.

Democratic and human rights values are properly a part of U.S. foreign policy. The U.S. government has long raised human rights concerns with the Russian government and should continue to do so. It is difficult to envisage bilateral relations with Russia becoming truly "normal" while these problems persist.

U.S. officials should continue to make clear American concerns publicly and privately with Russian officials, including at senior levels. The U.S. government should, as it does now, maintain a policy of denying visas to those Russian officials associated with the Magnitsky case. This is a tool that the executive branch might consider applying in other egregious cases. Washington should consider other ways in which it might assist the growth of a robust civil society in Russia. And U.S. officials should maintain contact with the full spectrum of Russian society. It was an important signal that, during his one visit to Moscow as president, Mr. Obama met with a broad range of civil society activists, opposition leaders and other non-official Russians.

Unfortunately, the Russian legislative branch has been virtually absent in the discussion of democracy and human rights within Russia. Members of Congress and senators might consider how they might directly engage their Russian counterparts on these issues.

Washington should bear in mind, however, that its ability to affect internal change in Russia is limited at best. Real, lasting political reform must come from within. Hopefully, the opposition movement that has emerged over the past four months will strengthen, will not be suppressed by the government, and will grow into a vehicle through which ordinary Russians can gain a greater say in their politics and governance. There are ways in which the United States can encourage this on the margins, but this is an issue that Russians themselves must drive.

The United States should continue to explore ways to work with Russia to advance American interests and to build a more positive, sustainable bilateral relationship. Doing so will increase American influence with and in Russia. It would be unwise for Washington, out of anger over differences over Syria or democratic backsliding within Russia, to hold back on working with Moscow on issues where cooperation can accomplish things of benefit to the United States. The U.S. government should be able to cooperate on issues where interests coincide while confronting Russia on other questions and making clear its democracy and human rights concerns—Washington should be able to walk and chew gum at the same time. Doing less would mean passing up opportunities to make Americans safer, more secure and more prosperous.

# EXPLORING THE ISSUE

## Should Russia Be Considered a Hostile Country?

## Questions for Critical Thinking and Reflection

1. Should it make any difference in U.S. foreign policy toward Russia whether or not the country is authoritarian or democratic?
2. Some analysts argue that it is naive to not recognize Russia as hostile and that failing to do so can lead to danger in such ways as making arms agreements that Russia will not keep. Other analysts argue that treating Russia as hostile will become a self-fulfilling prophecy by promoting Russia to react with hostility to U.S. policy proposals. Which position do you find more plausible?
3. What steps would you take to either improve U.S. relations with Russia or to guard against Russian policies or actions that contravene U.S. national interests?

## Is There Common Ground?

The debate over how to deal with Russia is not a matter of idle speculation. There are two very real policy considerations. The first involves the fact that the direction Russia takes in the future is likely to have important consequences for the world. During the decade after the collapse of the Soviet Union in 1991, Russia was in great economic and military disarray. President Yeltsin and President Putin sometimes strongly criticized such U.S.-favored actions as the expansion of NATO, but Moscow's weakness constrained it from trying to block U.S. preferences.

More recently, Russia's economic fortunes have improved. The global demand for energy and the increasing revenue that Russian gets from its oil and natural gas exports have given a particular boost to Russia's economy. It is yet unclear how much Russian military has recovered, but there are some signs that its morale, training, and operational capability are on the upswing. All this has given Russia greater confidence to oppose U.S. policy preferences where the two countries disagree. Russia through its position on the UN Security Council has helped block Washington's effort to get stringent sanctions on Iran for its nuclear development program. Russian arms have reportedly gone to Syria to support the embattled and dictatorial Bashar Assad regime. Russia has also grown increasingly vocal about the U.S. effort to build and deploy a ballistic missile defense (BMD) system in part in Eastern Europe.

The Obama administration has continued to support the reset idea. In June 2012, Deputy National Security Advisor for Strategic Communications

Ben Rhodes contended, "The reset with Russia is based on the belief that we can cooperate with them on areas of common interest, understanding that we still have some differences. And I think we continue to see very positive results from that reset policy." Others disagreed; the campaign site of Republican presidential candidate Mitt Romney labeled Obama's reset policy a failure and pledged, "Upon taking office [as president], Mitt Romney will reset the reset. He will implement a strategy that will seek to discourage aggressive or expansionist behavior on the part of Russia and encourage democratic political and economic reform."

## Additional Resources

More on the global relations of Russia and the United States can be found in Jeffrey Mankoff, *Russian Foreign Policy: The Return of Great Power Politics* (Rowman & Littlefield, 2011); and Martin S. Indyk, Kenneth G. Lieberthal, and Michael E. O'Hanlon, *Bending History: Barack Obama's Foreign Policy* (Brookings, 2012). For a focus on President Putin, read Andrew C. Kuchins, "The End of the 'Reset': Why Putin's Re-Election Means Turbulence Ahead," *Foreign Affairs* (March 1, 2012). He argues, "When it comes to Russia's political future, the only guarantee is uncertainty."

# ISSUE 3

## Is China Becoming a Dangerous Superpower?

**YES: Dean Cheng**, from Testimony during Hearings on "Investigating the Chinese Threat, Part I: Military and Economic Aggression" before the Committee on Foreign Affairs, U.S. House of Representatives (March 28, 2012)

**NO: Hu Jintao**, from "Building a China-U.S. Cooperative Partnership Based on Mutual Respect and Mutual Benefit," address to a welcome banquet, Marriott Wardman Park Hotel, Washington, DC (January 2, 2011)

### ISSUE SUMMARY

**YES:** Dean Cheng, the research fellow for Chinese political and security affairs at the Heritage Foundation, argues that China's increasing military and economic power and its comprehensive policy of harnessing all aspects of its military, economic, and diplomatic assets to assert its power are creating a powerful rival to U.S. power and interests in Asia and the Pacific region.

**NO:** Hu Jintao, the president of China and Communist Party chairman, tells an American audience that his country and theirs share an ultimate goal of creating a stable and prosperous international order and that both countries can and should cooperate and work with people across the world to share opportunities, meet challenges, and build a better future for mankind.

**C**hina has a history as one of the oldest and at times most powerful countries (and empires) in the world. During the Yuan dynasty (1271–1368) and most of the Ming dynasty (1368–1644), China was also arguably the world's most powerful empire, dominating most of Asia.

However, China's power compared with Europe's began to ebb, with the Industrial Revolution beginning in Europe in the mid-1700s playing a major role. By the 1800s, the European powers, joined by the United States in the last years of the century, came to increasingly dominate China. The Chinese consider these years a period of humiliation, emblemized by a park in a European enclave in Shanghai that bore the sign, "Dogs and Chinese Not Allowed." China's road back began in 1911 when Nationalist forces under Sun Yatsen overthrew the last emperor. Internal struggles and the invasion by Japan (1931–1945) blocked much advance in China's economic and political power until the Communists under Mao Zedong defeated the Nationalists under Chiang Kai-shek, who fled and set up the remnants of the Nationalist government on Formosa (Taiwan) as the Republic of China. Gradually, Communist China (the People's Republic of China, PRC) built up its strength. Military power came first. China's military was saddled by obsolete weapons, but it was the world's largest military force, numbering as many as 4.2 million troops in the 1980s. China also sought to acquire nuclear weapons and delivery capability, and succeeded in that quest by the mid-1960s. Fundamental changes in China's status began in the 1970s. In 1971, the United Nations changed the rightful owner of China's seat, including its position as a permanent member of the Security Council, from the Nationalist government on Taiwan to the PRC. The following year, the United States relaxed its hostility, and President Richard Nixon visited China. In 1979, President Jimmy Carter shifted U.S. diplomatic recognition of the "legitimate" government of China from the Taiwan government to the PRC government. Domestically, the two great leaders of the Communist Revolution and government, Premier Zhou Enlai and Communist Party Chairman Mao Zedong, both died in 1976. This opened the way for a less ideological approach to improving China's economy.

Since then, China has changed rapidly. It retains a communist government, but it has adopted many of the trappings of a capitalist economy. Where once China rejected global trade and other international economic organizations, it has now embraced them.

Economically, it is possible to argue that China is still a poor country, one whose 2011 per capita gross domestic product (GDP) of $5,414 was far below the U.S. per capita GDP of $48,387. But China has also become one of the largest economies in the world. China's 2011 GDP was $ 7.3 trillion. That makes it the second largest economy in the world, although still far behind the United States ($15.1 trillion). China has also become the second largest global trader, with its $4.0 trillion in exports and imports behind only the United States ($4.7 trillion). China is also the fastest growing large economy, expanding by an annual average of over 8 percent since 1975. Much of this is industrial growth, and China is the world's fourth largest producer of automobiles and commercial vehicles and third greatest steel manufacturer.

China's growing economy and industrialization have allowed it to upgrade its military technology. China is also second in military spending. The country's 2011 official defense budget was $143 billion dollars, but there is little doubt that actual spending is higher than that, with some estimates putting it at over $200 billion. Still, the amount, whatever it is, falls far short of the 2011 U.S. defense budget ($711 billion).

What all this portends is the issue here. In the first reading, Dean Cheng warns that it is time to take China's military expansion seriously. Hu Jintao projects a very different image of China in the second reading, claiming it wishes to work with the United States and the rest of the world toward a peaceful, prosperous world.

# YES ↵

Dean Cheng

# Investigating the Chinese Threat, Part I: Military and Economic Aggression

**M**y comments today discuss the issue of the threats posed by the People's Republic of China (PRC) to the United States. They will focus on the security aspect of the threat, but I would like to emphasize that the Chinese concept of national security is a holistic one, rooted in the idea of "comprehensive national power." Comprehensive national power assumes that a nation's standing, and its relative power, is rooted not solely in its military, but must also take into account its economic capabilities, its scientific and technical capacity, the diplomatic respect it receives, and its political unity. There is even a cultural component, as Chinese President Hu Jintao noted in a speech last year.

This is not to equate "comprehensive national power" with "threat." Indeed, Chinese economic growth and prosperity cannot be properly called a threat in any direct sense; China's economic development does not, in and of itself, jeopardize American security. But it is a part of the security calculus because it enables China's military modernization as currently conceived, and because it represents, as the Chinese phrase it, part of the overall military potential of a nation. In terms of the military-security aspect, there are many visible elements. That being said, the military-security aspect is, in many ways, the most visible element of the China threat. The People's Liberation Army (PLA) is the world's largest military, numbering approximately 2.3 million troops. By contrast, the United States active duty military is approximately 1.5 million.

The recently concluded National People's Congress (NPC) declared that the PLA budget would increase by 11.2% in 2012, continuing a two-decade long pattern of double-digit increases, which has seen the official spending figures more than double. These figures, widely acknowledged to be substantially understating China's actual defense spending, have now passed the $100 billion mark.

The PLA military has been steadily modernizing across a range of capabilities, including land, sea, air, and space forces. This effort gained impetus in the wake of the first Gulf War, when the Coalition performance took the Chinese by surprise. The direction of that effort was codified in the "Military Strategic Guidelines for the New Period." These guidelines, issued in 1993, introduced the concept of "local wars under modern, high-tech conditions." These guidelines constitute "the highest level of national guidance and direction" to the Chinese armed forces.

U.S. House of Representatives, March 28, 2012.

In a December 1995 speech by then Party General Secretary and Chinese President Jiang Zemin to the Central Military Commission further clarified the direction of Chinese military modernization. In that speech, Jiang emphasized the importance of the new guidelines, and charged the PLA with undertaking the "Two Transformations." These entailed a shift from a military focused on quantity to one focused on quality, and from a military preparing for "local wars under modern conditions," to one that was preparing for "local wars under modern, high-tech conditions."

This modernization is reflected in the steady acquisition of a range of new systems by the PLA Air Force, PLA Navy, and Second Artillery, which are growing in importance relative to the ground forces, the traditional senior service in the PLA, due to their greater reliance on technology.

For the PLA Air Force, the modernization effort has seen the steady introduction of new fighters, including Su-27s and Su-30s acquired from Russia, as well as the indigenously developed J-10. The new J-20 stealthy combat aircraft was tested on the eve of Secretary of Defense Gates' visit in 2010. Other PLA acquisitions include tanker, transport, and electronic warfare aircraft, reflecting the broad modernization of PLAAF capabilities extending to the combat support functions. The PLA XV Airborne Corps, under the control of the PLAAF, has also seen its equipment modernized, including new airborne combat vehicles.

For the PLA Navy, the modernization effort has seen the introduction of at least two new submarine classes, including the domestically designed Yuan-class diesel-electric boat, and continued work on a new nuclear-powered attack submarine. China's missile forces, meanwhile, are believed to be steadily acquiring both ballistic and cruise missiles. They are also believed to have reached initial operational capability with the DF-21D anti-ship ballistic missile system.

More important than individual weapons is the steady Chinese effort to improve their command, control, communications, computers, intelligence, surveillance, and reconnaissance, or C4ISR, capabilities. This is a reflection of the shift in focus from "local wars under modern, high-technology conditions" to "local wars under informationized conditions." In essence, the PLA has made clear that it considers the most important high technology areas were those associated with information, i.e., communications, computers, advance sensors, space systems. Moreover, Chinese military writings regularly note that future warfare will not be platform against platform, or even system (*xitong*) against system, but a contest between systems-of-systems. Thus, the creation of networks of sensors and communications is at least as important as the acquisition of particular weapons.

In this regard, the recent Chinese space white paper highlighted the plan to field, in the next five years or so, a constellation of high-resolution, multispectral earth observation satellites—in short, China is entering the "spy satellite" business to provide the PLA with global surveillance and tracking capabilities. At the same time, Chinese tests of anti-satellite capabilities, not only in 2007, but in 2010, underscore the growing ability of the PLA to deny opponents the same C4ISR capabilities that the PLA is acquiring.

# Additional Threat Considerations

While much of the discussion of the potential threat from China tends to focus on hardware, this "bean count" type of analysis can be somewhat misleading. It is important to recognize that China, as the world's most populous country, and also the second largest economy, is bound to have a very large military. It has more people to draw upon, and an increasing portfolio of interests that require defending. And, as has been noted, there is nothing more expensive, and more useless, than a second-best military. Chinese defense spending, too, needs to be seen in the context of Chinese strategy.

China's defense spending is generally accepted to be significantly higher than its official figures, but that is not to say that China is necessarily spending for defense on the scale of the former Soviet Union. Indeed, as close students of the collapse of the USSR, it is mistaken to expect that China will follow the Soviet path and bankrupt itself on defense spending while neglecting the other components of comprehensive national power. Instead, the Chinese leadership regularly emphasizes that national economic construction continues to hold higher priority than army-building. This emphasis on building up national economic power, and keeping military spending on a relatively lower priority, was reiterated in Hu Jintao's December 2004 speech, when he laid out the "historic missions of the PLA in the new phase of the new century," often referred to as the "New."

# Historic Missions of the PLA

What should worry us about the PRC, and in particular about its military build-up, are the underlying context within which we should be examining China's military modernization effort. The first issue is that the Chinese do not think the way we do. By this, I am referring to the issues of deterrence and also of crisis management. The American outlook on both has been shaped in no small part by the Cuban Missile Crisis, itself affected by President Kennedy's lessons drawn from World War I. The great fear has been that war would result from inadvertent escalation; thus, Kennedy worried about pushing the Russians too far, paralleling the path to World War I.

The President's ambassador-at-large, Chester Bowles, meanwhile recommended Barbara Tuchman's *The Guns of August* to Ambassador Dobrynin in the midst of the crisis, in order to avoid a repetition of the "pattern of politico-military action and counter-action."

Consequently, there is a common belief on the part of many American analysts that "nuclear armed nations do not go to war with each other." This conclusion implies that the main danger is accidental conflict, rather than deliberate action. It is not at all clear, however, that the PRC necessarily subscribes to a comparable view. In this regard, it is important to recognize that, whereas the western focus of deterrence has tended to be on dissuasion, the Chinese term *weishe*, which is commonly translated into "deterrence" in fact embodies not only dissuasion, but also coercion. This is not simply a terminological difference or issue of translation; rather, it indicates that, at a fundamental, conceptual level, American and Chinese policy-makers approach the concept of deterrence, and therefore international relations, from wholly different starting points.

This is reflected in Chinese historical behavior. It is useful to recall that the PRC chose to precipitate a conflict with the USSR in 1969, when both were nuclear-armed, over the disputed border. That conflict not only suggests that the Chinese view of what successfully deters is different from our own, but also betrays a very different sense of crisis management. The Chinese seem to believe that crises are fundamentally controllable. Thus, in recent discussions to limit the potential for aerial or maritime incidents, the Chinese stance has been to reject "the possibility of accidents, blaming continued US operations for any risks."

This stance is especially disturbing, as recent crises suggest a reluctance to engage in communications during a crisis. Thus, during the EP-3 incident in 2001, Chinese officials could not be contacted for some time. The commander of the US Seventh Fleet has also indicated that Chinese naval forces currently tend to ignore ship-to-ship communications in the Asian region.

Indeed, Chinese crisis response often seems to be sluggish, with officials reacting at telex-speeds in an increasingly Twitter-based world. This fundamentally different approach to deterrence and crisis management would not be so worrisome, but for the reality that China is such a major player on the world stage. Indeed, by dint of its population, economy, and technological base, as well as its military, China is different from all other post-Cold War antagonists of the United States. Unlike Iraq, Serbia, or Afghanistan, China has a substantial indigenous military industrial base, and possesses space and cyber capabilities on a rough par with the United States, as well as a substantial nuclear arsenal. In any threat assessment of the PRC, then, one must consider not only China's substantial actual capabilities, but its approach to crises which is potentially destabilizing. Thus, in assessing the potential risks of conflict, the PLA poses a fundamentally different scale of threat than have other states in the past, or even than North Korea or Iran would in any calculation of the future.

This is further exacerbated by the choices the PRC has made in terms of what programs to pursue, which would not suggest benignant intentions. US analysts have characterized China's military approach as one of anti-access/area denial. In essence, the PLA's efforts appear aimed at preventing the United States from deploying to the western Pacific, and therefore jeopardize the ability of the United States to support its allies, assist its friends, or otherwise fulfill its security obligations. Some of the programs that recent DOD reports on Chinese military capabilities have highlighted in this regard include anti-ship ballistic missiles, anti-ship cruise missiles, and modernization of various Chinese strike aircraft.

But Chinese efforts opposing American access extend beyond simply the acquisition of systems, and involve strategic and operational activities, which are equally problematic in their effect on US abilities to operate in the western Pacific. At the strategic level, the Chinese write regularly about the importance of political warfare, which is aimed at fundamentally altering the framework of regional activity, raising doubts about the very legitimacy of the American presence. This includes the pursuit of the so-called three warfares, i.e., public opinion warfare, psychological warfare, and legal warfare.

Public opinion/media warfare is the venue for implementing psychological and legal warfare. It refers to the use of various mass information channels, including the Internet, television, radio, newspapers, movies, and other forms of media, in accordance with an overall plan and with set objectives in mind, to transmit selected news and other materials to the intended audience. The goal is to generate public support both at home and abroad for one's own position and create opposition to one's enemy. It seeks to guide public perceptions and opinion so as to effect shifts in the overall balance of strength between oneself and one's opponent.

Public opinion warfare is seen as a stand-alone form of warfare or conflict, as it may occur independent of whether there is an actual outbreak of hostilities. Indeed, it is perhaps best seen as a constant, ongoing activity, aimed at long-term influence of perceptions and attitudes. One of the main tools of public opinion/media warfare is the news media, including both domestic and foreign entities. The focus of public opinion/media warfare is not limited to the press, however, but involves all the instruments that inform and influence public opinion (e.g., movies, television programs, books).

Psychological warfare is the most basic of the "three warfares." It is defined as conflict in the spiritual and psychological area; its purpose is to influence, constrain, and/or alter an opponent's thoughts, emotions, and habits, while at the same time strengthening friendly psychology.

Although much of the focus is on commanders and key decisionmakers, psychological warfare is also aimed at the broader civilian and military populations. It encompasses the range of actions that will affect an opponent's population, social groups, military, government, and/or leadership, in terms of their beliefs and attitudes, including their will to resist. Thus, psychological warfare is seen as more than simply military propaganda, but is a reflection of comprehensive national power and overall national strength, in psychological terms.

Legal warfare, as one Chinese article defines it, involves "arguing that one's own side is obeying the law, criticizing the other side for violating the law, and making arguments for one's own side in cases where there are also violations of the law." It is one of the key instruments of psychological and public opinion/media warfare, by raising doubts among adversary and neutral military and civilian authorities, as well as the broader population, about the legality of adversary actions, thereby sapping political will and support, and potentially retarding military activity. It also provides material for public opinion/media warfare.

What makes the Chinese conception of legal warfare unique is that it is an offensive, rather than defensive, orientation towards the use of the law in times of crisis or conflict. American JAGs are focused on advising American officers on when their actions may violate the law; the case where a JAG advised against firing a missile against Mullah Omar because of the presence of civilians in his convoy is perhaps the best example.

By contrast, the Chinese conception is to use the law to attack and constrain opponents by seizing the initiative on the legal battlefield and thereby disrupt enemy operations. This includes efforts at legal deterrence or coercion, which would warn an opponent that their every action will be scrutinized for possible violations of international law or the laws of armed conflict, in order to impose self-constraint; legal strikes, which would officially charge the enemy with operational activities that violated the law; and legal counterattacks, which would highlight enemy efforts at slanting or misrepresenting international law in their favor.

At the operational level, Chinese military writings suggest that they are intent upon establishing information superiority or dominance over an opponent, that is, the ability to exploit information more rapidly and effectively, while preventing an adversary from doing so. As one Chinese military textbook observes, the focus of the "campaign basic guiding concept" is to establish superiority, or dominance, over the information realm. Seizing information superiority or dominance (*zhi xinxi quan*) is seen as vital.

An essential means of attaining information dominance, in turn, would be through military space operations. "Establishing space dominance, establishing information dominance, and establishing air dominance in a conflict will have influential effects." By attacking opposing space forces, the PLA would deny an opponent the elements crucial for coordinating forces, targeting advanced weapons, and determining the effectiveness of operations countering China's anti-access/area denial capabilities. By engaging in computer network attacks, the PLA potentially threatens the entire information infrastructure upon which national militaries and national economies depend. In combination, it would nullify much of the advantage that American forces have enjoyed in previous conflicts.

Again, this suggests that the overall Chinese military development effort is focused on countering the American ability to uphold its alliance commitments and support friends and allies in the region. In a situation where the "three warfares" were already raising doubts about the legitimacy of an American role, the Chinese ability to demonstrate information dominance through the establishment of space and cyber superiority would raise real questions about whether the United States could respond at an acceptable cost.

By raising the cost of American intervention, such efforts also serve to influence other Asian states, by raising doubts about whether the United States can and will fulfill its commitments. Chinese demonstrations of their capabilities, whether the anti-satellite tests of 2007 and 2010, or persistent Chinese cyber intrusions into various nations' networks, serve as a warning to all states, conforming with the old Chinese saying, "Kill the chicken to scare the monkey." By showing that the PLA has the ability to challenge the United States in the most advanced technology domains, space and cyber, the Chinese leadership is making clear that any American intervention will be potentially costly. That Beijing is doing this while simultaneously pushing assertively against its neighbors is likely intended to raise doubts in Tokyo, Seoul, Manila, and Taipei about how effective an American response would be—and therefore whether those states should seek it in the first place. The more longstanding the doubts, the greater the hesitancy to call upon the US in the midst of a crisis.

In this light, the Chinese acquisition of tactical capabilities, such as the anti-ship ballistic missile, reinforces the strategic objectives. The more capable the PLA appears to be in effecting an anti-access/area denial capability, the more likely Chinese strategic political warfare moves are to raise questions about the desirability as well as viability of opposing Beijing. Persuading China's neighbors that it is better to concede to Chinese wishes than to call upon an America that cannot effectively do anything would allow Chinese leaders to obtain victory without fighting. At the same time, if America finds its allies reluctant to provide or request support and assistance, then Washington is less likely to intervene, especially when that intervention is more likely to be costly.

## Conclusions

It cannot be emphasized enough that China's approach to its security is not solely focused on military measures, but instead incorporates all the instruments of national power. The PRC conceives of its foreign and security policy in a holistic manner, and is employing all of its available resources, military, science and technology, economic and diplomatic resources, in order to influence its neighbors, many of which are American allies and friends.

China, for example, has used its space program, not only to create anti-satellite capabilities, but also to demonstrate its technological prowess. As important, it has also employed it as a diplomatic tool, creating the Asia-Pacific Space Cooperation Organization (APSCO) which is headquartered in Beijing.

China has also established a global, 24-hour English language news service as part of Xinhua, the Chinese state news agency, and is opening news bureaus around the world. Meanwhile CCTV has now opened an office here in Washington, DC. In response, the United States needs to establish a consistent policy, comprising persistent actions across the spectrum of capabilities to make clear that the United States will remain a steadfast partner.

Yet, the Chinese challenge does not appear to be evoking a sufficient American response. Despite NASA's excellent "branding" globally, it is not clear that the United States has been nearly as diligent in utilizing its space assets for terrestrial, political gains. And while China has been expanding its global media presence, the US has tried to cut Chinese language services on Voice of America, and AP, as well as AFP, Reuters and other western news agencies are limiting their news bureaus to a handful of capitals. Thus, around the world, the first and sometimes only view of the news is through Beijing's eyes. In terms of strategic communications, it would seem China has a far better understanding of the myriad ways to influence global opinion than does the nation of Madison Avenue.

Even the much-discussed "pivot to Asia" contained in the recent Defense Strategic Guidance falls short. For all the publicity accorded the phrase, there is a remarkable lack of concrete commitments of resources to match the rhetoric.

Both Secretary Panetta and Secretary Clinton have emphasized that the United States still looks to Europe. "Europe remains America's partner of first resort," Mrs. Clinton said, and Mr. Panetta described Europe as the United States' "security partner of choice for military operations and diplomacy around the world." This raises questions about just how much of a pivot is actually involved, especially as budgetary resources are cut.

The United States remains the predominant power. In Asia, it is far more welcome and far less distrusted than the PRC. The 21st Century can be "America's Pacific Century" as Secretary of State Clinton has called it, but it requires a willingness to demonstrate leadership and resolve to make clear to the region that we are, as Robert Kennedy phrased it, "just friends and brave enemies."

# Building a China-U.S. Cooperative Partnership Based on Mutual Respect and Mutual Benefit

I wish to begin by thanking the U.S.-China Business Council, the National Committee on U.S.-China Relations and other friendly organizations for hosting this welcoming luncheon. I am delighted to have this opportunity to meet friends, old and new, to renew friendship and plan for the future. I would like to extend cordial greetings and best wishes to you and to people from various sectors of the United States who have long cared for and supported the growth of China-U.S. relations.

On this day 74 years ago, President Franklin Roosevelt made his inaugural speech "The Road of Enduring Progress." He called on the American people who were coming out of the depression to unite as one and redouble their efforts to forge ahead along the road of enduring progress. Today, the turbulence caused by the international financial crisis is receding and the world economy is returning to growth. Yet there still exist many uncertainties and destabilizing factors, making the world economic recovery a tortuous process. All countries in the world, including China and the United States, want to fully emerge from the crisis as soon as possible and achieve a full recovery of the world economy. In the face of the complex and fluid international situation and various risks and challenges, the people of our two countries should step up cooperation and work with people across the world to share opportunities, meet challenges and build a better future for mankind.

Thirty-two years ago, Mr. Deng Xiaoping, chief architect of China's reform and opening-up, paid a historic visit to the United States. He said during the visit that the Pacific Ocean should no longer be an obstacle that sets us apart. Rather, it should be a bond that links us together. History has proved the correctness of this important statement.

In the first decade of this century, China and the United States worked together and made steady progress in building a positive, cooperative and comprehensive relationship for the 21st century. China-U.S. relations have reached unprecedented breadth and depth. Given the ever changing circumstances in the world and in our respective countries, what should we do to take a sound and steady China-U.S. relationship into the new decade?

Jintao, Hu. From speech given by China's President at a welcome banquet in Washington, DC, on January 2, 2011.

To answer this question, one must, first and foremost, identify the basis for the development of China-U.S. relations. It is fair to say our two countries have never enjoyed such broad common interests and shouldered such important common responsibilities as we do today.

Both China and the United States are committed to upholding world peace and stability and reforming the international system. China is the largest developing country while the United States the largest developed one. The steady growth of our relations is, in itself, a major contribution to world peace and stability. Our two countries have engaged in coordination and cooperation on a range of regional hotspot issues and maintained close communication and coordination in both the traditional and non-traditional security fields. Together, we pushed for major progress in the international efforts on climate change and nonproliferation, and facilitated positive outcomes at the G20 [Group of 20] summits and other meetings. We have joined the rest of the international community in a common effort to safeguard overall stability in the international order and advance the reform and development of the international system.

Both China and the United States are committed to the development and prosperity of the Asia-Pacific region. The Asia-Pacific region is where China and the United States have the most overlapping interests. Cooperation between our two countries in the region is crucial to the regional situation and the growth of our bilateral relations. China and the United States have maintained close communication and coordination on regional hotspot issues such as the Korean nuclear issue, Afghanistan and South Asia and played a constructive role in promoting peace, development, good-neighborliness, mutual trust and mutually beneficial cooperation in the region.

Both China and the United States are committed to stronger bilateral cooperation in all fields to the benefit of the two peoples. The United States is China's second largest export market and main source of investment. China is the United States' third largest export market and also the fastest growing one. Preliminary statistics show that, over the past 10 years, quality yet inexpensive Chinese products have saved American consumers over 600 billion U.S. dollars. For many American companies, their businesses in China have become the biggest source of profits in their global operations. Even in 2008 and 2009 when the international financial crisis was most severe, over 70 percent of American companies in China remained profitable. Today, some 3 million tourists travel between the two countries every year. The friendly exchanges between the Chinese and American people have contributed not only to their own cultural progress, but also to the exchanges and mutual learning between the Eastern and the Western civilizations. And they have given a strong boost to the overall progress of human civilization.

Looking ahead, we are fully confident about the prospects of China-U.S. relations. Here I would like to propose that we take the following steps to advance the sound and steady growth of our relations.

First, bear in mind the overall interests, take a long-term perspective and make active efforts to advance China-U.S. cooperative partnership. The China-U.S. relationship is not one in which one side's gain means the other side's loss. Rather, it should be a relationship in which the two sides respect each other and endeavor to deepen strategic mutual trust. It should be a relationship that highlights common interests and stronger cooperation in all fields. The two sides should view and handle the bilateral relations from a global perspective and in keeping with the trend of the times. We should keep our relations on the path of equality, mutual respect, mutual trust, mutual benefit and common development. And to do that, we should increase high-level exchanges, deepen and expand communication at all levels, better appreciate each other's strategic intentions and development paths, and further increase mutual trust, dispel misgivings and build consensus.

Second, seize opportunities and take innovative steps to build a new pattern of mutually beneficial economic cooperation. Both China and the United States are advancing economic restructuring, increasing inputs in environmental protection, new energy and technological innovation, and promoting the development of health, education and other social programs. All this presents new opportunities for us to foster new areas of economic cooperation. China wants to work with the United States to forge a framework of broader and stronger economic cooperation. We can carry out fiscal, financial, and business cooperation on a larger scale, expand exchanges and cooperation in energy, the environment, agriculture, health and other fields, and broaden cooperation in new areas such as aviation and space, infrastructure and smart power grids. In this way, we will make our business ties even stronger and create more jobs and wealth for our people.

Third, intensify communication and consultation and deepen coordination and cooperation in addressing global challenges and international and regional hotspot issues. China and the United States should pursue global cooperation as partners to fulfill common responsibilities and meet common challenges. We should enhance consultation and coordination on global issues such as the Doha Round negotiations, climate change, energy and resources security, food security and public health security through bilateral and multilateral channels, maintain dialogue and exchanges on regional security, regional cooperation and hotspot issues, and work together for a more equitable, just, inclusive and better-managed international system. We should stay committed to promoting peace, stability and prosperity in the Asia-Pacific region, engage in open and inclusive regional cooperation, and turn the Asia Pacific into an important region where China and the United States work closely with each other on the basis of mutual respect.

Fourth, deepen friendship, be forward-looking, and vigorously promote friendly exchanges between various sectors of our two countries. The development of China-U.S. relations, in the final analysis, hinges on the broad support and active involvement of people from all walks of life in the two countries. We should draw up a good plan for our exchanges and cooperation in culture, education, science and technology and other fields, and encourage more dialogue and exchanges between the legislatures, local authorities, business communities, academic institutions, media organizations and other sectors so that more and more people will become supporters of stronger China-U.S. relations and get actively involved in this worthy cause. We need to put in extra efforts to boost exchanges between our young people and carry out diverse forms of youth exchange to ensure that the younger generation will carry forward China-U.S. friendship.

Fifth, treat each other with respect and as equals, and handle major, sensitive issues in a proper manner. A review of the history of our relations tells us that China-U.S. relations will enjoy smooth and steady growth when the two countries handle well issues involving each other's major interests. Otherwise, our relations will suffer constant trouble or even tension. Taiwan and Tibet-related issues concern China's sovereignty and territorial integrity, and they represents China's core interests. They touch upon the national sentiments of the 1.3 billion Chinese. We hope that the U.S. side will honor its commitments and work with us to preserve the hard-won progress of our relations.

China and the United States are different in history, culture, social system and development level. It is thus only normal that we have some disagreements and frictions. We should view and handle bilateral relations from a strategic and long-term perspective and with a sense of responsibility to history and to the future. We should prevent our relations from being affected or held back by any individual incident at any particular time. We should increase mutual trust, remove obstacles and work together to build a China-U.S. cooperative partnership based on mutual respect and mutual benefit.

The first decade of the 21st century has just passed. It is a decade when China made remarkable achievements in its reform and development endeavor and its relations with the rest of the world notably strengthened. The Chinese economy grew at an average annual rate of around 11 percent. And the Chinese people's livelihood markedly improved. During these 10 years, China imported 687 billion U.S. dollars worth of goods on average every year and created more than 14 million jobs in the relevant countries and regions. China joined the international community in an active effort to counter the international financial crisis, advance the reform of the international economic system, and promote the peaceful settlement of international disputes and hotspot issues. China took an active part in the international cooperation in addressing global issues and worked with countries around the world to safeguard world peace and promote common development.

Despite the remarkable achievements in China's development, we are keenly aware that China is still the largest developing country in the world. We still have a long way to go before we can achieve our national development goals. Development holds the key to resolve all problems in China, and we must pursue scientific development that puts people first and emphasizes comprehensive, coordinated and sustainable development. We need to adopt a more holistic approach to development and attach greater importance to ensuring and improving people's well-being and promoting social equity and justice. China has set out the guiding principles, strategic objectives and major tasks for economic and social development in the coming five years. We will continue to deepen reform and opening-up, advance economic, political, cultural and social restructuring in an all-round way, and improve the socialist market economy. We will develop socialist democracy and build a socialist country under the rule of law. We will work for vigorous cultural development and prosperity, enhance social harmony and improve our open economy in all respects. Through these efforts, we will make continuous progress in our endeavor to build a prosperous, strong, democratic, culturally advanced and harmonious modern socialist country.

We will stick to the basic state policy of opening to the outside world and follow a win-win strategy of opening-up. We will continue to advance China's interests in the broader context of the common interests of the international community, and expand and deepen the converging interests with others. We welcome the participation of other countries in China's development to share our development opportunities. And we will explore new areas and space for opening-up and contribute to the common development of the region and the world through our development. We will remain committed to the path of peaceful development, continue to strive for a peaceful international environment to develop ourselves, and uphold and promote world peace through our own development. China stands for peaceful settlement of international disputes and hotspot issues, and we follow a national defense policy that is defensive in nature. We do not engage in an arms race or pose a military threat to any country. China will never seek hegemony or pursue an expansionist policy.

To advance the sustained, sound and steady development of China-U.S. relations serves the fundamental interests of our two peoples. It is also conducive to world peace and development. Working together hand in hand, we will build a China-U.S. cooperative partnership based on mutual respect and mutual benefit and deliver greater benefits to the people of our two countries and the world over.

# EXPLORING THE ISSUE

## Is China Becoming a Dangerous Superpower?

### Questions for Critical Thinking and Reflection

1. Would it be wiser for the United States to follow policies that try to restrain China's power and/or build alliances, weapons systems, and other measure to counterbalance it or to try to accommodate China now to ensure good relations with a budding superpower?
2. Which is a more valid measure of China's economic power: China's overall GDP, which is the world's second largest, or China's per capita GDP, which ranks China 91st of the 190 of countries measured by the World Bank and is one-ninth the size of the U.S. per capita GDP?
3. Assume China is on the road to becoming a superpower. Other than the unlikely scenario of a nuclear attack on the United States, how specifically would that status for China threaten the United States?

## Is There Common Ground?

One of the reasons that Richard Nixon sought to begin the process of normalizing relations with China more than three decades ago was that he believed China was not only on the road to becoming a superpower but also that it might become the predominant country in the twenty-first century. While it remains unclear if Nixon was correct or not, there can be no doubt that China's power continues to develop. It still has the world's largest military (2.3 million troops on active duty; the United States has 1.5 million), and its array of nuclear weapons and delivery systems, while still smaller than those of the United States and Russia, is substantial. Preliminary data for 2012 indicate that China's economy and its defense spending continue to grow rapidly, although a bit less quickly than in recent years.

How to react to the growth of China is one of the hottest topics in national security circles. To a degree, it is only natural for China to seek a military capability to protect itself and to promote its interests in Asia and perhaps globally. That is what the United States does and, to a lesser degree, other countries do as well. Certainly China has come a long way toward that goal, but the Chinese began from a very low military technology point and their weaponry remains far behind U.S. standards. Still, China's military technology has improved substantially, and it is most likely to use its military muscle in Asia, where it has a geographical advantage over the far distant United States. Moreover, China's forces are concentrated in Asia; those of the United States are dispersed globally.

Most recently, tensions have risen between China and many of its neighbors including Japan, Vietnam, and the Philippines over competing claims to islands in the region. This has set off something of an arms race in the region. Partly in response to that, the United States has moved to shift forces from other regions to its Pacific commands. In China, it is the Communist Party, not the government, that decides policy, and President Hu is scheduled to step down from his post as head (general secretary) of the party in late 2012 and to also retire from the presidency in 2013. Part of the future will rest on the views of the country's new leadership. It is not certain yet, but most analysts believe that Xi Jinping, the current vice president, will follow Hu both as general secretary and as president. It should be added that the unilateral power of the general secretary/president is considerably diminished from what it once was, and whoever is the leader often needs to seek consensus among the Communist Party's top decision making body, the Politburo.

## Additional Resources

*Time* magazine's cover story, "Big Brotherhood" (October 22, 2012) gives insights into these presumed new leaders. A recent study of China's views of the United States can be found in Biwu Zhang, *Chinese Perceptions of the U.S.: An Exploration of China's Foreign Policy Motivations* (Lexington Books, 2012). A broader analysis of China's foreign policy is Robert G. Sutter, *Chinese Foreign Relations: Power and Policy Since the Cold War* (Rowman & Littlefield, 2012). For a somewhat contrasting view on China military power, read Tai Ming Cheung, "China's Emergence as a Defense Technological Power: Introduction," and other articles in *Journal of Strategic Studies* (June 2011), Special Issue: China's Emergence as a Defense Technological Power; and Andrew Scobell and Andrew J. Nathan, "China's Overstretched Military," *The Washington Quarterly* (October 2012).

# ISSUE 4

# Are the Palestinians Blocking the Path to Peace in the Middle East?

YES: Benjamin Netanyahu, from *Address to the 66th session of the General Assembly of United Nations at Its Headquarters in New York City* (September 23, 2011)

NO: Mahmoud Abbas, from *Address to the 66th Session of the General Assembly of United Nations at Its Headquarters in New York City* (September 23, 2011)

## ISSUE SUMMARY

YES: Benjamin Netanyahu, prime minister of Israel, tells the UN General Assembly that on behalf of the people of Israel, "I extend my hand to the Palestinian people, with whom we seek a just and lasting peace," and claims this has always been Israel's position but that the Palestinians have not reciprocated.

NO: Mahmoud Abbas, president the Palestinian National Authority, tells the UN General Assembly that the Palestinian people want to "achieve a just and comprehensive peace in our region that ensures the inalienable, legitimate national rights of the Palestinian people as defined by the resolutions of international legitimacy of the United Nations," but that, "The Israeli government refuses to commit to . . . negotiations that are based on international law and United Nations resolutions."

T he history of Israel/Palestine dates back to biblical times when there were both Hebrew and Arab kingdoms in the area. In later centuries, the area was conquered by many others; from 640 to 1917 it was almost continually controlled by Muslim rulers. In 1917 the British captured the area, Palestine, from Turkey.

Concurrently, a Zionist movement for a Jewish homeland arose. In 1917 the Balfour Declaration by Great Britain promised increased Jewish immigration to Palestine. The Jewish population in the region increased slowly, then more rapidly, because of refugees from the Holocaust. Soon after World War II, the Jewish population in Palestine stood at 650,000 and the Arab population was 1,350,000. Zionists increasingly agitated for an independent Jewish state. When the British withdrew in 1947, war immediately broke out between Jewish and Arab forces. The Jews won, establishing Israel in 1948 and doubling their territory. Most Palestinian Arabs fled (or were driven) from Israel to refugee camps in Gaza and the West Bank (of the Jordan River), two areas that had been part of Palestine but were captured in the war by Egypt and Jordan, respectively. As a result of the 1967 Six Day War between Israel and Egypt, Jordan, and Syria, the Israelis again expanded their territory by capturing several areas, including the Sinai Peninsula, Gaza, the Golan Heights, and the West Bank. Also in this period the Palestine Liberation Organization (PLO) became the major representative of Palestinian Arabs. True peace was not possible because the PLO and the Arab states would not recognize Israel's legitimacy and because Israel refused to give up some of the captured territory.

Since then, however, continuing violence, including another war in 1973, has persuaded many war-exhausted Arabs and Israelis that there has to be mutual compromise to achieve peace. Pressure from a number of quarters, including the United States, has kept the government of Israel and the Palestinians talking, at least at times. President George W. Bush announced his support of a Palestinian state, and President Barack Obama has continued that position.

Perhaps the most serious sore point between the Arabs and Israelis is the fate of the Palestinians, who live primarily in the West Bank and Gaza. Complicating the West Bank issue is that fact that Jerusalem is in or on the border of the West Bank (depending on one's views), and the Israelis claim all of it as their national capital and the Palestinians lay claim to part of it, East Jerusalem. About 400,000 Jews live in settlements in the West Bank and in East Jerusalem, both potentially part of an independent Palestine. For the most part, negotiations between Israel and the Palestinians have gone nowhere, and there have been times of violence between Arabs and Jews. A particular issue has been the expansion of violence at times, though there have been steps toward peace. Secret peace talks occurred between the Israelis and Palestinians in Norway and led to the Oslo Agreement in 1993. Palestinians gained limited control over Gaza and parts of the West Bank and established a quasi-government, the Palestinian National Authority, led by Yasser Arafat.

And another hopeful time came after Arafat died in 2004 and was succeeded by a seeming moderate, Mahmoud Abbas. Then Israel withdrew the last of its troops from Gaza in 2005, leaving it under full Palestinian control. Just a few months later, though, much of the world was appalled when the Palestinians gave representatives of Hamas, a terrorist organization, control of the Palestinian parliament. Matters worsened in 2006 with attacks launched against Israel from Gaza, followed by Israeli retaliation. Since then, there has been little significant violence between the two sides, but there has also been not progress toward a permanent solution. The Palestinians, however, have sought recognition as a country by seeking admissions to the United Nations.

That is opposed by not only Israel, but also by many other countries, including the United States, which believes that statehood for Palestine needs to come through a resolution of the issues with Israel. In the YES and NO selections, the leaders of Israel and of the Palestinians, in speeches given the same day before the UN General Assembly, both profess the desire for peace and blame each other for the failure to achieve that goal.

# YES ↵

Benjamin Netanyahu

# Address to the 66th Session of the General Assembly of United Nations at Its Headquarters in New York City

Israel has extended its hand in peace from the moment it was established 63 years ago [in 1948]. On behalf of Israel and the Jewish people, I extend that hand again today. I extend it to the people of Egypt and Jordan, with renewed friendship for neighbors with whom we have made peace. I extend it to the people of Turkey, with respect and good will. I extend it to the people of Libya and Tunisia, with admiration for those trying to build a democratic future. I extend it to the other peoples of North Africa and the Arabian Peninsula, with whom we want to forge a new beginning. I extend it to the people of Syria, Lebanon and Iran, with awe at the courage of those fighting brutal repression.

But most especially, I extend my hand to the Palestinian people, with whom we seek a just and lasting peace.

In Israel our hope for peace never wanes. Our scientists, doctors, innovators, apply their genius to improve the world of tomorrow. Our artists, our writers, enrich the heritage of humanity. Now, I know that this is not exactly the image of Israel that is often portrayed in this hall. After all, it was here in 1975 that the age-old yearning of my people to restore our national life in our ancient biblical homeland—it was then that this was braided—branded, rather—shamefully, as racism. And it was here in 1980, right here, that the historic peace agreement between Israel and Egypt wasn't praised; it was denounced! And it's here year after year that Israel is unjustly singled out for condemnation. It's singled out for condemnation more often than all the nations of the world combined. Twenty-one out of the 27 General Assembly resolutions condemn Israel—the one true democracy in the Middle East.

Well, this is an unfortunate part of the UN institution. It's the—the theater of the absurd. It doesn't only cast Israel as the villain; it often casts real villains in leading roles: Gadhafi's Libya chaired the UN Commission on Human Rights; Saddam's Iraq headed the UN Committee on Disarmament.

You might say: That's the past. Well, here's what's happening now—right now, today. Hezbollah-controlled Lebanon now presides over the UN Security Council. This means, in effect, that a terror organization presides over the body entrusted with guaranteeing the world's security.

Netanyahu, Benjamin. From *A Report to the Secretary General of the United Nations,* September 23, 2011.

You couldn't make this thing up.

So here in the UN, automatic majorities can decide anything. They can decide that the sun sets in the west or rises in the west. I think the first has already been pre-ordained. But they can also decide—they have decided that the Western Wall in Jerusalem, Judaism's holiest place, is occupied Palestinian territory.

And yet even here in the General Assembly, the truth can sometimes break through. In 1984 when I was appointed Israel's ambassador to the United Nations, I visited the great rabbi of Lubavich. He said to me—and ladies and gentlemen, I don't want any of you to be offended because from personal experience of serving here, I know there are many honorable men and women, many capable and decent people serving their nations here. But here's what the rebbe said to me. He said to me, you'll be serving in a house of many lies. And then he said, remember that even in the darkest place, the light of a single candle can be seen far and wide.

Today I hope that the light of truth will shine, if only for a few minutes, in a hall that for too long has been a place of darkness for my country. So as Israel's prime minister, I didn't come here to win applause. I came here to speak the truth. (Cheers, applause.) The truth is—the truth is that Israel wants peace. The truth is that I want peace. The truth is that in the Middle East at all times, but especially during these turbulent days, peace must be anchored in security. The truth is that we cannot achieve peace through UN resolutions, but only through direct negotiations between the parties. The truth is that so far the Palestinians have refused to negotiate. The truth is that Israel wants peace with a Palestinian state, but the Palestinians want a state without peace. And the truth is you shouldn't let that happen.

When I first came here 27 years ago, the world was divided between East and West. Since then the Cold War ended, great civilizations have risen from centuries of slumber, hundreds of millions have been lifted out of poverty, countless more are poised to follow, and the remarkable thing is that so far this monumental historic shift has largely occurred peacefully. Yet a malignancy is now growing between East and West that threatens the peace of all. It seeks not to liberate, but to enslave, not to build, but to destroy.

That malignancy is militant Islam. It cloaks itself in the mantle of a great faith, yet it murders Jews, Christians and Muslims alike with unforgiving impartiality. On September 11th it killed thousands of Americans, and it left the twin towers in smoldering ruins. Last night I laid a wreath on the 9/11 memorial. It was deeply moving. But as I was going there, one thing echoed in my mind: the outrageous words of the president of Iran on this podium yesterday. He implied that 9/11 was an American conspiracy. Some of you left this hall. All of you should have.

Since 9/11, militant Islamists slaughtered countless other innocents—in London and Madrid, in Baghdad and Mumbai, in Tel Aviv and Jerusalem, in every part of Israel. I believe that the greatest danger facing our world is that this fanaticism will arm itself with nuclear weapons. And this is precisely what Iran is trying to do.

Can you imagine that man who ranted here yesterday—can you imagine him armed with nuclear weapons? The international community must stop Iran before it's too late. If Iran is not stopped, we will all face the specter of nuclear terrorism, and the Arab Spring could soon become an Iranian winter. That would be a tragedy. Millions of Arabs have taken to the streets to replace tyranny with liberty, and no one would benefit more than Israel if those committed to freedom and peace would prevail.

This is my fervent hope. But as the prime minister of Israel, I cannot risk the future of the Jewish state on wishful thinking. Leaders must see reality as it is, not as it ought to be. We must do our best to shape the future, but we cannot wish away the dangers of the present.

And the world around Israel is definitely becoming more dangerous. Militant Islam has already taken over Lebanon and Gaza. It's determined to tear apart the peace treaties between Israel and Egypt and between Israel and Jordan. It's poisoned many Arab minds against Jews and Israel, against America and the West. It opposes not the policies of Israel but the existence of Israel. Now, some argue that the spread of militant Islam, especially in these turbulent times—if you want to slow it down, they argue, Israel must hurry to make concessions, to make territorial compromises. And this theory sounds simple. Basically it goes like this: Leave the territory, and peace will be advanced. The moderates will be strengthened, the radicals will be kept at bay. And don't worry about the pesky details of how Israel will actually defend itself; international troops will do the job.

These people say to me constantly: Just make a sweeping offer, and everything will work out. You know, there's only one problem with that theory. We've tried it and it hasn't worked. In 2000 Israel made a sweeping peace offer that met virtually all of the Palestinian demands. Arafat rejected it. The Palestinians then launched a terror attack that claimed a thousand Israeli lives. Prime Minister Olmert afterwards made an even more sweeping offer, in 2008. President Abbas didn't even respond to it.

But Israel did more than just make sweeping offers. We actually left territory. We withdrew from Lebanon in 2000 and from every square inch of Gaza in 2005. That didn't calm the Islamic storm, the militant Islamic storm that threatens us. It only brought the storm closer and make it stronger.

Hezbollah and Hamas fired thousands of rockets against our cities from the very territories we vacated. See, when Israel left Lebanon and Gaza, the moderates didn't defeat the radicals, the moderates were devoured by the radicals. And I regret to say that international troops like [UN peacekeepers] UNIFIL in Lebanon and in Gaza didn't stop the radicals from attacking Israel. We left Gaza hoping for peace.

We didn't freeze the settlements in Gaza, we uprooted them. We did exactly what the theory says: Get out, go back to the 1967 borders, dismantle the settlements.

And I don't think people remember how far we went to achieve this. We uprooted thousands of people from their homes. We pulled children out of—out of their schools and their kindergartens. We bulldozed synagogues. We even—we even moved loved ones from their graves. And then, having done all that, we gave the keys of Gaza to President Abbas.

Now the theory says it should all work out, and President Abbas and the Palestinian Authority now could build a peaceful state in Gaza. You can remember that the entire world applauded. They applauded our withdrawal as an act of great statesmanship. It was a bold act of peace. But ladies and gentlemen, we didn't get peace. We got war. We got Iran, which through its proxy Hamas promptly kicked out the Palestinian Authority. The Palestinian Authority collapsed in a day—in one day.

President Abbas just said on this podium that the Palestinians are armed only with their hopes and dreams. Yeah, hopes, dreams and 10,000 missiles and Grad rockets supplied by Iran, not to mention the river of lethal weapons now flowing into Gaza from the Sinai, from Libya, and from elsewhere.

Thousands of missiles have already rained down on our cities. So you might understand that, given all this, Israelis rightly ask: What's to prevent this from happening again in the West Bank? See, most of our major cities in the south of the country are within a few dozen kilometers from Gaza. But in the center of the country, opposite the West Bank, our cities are a few hundred meters or at most a few kilometers away from the edge of the West Bank.

So I want to ask you. Would any of you—would any of you bring danger so close to your cities, to your families? Would you act so recklessly with the lives of your citizens? Israel is prepared to have a Palestinian state in the West Bank, but we're not prepared to have another Gaza there. And that's why we need to have real security arrangements, which the Palestinians simply refuse to negotiate with us.

Israelis remember the bitter lessons of Gaza. Many of Israel's critics ignore them. They irresponsibly advise Israel to go down this same perilous path again. Your read what these people say and it's as if nothing happened—just repeating the same advice, the same formulas as though none of this happened.

And these critics continue to press Israel to make far-reaching concessions without first assuring Israel's security. They praise those who unwittingly feed the insatiable crocodile of militant Islam as bold statesmen. They cast as enemies of peace those of us who insist that we must first erect a sturdy barrier to keep the crocodile out, or at the very least jam an iron bar between its gaping jaws.

So in the face of the labels and the libels, Israel must heed better advice. Better a bad press than a good eulogy, and better still would be a fair press whose sense of history extends beyond breakfast, and which recognizes Israel's legitimate security concerns.

I believe that in serious peace negotiations, these needs and concerns can be properly addressed, but they will not be addressed without negotiations. And the needs are many, because Israel is such a tiny country. Without Judea and Samaria, the West Bank, Israel is all of 9 miles wide. I want to put it for you in perspective, because you're all in the city. That's about two-thirds the length of Manhattan. It's the distance between Battery Park and Columbia University. And don't forget that the people who live in Brooklyn and New Jersey are considerably nicer than some of Israel's neighbors.

So how do you—how do you protect such a tiny country, surrounded by people sworn to its destruction and armed to the teeth by Iran? Obviously you can't defend it from within that narrow space alone. Israel needs greater strategic depth, and that's exactly why Security Council Resolution 242 didn't require Israel to leave all the territories it captured in the Six-Day War. It talked about withdrawal from territories, to secure and defensible boundaries. And to defend itself, Israel must therefore maintain a long-term Israeli military presence in critical strategic areas in the West Bank.

I explained this to President Abbas. He answered that if a Palestinian state was to be a sovereign country, it could never accept such arrangements. Why not? America has had troops in Japan, Germany, and South Korea for more than a half a century. Britain has had an airspace in Cyprus or rather an air base in Cyprus. France has forces in three independent African nations. None of these states claim that they're not sovereign countries.

And there are many other vital security issues that also must be addressed. Take the issue of airspace. Again, Israel's small dimensions create huge security problems. America can be crossed by jet airplane in six hours. To fly across Israel, it takes three minutes. So is Israel's tiny airspace to be chopped in half and given to a Palestinian state not at peace with Israel?

Our major international airport is a few kilometers away from the West Bank. Without peace, will our planes become targets for antiaircraft missiles placed in the adjacent Palestinian state? And how will we stop the smuggling into the West Bank? It's not merely the West Bank, it's the West Bank mountains. It just dominates the coastal plain where most of Israel's population sits below. How could we prevent the smuggling into these mountains of those missiles that could be fired on our cities?

I bring up these problems because they're not theoretical problems. They're very real. And for Israelis, they're life-and-death matters. All these potential cracks in Israel's security have to be sealed in a peace agreement before a Palestinian state is declared, not afterwards, because if you leave it afterwards, they won't be sealed. And these problems will explode in our face and explode the peace.

The Palestinians should first make peace with Israel and then get their state. But I also want to tell you this. After such a peace agreement is signed, Israel will not be the last country to welcome a Palestinian state as a new member of the United Nations. We will be the first. (Applause.)

And there's one more thing. Hamas has been violating international law by holding our soldier Gilad Shalit captive for five years.

They haven't given even one Red Cross visit. He's held in a dungeon, in darkness, against all international norms. Gilad Shalit is the son of Aviva and Noam Shalit. He is the grandson of Zvi Shalit, who escaped the Holocaust by coming to the—in the 1930s as a boy to the land of Israel. Gilad Shalit is the son of every Israeli family. Every nation represented here should demand his immediate release. (Applause.) If you want to—if you want to pass a resolution about the Middle East today, that's the resolution you should pass.

Ladies and gentlemen, last year in Israel in Bar-Ilan University, this year in the Knesset and in the U.S. Congress, I laid out my vision for peace in which a demilitarized Palestinian state recognizes the Jewish state. Yes, the Jewish state. After all, this is the body that recognized the Jewish state 64 years ago. Now, don't you think it's about time that Palestinians did the same? The Jewish state of Israel will always protect the rights of all its minorities, including the more than 1 million Arab citizens of Israel.

I wish I could say the same thing about a future Palestinian state, for as Palestinian officials made clear the other day—in fact, I think they made it right here in New York—they said the Palestinian state won't allow any Jews in it. They'll be Jew-free—Judenrein. That's ethnic cleansing. There are laws today in Ramallah that make the selling of land to Jews punishable by death. That's racism. And you know which laws this evokes.

Israel has no intention whatsoever to change the democratic character of our state. We just don't want the Palestinians to try to change the Jewish character of our state. (Applause.) We want to give up—we want them to give up the fantasy of flooding Israel with millions of Palestinians. President Abbas just stood here, and he said that the core of the Israeli–Palestinian conflict is the settlements. Well, that's odd. Our conflict has been raging for—was raging for nearly half a century before there was a single Israeli settlement in the West Bank. So if what President Abbas is saying was true, then the—I guess that the settlements he's talking about are Tel Aviv, Haifa, Jaffa, Be'er Sheva. Maybe that's what he meant the other day when he said that Israel has been occupying Palestinian land for 63 years. He didn't say from 1967; he said from 1948. I hope somebody will bother to ask him this question because it illustrates a simple truth: The core of the conflict is not the settlements. The settlements are a result of the conflict.

The settlements have to be—it's an issue that has to be addressed and resolved in the course of negotiations. But the core of the conflict has always been and unfortunately remains the refusal of the Palestinians to recognize a Jewish state in any border.

I think it's time that the Palestinian leadership recognizes what every serious international leader has recognized, from Lord Balfour and Lloyd George in 1917, to President Truman in 1948, to President Obama just two days ago right here: Israel is the Jewish state. (Applause.) President Abbas, stop walking around this issue. Recognize the Jewish state, and make peace with us. In such a genuine peace, Israel is prepared to make painful compromises. We believe that the Palestinians should be neither the citizens of Israel nor its subjects. They should live in a free state of their own. But they should be ready, like us, for compromise. And we will know that they're ready for compromise and for peace when they start taking Israel's security requirements seriously and when they stop denying our historical connection to our ancient homeland. I often hear them accuse Israel of Judaizing Jerusalem. That's like accusing America of Americanizing Washington, or the British of Anglicizing London. You know why we're called "Jews"? Because we come from Judea.

In my office in Jerusalem, there's a—there's an ancient seal. It's a signet ring of a Jewish official from the time of the Bible. The seal was found right next to the Western Wall, and it dates back 2,700 years, to the time of King Hezekiah. Now, there's a name of the Jewish official inscribed on the ring in Hebrew. His name was Netanyahu. That's my last name. My first name, Benjamin, dates back a thousand years earlier to Benjamin—Binyamin—the son of Jacob, who was also known as Israel. Jacob and his 12 sons roamed these same hills of Judea and Sumeria 4,000 years ago, and there's been a continuous Jewish presence in the land ever since. And for those Jews who were exiled from our land, they never stopped dreaming of coming back: Jews in Spain, on the eve of their expulsion; Jews in the Ukraine, fleeing the pogroms; Jews fighting the Warsaw Ghetto, as the Nazis were circling around it. They never stopped praying, they never stopped yearning. They whispered: Next year in Jerusalem. Next year in the promised land.

As the prime minister of Israel, I speak for a hundred generations of Jews who were dispersed throughout the lands, who suffered every evil under the Sun, but who never gave up hope of restoring their national life in the one and only Jewish state.

Ladies and gentlemen, I continue to hope that President Abbas will be my partner in peace. I've worked hard to advance that peace. The day I came into office, I called for direct negotiations without preconditions. President Abbas didn't respond. I outlined a vision of peace of two states for two peoples. He still didn't respond. I removed hundreds of roadblocks and checkpoints, to ease freedom of movement in the Palestinian areas; this facilitated a fantastic growth in the Palestinian economy. But again—no response. I took the unprecedented step of freezing new buildings in the settlements for 10 months. No prime minister did that before, ever. (Scattered applause.) Once again—you applaud, but there was no response. No response. In the last few weeks, American officials have put forward ideas to restart peace talks. There were things in those ideas about borders that I didn't like. There were things there about the Jewish state that I'm sure the Palestinians didn't like.

But with all my reservations, I was willing to move forward on these American ideas. President Abbas, why don't you join me? We have to stop negotiating about the negotiations. Let's just get on with it. Let's negotiate peace.

I spent years defending Israel on the battlefield. I spent decades defending Israel in the court of public opinion. President Abbas, you've dedicated your life to advancing the Palestinian cause. Must this conflict continue for generations, or will we enable our children and our grandchildren to speak in years ahead of how we found a way to end it? That's what we should aim for, and that's what I believe we can achieve.

In two and a half years, we met in Jerusalem only once, even though my door has always been open to you. If you wish, I'll come to Ramallah. Actually, I have a better suggestion. We've both just flown thousands of miles to New York. Now we're in the same city. We're in the same building. So let's meet here today in the United Nations. Who's there to stop us? What is there to stop us? If we genuinely want peace, what is there to stop us from meeting today and beginning peace negotiations?

And I suggest we talk openly and honestly. Let's listen to one another. Let's do as we say in the Middle East: Let's talk "doogri." That means straightforward. I'll tell you my needs and concerns. You'll tell me yours. And with God's help, we'll find the common ground of peace. There's an old Arab saying that you cannot applaud with one hand. Well, the same is true of peace. I cannot make peace alone. I cannot make peace without you. President Abbas, I extend my hand—the hand of Israel—in peace. I hope that you will grasp that hand. We are both the sons of Abraham. My people call him Avraham. Your people call him Ibrahim. We share the same patriarch. We dwell in the same land. Our destinies are intertwined. Let us realize the vision of Isaiah, "The people who walk in darkness will see a great light." Let that light be the light of peace.

Mahmoud Abbas         ➜ **NO**

# Address to the 66th Session of the General Assembly of United Nations at Its Headquarters in New York City

$\mathbf{T}$he Question Palestine is intricately linked with the United Nations via the resolutions adopted by its various organs and agencies and via the essential and lauded role of the United Nations Relief and Works Agency for Palestine Refugees in the Near East—UNRWA—which embodies the international responsibility towards the plight of Palestine refugees, who are the victims of Al-Nakba (Catastrophe) that occurred in 1948. [Palestinians and some others commemorate *Yawm al-Nakba,* the Day of Catastrophe on May 15. The date coincides with Israel's declaration of independence in 1948 and what the Palestinians claim is the expulsion by violence and intimidation of many of their people from their lands in what is now Israel.] We aspire for and seek a greater and more effective role for the United Nations in working to achieve a just and comprehensive peace in our region that ensures the inalienable, legitimate national rights of the Palestinian people as defined by the resolutions of international legitimacy of the United Nations.

A year ago, at this same time, distinguished leaders in this hall addressed the stalled peace efforts in our region. Everyone had high hopes for a new round of final status negotiations, which had begun in early September in Washington under the direct auspices of President Barack Obama and with participation of the Quartet, and with Egyptian and Jordanian participation, to reach a peace agreement within one year. We entered those negotiations with open hearts and attentive ears and sincere intentions, and we were ready with our documents, papers and proposals. But the negotiations broke down just weeks after their launch.

After this, we did not give up and did not cease our efforts for initiatives and contacts. Over the past year we did not leave a door to be knocked or channel to be tested or path to be taken and we did not ignore any formal or informal party of influence and stature to be addressed. We positively considered the various ideas and proposals and initiatives presented from many countries and parties. But all of these sincere efforts and endeavors undertaken by international parties were repeatedly wrecked by the positions of the Israeli government, which quickly dashed the hopes raised by the launch of negotiations last September.

Abbas, Mahmoud. From *A Report to the Secretary General of the United Nations,* September 23, 2011.

The core issue here is that the Israeli government refuses to commit to terms of reference for the negotiations that are based on international law and United Nations resolutions, and that it frantically continues to intensify building of settlements on the territory of the State of Palestine. Settlement activities embody the core of the policy of colonial military occupation of the land of the Palestinian people and all of the brutality of aggression and racial discrimination against our people that this policy entails. This policy, which constitutes a breach of international humanitarian law and United Nations resolutions, is the primary cause for the failure of the peace process, the collapse of dozens of opportunities, and the burial of the great hopes that arose from the signing of the Declaration of Principles in 1993 between the Palestine Liberation Organization and Israel to achieve a just peace that would begin a new era for our region.

The reports of United Nations missions as well as by several Israeli institutions and civil societies convey a horrific picture about the size of the settlement campaign, which the Israeli government does not hesitate to boast about and which it continues to execute through the systematic confiscation of the Palestinian lands and the construction of thousands of new settlement units in various areas of the West Bank, particularly in East Jerusalem, and accelerated construction of the annexation Wall that is eating up large tracts of our land, dividing it into separate and isolated islands and cantons, destroying family life and communities and the livelihoods of tens of thousands of families. The occupying Power also continues to refuse permits for our people to build in Occupied East Jerusalem, at the same time that it intensifies its decades-long campaign of demolition and confiscation of homes, displacing Palestinian owners and residents under a multi-pronged policy of ethnic cleansing aimed at pushing them away from their ancestral homeland. In addition, orders have been issued to deport elected representatives from the city of Jerusalem. The occupying Power also continues to undertake excavations that threaten our holy places, and its military checkpoints prevent our citizens from getting access to their mosques and churches, and it continues to besiege the Holy City with a ring of settlements imposed to separate the Holy City from the rest of the Palestinian cities.

The occupation is racing against time to redraw the borders on our land according to what it wants and to impose a fait accompli on the ground that changes the realities and that is undermining the realistic potential for the existence of the State of Palestine.

At the same time, the occupying Power continues to impose its blockade on the Gaza Strip and to target Palestinian civilians by assassinations, air strikes and artillery shelling, persisting with its war of aggression of three years ago on Gaza, which resulted in massive destruction of homes, schools, hospitals, and mosques, and the thousands of martyrs and wounded.

The occupying Power also continues its incursions in areas of the Palestinian National Authority through raids, arrests and killings at the checkpoints. In recent years, the criminal actions of armed settler militias, who enjoy the special protection of the occupation army, have intensified with the perpetration of frequent attacks against our people, targeting their homes, schools, universities, mosques, fields, crops and trees. Despite our repeated warnings, the occupying Power has not acted to curb these attacks and we hold them fully responsible for the crimes of the settlers.

These are just a few examples of the policy of the Israeli colonial settlement occupation, and this policy is responsible for the continued failure of the successive international attempts to salvage the peace process.

This policy will destroy the chances of achieving a two-State solution upon which there is an international consensus, and here I caution aloud: This settlement policy threatens to also undermine the structure of the Palestinian National Authority and even end its existence. In addition, we now face the imposition new conditions not previously raised, conditions that will transform the raging conflict in our inflamed region into a religious conflict and a threat to the future of a million and a half Christian and Muslim Palestinians, citizens of Israel, a matter which we reject and which is impossible for us to accept being dragged into.

All of these actions taken by Israel in our country are unilateral actions and are not based on any earlier agreements. Indeed, what we witness is a selective application of the agreements aimed at perpetuating the occupation. Israel reoccupied the cities of the West Bank by a unilateral action, and reestablished the civil and military occupation by a unilateral action, and it is the one that determines whether or not a Palestinian citizen has the right to reside in any part of the Palestinian Territory. And it is confiscating our land and our water and obstructing our movement as well as the movement of goods. And it is the one obstructing our whole destiny. All of this is unilateral.

In 1974, our deceased leader Yasser Arafat came to this hall and assured the Members of the General Assembly of our affirmative pursuit for peace, urging the United Nations to realize the inalienable national rights of the Palestinian people, stating: "Do not let the olive branch fall from my hand."

In 1988, President Arafat again addressed the General Assembly, which convened in Geneva to hear him, where he submitted the Palestinian peace program adopted by the Palestine National Council at its session held that year in Algeria.

When we adopted this program, we were taking a painful and very difficult step for all of us, especially those, including myself, who were forced to leave their homes and their towns and villages, carrying only some of our belongings and our grief and our memories and the keys of our homes to the camps of exile and the Diaspora in the 1948 Al-Nakba, one of the worst operations of uprooting, destruction and removal of a vibrant and cohesive society that had been contributing in a pioneering and leading way in the cultural, educational and economic renaissance of the Arab Middle East.

Yet, because we believe in peace and because of our conviction in international legitimacy, and because we had the courage to make difficult decisions for our people, and in the absence of absolute justice, we decided to adopt the path of relative justice—justice that is possible and could correct part of the grave historical injustice committed against our people. Thus, we agreed to establish the State of Palestine on only 22% of the territory of historical Palestine—on all the Palestinian Territory occupied by Israel in 1967.

We, by taking that historic step, which was welcomed by the States of the world, made a major concession in order to achieve a historic compromise that would allow peace to be made in the land of peace. In the years that followed—from the Madrid Conference and the Washington negotiations leading to the Oslo agreement, which was signed 18 years ago in the garden of the White House and was linked with the letters of mutual recognition between the PLO and Israel, we persevered and dealt positively and responsibly with all efforts aimed at the achievement of a lasting peace agreement. Yet, as we said earlier, every initiative and every conference and every new round of negotiations and every movement was shattered on the rock of the Israeli settlement expansion project.

I confirm, on behalf of the Palestine Liberation Organization, the sole legitimate representative of the Palestinian people, which will remain so until the end of the conflict in all its aspects and until the resolution of all final status issues, the following:

1. The goal of the Palestinian people is the realization of their inalienable national rights in their independent State of Palestine, with East Jerusalem as its capital, on all the land of the West Bank, including East Jerusalem, and the Gaza Strip, which Israel occupied in the June 1967 war, in conformity with the resolutions of international legitimacy and with the achievement of a just and agreed upon solution to the Palestine refugee issue in accordance with resolution 194, as stipulated in the Arab Peace Initiative which presented the consensus Arab vision to resolve the core the Arab–Israeli conflict and to achieve a just and comprehensive peace. To this we adhere and this is what we are working to achieve. Achieving this desired peace also requires the release of political prisoners and detainees in Israeli prisons without delay.
2. The PLO and the Palestinian people adhere to the renouncement of violence and rejection and condemning of terrorism in all its forms, especially State terrorism, and adhere to all agreements signed between the Palestine Liberation Organization and Israel.
3. We adhere to the option of negotiating a lasting solution to the conflict in accordance with resolutions of international legitimacy. Here, I declare that the Palestine Liberation Organization is ready to return immediately to the negotiating table on the basis of the adopted terms of reference based on international legitimacy and a complete cessation of settlement activities.
4. Our people will continue their popular peaceful resistance to the Israeli occupation and its settlement and apartheid policies and its construction of the racist annexation Wall, and they receive support for their resistance, which is consistent with international humanitarian law and international conventions and has the support of peace activists from Israel and around the world, reflecting an impressive, inspiring and courageous example of the strength of this defenseless people, armed only with their dreams, courage, hope and slogans in the face of bullets, tanks, tear gas and bulldozers.
5. When we bring our plight and our case to this international podium, it is a confirmation of our reliance on the political and diplomatic option and is a confirmation that we do not undertake unilateral steps.

Our efforts are not aimed at isolating Israel or de-legitimizing it; rather we want to gain legitimacy for the cause of the people of Palestine. We only aim to de-legitimize the settlement activities and the occupation and apartheid and the logic of ruthless force, and we believe that all the countries of the world stand with us in this regard.

I am here to say on behalf of the Palestinian people and the Palestine Liberation Organization: We extend our hands to the Israeli government and the Israeli people for peace-making. I say to them: Let us urgently build together a future for our children where they can enjoy freedom, security and prosperity. Let us build the bridges of dialogue instead of checkpoints and walls of separation, and build cooperative relations based on parity and equity between two neighboring States—Palestine and Israel—instead of policies of occupation, settlement, war and eliminating the other.

Despite the unquestionable right of our people to self-determination and to the independence of our State as stipulated in international resolutions, we have accepted in the past few years to engage in what appeared to be a test of our worthiness, entitlement and eligibility. During the last two years our national authority has implemented a program to build our State institutions. Despite the extraordinary situation and the Israeli obstacles imposed, a serious extensive project was launched that has included the implementation of plans to enhance and advance the judiciary and the apparatus for maintenance of order and security, to develop the administrative, financial, and oversight systems, to upgrade the performance of institutions, and to enhance self-reliance to reduce the need for foreign aid. With the thankful support of Arab countries and donors from friendly countries, a number of large infrastructure projects have been implemented, focused on various aspects of service, with special attention to rural and marginalized areas.

In the midst of this massive national project, we have been strengthening what we seeking to be the features of our State: from the preservation of security for the citizen and public order; to the promotion of judicial authority and rule of law; to strengthening the role of women via legislation, laws and participation; to ensuring the protection of public freedoms and strengthening the role of civil society institutions; to institutionalizing rules and regulations for ensuring accountability and transparency in the work of our Ministries and departments; to entrenching the pillars of democracy as the basis for the Palestinian political life.

When division struck the unity of our homeland, people and institutions, we were determined to adopt dialogue for restoration of our unity. We succeeded months ago in achieving national reconciliation and we hope that its implementation will be accelerated in the coming weeks. The core pillar of this reconciliation was to turn to the people through legislative and presidential elections within a year, because the State we want will be a State characterized by the rule of law, democratic exercise and protection of the freedoms and equality of all citizens without any discrimination and the transfer of power through the ballot box.

The reports issued recently by the United Nations, the World Bank, the Ad Hoc Liaison Committee (AHLC) and the International Monetary Fund confirm and laud what has been accomplished, considering it a remarkable and unprecedented model. The consensus conclusion by the AHLC a few days ago here described what has been accomplished as a "remarkable international success story" and confirmed the readiness of the Palestinian people and their institutions for the immediate independence of the State of Palestine.

It is no longer possible to redress the issue of the blockage of the horizon of the peace talks with the same means and methods that have been repeatedly tried and proven unsuccessful over the past years. The crisis is far too deep to be neglected, and what is more dangerous are attempts to simply circumvent it or postpone its explosion.

It is neither possible, nor practical, nor acceptable to return to conducting business as usual, as if everything is fine. It is futile to go into negotiations without clear parameters and in the absence of credibility and a specific timetable. Negotiations will be meaningless as long as the occupation army on the ground continues to entrench its occupation, instead of rolling it back, and continues to change the demography of our country in order to create a new basis on which to alter the borders.

It is a moment of truth and my people are waiting to hear the answer of the world. Will it allow Israel to continue its occupation, the only occupation in the world? Will it allow Israel to remain a State above the law and accountability? Will it allow Israel to continue rejecting the resolutions of the Security Council and the General Assembly of the United Nations and the International Court of Justice and the positions of the overwhelming majority of countries in the world?

I come before you today from the Holy Land, the land of Palestine, the land of divine messages, ascension of the Prophet Muhammad (peace be upon him) and the birthplace of Jesus Christ (peace be upon him), to speak on behalf of the Palestinian people in the homeland and in the Diaspora, to say, after 63 years of suffering of the ongoing Nakba: Enough. It is time for the Palestinian people to gain their freedom and independence.

The time has come to end the suffering and the plight of millions of Palestine refugees in the homeland and the Diaspora, to end their displacement and to realize their rights, some of them forced to take refuge more than once in different places of the world.

At a time when the Arab peoples affirm their quest for democracy—the Arab Spring—the time is now for the Palestinian Spring, the time for independence.

The time has come for our men, women and children to live normal lives, for them to be able to sleep without waiting for the worst that the next day will bring; for mothers to be assured that their children will return home without fear of suffering killing, arrest or humiliation; for students to be able to go to their schools and universities without checkpoints obstructing them. The time has come for sick people to be able to reach hospitals normally, and for our farmers to be able to take care of their good land without fear of the occupation seizing the land and its water, which the wall prevents access to, or fear of the settlers, for whom settlements are being built on our land and who are uprooting and burning the olive trees that have existed for hundreds of years. The time has come for the thousands of prisoners to be released from the prisons to return to their families and their children to become a part of building their homeland, for the freedom of which they have sacrificed.

My people desire to exercise their right to enjoy a normal life like the rest of humanity. They believe what the great poet Mahmoud Darwish said: Standing here, staying here, permanent here, eternal here, and we have one goal, one, one: to be.

We profoundly appreciate and value the positions of all States that have supported our struggle and our rights and recognized the State of Palestine following the Declaration of Independence in 1988, as well as the countries that have recently recognized the State of Palestine and those that have upgraded the level of Palestine's representation in their capitals. I also salute the Secretary-General, who said a few days ago that the Palestinian State should have been established years ago.

Be assured that this support for our people is more valuable to them than you can imagine, for it makes them feel that someone is listening to their narrative and that their tragedy and the horrors of Al-Nakba and the occupation, from which they have so suffered, are not being ignored. And, it reinforces their hope that stems from the belief that justice is possible . . . in this world. The loss of hope is the most ferocious enemy of peace and despair is the strongest ally of extremism. I say: The time has come for my courageous and proud people, after decades of displacement and colonial occupation and ceaseless suffering, to live like other peoples of the earth, free in a sovereign and independent homeland.

I would like to inform you that, before delivering this statement, I submitted, in my capacity as the President of the State of Palestine and Chairman of the Executive Committee of the Palestine Liberation Organization, to H.E. Mr. Ban Ki-moon, Secretary-General of the United Nations, an application for the admission of Palestine on the basis of the 4 June 1967 borders, with Al-Quds Al-Sharif as its capital, as a full member of the United Nations.

I call upon Mr. Secretary-General to expedite transmittal of our request to the Security Council, and I call upon the distinguished members of the Security Council to vote in favor of our full membership. I also call upon the States that did not recognize the State of Palestine as yet to do so.

The support of the countries of the world for our endeavor is a victory for truth, freedom, justice, law and international legitimacy, and it provides tremendous support for the peace option and enhances the chances of success of the negotiations.

Your support for the establishment of the State of Palestine and for its admission to the United Nations as a full member is the greatest contribution to peacemaking in the Holy Land.

# EXPLORING THE ISSUE

## Are the Palestinians Blocking the Path to Peace in the Middle East?

## Questions for Critical Thinking and Reflection

1. Under what terms other than a Palestinian state is there any chance of establishing a stable peace?
2. Is it possible to have a truly stable Palestinian state if, as is true now, about 17 percent of its population is made up of Jewish "settlers" living in enclaves within West Bank that are not subject to the authority of the Palestinian government?
3. Given the history of violence against Israel and the continuing strength of Hamas among the Palestinians, how would it be possible to make Israel feel secure enough to allow a Palestinian state to come into existence?

## Is There Common Ground?

A comprehensive overview of the issues in this debate is available in Joel Peters and David Newman (eds.), *Routledge Handbook on the Israeli-Palestinian Conflict* (Routledge, 2013).

It must also be remembered that Arab Muslims make up 21 percent of Israel's population. An analysis of the relations between Israel's Jewish majority and Muslim minority can be found in Ilan Peleg and Dov Waxman. *Israel's Palestinians: The Conflict Within* (Cambridge University Press, 2011).

Complicating matters for Israel is its division between relatively secular Jews, who tend to be moderate in their attitudes toward the Palestinians, and Orthodox Jews, who regard the areas in dispute as land given by God to the Jewish nation and who regard giving up the West Bank and, especially, any part of Jerusalem as sacrilege. Furthermore, more than 400,000 Israelis live in the West Bank, and removing them would be traumatic for Israel. The issue is also a matter of grave security concern. The Jews have suffered mightily throughout history; repeated Arab terrorism represents the latest of their travails. It is arguable that the Jews can be secure only in their own country and that the West Bank (which cuts Israel almost in two) is crucial to Israeli security. If an independent Palestine centered in the West Bank is created, Israel will face a defense nightmare, especially if new hostilities with the Palestinians occur. Additional material on a prospective Palestinian state is available in

Virginia Tilley, *The One-State Solution: A Breakthrough for Peace in the Israeli–Palestinian Deadlock* (University of Michigan Press, 2010).

Thus, for the Israelis the "land for peace" choice is a difficult one. Some Israelis are unwilling to cede any of what they consider the land of ancient Israel. Other Israelis would be willing to swap land for peace, but they doubt that the Palestinians would be assuaged. Still other Israelis think that the risk is worth the potential prize: peace.

Palestinians do not march in political lockstep any more than do Israelis. Indeed, there has been serious tension and even fighting between Fatah, the more moderate Palestinian faction led by Palestinian National Authority President Mahmoud Abbas, and the more militant group Hamas, which the United States considers a terrorist organization. Further complicating matters, Israel's government has been somewhat unstable in recent years. In 2012, 12 political parties have seats in the Knesset, with no party holding more than 23 percent of the seats. The United States has tried to encourage peace in the area, but failed to achieve it. At the urging of the United States, Israel and the Palestinians agreed in early September 2010 to resume direct negotiations for the first time in two years. "This moment of opportunity may not soon come again," Obama said heralding the talks, and Palestinian President Mahmoud Abbas and Israeli Prime Minister Benjamin Netanyahu expressed cautious optimism. Yet, the same obstacles have remained and such hopeful statements yield the dueling accusations in the YES and NO selections.

## Additional Resource

A look at U.S. policy is in Robert O. Freedman, ed., *Israel and the United States: Six Decades of US-Israeli Relations* (Westview Press, 2012).

# ISSUE 5

## Should Force Be Used if Necessary to Prevent Iran from Acquiring Nuclear Weapons?

YES: **Norman Podhoretz**, from "Stopping Iran: Why the Case for Military Action Still Stands," *Commentary* (February 2008)

NO: **Paul R. Pillar**, from "We Can Live with a Nuclear Iran," *Washington Monthly* (April 2012)

### ISSUE SUMMARY

YES: Norman Podhoretz, editor-at-large of the opinion journal *Commentary*, argues that the consequences of Iran acquiring nuclear weapons will be disastrous and that there is far less risk using whatever measures are necessary, including military force, to prevent the consequences than there is in dealing with a nuclear-armed Iran.

NO: Paul R. Pillar, who teaches in the Security Studies Program at Georgetown University, maintains that a nuclear-armed Iran with a bomb would be much less dangerous than many people contend it would be and that war with Iran would be much more costly than many people contend it would be.

$T$he global effort to control the spread of nuclear weapons centers around the nuclear Non-Proliferation Treaty (NPT) of 1968. Under it, 85 percent of the world's countries that adhere to the NPT pledge not to transfer nuclear weapons or assist a nonnuclear state to make or otherwise acquire nuclear weapons. Nonnuclear countries also agree not to build or accept nuclear weapons and to allow the UN's International Atomic Energy Agency (IAEA) to monitor their nuclear facilities to ensure their exclusive use for peaceful purposes.

The NPT has not been a complete success. India and Pakistan both tested nuclear weapons in 1998. Israel's possession of nuclear weapons is an open secret. None of them agreed to the treaty. Currently, there are tensions over two countries that have agreed to the NPT. One of those countries is North Korea, which adhered to the NPT in 1970, then violated the treaty in the early 1990s by moving toward building nuclear weapons. Diplomacy failed to halt the development program, and North Korea tested a nuclear weapon in 2006. Iran, like North Korea, agreed to the NPT in 1970. At that time, Iran was ruled by a pro-Western monarch, Shah Mohammad Reza Pahlavi, who was overthrown in 1979. After the Shah fled, the Ayatollah Ruhollah Khomeini returned from exile and founded a theocratic political system that condemned Western values and influence.

During the 1980s, Iran fought a horrendous 8-year war with Iraq, one in which Iraq used chemical weapons. Partly because of that war and the assumption that Iraq had nuclear weapon ambitions, Iran moved not only to generate enriched uranium and take other steps necessary to generate nuclear fuel for energy, but also to build nuclear weapons. This program also reflected a combination of Iran's desire to become a regional power and its fear of the United States. Among other concerns, the United States had sent troops into two neighboring Muslim countries, Afghanistan in 2001 and Iraq in 2003. The United States by 2003 was urging international pressure to force Iran to give up its program. Three European Union countries—France, Germany, and Great Britain (the EU-3)—took the lead trying to persuade Iran to end its dual-use efforts. Iran negotiated, but also claimed that its intentions were peaceful and that it had the sovereign right to develop nuclear power. With no progress being made, the council of the IAEA voted overwhelmingly in February 2006 to refer the matter to the UN Security Council. Since then, the United States and the EU have become increasingly critical of Iran, and they have increasingly applied economic sanctions on Iran. The UN has also applied some sanctions, but these have been limited because Russia and China both oppose harsh sanctions and both also have a veto in the Security Council. There are indications that the sanctions are seriously damaging Iran's economy, but Iran has remained defiant, and it is clear that it has also moved closer to having the capability of building a nuclear weapon if it wishes to. In the YES selection, Norman Podhoretz writes that allowing Iran to acquire nuclear weapons will set the stage for the outbreak of a nuclear war that will become as inescapable then as it is avoidable now. Paul Pillar disagrees in the NO selection. He contends the only alternatives are not war with Iran or Iran with nuclear weapons. Pillar suggests that it is still worth trying to find a diplomatic solution that would permit Iran to have a peaceful nuclear program and also permit enough inspections by the IAEA to ensure that Iran is not building nuclear weapons.

# YES ⬅    Norman Podhoretz

# Stopping Iran: Why the Case for Military Action Still Stands

**U**p until a fairly short time ago, scarcely anyone dissented from the assessment offered with "high confidence" by the National Intelligence Estimate [NIE] of 2005 that Iran was "determined to develop nuclear weapons." Correlatively, no one believed the protestations of the mullahs ruling Iran that their nuclear program was designed strictly for peaceful uses.

The reason for this near-universal consensus was that Iran, with its vast reserves of oil and natural gas, had no need for nuclear energy, and that in any case, the very nature of its program contradicted the protestations.

Here is how *Time* magazine put it as early as March 2003—long before, be it noted, the radical Mahmoud Ahmadinejad had replaced the putatively moderate Mohamed Khatami as president:

> On a visit last month to Tehran, International Atomic Energy Agency [IAEA] director Mohamed ElBaradei announced he had discovered that Iran was constructing a facility to enrich uranium—a key component of advanced nuclear weapons—near Natanz. But diplomatic sources tell *Time* the plant is much further along than previously revealed. The sources say work on the plant is "extremely advanced" and involves "hundreds" of gas centrifuges ready to produce enriched uranium and "the parts for a thousand others ready to be assembled."

So, too, the Federation of American Scientists about a year later:

> It is generally believed that Iran's efforts are focused on uranium enrichment, though there are some indications of work on a parallel plutonium effort. Iran claims it is trying to establish a complete nuclear-fuel cycle to support a civilian energy program, but this same fuel cycle would be applicable to a nuclear-weapons development program. Iran appears to have spread their nuclear activities around a number of sites to reduce the risk of detection or attack.

And just as everyone agreed with the American intelligence community that Iran was "determined to develop nuclear weapons," everyone also agreed with President George W. Bush that it must not be permitted to succeed. Here, the reasons were many and various.

To begin with, Iran was (as certified even by the doves of the State Department) the leading sponsor of terrorism in the world, and it was therefore reasonable to fear that it would transfer nuclear technology to terrorists who would be only too happy to use it against us. Moreover, since Iran evidently aspired to become the hegemon of the Middle East, its drive for a nuclear capability could result (as, according to the *New York Times,* no fewer than 21 governments in and around the region were warning) in "a grave and destructive nuclear-arms race." This meant a nightmarish increase in the chances of a nuclear war. An even greater increase in those chances would result from the power that nuclear weapons—and the missiles capable of delivering them, which Iran was also developing and/or buying—would give the mullahs to realize their evil dream of (in the words of Ahmadinejad) "wiping Israel off the map."

Nor, as almost everyone also agreed, were the dangers of a nuclear Iran confined to the Middle East. Dedicated as the mullahs clearly were to furthering the transformation of Europe into a continent where Muslim law and practice would more and more prevail, they were bound to use nuclear intimidation and blackmail in pursuit of this goal as well. Beyond that, nuclear weapons would even serve the purposes of a far more ambitious aim: the creation of what Ahmadinejad called "a world without America." Although, to be sure, no one imagined that Iran would acquire the capability to destroy the United States, it was easy to imagine that the United States would be deterred from standing in Iran's way by the fear of triggering a nuclear war.

Running alongside the near-universal consensus on Iran's nuclear intentions was a commensurately broad agreement that the regime could be stopped from realizing those intentions by a judicious combination of carrots and sticks. The carrots, offered through diplomacy, consisted of promises that if Iran were (in the words of the Security Council) to "suspend all enrichment-related and reprocessing activities, including research and development, to be verified by the IAEA," it would find itself on the receiving end of many benefits. If, however, Iran remained obdurate in refusing to comply with these demands, sticks would come into play in the form of sanctions.

And indeed, in response to continued Iranian defiance, a round of sanctions was approved by the Security Council in December 2006. When these (watered down to buy the support of the Russians and the Chinese) predictably failed to bite, a tougher round was unanimously authorized three months later, in March 2007. When these in turn failed, the United States, realizing that the Russians and the Chinese would veto stronger medicine, unilaterally imposed a new series of economic sanctions—which fared no better than the multilateral measures that had preceded them.

What then to do? President Bush kept declaring that Iran must not be permitted to get the bomb, and he kept warning that the "military option"—by which he meant air strikes, not an invasion on the ground—was still on the table as a last resort. On this issue our Western European allies were divided. To the surprise of many who had ceased thinking of France as an ally because of [President] Jacques Chirac's relentless opposition to the policies of the Bush administration, Nicholas Sarkozy, Chirac's successor as president, echoed Bush's warning in equally unequivocal terms. If, Sarkozy announced, the Iranians pressed on with their nuclear program, the world would be left with a choice between "an Iranian bomb and bombing Iran"—and he left no doubt as to where his own choice would fall. On the other hand, Gordon Brown, who had followed Tony Blair as prime minister of the UK, seemed less willing than Sarkozy to contemplate military action against Iran's nuclear installations, even as a last resort. Like the new chancellor of Germany, Angela Merkel, Brown remained—or professed to remain—persuaded that more diplomacy and tougher sanctions would eventually work.

This left a great question hanging in the air: when, if ever, would Bush (and/or Sarkozy) conclude that the time had come to resort to the last resort?

Obviously the answer to that question depended on how long it would take for Iran itself to reach the point of no return. According to the NIE of 2005, it was "unlikely . . . that Iran would be able to make a nuclear weapon . . . before early-to-mid next decade"—that is, between 2010 and 2015. If that assessment, offered with "moderate confidence," was correct, Bush would be off the hook, since he would be out of office for two years at the very least by the time the decision on whether or not to order air strikes would have to be made. That being the case, for the remainder of his term he could continue along the carrot-and-stick path, while striving to ratchet up the pressure on Iran with stronger and stronger measures that he could hope against hope might finally do the trick. If he could get these through the Security Council, so much the better; if not, the United States could try to assemble a coalition outside the UN that would be willing to impose really tough sanctions.

Under these circumstances, there would also be enough time to add another arrow to this nonmilitary quiver: a serious program of covert aid to dissident Iranians who dreamed of overthrowing the mullocracy [rule by mullahs, Muslim clerics] and replacing it with a democratic regime. Those who had been urging Bush to launch such a program, and who were confident that it would succeed, pointed to polls showing great dissatisfaction with the mullocracy among the Iranian young, and to the demonstrations against it that kept breaking out all over the country. They also contended that even if a new democratic regime were to be as intent as the old one on developing nuclear weapons, neither it nor they would pose anything like the same kind of threat.

All well and good. The trouble was this: only by relying on the accuracy of the 2005 NIE would Bush be able in all good conscience to pass on to his successor the decision of whether or when to bomb the Iranian nuclear facilities. But that estimate, as he could hardly help knowing from the CIA's not exactly brilliant track record, might easily be too optimistic.

To start with the most spectacular recent instance, the CIA had failed to anticipate 9/11. It then turned out to be wrong in 2002 about Saddam Hussein's possession of weapons of mass destruction, very likely because it was bending over backward to compensate for having been wrong in exactly the opposite direction in 1991, when at the end of the first Gulf war the IAEA discovered that the Iraqi nuclear program was far more advanced than the CIA had estimated. Regarding that by now notorious lapse, Jeffrey T. Richelson, a leading (and devoutly nonpartisan) authority on the American intelligence community, writes in *Spying on the Bomb*:

> The extent that the United States and its allies underestimated and misunderstood the Iraqi program [before 1991] constituted a "colossal international intelligence failure," according to one Israeli expert. [IAEA's chief weapons inspector] Hans Blix acknowledged "that there was suspicion certainly," but "to see the enormity of it is a shock."

And these were only the most recent cases. Gabriel Schoenfeld, a close student of the intelligence community, offers a partial list of earlier mistakes and failures:

> The CIA was established in 1947 in large measure to avoid another surprise attack like the one the U.S. had suffered on December 7, 1941 at Pearl Harbor. But only three years after its founding, the fledgling agency missed the outbreak of the Korean war. It then failed to understand that the Chinese would come to the aid of the North Koreans if American forces crossed the Yalu river. It missed the outbreak of the Suez war in 1956. In September 1962, the CIA issued an NIE which stated that the "Soviets would not introduce offensive missiles in Cuba"; in short order, the USSR did precisely that. In 1968 it failed to foresee the Warsaw Pact invasion of Czechoslovakia. . . . It did not inform Jimmy Carter that the Soviet Union would invade Afghanistan in 1979.

Richelson adds a few more examples of hotly debated issues during the cold war that were wrongly resolved, including "the existence of a missile gap, the capabilities of the Soviet SS-9 intercontinental ballistic missile, [and] Soviet compliance with the test-ban and antiballistic missile treaties." This is not to mention perhaps the most notorious case of all: the fiasco, known as the Bay of Pigs, produced by the CIA's wildly misplaced confidence that an invasion of Cuba by the army of exiles it had assembled and trained would set off a popular uprising against the Castro regime.

On Bush's part, then, deep skepticism was warranted concerning the CIA's estimate of how much time we had before Iran reached the point of no return. As we have seen, Mohamed ElBaradei, the head of the IAEA, had "discovered" in 2003 that the Iranians were constructing facilities to enrich uranium. Still, as late as April 2007 the same ElBaradei was pooh-poohing the claims made by Ahmadinejad that Iran already had 3,000 centrifuges in operation. A month later, we learn from Richelson, ElBaradei changed his mind after a few spot inspections. "We believe," ElBaradei now said, that the Iranians "pretty much have the knowledge about how to enrich. From now on, it is simply a question of perfecting that knowledge."

We also learn from Richelson that another expert, Matthew Bunn of Harvard's Center for Science and International Affairs, interpreted the new information the IAEA came up with in April 2007 as meaning that "whether they're six months or a year away, one can debate. But it's not ten years." This chilling estimate of how little time we had to prevent Iran from getting the bomb was similar to the conclusion reached by several Israeli experts (though the official Israeli estimate put the point of no return in 2009).

Then in a trice, everything changed. Even as Bush must surely have been wrestling with the question of whether it would be on his watch that the decision on bombing the Iranian nuclear facilities would have to be made, the world was hit with a different kind of bomb. This took the form of an unclassified summary of a new NIE, published early last December. Entitled "Iran: Nuclear Intentions and Capabilities," this new document was obviously designed to blow up the near-universal consensus that had flowed from the conclusions reached by the intelligence community in its 2005 NIE. In brief, whereas the NIE of 2005 had assessed "with high confidence that Iran currently is determined to develop nuclear weapons," the new NIE of 2007 did "not know whether [Iran] currently intends to develop nuclear weapons."

This startling 180-degree turn was arrived at from new intelligence, offered by the new NIE with "high confidence": namely, that "in fall 2003 Tehran halted its nuclear-weapons program." The new NIE was also confident—though only moderately so—that "Tehran had not restarted its nuclear-weapons program as of mid-2007." And in the most sweeping of its new conclusions, it was even "moderately confident" that "the halt to those activities represents a halt to Iran's entire nuclear-weapons program."

Whatever else one might say about the new NIE, one point can be made with "high confidence": that by leading with the sensational news that Iran had suspended its nuclear-weapons program in 2003, its authors ensured that their entire document would be interpreted as meaning that there was no longer anything to worry about. Of course, being experienced bureaucrats, they took care to protect themselves from this very accusation. For example, after dropping their own bomb on the fear that Iran was hell-bent on getting the bomb, they immediately added "with moderate-to-high confidence that Tehran at a minimum is keeping open the option to develop nuclear weapons." But as they must have expected, scarcely anyone paid attention to this caveat. And as they must also have expected, even less attention was paid to another self-protective caveat, which—making doubly sure it would pass unnoticed—they relegated to a footnote appended to the lead sentence about the halt:

> For the purposes of this Estimate, by "nuclear-weapons program" we mean Iran's nuclear-weapon design and weaponization work and covert uranium conversion-related and uranium enrichment-related work; we do not mean Iran's declared civil work related to uranium conversion and enrichment.

Since only an expert could grasp the significance of this cunning little masterpiece of incomprehensible jargon, the damage had been done by the time its dishonesty was exposed.

The first such exposure came from John Bolton, who before becoming our ambassador to the UN had served as Under Secretary of State for Arms Control and International Security, with a special responsibility for preventing the proliferation of weapons of mass destruction. Donning this hat once again, Bolton charged that the dishonesty of the footnote lay most egregiously in the sharp distinction it drew between military and civilian programs. For, he said,

> the enrichment of uranium, which all agree Iran is continuing, is critical to civilian *and* military uses [emphasis added]. Indeed, it has always been Iran's "civilian" program that posed the main risk of a nuclear "breakout."

Two other experts, Valerie Lincy, the editor of Iranwatch.org, writing in collaboration with Gary Milhollin, the director of the Wisconsin Project on Nuclear Arms Control, followed up with an explanation of why the halt of 2003 was much less significant than a layman would inevitably be led to think:

> [T]he new report defines "nuclear-weapons program" in a ludicrously narrow way: it confines it to enriching uranium at secret sites or working on a nuclear-weapon design. But the halting of its secret enrichment and weapon-design efforts in 2003 proves only that Iran made a tactical move. It suspended work that, if discovered, would unambiguously reveal intent to build a weapon. It has continued other work, crucial to the ability to make a bomb, that it can pass off as having civilian applications.

Thus, as Lincy and Milhollin went on to write, the main point obfuscated by the footnote was that once Iran accumulated a stockpile of the kind of uranium fit for civilian use, it would "in a matter of months" be able "to convert that uranium . . . , to weapons grade."

Yet, in spite of these efforts to demonstrate that the new NIE did not prove that Iran had given up its pursuit of nuclear weapons, just about everyone in the world immediately concluded otherwise, and further concluded that this meant the military option was off the table. George Bush may or may not have been planning to order air strikes before leaving office, but now that the justification for doing so had been discredited by his own intelligence agencies, it would be politically impossible for him to go on threatening military action, let alone to take it.

But what about sanctions? In the weeks and months before the new NIE was made public, Bush had been working very hard to get a third and tougher round of sanctions approved by the Security Council. In trying to persuade the Russians and the Chinese to sign on, Bush argued that the failure to enact such sanctions would leave war as the only alternative. Yet if war was now out of the question, and if in any case Iran had for all practical purposes given up its pursuit of nuclear weapons for the foreseeable future, what need was there of sanctions?

Anticipating that this objection would be raised, the White House desperately set out to interpret the new NIE as, precisely, offering "grounds for hope that the problem can be solved diplomatically—without the use of force." These words by Stephen Hadley, Bush's National Security Adviser, represented the very first comment on the new NIE to emanate from the White

House, and some version of them would be endlessly repeated in the days to come. Joining this campaign of damage control, Sarkozy and Brown issued similar statements, and even Merkel (who had been very reluctant to go along with Bush's push for another round of sanctions) now declared that it was:

> dangerous and still grounds for great concern that Iran, in the face of the UN Security Council's resolutions, continues to refuse to suspend uranium enrichment. . . . The Iranian president's intolerable agitation against Israel also speaks volumes. . . . It remains a vital interest of the whole world community to prevent a nuclear-armed Iran.

As it happened, Hadley was right about the new NIE, which executed another 180-degree turn—this one, away from the judgment of the 2005 NIE concerning the ineffectiveness of international pressure. Flatly contradicting its "high confidence" in 2005 that Iran was forging ahead "despite its international obligations and international pressure," the new NIE concluded that the nuclear-weapons program had been halted in 2003 "primarily in response to international pressure." This indicated that "Tehran's decisions are guided by a cost-benefit approach rather than a rush to a weapon irrespective of the political, economic, and military costs."

Never mind that no international pressure to speak of was being exerted on Iran in 2003, and that at that point the mullahs were more likely acting out of fear that the Americans, having just invaded Iraq, might come after them next. Never mind, too, that religious and/or ideological passions, which the new NIE pointedly neglected to mention, have over and over again throughout history proved themselves a more powerful driving force than any "cost-benefit approach." Blithely sweeping aside such considerations, the new NIE was confident that just as the carrot-and-stick approach had allegedly sufficed in the past, so it would suffice in the future to "prompt Tehran to extend the current halt to its nuclear-weapons program."

The worldview implicit here has been described by Richelson (mainly with North Korea in mind) as the idea that "moral suasion and sustained bargaining are the proven mechanisms of nuclear restraint." Such a worldview "may be ill-equipped," he observes delicately:

> to accept the idea that certain regimes are incorrigible and negotiate only as a stalling tactic until they have attained a nuclear capability against the United States and other nations that might act against their nuclear programs.

True, the new NIE did at least acknowledge that it would not be easy to induce Iran to extend the halt, "given the linkage many within the leadership probably see between nuclear-weapons development and Iran's key national-security and foreign-policy objectives." But it still put its money on a:

> combination of threats of intensified international scrutiny and pressures, along with opportunities for Iran to achieve its security, prestige, and goals for regional influence in other ways.

It was this pronouncement, and a few others like it, that gave Stephen Hadley "grounds for hope that the problem can be solved diplomatically." But that it was a false hope was demonstrated by the NIE itself. For if Iran was pursuing nuclear weapons in order to achieve its "key national-security and foreign-policy objectives," and if those objectives explicitly included (for a start) hegemony in the Middle East and the destruction of the state of Israel, what possible "opportunities" could Tehran be offered to achieve them "in other ways"?

So much for the carrot. As for the stick, it was no longer big enough to matter, what with the threat of military action ruled out, and what with the case for a third round of sanctions undermined by the impression stemming from the NIE's main finding that there was nothing left to worry about. Why worry when it was four years since Iran had done any work toward developing the bomb, when the moratorium remained in effect, and when there was no reason to believe that the program would be resumed in the near future?

What is more, in continuing to insist that the Iranians must be stopped from developing the bomb and that this could be done by nonmilitary means, the Bush administration and its European allies were lagging behind a new consensus within the American foreign-policy establishment that had already been forming even before the publication of the new NIE. Whereas the old consensus was based on the proposition that (in Senator John McCain's pungent formulation) "the only thing worse than bombing Iran was letting Iran get the bomb," the emerging new consensus held the opposite—that the only thing worse than letting Iran get the bomb was bombing Iran.

What led to this reversal was a gradual loss of faith in the carrot-and-stick approach. As one who had long since rejected this faith and who had been excoriated for my apostasy by more than one member of the foreign-policy elites, I never thought I would live to see the day when these very elites would come to admit that diplomacy and sanctions had been given a fair chance and that they had accomplished nothing but to buy Iran more time. The lesson drawn from this new revelation was, however, a different matter.

It was in the course of a public debate with one of the younger members of the foreign-policy establishment that I first chanced upon the change in view. Knowing that he never deviated by so much as an inch from the conventional wisdom of the moment within places like the Council on Foreign Relations and the Brookings Institution, I had expected him to defend the carrot-and-stick approach and to attack me as a warmonger for contending that bombing was the only way to stop the mullahs from getting the bomb. Instead, to my great surprise, he took the position that there was really no need to stop them in the first place, since even if they had the bomb they could be deterred from using it, just as effectively as the Soviets and the Chinese had been deterred during the cold war.

Without saying so in so many words, then, my opponent was acknowledging that diplomacy and sanctions had proved to be a failure, and that there was no point in pursuing them any further. But so as to avoid drawing the logical conclusion—namely, that military action had now become necessary— he simply abandoned the old establishment assumption that Iran must at all costs be prevented from developing nuclear weapons, adopting in its place the complacent idea that we could learn to live with an Iranian bomb.

In response, I argued that deterrence could not be relied upon with a regime ruled by Islamofascist revolutionaries who not only were ready to die for their beliefs but cared less about protecting their people than about the spread of their ideology and their power. If the mullahs got the bomb, I said, it was not they who would be deterred, but we.

So little did any of this shake my opponent that I came away from our debate with the grim realization that the President's continued insistence on the dangers posed by an Iranian bomb would more and more fall on deaf ears—ears that would soon be made even deafer by the new NIE's assurance that Iran was no longer hell-bent on acquiring nuclear weapons after all. There might be two different ideas competing here—one, that we could live with an Iranian bomb; the other, that there would be no Iranian bomb to live with— but the widespread acceptance of either would not only preclude the military option but would sooner or later put an end even to the effort to stop the mullahs by nonmilitary means.

And yet there remained something else, or rather someone else, to factor into the equation: the perennially "misunderestimated" George W. Bush, a man who knew evil when he saw it and who had the courage and the determination to do battle against it. This was also a man who, far more than most politicians, said what he meant and meant what he said. And what he had said at least twice before was that if we permitted Iran to build a nuclear arsenal, people fifty years from now would look back and wonder how we of this generation could have allowed such a thing to happen, and they would rightly judge us as harshly as we today judge the British and the French for what they did at Munich in 1938. It was because I had found it hard to understand why Bush would put himself so squarely in the dock of history on this issue if he were resigned to an Iran in possession of nuclear weapons, or even of the ability to build them, that I predicted in these pages, and went on predicting elsewhere, that he would not retire from office before resorting to the military option.

But then came the new NIE. To me it seemed obvious that it represented another ambush by an intelligence community that had consistently tried to sabotage Bush's policies through a series of damaging leaks and was now trying to prevent him from ever taking military action against Iran. To others, however, it seemed equally obvious that Bush, far from being ambushed, had welcomed the new NIE precisely because it provided him with a perfect opportunity to begin distancing himself from the military option.

But I could not for the life of me believe that Bush intended to fly in the face of the solemn promise he had made in his 2002 State of the Union address:

> We'll be deliberate, yet time is not on our side. I will not wait on events, while dangers gather. I will not stand by, as peril draws closer and closer. The United States of America will not permit the world's most dangerous regimes to threaten us with the world's most destructive weapons.

To which he had added shortly afterward in a speech at West Point: "If we wait for threats to fully materialize, we will have waited too long."

How, I wondered, could Bush not know that in the case of Iran he was running a very great risk of waiting too long? And if he was truly ready to run that risk, why, in a press conference the day after the new NIE came out, did he put himself in the historical dock yet again by repeating what he had said several times before about the judgment that would be passed on this generation in the future if Iran were to acquire a nuclear weapon?

> If Iran shows up with a nuclear weapon at some point in time, the world is going to say, what happened to them in 2007? How come they couldn't see the impending danger? What caused them not to understand that a country that once had a weapons program could reconstitute the weapons program? How come they couldn't see that the important first step in developing a weapon is the capacity to be able to enrich uranium? How come they didn't know that with that capacity, that knowledge could be passed on to a covert program? What blinded them to the realities of the world? And it's not going to happen on my watch.

"It's not going to happen on my watch." What else could this mean if not that Bush was preparing to meet "the impending danger" in what he must by now have concluded was the only way it could be averted?

The only alternative that seemed even remotely plausible to me was that he might be fixing to outsource the job to the Israelis. After all, even if, by now, it might have become politically impossible for us to take military action, the Israelis could not afford to sit by while a regime pledged to wipe them off the map was equipping itself with nuclear weapons and the missiles to deliver them. For unless Iran could be stopped before acquiring a nuclear capability, the Israelis would be faced with only two choices: either strike first, or pray that the fear of retaliation would deter the Iranians from beating them to the punch. Yet a former president of Iran, Hashemi Rafsanjani, had served notice that his country would not be deterred by the fear of retaliation:

> If a day comes when the world of Islam is duly equipped with the arms Israel has in its possession, . . . application of an atomic bomb would not leave anything in Israel, but the same thing would just produce damages in the Muslim world.

If this was the view of even a supposed moderate like Rafsanjani, how could the Israelis depend upon the mullahs to refrain from launching a first strike? The answer was that they could not. Bernard Lewis, the leading contemporary authority on the culture of the Islamic world, has explained why:

> MAD, mutual assured destruction, [was effective] right through the cold war. Both sides had nuclear weapons. Neither side used them, because both sides knew the other would retaliate in kind. This will not work with a religious fanatic [like Ahmadinejad]. For him, mutual assured destruction is not a deterrent, it is an inducement. We know already that [the mullahs ruling Iran] do not give a damn about killing their own people in great numbers. We have seen it again and again. In the final scenario, and this applies all the more strongly if they kill

large numbers of their own people, they are doing them a favor. They are giving them a quick free pass to heaven and all its delights.

Under the aegis of such an attitude, even in the less extreme variant that may have been held by some of Ahmadinejad's colleagues among the regime's rulers, mutual assured destruction would turn into a very weak reed. Understanding that, the Israelis would be presented with an irresistible incentive to preempt—and so, too, would the Iranians. Either way, a nuclear exchange would become inevitable.

What would happen then? In a recently released study, Anthony Cordesman of the Center for Strategic and International Studies argues that Rafsanjani had it wrong. In the grisly scenario Cordesman draws, tens of millions would indeed die, but Israel—despite the decimation of its civilian population and the destruction of its major cities—would survive, even if just barely, as a functioning society. Not so Iran, and not its "key Arab neighbors," particularly Egypt and Syria, which Cordesman thinks Israel would also have to target in order "to ensure that no other power can capitalize on an Iranian strike." Furthermore, Israel might be driven in desperation to go after the oil wells, refineries, and ports in the Gulf.

"Being contained within the region," writes Martin Walker of UPI in his summary of Cordesman's study, "such a nuclear exchange might not be Armageddon for the human race." To me it seems doubtful that it could be confined to the Middle East. But even if it were, the resulting horrors would still be far greater than even the direst consequences that might follow from bombing Iran before it reaches the point of no return.

In the worst case of this latter scenario, Iran would retaliate by increasing the trouble it is already making for us in Iraq and by attacking Israel with missiles armed with non-nuclear warheads but possibly containing biological and/or chemical weapons. There would also be a vast increase in the price of oil, with catastrophic consequences for every economy in the world, very much including our own. And there would be a deafening outcry from one end of the earth to the other against the inescapable civilian casualties. Yet, bad as all this would be, it does not begin to compare with the gruesome consequences of a nuclear exchange between Israel and Iran, even if those consequences were to be far less extensive than Cordesman anticipates.

Which is to say that, as between bombing Iran to prevent it from getting the bomb and letting Iran get the bomb, there is simply no contest.

But this still does not answer the question of who should do the bombing. Tempting as it must be for George Bush to sit back and let the Israelis do the job, there are considerations that should give him pause. One is that no matter what he would say, the whole world would regard the Israelis as a surrogate for the United States, and we would become as much the target of the ensuing recriminations both at home and abroad as we would if we had done the job ourselves.

To make matters worse, the indications are that it would be very hard for the Israeli air force, superb though it is, to pull the mission off. Thus, an analysis by two members of the Security Studies Program at MIT concluded that while "the Israeli air force now possesses the capability to destroy even well-hardened targets in Iran with some degree of confidence," the problem is that for the mission to succeed, all of the many contingencies involved would have to go right. Hence an Israeli attempt could end with the worst of all possible outcomes: retaliatory measures by the Iranians even as their nuclear program remained unscathed. We, on the other hand, would have a much bigger margin of error and a much better chance of setting their program back by a minimum of five or ten years and at best wiping it out altogether.

The upshot is that if Iran is to be prevented from becoming a nuclear power, it is the United States that will have to do the preventing, to do it by means of a bombing campaign, and (because "If we wait for threats to fully materialize, we will have waited too long") to do it soon.

When I first predicted a year or so ago that Bush would bomb Iran's nuclear facilities once he had played out the futile diplomatic string, the obstacles that stood in his way were great but they did not strike me as insurmountable. Now, thanks in large part to the new NIE, they have grown so formidable that I can only stick by my prediction with what the NIE itself would describe as "low-to-moderate confidence." For Bush is right about the resemblance between 2008 and 1938. In 1938, as Winston Churchill later said, Hitler could still have been stopped at a relatively low price and many millions of lives could have been saved if England and France had not deceived themselves about the realities of their situation. Mutatis mutandis, it is the same in 2008, when Iran can still be stopped from getting the bomb and even more millions of lives can be saved—but only provided that we summon up the courage to see what is staring us in the face and then act on what we see.

Unless we do, the forces that are blindly working to ensure that Iran will get the bomb are likely to prevail even against the clear-sighted determination of George W. Bush, just as the forces of appeasement did against Churchill in 1938. In which case, we had all better pray that there will be enough time for the next President to discharge the responsibility that Bush will have been forced to pass on, and that this successor will also have the clarity and the courage to discharge it. If not—God help us all—the stage will have been set for the outbreak of a nuclear war that will become as inescapable then as it is avoidable now.

Paul R. Pillar

**→ NO**

# We Can Live with a Nuclear Iran

At around 8:30 in the morning on Wednesday, January 11 [2012], while much of Tehran [the capital of Iran] was snarled in its usual rush-hour traffic, a motorcyclist drew alongside a gray Peugeot and affixed a magnetic bomb to its exterior. The ensuing blast killed the car's thirty-two-year-old passenger, Mostafa Ahmadi Roshan, a professor of chemistry and the deputy director of Iran's premiere uranium enrichment facility. The assassin disappeared into traffic, and Roshan became the fifth Iranian nuclear scientist to die in violent or mysterious circumstances since 2007.

The attack was, in a sense, fairly typical of the covert war being waged against Iran's nuclear program, a campaign that has included computer sabotage as well as the serial assassination of Iranian scientists. Even the manner of the killing was routine; Roshan was the third scientist to die from a magnet bomb slapped onto his car during a commute. But the timing of the chemist's death—amid a series of diplomatic events that came fast and furious in January and February, each further complicating relations with Iran—had the effect of dramatizing how close this covert war may be to becoming an overt one.

On New Year's Eve, eleven days before the bombing that killed Roshan, President Barack Obama enacted a new round of sanctions that essentially blacklisted Iran's central bank by penalizing anyone who does business with it, a move designed to cripple the Islamic Republic's ability to sell oil overseas. Iran responded by threatening to militarily shut down the Strait of Hormuz, the narrow shipping lane out of the Persian Gulf through which 20 percent of the world's oil trade passes. On January 8, three days before the attack on Roshan, U.S. Defense Secretary Leon Panetta appeared on Face the Nation and reinforced America's commitment to keep Iran from acquiring a nuclear weapon. Just in December, Panetta had emphasized the damaging consequences that war with Iran would bring, but now he stressed that Iranian development of a nuclear weapon would cross a "red line." When the European Union announced its own sanctions of the Iranian central bank in late January, Iran redoubled its threat to block shipping lanes in the Strait of Hormuz [which connects the Persian Gulf to the Arabian Sea]. Panetta called this another "red line" that would provoke a military response from the U.S. February brought more posturing from Iran, along with two assassination attempts against Israelis living in New Delhi and Tbilisi that were widely attributed to Tehran.

Pillar, Paul R. From *Washington Monthly*, April 2012. Copyright © 2012 by Washington Monthly Publishing, LLC, 1319 F St. NW, Suite 710, Washington, DC 20004. (202) 393-5155. Reprinted by permission. www.washingtonmonthly.com

All of this has played out against the unhelpful backdrop of American election-year politics. The Republican presidential candidates, with the exception of the antiwar libertarian Ron Paul, have seized on Iran as a possible winning issue and have tried to outdo each other in sounding bellicose about it. Mitt Romney has repeatedly discussed the use of military force as one way of fulfilling his promise that, if he is elected, Iran "will not have a nuclear weapon." In short, both Democrats and Republicans have so ratcheted up their alarm about the possibility of an Iranian nuclear weapon that they are willing to commit to the extreme step of launching an offensive war—an act of aggression—to try to stop it.

Meanwhile, the Israeli government, which has led the way in talking up the danger of an Iranian bomb, represents a significant hazard outside Washington's control. It was most likely the Israelis, for instance, who orchestrated the provocatively timed attack on Roshan. Defense Minister Ehud Barak recently dialed down the heat somewhat by saying that an Israeli decision to strike Iran was "far off." But Prime Minister Benjamin Netanyahu, mindful of the U.S. electoral calendar and the possibility that Barack Obama might pull off a victory in November, may see a temporary opportunity to precipitate a conflict in which a preelection U.S. president would feel obliged to join in on Israel's side.

Yet even without an Israeli decision to start a war, recent U.S., Iranian, and Israeli actions already constitute an escalation toward one. Rising tensions have increased the chance that even a minor incident, such as a seaborne encounter in the Persian Gulf, could spiral out of control. And Iran's own covert actions—perhaps including the recent spate of car bombs targeting Israeli officials in India and Georgia and last year's bizarre alleged plot to blow up a restaurant in Washington, D.C., and kill the Saudi ambassador—feed even more hostility from the U.S. and Israel, escalating further the risk of open conflict.

Thus we find ourselves at a strange pass. Those in the United States who genuinely yearn for war are still a neoconservative minority. But the danger that war might break out—and that the hawks will get their way—has nonetheless become substantial. The U.S. has just withdrawn the last troops from one Middle Eastern country where it fought a highly costly war of choice with a rationale involving weapons of mass destruction. Now we find ourselves on the precipice of yet another such war—almost purely because the acceptable range of opinion on Iran has narrowed and ossified around the "sensible" idea that all options must be pursued to prevent the country from acquiring nuclear weapons.

Given the momentousness of such an endeavor and how much prominence the Iranian nuclear issue has been given, one might think that talk about exercising the military option would be backed up by extensive analysis of the threat in question and the different ways of responding to it. But it isn't. Strip away the bellicosity and political rhetoric, and what one finds is not rigorous analysis but a mixture of fear, fanciful speculation, and crude stereotyping. There are indeed good reasons to oppose Iranian acquisition of nuclear weapons, and likewise many steps the United States and the international community can and should take to try to avoid that eventuality. But an Iran with a bomb would not be anywhere near as dangerous as most people assume, and a war to try to stop it from acquiring one would be less successful, and far more costly, than most people imagine.

What difference would it make to Iran's behavior and influence if the country had a bomb? Even among those who believe that war with the Islamic Republic would be a bad idea, this question has been subjected to precious little careful analysis. The notion that a nuclear weapon would turn Iran into a significantly more dangerous actor that would imperil U.S. interests has become conventional wisdom, and it gets repeated so often by so many diverse commentators that it seldom, if ever, is questioned. Hardly anyone debating policy on Iran asks exactly why a nuclear-armed Iran would be so dangerous. What passes for an answer to that question takes two forms: one simple, and another that sounds more sophisticated.

The simple argument is that Iranian leaders supposedly don't think like the rest of us: they are religious fanatics who value martyrdom more than life, cannot be counted on to act rationally, and therefore cannot be deterred. On the campaign trail [Republican presidential nomination candidate] Rick Santorum has been among the most vocal in propounding this notion, asserting that Iran is ruled by the "equivalent of al-Qaeda," that its "theology teaches" that its objective is to "create a calamity," that it believes "the afterlife is better than this life," and that its "principal virtue" is martyrdom. Newt Gingrich speaks in a similar vein about how Iranian leaders are suicidal jihadists, and says "it's impossible to deter them."

The trouble with this image of Iran is that it does not reflect actual Iranian behavior. More than three decades of history demonstrate that the Islamic Republic's rulers, like most rulers elsewhere, are overwhelmingly concerned with preserving their regime and their power—in this life, not some future one. They are no more likely to let theological imperatives lead them into self-destructive behavior than other leaders whose religious faiths envision an afterlife. Iranian rulers may have a history of valorizing martyrdom—as they did when sending young militiamen to their deaths in near-hopeless attacks during the Iran–Iraq War in the 1980s—but they have never given any indication of wanting to become martyrs themselves. In fact, the Islamic Republic's conduct beyond its borders has been characterized by caution. Even the most seemingly ruthless Iranian behavior has been motivated by specific, immediate concerns of regime survival. The government assassinated exiled Iranian dissidents in Europe in the 1980s and '90s, for example, because it saw them as a counterrevolutionary threat. The assassinations ended when they started inflicting too much damage on Iran's relations with European governments. Iran's rulers are constantly balancing a very worldly set of strategic interests. The principles of deterrence are not invalid just because the party to be deterred wears a turban and a beard.

If the stereotyped image of Iranian leaders had real basis in fact, we would see more aggressive and brash Iranian behavior in the Middle East than we have. Some have pointed to the Iranian willingness to incur heavy losses in continuing the Iran–Iraq War. But that was a response to Saddam Hussein's invasion of the Iranian homeland, not some bellicose venture beyond Iran's borders. And even that war ended with Ayatollah Khomeini [the former supreme religious leader of Iran] deciding that the "poison" of agreeing to a cease-fire was better than the alternative. (He even described the ceasefire as "God's will"—so much for the notion that the Iranians' God always pushes them toward violence and martyrdom.)

Throughout history, it has always been worrisome when a revolutionary regime with ruthless and lethal internal practices moves to acquire a nuclear weapon. But it is worth remembering that we have contended with far more troubling examples of this phenomenon than Iran. Millions died from forced famine and purges in Stalin's Soviet Union, and tens of millions perished during the Great Leap Forward in Mao Tse-tung's China. China's development of a nuclear weapon (it tested its first one in 1964) seemed all the more alarming at the time because of Mao's openly professed belief that his country could lose half its population in a nuclear war and still come out victorious over capitalism. But deterrence with China has endured for half a century, even during the chaos and fanaticism of Mao's Cultural Revolution. A few years after China got the bomb, [U.S. President] Richard Nixon built his global strategy around engagement with Beijing.

The more sophisticated-sounding argument about the supposed dangers of an Iranian nuclear weapon—one heard less from politicians than from policy-debating intelligentsia—accepts that Iranian leaders are not suicidal but contends that the mere possession of such a weapon would make Tehran more aggressive in its region. A dominant feature of this mode of argument is "worst-casing," as exemplified by a pro-war article by Matthew Kroenig in a recent issue of *Foreign Affairs*. Kroenig's case rests on speculation after speculation about what mischief Iran "could" commit in the Middle East, with almost no attention to whether Iran has any reason to do those things, and thus to whether it ever would be likely to do them.

Kroenig includes among his "coulds" a scary possibility that also served as a selling point of the Iraq War: the thought of a regime giving nuclear weapons or materials to a terrorist group. Nothing is said about why Iran or any other regime ever would have an incentive to do this. In fact, Tehran would have strong reasons not to do it. Why would it want to lose control over a commodity that is scarce as well as dangerous? And how would it achieve deniability regarding its role in what the group subsequently did with the stuff? No regime in the history of the nuclear age has ever been known to transfer nuclear material to a nonstate group. That history includes the Cold War, when the USSR had both a huge nuclear arsenal and patronage relationships with a long list of radical and revolutionary clients. As for deniability, Iranian leaders have only to listen to rhetoric coming out of the United States to know that their regime would immediately be a suspect in any terrorist incidents involving a nuclear weapon.

The more sophisticated-sounding argument links Iran with sundry forms of objectionable behavior, either real or hypothetical, without explaining what difference the possession of a nuclear weapon would make. Perhaps the most extensive effort to catalog what a nuclear-armed Iran might do outside its borders is a monograph published last year by Ash Jain of the Washington Institute for Near East Policy. Jain's inventory of possible Iranian nastiness is comprehensive, ranging from strong-arming Persian Gulf states to expanding a strategic relationship with [President] Hugo Chavez's Venezuela. But nowhere is there an explanation of how Iran's calculations—or anyone else's—would change with the introduction of a nuclear weapon. The most that Jain can offer is to assert repeatedly that because Iran would be "shielded by a nuclear weapons capability," it might do some of these things. We never get an explanation of how, exactly, such a shield would work. Instead there is only a vague sense that a nuclear weapon would lead Iran to feel its oats.

Analysis on this subject need not be so vague. A rich body of doctrine was developed during the Cold War to outline the strategic differences that nuclear weapons do and do not make, and what they can and cannot achieve for those who possess them. Such weapons are most useful in deterring aggression against one's own country, which is probably the main reason the Iranian regime is interested in developing them. They are much less useful in "shielding" aggressive behavior outside one's borders, except in certain geopolitical situations in which their use becomes plausible.

The Pakistani–Indian conflict may be such a situation. Pakistan's nuclear arsenal may have enabled it to engage in riskier behavior in Kashmir than it otherwise would attempt, because nuclear weapons help to deter Pakistan's ultimate nightmare: an assault by the militarily superior India, which could slice Pakistan in two and perhaps destroy it completely. But if you try to apply that logic to Iran, no one is playing the role of India. Iran has its own tensions and rivalries with its neighbors—including Iraq, Saudi Arabia, other states on the Persian Gulf, and Pakistan. But none of these pose the kind of existential threat that Pakistan sees coming from India. Moreover, none of the current disputes between Iran and its neighbors (such as the one over ownership of some small islands also claimed by the United Arab Emirates) come close to possessing the nation-defining significance that the Kashmir conflict poses for both Pakistan and India.

Nuclear weapons matter insofar as there is a credible possibility that they will be used. This credibility is hard to achieve, however, in anything short of circumstances that might involve the destruction of one's nation. In the case of Iran, there would need to be some specific aggressive or subversive act that Tehran is holding back from performing now for fear of retaliation—from the Americans, the Israelis, the Saudis, or someone else. Further, in order for Iran to neutralize the threat of retaliation, the desired act of mischief would have to be so important to Tehran that it could credibly threaten to escalate the matter to the level of nuclear war. Proponents of a war with Iran have been unable to provide an example of a scenario that meets these criteria, however. The impact of Iran possessing a bomb is therefore far less dire than the alarmist conventional wisdom suggests.

To be sure, the world would be a better place without an Iranian nuclear weapon. An Iranian bomb would be a set-back for the global nuclear nonproliferation regime, for example, and the arms control community is legitimately concerned about it. It would also raise the possibility that other regional states, such as Saudi Arabia or Egypt, might be more inclined to try to acquire nuclear weapons as well. But that raises the question of why these states have not already done so, despite decades of facing both Israel's nuclear force and tensions with Iran. Ever since [U.S. President] John F. Kennedy mused [in 1963] that there might be fifteen to twenty-five states with nuclear weapons by the 1970s, estimates of the pace of proliferation—like estimates of the pace of Iran's nuclear program—have usually been too high.

Furthermore, it's not clear that any of this would cause substantial and direct damage to U.S. interests. Indeed, the alarmists offer more inconsistent arguments when discussing the dynamics of a Middle East in which rivals of Iran acquire their own nuclear weapons. If, as the alarmists project, nuclear weapons would appreciably increase Iranian influence in the region, why wouldn't further nuclear proliferation—which the alarmists also project—negate this effect by bestowing a comparable benefit on the rivals?

In the absence of further proliferation among Iran's rivals, there is a chance that Iran would be marginally bolder if it possessed a nuclear weapon—and that the United States and other countries in the Middle East would be correspondingly less bold. Perceptions of strength do matter. But two further observations are important. First, once concrete confrontations occur, strategic realities trump perceptions. One of the conjectures in Jain's monograph, for instance, is that Hezbollah and Hamas might become emboldened if Iran extended a nuclear umbrella over them. But in the face of Israel's formidable nuclear superiority, would Iranian leaders really be willing to risk Tehran to save Gaza [the Palestinian controlled territory between Israel and Egypt]? The Iranians could not get anyone to believe such a thing.

Second, one must ultimately ask whether the conjectured consequences of an Iranian bomb would be worse than a war with Iran. The conjectures are just that. They are not concrete, not based on nuclear doctrine or rigorous analysis, and not even likely. They are worst-case speculations, and not adequate justifications for going to war.

When the debate turns from discussing the consequences that would flow from Iran's acquisition of a nuclear weapon to discussing the consequences of a U.S. military attack on Iran, the mode of argument used by proponents of an attack changes entirely. Instead of the worst case, the emphasis is now on the best case. This "best-casing" often rests on the assumption that military action would take the form of a confined, surgical use of air power to take out Iran's nuclear facilities. But the dispersed nature of the target and the U.S. military's operational requirements (including the suppression of Iranian air defenses) would make this a major assault. It would be the start of a war with Iran. As Richard Betts remarks in his recent book about the American use of military force, anyone who hears talk about a surgical strike should get a second opinion.

If the kind of worst-casing that war proponents apply to the implications of a nuclear Iran were applied to this question, the ramifications would be seen as catastrophic: we would be hearing about a regional conflagration involving multiple U.S. allies, sucking in U.S. forces far beyond the initial assault. When the Brookings Institution ran a war-games simulation a couple of years ago, an

Israeli strike on Iranian nuclear facilities escalated into a region-wide crisis in which Iranian missiles were raining down on Saudi Arabia as well as Israel, and Tehran launched a worldwide terrorist campaign against U.S. interests.

No one knows what the full ramifications of such a war with Iran would be, and that is the main problem with any proposal to use military force against the Iranian nuclear program. But the negative consequences for U.S. interests are likely to be severe. In December, Secretary Panetta identified some of those consequences when he warned of the dangers of war: increased domestic support for the Iranian regime; violent Iranian retaliation against U.S. ships and military bases; "severe" economic consequences; and, perhaps, escalation that "could consume the Middle East in a confrontation and a conflict that we would regret."

Surely, Iran would strike back, in ways and places of its own choosing. That should not be surprising; it is what Americans would do if their own homeland were attacked. Proponents of an attack and some Israeli officials offer a more sanguine prediction of the Iranian response, and this is where their image of Iran becomes most inconsistent. According to this optimistic view, the same regime that cannot be trusted with a nuclear weapon because it is recklessly aggressive and prone to cause regional havoc would suddenly become, once attacked, a model of calm and caution, easily deterred by the threat of further attacks. History and human behavior strongly suggest, however, that any change in Iranian conduct would be exactly the opposite—that as with the Iran–Iraq War, an attack on the Iranian homeland would be the one scenario that would motivate Iran to respond zealously. Iran's specific responses would probably include terrorism through its own agents as well as proxy groups, other violent reprisals against U.S. forces in the region, and disruption of the exports of other oil producers.

An armed attack on Iran would be an immediate political gift to Iranian hard-liners, who are nourished by confrontation with the West, and with the United States in particular. Armed attack by a foreign power traditionally produces a rally-round-the-flag effect that benefits whatever regime is in power. Last year a spokesperson for the opposition Green Movement in Iran said the current regime "would really like for someone" to bomb the nuclear facilities because "this would then increase nationalism and the regime would gather everyone and all the political parties around itself." Over the longer term, an attack would poison relations between the United States and generations of Iranians. It would become an even more prominent and lasting grievance than the U.S.-engineered overthrow of [Iran's] Prime Minister Mohammad Mosaddeq in 1953 or the accidental shooting down of an Iranian airliner over the Persian Gulf in 1988. American war proponents who optimistically hope that an attack would somehow stir the Iranian political pot in a way that would undermine the current clerical regime are likely to be disappointed. Even if political change in Iran occurred, any new regime would be responsive to a populace that has more reason than ever to be hostile to the United States.

Regional political consequences would include deepened anger at the United States for what would be seen as unprovoked killing of Muslims—with everything such anger entails in terms of stimulating more extremist violence against Americans. The emotional gap between Persians and Arabs would lessen, as would the isolation of Iran from other states in the region. Contrary to a common misconception, the Persian Gulf Arabs do not want a U.S. war with Iran, notwithstanding their own concerns about their neighbor to the north. The misconception stems mainly from misinterpretation of a Saudi comment in a leaked cable about "cutting off the head of the snake." Saudi and other Gulf Arab officials have repeatedly indicated that while they look to U.S. leadership in containing Iranian influence, they do not favor an armed attack. The former Saudi intelligence chief and ambassador to the United States, Prince Turki Al Faisal, recently stated, "It is very clear that a military strike against Iran will be catastrophic in its consequences, not just on us but the world in general."

Then there are the economic consequences that would stem from a U.S.–Iranian war, which are incalculable but likely to be immense. Given how oil markets and shipping insurance work, the impact on oil prices of any armed conflict in the vicinity of the Persian Gulf would be out of proportion to the amount of oil shipments directly interdicted, even if the U.S. Navy largely succeeded in keeping the Strait of Hormuz open. And given the current fragility of Western economies, the full economic cost of a war would likewise be out of proportion to the direct effect on energy prices, a sudden rise in which might push the U.S. economy back into recession.

In return for all of these harmful effects, an attack on Iran would not even achieve the objective of ensuring a nuclear-weapons-free Iran. Only a ground invasion and occupation could hope to accomplish that, and not even the most fervent anti-Iranian hawks are talking about that kind of enormous undertaking. Panetta's estimate that an aerial assault would set back the Iranian nuclear program by only one or two years is in line with many other assessments. Meanwhile, an attack would provide the strongest possible incentive for Iran to move forward rapidly in developing a nuclear weapon, in the hope of achieving a deterrent to future attacks sooner rather than later. That is how Iraq reacted when Israel bombed its nuclear reactor in 1981. Any prospect of keeping the bomb out of Iranian hands would require still more attacks a couple of years hence. This would mean implementing the Israeli concept of periodically "mowing the lawn"—a prescription for unending U.S. involvement in warfare in the Middle East.

"There's only one thing worse than military action against Iran," Senator John McCain has said, "and that is a nuclear-armed Iran." But any careful look at the balance sheet on this issue yields the opposite conclusion. Military action against Iran would have consequences far worse than a nuclear-armed Iran.

War or a world with an Iranian bomb are not the only alternatives. The judgment of the U.S. intelligence community, as voiced publicly by Director of National Intelligence James Clapper, is that Iran is retaining the option to build nuclear weapons but has not yet decided to do so. Much diplomatic ground has yet to be explored in searching for a formula that would permit Iran to have a peaceful nuclear program with enough inspections and other safeguards to assuage Western concerns about diversion of nuclear material to military use. As Trita Parsi reports in a recent book, the Obama administration's brief fling at diplomacy in 2009 was, in the words of a senior State Department official, "a gamble on a single roll of the dice." Now the administration, having seen how stridency toward Iran has threatened to get out of hand, seems willing to try diplomacy again in talks with Iran that will also include Britain, France, Germany, Russia, and China.

The sanctions on Iran have probably contributed to Tehran's willingness to negotiate as well. Unless carefully wedded to diplomacy, however, sanctions risk being a counterproductive demonstration of Western hostility. Besides being serious about searching for a mutually acceptable formula of inspections and procedures that would safeguard against Iranian use of nuclear material for military purposes (and which may need to permit some Iranian enrichment of uranium), Western negotiators need to persuade the Iranians that concessions on their part will lead to the lifting of sanctions. This may be hard to do, partly because the legislation that imposes U.S. sanctions on Iran mentions human rights and other issues besides the nuclear program, and partly because many U.S. hawks openly regard sanctions only as a tool to promote regime change or as a necessary step toward being able to say that "diplomacy and sanctions have failed," and thus launching a war is the only option left. The challenge for the Obama administration is to persuade Tehran that this attitude does not reflect official policy.

Why would anyone, weighing all the costs and risks on each side of this issue, even consider starting a war with Iran? The short answer is that neocon habits die hard. It might seem that the recent experience of the Iraq War should have entirely discredited such proclivities, or at least dampened policymakers' inclination to listen to those who have them. But the war in Iraq may have instead inured the American public to the extreme measure of an offensive war, at least when it involves weapons of mass destruction and loathsome Middle Eastern regimes.

The Iranian government has provided good reason for Americans to loathe it, from its harsh suppression of the Green Movement to the anti-Semitic rants and other outrageous statements of President Mahmoud Ahmadinejad. Unfortunately the belligerent rhetoric in Iran feeds belligerent rhetoric in the United States and vice versa, in a process that yields beliefs on each side that go beyond the reality on the other side. The demonization of Iran in American discourse has gone on for so long that even unsupported common wisdom is taken for granted. The excesses of the Republican primary campaign have contributed to the pattern. Minnesota Representative] Michele Bachmann, for example, may be out of the race [for the Republican presidential nomination in 2012], but when she stated that the Iranian president "has said that if he has a nuclear weapon he will use it to wipe Israel off the face of the Earth," it was the sort of untruth that has tended to stick in the current climate (never mind that Iran claims it doesn't even want nuclear weapons).

As for Israel, it is impossible to ignore how much, in American politics, the Iran issue is an Israel issue. The Netanyahu government's own repeated invocation of an Iranian nuclear threat has several roots, including the desire to preserve Israel's regional nuclear weapons monopoly, the usefulness of having

Iran stand in as the region's "real problem" to divert attention from the festering Israeli–Palestinian conflict, and simple emotion and fear. What American politicians don't seem to understand but any reader of Haaretz would know is that many leading Israelis, whose experience demonstrates both their deep commitment to Israel's security and their expertise in pronouncing on it, see the issue differently. Former Mossad chief Meir Dagan described the idea of an Israeli air strike on Iranian nuclear facilities as "the stupidest thing I have ever heard." Another former Mossad head, Efraim Halevy, and the current director of the service, Tamir Pardo, have both recently denied that an Iranian nuclear weapon would be an existential threat to Israel. Even Defense Minister Barak, in an interview answer from which he later tried to backtrack, acknowledged that any Iranian interest in a nuclear weapon was "not just about Israel" but an understandable interest given the other countries that are already in the nuclear club.

If Iran acquired the bomb, Israel would retain overwhelming military superiority, with its own nuclear weapons—which international think tanks estimate to number at least 100 and possibly 200—conventional forces, and delivery systems that would continue to outclass by far anything Iran will have. That is part of the reason why an Iranian nuclear weapon would not be an existential threat to Israel and would not give Iran a license to become more of a regional troublemaker. But a war with Iran, begun by either Israel or the United States, would push Israel farther into the hole of perpetual conflict and regional isolation. Self-declared American friends of Israel are doing it no favor by talking up such a war.

# EXPLORING THE ISSUE

## Should Force Be Used if Necessary to Prevent Iran from Acquiring Nuclear Weapons?

### Questions for Critical Thinking and Reflection

1. Why would a nuclear-armed Iran be a particular threat to the United States?
2. If it comes down to letting Iran build nuclear weapons or sending in U.S. troops to topple Iran's government and destroy its nuclear weapons and its ability to produce more, which option do you favor?
3. Iran claims that it has a sovereign right to build nuclear facilities and enrich uranium, just as numerous nonnuclear weapon countries, like Japan and Germany, do. What are Iran's rights as a country?

### Is There Common Ground?

During 2012, tensions between the West and Iran continued to grow. Driving this was that fact that Iran's uranium enrichment program continued to progress toward a capability of making enough highly enriched uranium to make a nuclear weapons. Natural uranium is made up of two radioactive isotopes, and is about 93 percent U-238 and 7 percent U-235. The process of enriching uranium involves increasing the percentage of U-235 in it. Fuel for nuclear power reactions producing electricity needs to be enriched to about 4 percent U-235. There are some peaceful applications in medical research and other areas that need uranium enriched up to 20 percent U-235. The threshold for uranium to make a crude nuclear weapons is about 20 percent U-235, although most advanced nuclear weapons are based on uranium enriched to 85 percent U-235 or more. It takes a little more than 100 pounds of highly enriched uranium to make a nuclear explosive device.

By all estimates, Iran is near the threshold. In August 2012, the IAEA reported that Iran had dramatically increased its number of centrifuges for making enriched uranium and had amassed about 420 pounds of 20 percent U-235 uranium. Iran would also have to master the complex technology to make an explosive device, but that is probably within its near-term capability also. The prime minister of Israel, the foreign minister of France, and others have predicted that Iran could be able to produce a nuclear weapon by mid-2013. Other estimates put the date further away, but at most by a few years. Iran already has missiles capable of carrying a nuclear warhead over 900 miles, putting Israel in range. Some estimates of Iran's missile development put Western Europe in range by 2014 or 2015 and the United States in range by about 2020.

As Iran has approached the point where it could build a nuclear device, the pressure to attack Iran's nuclear facilities has grown. Prime Minister Benjamin Netanyahu of Israel has said Israel will do so and urged other countries, especially the United States, to join or at least back such a strike. President Barack Obama has said the United States will use all its powers to prevent Iran from acquiring nuclear weapons. But he has never said specifically that included using military force and he has also said he is opposed an Israeli attack in the near term. Moreover, U.S. defense officials have estimated that an Israeli attack could only delay Iran's capability by perhaps two years, not destroy it.

The issue also became tied up in the U.S. presidential election in 2012, with Republican candidate Mitt Romney accusing Obama of not being steadfast enough. Late in the campaign, *The New York Times* reported that Iran and the United States had agreed to direct talks, but not until after the U.S. election. Both Iran and the White House denied the report, but most analysts continued to give it creditability.

Also in late 2012, sanctions on Iran continued to increase. In October, for example, the European Union banned the importation of natural gas from Iran. These economic pressures continued to degrade Iran's economy. Between 2002 and late 2012, for instance, the exchange rate of Iran's currency, the real, against the U.S. dollar had dropped from 8,000 per dollar to 33,000 reals per dollar, making it very expensive for Iran to import needed foreign goods and services. Nevertheless, Iran is steadfast in its refusal to abandon its program. Iran has said it would agree to limit enrichment to 20 percent if sanctions ended, but the United States and Europe take the position that 20 percent if much higher than needed for most peaceful uses and that without strict inspections it would be hard to ensure that Iran was keeping to the 20 percent standard.

# Additional Resources

To understand Iran better, read Ervand Abrahamian, *A History of Modern Iran* (Cambridge University Press, 2008). For a periodically updated background article on this nuclear issue, go to the Council on Foreign Relations' "backgrounder," Iran's Nuclear Program, at www.cfr.org/publication/16811/. The very latest news accounts and an opportunity to join the debate are at the site of Iran Nuclear Watch at www.irannuclearwatch.blogspot.com/. A recent overview is contained in Dana Allin and Steven Simon, *The Sixth Crisis: Iran, Israel, America, and the Rumors of War* (Oxford University Press, 2010).

# ISSUE 6

# Is U.S. Policy Toward Latin America on the Right Track?

**YES: Arturo A. Valenzuela,** from Testimony during Hearings on "U.S. Policy Toward the Americas in 2010 and Beyond" before the Subcommittee on the Western Hemisphere, Committee on Foreign Affairs, U.S. House of Representatives (March 10, 2010)

**NO: Otto J. Reich,** from Testimony during Hearings on "U.S. Policy Toward the Americas in 2010 and Beyond" before the Subcommittee on the Western Hemisphere, Committee on Foreign Affairs, U.S. House of Representatives (March 10, 2010)

### ISSUE SUMMARY

**YES:** Arturo A. Valenzuela, the U.S. assistant secretary of state for Western Hemisphere affairs, describes the views and policies of the Obama administration regarding the Western Hemisphere, as focused on three priorities critical to everyone in the region: promoting social and economic opportunity, ensuring safety, and strengthening effective institutions of democratic governance.

**NO:** Otto J. Reich, the U.S. assistant secretary of state for Western Hemisphere affairs during the administration of President George H. W. Bush, tells Congress that he believes the U.S. government today is underestimating the security threats in the Western Hemisphere.

For most of U.S. history, policy toward Latin America and the Caribbean has been marked by conquest and domination. In 1819, the United States first acquired territory in what was arguably Latin America when threats forced Spain to surrender Florida and parts of what are now Alabama and Mississippi. Less directly, the United States acquired a huge tract of formerly Mexican territory after American settlers had seized the territory, briefly created the Republic of Texas, and then agreed to annexation by the United States (1845). The Mexican–American War (1846–1848) broke out the following year, and the U.S. victory diminished Mexico's remaining territory by about 50 percent and increased U.S. territory by about one-third.

During these early years, Washington had also declared that much of the Western Hemisphere was, in essence, a U.S. sphere of influence. The (President

James) Monroe Doctrine (1823) proclaimed that the United States would view any move by a country outside the Western Hemisphere to colonize land or interfere with countries in the Americas as acts of aggression requiring U.S. intervention. This unilateral U.S. move gave some protection to the newly independent countries in Latin America and the Caribbean, but it also included the U.S. presumption that it had special authority over the hemisphere. In 1904 the (President Theodore) Roosevelt Corollary (to the Monroe Doctrine), by which the United States granted itself the authority to intervene in the domestic affairs of all countries to the south in cases of "flagrant . . . wrongdoing" by them, was declared. During the decades that followed, the corollary was used to justify repeated interventions, including military occupations of Cuba (1898–1992), the Dominican Republic (1916–1924), Haiti (1915–1934), Honduras (1924–1925), Mexico (1914–1917), and Nicaragua (1912–1913).

The Roosevelt Corollary came at a time of distinct U.S. imperialism. The Spanish–American war had led to the U.S. acquisition of Puerto Rico and the temporary control of Cuba. Elsewhere, the war and other events led to such U.S. colonial possessions as the Philippines, Guam, and Hawaii. Roosevelt's maneuvering was critical in creating the new country of Panama, which then dutifully agreed to U.S. control over the Panama Canal Zone.

Efforts to establish a more benevolent, partner-like U.S. policy began when President Franklin Roosevelt declared the "Good Neighbor Policy" in 1933, pledging to avoid the heavy-handed excesses of the past. Washington was also instrumental in creating the Organization of American States (OAS), which was created in 1948. Although originally meant primarily as a cold war alliance, the OAS did advance the ideal of equality and cooperation among the countries of the Western Hemisphere. Also spurred by cold war worries about the spread of communism, President John F. Kennedy launched the Alliance for Progress to increase U.S. economic aid to the hemisphere. Since then, new U.S. presidents have routinely pledged friendship toward and respect for the region's other countries. It is also the case that on average U.S. policy has been less assertive and more cooperative than it was. Still, American actions have not fully matched the rhetoric. Instead, the U.S. sphere-of-influence approach to hemispheric relations has continued in many ways. There have been occasional military interventions (Dominican Republic, 1965; Grenada, 1983; Panama, 1988; and Haiti, 1994) and a number of other instances where a government in a country to the south was brought to power, kept in power, or toppled from power because of less direct actions by Washington.

Currently, U.S.–Latin American relations are being roiled by a number of issues. The most prominent of these is the coming to power of government leaders who are populists and critical of the United States. President Hugo Chávez of Venezuela and President Evo Morales of Bolivia are prime examples. In the following debate, two individuals who have been the top U.S. diplomat for Latin America represent different streams of U.S. approach to the region. Arturo Valenzuela, who is Chilean American, argues from the Obama administration's somewhat more cooperative approach. Cuban American Otto Reich favors the more assertive approach that marked the previous Bush administration.

# YES ✒

**Arturo A. Valenzuela**

# U.S. Policy Toward the Americas in 2010 and Beyond

T hank you for the opportunity to talk about U.S. policy in the Americas. I am just back from a six-nation trip to Latin America with Secretary [of State Hillary] Clinton, where we had the chance to meet with over a dozen heads of state, and many leaders in civil society and the private sector, and talk about our highest priorities and responsibilities. We were particularly moved by the eloquent words of President-elect [José] Mujica who in his inaugural address outlined a bold vision of progress for Uruguay and a powerful defense of democratic values and institutions, including the respect for opposition parties and the value of dialogue and compromise in public affairs. So this is a particularly welcome opportunity to take stock of where we are and, more importantly, where we want to go in our relations with the countries of the Americas. It is very important, at the outset, to recognize how much our growing interdependence makes the success of our neighbors a compelling U.S. national security interest. Advancing that interest is a fundamental goal of our engagement in the Americas.

In 1961 the Alliance for Progress captured the imagination of the Americas with a bold shared vision. We live in a very different world at the beginning of the 21st century. With few exceptions, the countries of the region are much more inclusive, prosperous, and democratic. But, today, much of what we must help accomplish in this hemisphere also hinges on the power of a shared vision: a vision of an Inter-American community with shared values, shared challenges, a shared history and, most importantly, shared responsibility. Advancing that vision will require sustained, informed, creative, and competent engagement. That engagement must be sophisticated and variegated. We speak, accurately, of a "region," and of big unifying agendas, but we know at the same time that our community comprises profoundly diverse nations and sub-regions. To be successful, our approach must be able to disaggregate when necessary.

Our challenge is to carefully use our diplomatic and development tools, and our limited resources, to optimal effect. We need to help catalyze networks of practical partnerships, among all capable stakeholders in the Americas, focused on three priorities critical to people in every country of this region: promoting social and economic opportunity for everyone; ensuring the safety of all of our citizens; and strengthening effective institutions of democratic governance, respect for human rights, and accountability. Across all of these

U.S. House of Representatives, March 10, 2010.

priorities, I want to emphasize, we are also working on practical initiatives to advance us toward a secure, clean energy future.

There is a strong element of community in the Americas today, and it will only get stronger with time. That feeling was nowhere more evident than in the extraordinary outpouring of support and assistance to the people of Haiti following the devastating earthquake there. Or in the region's unanimous feelings of solidarity with Chile after it, too, was hit by one of the biggest earthquakes the world has ever experienced.

Haiti is a special case. Shortly after taking office, well before the earthquake, President [Barack] Obama and Secretary Clinton emphasized their personal commitment to helping Haiti break the cycles of poverty and poor government that have crippled its development. We have reaffirmed our commitment in the aftermath of the earthquake. You know the extent of the damage, the loss of life, and the urgent need. The Government of Haiti faces daunting tasks. Meeting them will require a sustained and substantial commitment from the international community, in support of the Government and people of Haiti as they define what their future should look like. On March 4, the United States and United Nations announced that in cooperation with the Government of Haiti, and with the support of Brazil, Canada, the European Union, France, and Spain, they will co-host a ministerial—the *International Donors' Conference Toward a New Future for Haiti*—at the United Nations in New York on March 31, 2010. The goal of the conference is to mobilize international support for Haiti's development needs and to begin to lay the foundation for Haiti's long-term recovery.

We in the Americas are joined together by many intersecting and overlapping interests, needs, and affinities. We share the common, though sometimes contentious, history of the Americas, developing from diverse European colonization, displacement of indigenous peoples, forced African immigration, assimilation of later immigrant groups, and the gradual coalescence of adaptable new societies. The populations of our countries reflect a particularly rich and largely harmonious racial and cultural diversity that differentiates this hemisphere from large parts of Europe, Asia, and Africa.

We share a common history of independence movements inspired by the human ideals of the enlightenment, followed by the long and difficult processes by which our peoples have struggled to build the just, free, inclusive, and successful societies envisioned by our founding fathers. Many of our nations have followed policies in the past that have hindered this process, as when the United States put Cold War priorities ahead of democratization in the region.

Today, however, fundamental values of democracy, respect for human rights, accountability, tolerance, and pluralism are increasingly ingraining themselves into practice throughout the Americas. So many of the Americas' leading democracies have recently gone through, or are preparing for, peaceful electoral transfers of power. Alternation in power, increasingly effective institutions, responsible fiscal policies, open trade policies, and greater accountability—exemplified by such countries as Brazil, Chile, Colombia, Costa Rica, Peru, Uruguay, and El Salvador—embody the hemispheric reality. The significance of this trend cannot be overstated.

Our common legacy, our shared values, and the nature of today's global challenges must underpin a new and converging agenda for cooperation that helps unite diverse peoples and governments around a shared task: building stable, safe, inclusive societies that are supported by effective and legitimate institutions of governance. This agenda should also protect our diversity through tolerance and pluralism as a key factor in our region's success and competitiveness in a globalized economy. Energy security and global climate change are crucial issues for our partners and us and offer opportunities for deeper collaboration. Our broad common agenda, not individual differences or outliers, should define our interaction in the Americas. I know some governments in the region will not embrace this approach, will do so only very selectively, or will seek to undermine this common cause. Working together with others, we need to be clear-eyed and proactive in countering efforts to undermine our common agenda. These can include attempts to expand authoritarian or populist rule at the expense of effective democratic governance based on the rule of law and representative government. They can also include the ill-conceived embrace of dangerous or problematic external actors.

We are concerned about the persistent erosion of democratic institutions and fundamental freedoms in several countries, particularly freedom of the press. These freedoms reflect the regional consensus and are enshrined in fundamental instruments of the Inter-American system. The recent Inter-American Human Rights Commission report on Venezuela was a complete and dispassionate review of the current state of affairs, and it represents an opportunity for Venezuela's government to begin a dialogue internally and with the hemispheric community. In Cuba, we want to promote respect for human rights and fundamental freedoms. We have taken measures to increase contact between separated families and to promote the free flow of information to, from, and within Cuba. We have engaged the Cuban government on key bilateral matters like migration and direct mail service and will continue to engage Cuba to advance U.S. national interests, as in our effort to respond to the humanitarian crisis in Haiti. We remain deeply concerned by the poor human rights situation in Cuba, which contributed to the recent death of prisoner of conscience Orlando Zapata as a result of a hunger strike. We are also focused on securing the release of the U.S. citizen jailed in Cuba in December; a matter of great importance to the United States.

Our response to the coup d'état in Honduras [the January 2009 overthrow of somewhat-to-the-left President Manuel Zelaya by the military] shows that our interests are served by leveraging multilateral mechanisms, in concert with our partners, to support the implementation of principled policies. In Honduras we helped to strengthen the "collective defense of democracy" as a cornerstone of the Inter-American System. Today, Honduras is governed by elected leaders who are moving quickly to promote national reconciliation and their country's return to the fold of hemispheric democracies. [After a long crisis, new presidential election was held in November 2009 and won by somewhat rightist candidate Porfirio Lobo.] As Honduras moves forward, we will continue to maintain a vigilant eye on the human rights situation there in light of serious concerns that have been raised.

To help advance our national interests, as reflected in the broad common agenda I outlined, the President has submitted an FY 2011 [fiscal year 2011; the U.S. fiscal year runs from October 1, 2011, to September 30, 2012] request for foreign assistance in the region that reflects a continuing shift toward greater economic and development assistance, over traditional security assistance. Specifically, of the total FY 2011 request, 62 percent is economic and development assistance, versus only 50 percent in the FY 2009 and FY 2010 enacted levels.

This does not mean we face a diminished threat to our national security from transnational crime and other menaces. These include the global drug trade, the largest criminal industry in the world, involving every country in the region. Nor does it mean we are shying away from doing our utmost to safeguard the security of our citizens and citizens throughout the region. Instead, our request recognizes the critical importance of strong institutions, broad economic opportunity, and social inclusion in building resilient societies that can protect people from threats to their safety. For example, the request includes specific funding for innovative regional initiatives reflecting our commitment to shared prosperity and a sustainable future—such as the Inter-American Social Protection Network and the Energy and Climate Partnership of the Americas.

Our request also reflects our continued commitment to key hemispheric citizen safety initiatives including the Merida Initiative, our programs in Colombia, the Caribbean Basin Security Initiative, and the Central America Regional Security Initiative. [The Merida Initiative is a U.S. program that the State Department characterizes as helping "Mexico, the nations of Central America, the Dominican Republic, and Haiti to confront criminal organizations whose illicit actions undermine public safety, erode the rule of law, and threaten the national security of the United States."] The security challenges in the region are profoundly interconnected. Our initiatives are grounded in a common strategic vision and coordinated internally and with the interagency to ensure comprehensive and coherent planning and implementation. While these initiatives are mutually reinforcing, sharing broad objectives and some key activities, they vary considerably in size, level of U.S. support, complexity, and level of development. The combination of a common strategic approach and distinct, but interlocking, regional initiatives provides the necessary unity of effort as well as the flexibility necessary to help address unique circumstances that vary by country or sub-region.

The evolving mix of our assistance is also a function of successful partnerships—such as those with Colombia and Mexico—that have enabled others to assume an increasing share of responsibility for their own citizens' safety. It is also a function of the leadership of many members of this committee, and the administration's clear understanding of the connection between major security challenges and a combination of weak institutions, social exclusion, and lack of economic opportunity that plague many societies.

Earlier I referred to three priorities critical to people throughout the Americas. They are mutually reinforcing, and they inform and influence our diplomatic and development policy throughout the Americas, so I would like to expand upon them in that context.

# Opportunity

Through social and economic partnerships with governments, civil society, and the private sector we can leverage investments in people and infrastructure to make societies more competitive in the world and inclusive at home. Our public diplomacy initiatives—scholarships, exchange programs, in-country language programs, other activities through our bi-national centers—advance these goals, bringing huge return on our investment. We are now exploring the potential to significantly expand such programs. The inclusion into the economic mainstream of traditionally marginalized groups is crucial to economic growth.

The Pathways to Prosperity initiative, which we have re-cast as a strategic platform for promoting sustainable development, trade capacity building and regional competitiveness, is also key to promoting more equitable economic growth. The initiative, which includes those countries in the hemisphere that are committed to trade and market economies, comprises a number of programs to help ensure that the benefits of trade and economic growth are equitably shared among all sectors of society. Despite its macroeconomic growth, poverty and income inequality remain key challenges in this hemisphere. Pathways countries share a commitment to promote a more inclusive prosperity and responsive democratic institutions.

Countries throughout the Americas have experience, creativity, and talent to address these challenges and through Pathways we are working with partners to help exchange information and share best practices to benefit all. Secretary Clinton participated in the Pathways ministerial last week and cited a number of areas that we have identified for cooperation under Pathways. These include the creation of small business development centers; support for women entrepreneurs; modernizing customs procedures; expanded opportunities for English and Spanish language instruction; helping small- and medium-sized enterprises decrease their carbon footprint; and promoting the use of secured transaction to help small businesses better access capital.

We are also working with partners in the Western Hemisphere to fight poverty through the Inter-American Social Protection Network, which our leaders committed to support at the Summit of the Americas in Trinidad and Tobago last April. The launch of the Network in New York City in September 2009 was important—demonstrating the commitment of governments and citizens throughout the Americas to helping each other achieves social justice in creative and innovative ways. Examples of innovative social protection strategies include Conditional Cash Transfers (CCTs)—a simple idea linking responsibility with opportunity.

We will continue to work closely with partner nations such as Canada in promoting greater opportunity in the region. Canada's major development commitment to Haiti—both before and after the earthquake—as well as their programs in the Caribbean, Bolivia, Honduras, and Peru are effective multipliers to our own efforts.

We are also in serious discussion with other nations, such as Spain, and the EU, who provide substantial development assistance in the Americas.

In particular, we see important opportunities to more effectively coordinate our programs in Central America, bilaterally and through SICA [Sistema de Integración Centroamericana]. When I met in Madrid with my Spanish counterparts last month we agreed to move quickly to assess and take advantage of these opportunities. It is very important to address too our pending free trade agreements with Colombia and Panama. These accords are important components of economic engagement with the Americas. As the President has made clear, we remain committed to working with both Panama and Colombia to address outstanding issues, including concerns voiced by members of Congress and other critical stakeholders. We are confident that together we can advance our interests and values through these agreements and our deep and diverse relationships with both Panama and Colombia.

Sustaining the opportunity generated by economic growth requires vastly enhanced cooperation on energy and climate change. The Energy and Climate Partnership of the Americas helps achieve this. The State Department is working together with the Department of Energy to lead U.S. efforts under the Partnership, and we and other governments in the region (Brazil, Chile, Colombia, Costa Rica, Mexico, and Peru) have developed initiatives focused on energy efficiency, renewable energy, infrastructure, energy poverty, and cleaner fossil fuels. Secretary of Energy Steven Chu will host an ECPA [Energy and Climate Partnership of the Americas] Ministerial April 15–16 in Washington, with Secretary Clinton's participation. There, we will further existing ECPA initiative and identifying new ones. We are excited about the countless opportunities for cooperation under ECPA.

Scientific partnerships in our Hemisphere also hold the promise of opportunity. Economic growth, promoting security, and unleashing the potential of developing countries are inextricable from the sustainable development of our common resources and building our capacity for innovation. The number of researchers in the workforce, doctoral degrees awarded, and research and development expenditures in Latin America are well below that of OECD [Organization of Economic Cooperation and Development] countries. Even so, scientific publications and patent applications have increased steadily in the region particularly in Argentina, Brazil, Chile, Mexico, and Uruguay. It is vital that we encourage this continued growth and use international scientific cooperation as the way to build further capacity. Increased cooperation in science addresses key development goals for the countries in the region, but also directly benefits the U.S. economy. The countries of Latin America and the Caribbean not only look to the United States for leadership in S&T [science and technology] activities, but we are their largest trading partners, their largest source of foreign direct investment, and our universities are the destination of many of the best and brightest Latin American students. Investing in S&T cooperation with Latin America today will strengthen our U.S. universities and research institutions, but as we look past the immediate financial crisis, will help position American companies in the innovative industries of the future, ranging from clean energy to biotechnology. Bringing prosperity and economic growth to some of our strongest trading partners will also have a positive impact for traditional U.S. exporters.

# Citizen Safety

Citizen Safety encompasses a similarly multi-dimensional set of partnerships that broker cooperation and institution building to fight transnational crime and assure a secure daily existence for individuals throughout the Inter-American community. To get sustained buy-in, it is vital that our security partnerships be understood by publics as *responsive* to the very local insecurity they face (crime, human trafficking, drug addiction, and poor environment, lack of reliable energy, or clean water), and not simply a means of securing the United States regardless of the cost to others.

Strong public diplomacy has a vital tactical role in building wider awareness of the ways these jointly developed partnerships, for example, with Colombia, Peru, Mexico, Central America, and the Caribbean address shared concerns, strengthen institutions, and help build resilient communities in which people can thrive. Our diplomacy must also emphasize to publics all we do domestically to live up to our responsibility to address some of the key factors of transnational crime, including demand for drugs, and illicit traffic in firearms and bulk cash.

A variety of security partnerships in the region, the Merida Initiative, the Central American Regional Security Initiative (CARSI), and the Caribbean Basin Security Initiative (CBSI), seek to strengthen partners' ability to fight transnational crime, protect citizens, and prevent the spread of illicit goods and violence to the United States. In the process these partnerships are transforming relationships, brokering growing cooperation and trust between those countries and the United States, and between the partner nations themselves.

The United States and Mexico have forged a strong partnership to enhance citizen safety and fight organized crime and drug trafficking organizations. In 2009, the United States and Mexico agreed to new goals to broaden and deepen the cooperation between the two countries. These include expanding the border focus beyond interdiction of contraband to include facilitating legitimate trade and travel; cooperating to build strong communities resilient to the corrupting influence of organized crime; disrupting organized crime; and institutionalizing reforms to sustain the rule of law and respect for human rights. The Caribbean Basin Security Initiative (CBSI) seeks to substantially reduce illicit trafficking, increase safety for our people, and promote social justice. More than a series of programs, this partnership will be an ongoing collaboration that draws upon, and helps develop, the capacity of all to better address common and inter-related challenges. Partnership activities will be designed in a manner that maximizes synergies with other regional efforts (e.g. Merida). Under CBSI we will jointly seek the greatest possible support from extra-regional partners in pursuit of key objectives.

The Central American Regional Security Initiative (CARSI), in coordination with Merida Initiative and CBSI, strengthens and integrates security efforts from the U.S. Southwest border to Panama, including the littoral waters of the Caribbean. The desired end-state is a safer and more secure hemisphere—in which the U.S., too, is protected from spread of illicit drugs, violence, and transnational threats. CARSI recognizes a sequenced approach to resolving the challenges, consisting of: the immediate need to address the rapidly deteriorating security environment; the medium-term requirement to augment civilian law enforcement and security entities; the capabilities to reestablish control and exert the rule of law; and the long-term necessity to strengthen the justice sector and other state institutions.

In the Andes, it remains in our national interest to help the Colombian people achieve the lasting and just peace they want, making irreversible the gains they have sacrificed so hard to achieve. Colombia has made major progress reducing violence and kidnappings, improving human rights, expanding the rule of law, and advancing the country's social and economic development. Important challenges remain including in the area of human rights. We will continue to work closely with the Colombian government to promote respect for human rights, ensure access to justice, and end impunity. We will also continue to collaborate with Colombia to prevent and respond to the disturbingly high rates of internal displacement. The Colombia Strategic Development Initiative (CSDI) is our plan to support the government of Colombia's "National Consolidation Plan." CSDI is a whole-of-government approach that integrates civilian institution–building, rule of law, and alternative development programs with security and counternarcotics efforts.

In Colombia, Mexico, and elsewhere in the region the Secretary has emphasized that we understand that effective and collaborative counterdrug policies must be based holistically on four key goals: demand reduction, eradication and interdiction, just implementation of the law, and public health. To be sustainable, any gains will require economic and social opportunity sufficiently strong to provide compelling alternatives to involvement in illicit drug production and trafficking.

We tend to speak of U.S. security initiatives in the region, but in reality these are overwhelmingly joint in their development increasingly plurilateral [a few more than two countries or other partners] in their implementation, and multi-faceted in their impact. As countries strengthen their internal capacity to address security challenges they are forming their own partnerships with neighbors in ways that multiply the effectiveness of programs. Canada is an increasingly important and committed security partner with regional countries; Mexico and Colombia are sharing vital capacity and experience; countries such as Uruguay, Chile, and Brazil are showing notable leadership in international security initiatives such as MINUSTAH [La Mission des Nations Unies pour la Stabilisation en Haïti, the UN peacekeeping force] in Haiti.

## Effective Democratic Governance

Capable and legitimate institutions, including a vibrant civil society, are vital to successful societies that meet their citizens' needs. Our strong support for democracy and human rights is rooted in this fundamental fact. The capacity and integrity of democratic institutions [are] uneven in the Americas. All our nations have a broad co-responsibility to help strengthen both. Many are, in fact, reaching beyond their national success to share experience and technical capacity in the region and beyond.

U.S. democracy programs focus on broadening citizen participation, supporting free elections and justice sector reform, developing anti-corruption initiatives and governmental transparency, supporting human rights and fostering social justice through stronger rule of law. Strong and effective multilateral institutions in the Americas can play a vital role in strengthening effective democratic institutions. The Organization of American States (OAS), at the center of the inter-American system, has a mandate from its membership to do so.

We must work through the OAS to strengthen democratic institutions at a time in which these institutions are being seriously challenged in some countries in the region. As part of this effort, we should apply the valuable lessons of the success of the independent Inter-American Commission on Human Rights, as an impartial arbiter on human rights issues, to address critical governance issues affecting our region. We must also build the political will necessary among OAS member states to fulfill the promise of the Inter-American Democratic Charter as an effective tool in the collective defense of democracy.

Recent experience should demonstrate to us that both the Secretary General [SYG] and the Permanent Council should be less hesitant to use their existing authorities under the OAS Charter and the Inter-American Democratic Charter to take preventive action in situations that may affect the viability of democratic institutions in a member state. Such actions must be undertaken with the consent of the member state involved, of course.

As an organization, the OAS can do a better job of defending and promoting democracy and human rights, consistent with our shared commitment to implement and apply the Inter-American Democratic Charter. We need more effective mechanisms for foreseeing and counteracting emerging threats to democracy before they reach the crisis stage. The SYG's 2007 Report to the Permanent Council contained some useful recommendations in this regard that warrant further examination. The 2007 Report stressed the need for a "graduated response" to brewing political crises, and called for a more comprehensive linkage of the existing mechanisms of the OAS—particularly our peer review processes—into a coordinated response mechanism in support of member states' democratic institutions. We would welcome a serious discussion on the operationalization of these recommendations. We need to view the Democratic Charter more as resource states can call on when they need it and less as a punitive instrument to be feared and avoided. After all, the Democratic Charter was initially envisioned to function as a preventive toolbox in support of our region's democratic institutions. New regional or subregional institutions may also be able to promote democratic integration and effective governance. The extent to which they do so may ultimately determine their usefulness, staying power, or even legitimacy in their members' eyes. We are willing partners with new collectives that are capable instruments of this common cause.

We already work closely and successfully with many multilateral groupings of which we are not part, such as SICA and CARICOM [Caribbean Community: an international organization with 15 members and 4 associate members]. This engagement is about much more than just aid—it is about co-responsibility, a point Secretary Clinton highlighted during her recent trip to South and Central America. In a time of budgetary challenge in the United States, it is difficult to ask our Congress for assistance resources for countries unable to invest in social programs because they fail to collect taxes from those in their own country who should be contributing to their societies. In many countries in the region tax collection represents less than 15 percent, sometimes less than 10 percent, of GDP.

Mr. Chairman, I cannot close without reiterating here something that I have had occasion to say privately to you and some of the members on the sub-committee. Last April in Trinidad and Tobago President Obama asked his elected counterparts from throughout the Americas to look forward, together, toward the great tasks before us. He signaled clearly that partnership would be the leitmotif of the United States' engagement in the Americas.

That partnership is not just something we seek externally. It is something to which I commit, with you, and the other members of the sub-committee, as we work together to sustain smart policies that advance our national interests, and advance critical agendas we share with people all over the hemisphere. . . . I look forward to continuing this dialogue, and working with Congress to advance our positive agenda with the Americas.

**Otto J. Reich**                                    ➡ **NO**

# U.S. Policy Toward the Americas in 2010 and Beyond

Thank you . . . for this opportunity to address the topic of US policy toward Latin America. The overriding objective of US policy—in Latin America and elsewhere—should be to advance US national interests, not to win international popularity contests. If we can be liked while advancing our interests, so much the better. But let's be realistic: when we try to befriend undemocratic leaders and ignore their belligerence, we are *neither* liked *nor* do we advance our interests. Some of the despots in this hemisphere to whom the [President Barack] Obama Administration extended an open hand only to encounter a clenched fist include the rulers of Cuba, Venezuela, Bolivia, Nicaragua, Ecuador, and Honduras' former President [Manuel] Zelaya. Foremost among our national interests is security. Without security we cannot promote other goals such as democracy, human rights and socio-economic growth. I believe the US government today is underestimating the security threats in the Western Hemisphere. Rather, we seem to be fighting the ghosts of dictatorships past and trying too hard to be liked.

The main threat to the peace, freedom, prosperity and security of the US and the hemisphere does not come from military coups, but from a form of creeping totalitarianism self-described as 21st-Century socialism and allied with some of the most virulent forms of tyranny and anti-Western ideology in the world.

Today in Latin America, democracy is being undermined by a new gang of autocrats who, counseled by the oldest dictator in history, gain power through elections and then dismantle democracy from within. Following Fidel Castro's direction, that has already happened in Venezuela and Bolivia; is happening in Nicaragua and Ecuador; almost happened in Honduras; and could happen in any other nation that falls into the grasp of something called ALBA [Alternativa Bolivariana para las Américas], or the Bolivarian Alternative for the Americas.

ALBA's ruling pattern is clear: after gaining power democratically, they use force to intimidate political adversaries and the media; politicize the police and the military and place them at the orders of the ruling party; pack the judiciary with compliant judges; rewrite electoral laws to eliminate opposition candidates and parties; seize private property or force businesses to close using

U.S. House of Representatives, March 10, 2010.

bogus charges; incite mob violence to force potential opponents into silence or exile; and attack the churches, civic associations, the press, labor unions and any other civil institution that dares to challenge the government. Their stated model is Cuba, and the result will be an Orwellian dictatorship, a pauperized prison-nation whose citizens risk everything to flee.

ALBA was conceived in Havana and is financed by Venezuela's petro-dollars. It is actually the revival of Fidel Castro's half-century goal of uniting international radical and terrorist movements of the developing world under his leadership, a movement that in the 1960s he financed and called "The Tricontinental."

The first foreign country Fidel Castro visited after the overthrow of the [President Fulgencio] Batista dictatorship, in 1959, was Venezuela. While there, he secretly asked Venezuelan President Romulo Betancourt for $300 million (about $3 billion in today's dollars) to "undermine the Yankees (the US) . . ." in Latin America. Betancourt, a center-left leader but a committed democrat, flatly turned Castro down. Three years later Castro was supporting guerrilla warfare in Venezuela and sending an armed expedition of Cuban soldiers to join Marxist rebels in an attempt to destroy Venezuelan democracy and acquire its oil wealth. Today thanks to [Venezuela's President] Hugo Chavez, Castro has finally achieved his goal. Castro also targeted Bolivia in the 1960s, because of its strategic location and enormous mineral wealth. Bolivia has land borders with Argentina, Brazil, Paraguay, Peru and Chile—more than two thirds of South America. In 1967 Castro's lieutenant Ernesto (Che) Guevara selected Bolivia as the site to begin his communist takeover of the continent. Guevara failed miserably, but today a Castro disciple, [President] Evo Morales, is turning Bolivia into one of those 21st-Century dictatorships.

US policy cannot be solely focused on the ALBA Axis, but neither can we ignore it, because the Havana-Caracas-La Paz Axis is undermining the peace and prosperity of the rest of the hemisphere.

I cannot mention in our limited time all the bilateral relationships we have in the hemisphere. But the most sensitive dealings for the US remain those with Mexico, Brazil and Colombia. I contend that these nations and those of the rest of the hemisphere are confused by the signals sent by the Obama Administration in its first year. These three countries are following free market economic policies, providing greater opportunities for their population within a framework of civil liberties, and therefore making steady socio-economic progress. Yet, with the exception of Colombia, their foreign policy seems oddly antagonistic and even self-defeating.

We see Brazil, for example, distancing itself from the US and from Europe on critical matters such as Iran sanctions. Mexico, the Latin American country closest to the US in geography and economy, last month hosted a summit of Latin American leaders that included two military rulers, General Raul Castro of Cuba and Lieutenant Colonel Hugo Chavez of Venezuela, both of whom still wear their rank and uniform at home, but excluded the freely elected civilian leader of Honduras, Pepe [Porfirio] Lobo. This is bizarre, unless they are trying to send a message that they do not share our values or else are misreading the signals sent from Washington. I believe it is the latter.

Some observers explain Brazil's behavior as diplomatic "muscleflexing" by an economically emergent nation, or in the case of Mexico as a return to the traditional nationalistic foreign policy of decades past. Under the undemocratic 70-year rule of the PRI party [*Partido Revolucionario Institucional*], Mexico steered its foreign policy to the left, so as to distract its domestic radicals and keep them from interfering with the management of the more important domestic security and financial policies. These explanations are plausible, but US national interests are nevertheless damaged by the behavior of these friends. And while Mexico and Brazil are still friends, the ALBA nations are not, and are openly and actively undermining US interests.

For example, Venezuela has played an active destabilizing role in Ecuador, Peru, Nicaragua, and above all Colombia, where Hugo Chavez maintains explicit strategic and political alliances with the narco-terrorist Revolutionary Armed Forces of Colombia (FARC). (By the way, the term narco-terrorist is not mine, it is applied to the FARC by various agencies of the US and European governments.) Just last week the Spanish government accused Chavez of supporting with the Spanish Basque terrorist group ETA [Euskadi Ta Askatasuna/ Basque Homeland and Freedom] as well as the FARC. Not satisfied with merely supporting the FARC and allowing guerilla leaders and fighters to hide, train and recuperate inside Venezuelan territory, Chavez has repeatedly closed the commercial border and threatened war against Colombia. The impact on the Colombian economy has been devastating. But Chavez is not just involved in armed intervention against Colombia.

The US, Colombia, and other governments in the region have abundant evidence of massive flows of FARC-controlled cocaine through Venezuela. Senior Chavez regime officials have been designated by the US DEA [Drug Enforcement Agency] as drug kingpins and active collaborators of FARC drug trafficking. These kingpins include the current head of Venezuela's military intelligence services, General Hugo Carvajal, former Interior and Justice Minister Ramon Rodriguez Chacin, and former political police [intelligence service] chief Henry Rangel Silva. Weapons are smuggled to the FARC through Venezuela with the active collusion of senior Chavez regime officials including Army General Cliver Alcala Cordones. This is public record.

Last year, Peruvian intelligence services found evidence that Hugo Chavez actively supported the indigenous groups responsible for violent protests in that country. Former Bolivian Presidents Jorge Quiroga and Gonzalo Sanchez de Lozada have charged that the Chavez regime clandestinely financed and supported riots in that country as far back as 2002, which toppled two governments in quick succession and led to the election of Evo Morales. Chavez also actively supports radical groups in Ecuador, which under President Rafael Correa became a command, control, operations and training base for the Colombian FARC.

In Central America, Chavez actively supports the regime of Nicaraguan President Daniel Ortega. Chavez financed and encouraged Manuel Zelaya's efforts to violate the constitution and laws of Honduras. The disruption to the economy of Central America of the six-month-long Honduran political crisis is said to have cost hundreds of millions of dollars to those impoverished economies. Chavez used Venezuela's oil resources to strengthen El Salvador's

Marxist FMLN [Frente Farabundo Martí para la Liberación Nacional] party, and poured millions of dollars into both El Salvador and Panama's presidential elections. He succeeded in one and failed in the other. Mexico's intelligence services have found links between the Chavez regime and radical groups in that country.

Venezuela's oil wealth has been used to influence Caribbean states through the PetroCaribe program [Venezuelan program that allows favored nations in the region to buy oil at low prices]. PetroCaribe, however, merely postpones the payment for oil purchased today. A few forward thinking Caribbean leaders, in Trinidad-Tobago and Barbados for example, have warned that the PetroCaribe program is saddling the Caribbean's poor island nations with a debt burden they will never be able to repay. But cheap oil today is politically appealing to elected leaders who wish to continue winning elections even at the expense of future generations.

What PetroCaribe has done is to allow Chavez to manipulate the OAS, as evidenced before and during the Honduras crisis. This past week Chavez named Honduras' ousted would-be dictator Manuel Zelaya as the head of PetroCaribe's "Political Council"—a body that does not yet exist, obviously a position created to give Zelaya a salary with which to travel the Americas doing Chavez's bidding.

There is another country, Argentina, that although not a member of ALBA bears watching because of authoritarian tendencies by its ruling presidential couple and close ties to Cuba and Venezuela, lack of official transparency, massive corruption, harassment of private enterprise, and interference with the free market and with the institutions of democracy.

It is no secret that President Cristina Kirchner received millions of dollars from Hugo Chavez for her election campaign, money that was taken illegally from the Venezuelan state, introduced illegally into Argentina, and given to the Kirchner campaign in violation of Argentine law. We know much about the transfer of that money because of a Federal trial that took place in Miami, Florida, and because of an accidental search of a suitcase by an Argentine customs officer who was doing her job. It is well known that similar transfers have taken place in at least a half dozen countries in this region, but that have not yet been publicized.

Like Castro's before him, Chavez's ambitions are global, and the principal goal of his international activities is to weaken, undermine or cripple US strategic interests in the world, not just in the Americas. Chavez is very open about his determination to bring down what he calls the US Empire.

To this end, Chavez has forged strong bonds with undemocratic states such as Russia, Belarus and Iran. Chavez has signed numerous economic and military agreements with all three countries. He has purchased over $4 billion in Russian military equipment. He invited the Russian Navy to maneuver in the Caribbean, which it did, for the first time since the end of the Cold War. Russia's hard-line Prime Minister Vladimir Putin is going to Venezuela soon, reportedly to sign a nuclear energy deal with Chavez.

Chavez has visited Teheran [Iran] numerous times, has signed many commercial, financial and other agreements with Iran, hosted Iranian leader

[President Mahmoud] Ahmadinejad in Caracas and sponsored Ahmadinejad's travel to Bolivia and Nicaragua. He has supported Iran's efforts to acquire nuclear weapons capable of striking targets in Europe and throughout the Middle East. He is a vociferous enemy of Israel and a supporter of regimes dedicated to the destruction of Israel and the US, and the sponsorship of terrorism, such as Iran and Syria.

During Chavez's 11 years in power, Hamas and Hezbollah [Middle East-based terrorist groups] have established a presence in Venezuela. Israeli military intelligence recently disclosed that a shipment of arms seized last November by Israeli commandos departed from a Venezuelan port and docked in an Iranian port before sailing through the Suez Canal bound for Lebanon. The weapons, including missiles, reportedly were to be delivered to Hezbollah.

Chavez also has turned Venezuela over to the Castro regime. Today there are between 40,000 and 50,000 Cubans in Venezuela on official missions, by the Chavez regime's own admission. Since 2005 Venezuela's armed forces have been obliged to embrace Cuba's national security doctrine, which considers the US the greatest external threat to the survival of the 21st-Century socialist revolutionary regime in Caracas.

In spite of its alliances with Russia, China, Belarus, Iran, Syria, FARC, Hezbollah and other criminal, terrorist or rogue governments and non-state actors, there are still policymakers in Washington, D.C., who maintain that the Castro-Chavez-Morales alliance is no more than a nuisance to US interests.

It is time to care less about what others think of us and focus more on what they do to us.

# EXPLORING THE ISSUE

## Is U.S. Policy Toward Latin America on the Right Track?

## Questions for Critical Thinking and Reflection

1. Imagine that you are the U.S. secretary of state and that a Latin American country has democratically elected a very left-wing president. The new president is strongly critical of the United States and its policies in the region, pledges to give financial support to left-wing movements throughout the hemisphere, and otherwise makes every effort to thwart U.S. foreign policy goals. A secret emissary from dissidents in the other country comes to you and says that pro-U.S. groups, including the army, are ready to overthrow the antagonistic president if the United States signals that after a decent interval it will recognize the new government and resume economic and military aid. What would your response be and why?
2. Throughout history it has been common for major powers to control a sphere of influence in regions near their border. Is it appropriate for the United States to operate under the assumption that Latin America and the Caribbean are its sphere of influence?
3. In the NO selection, Otto Reich argues, "It is time to care less about what others think of us [the United States/Americans] and focus more on what they do to us." Is this a sound foundation for a successful foreign policy?

## Is There Common Ground?

The ongoing tensions between the older sphere-of-influence U.S. approach to Latin America and the Caribbean and the more recent good neighbor approach are evident in events that unfolded in Honduras beginning in 2009. That year, an attempt by left-leaning President Manuel Zelaya to hold an assembly to change the Constitution sparked a crisis that led the Honduran military to arrest Zelaya and send him into exile. Most countries condemned the coup and refused to recognize the new government. Additionally, the OAS suspended Honduras' membership for violating the democratic process. After some months, a new election was held, and right-leaning Porfirio Lobo was elected president. The duality of U.S. thinking is evident in Washington's reactions. At first, the Obama administration took a clear good neighbor approach by condemning Zelaya's overthrow, refusing to recognize the interim government, and supporting the suspension of Honduras by the OAS. Critics charge, however, that once the new elections were held, the sphere-of-influence

121

approach reemerged in the U.S. policy, with Washington too willing to accept the new, rightist president, when, arguably, what should have occurred was to restore the deposed leftist president to power. One flash point is at the OAS, where U.S. efforts to restore Honduras' membership were being blocked by a number of countries such as Argentina, Brazil, and Mexico. The episode ended in mid-2011 when, through a deal brokered by Colombia and Venezuela, the OSA by a 32 to 1 (Ecuador) vote restored Honduras' membership after the country permitted Zelaya to return from exile and agreed that he and his supporters could become involved in politics.

As for Venezuela, its relations with the United States remain poor. The high price of oil has aided Venezuela in recent years, and in 2012, President Hugo Chávez was reelected to a fourth term as president by a 55 percent vote in what by all accounts was a fair election.

## Additional Resources

A good place to begin learn more about Latin America is in Robert H. Holden and Rina Villars, *Contemporary Latin America: 1970 to the Present* (Wiley-Blackwell, 2012). For an overview of U.S. policy in the region, consult Peter H. Smith, *Talons of the Eagle: Latin America, the United States, and the World* (Oxford University Press, 2012). A specific look at United States–Venezuela relations can be found in Javier Corrales and Carlos A. Romero, *U.S.–Venezuela Relations since the 1990s: Coping with Midlevel Security Threats* (Routledge, 2012).

# ISSUE 7

# Does the Islamist Movement Threaten the Democracy Gained in the "Arab Spring"?

**YES: Andrew C. McCarthy,** from "Islam Is Islam, and That's It," *National Review* (no. 1, January 23, 2012)

**NO: Hillary Rodham Clinton,** from *Keynote Address at the National Democratic Institute's 2011 Democracy Awards Dinner* (U.S. Department of State, November 7, 2011)

### ISSUE SUMMARY

**YES:** Andrew C. McCarthy, a columnist for the *National Review*, argues that it is dangerously misleading to portray the Arab/Muslim world as a separate civilization that has values and goals that are fundamentally at odds with those of the United States and the rest of the West.

**NO:** U.S. Secretary of State Hillary Rodham Clinton welcomes the Arab democratization movement and contends that it is a positive development for the national interest of the United States.

**D**emocracy's genesis dates back about 2,500 years to its birth in the ancient Greek city-states. For more than 2,000 of those years, however, democracies existed only rarely and usually died out. This tenuous hold on political life began to strengthen with the rise of English democracy in the 1600s, and the American and French Revolutions in the late 1700s. Nevertheless, democracy continued to spread slowly and was limited mostly to Western Europe and North America. But during the past few decades, the pace of democratization picked up considerably.

Freedom House, an organization that measures political freedom and democracy, reports that in 1973, the first year it compiled its "Freedom Index," only 29 percent of all countries were free. Another 25 percent were partly free, while nearly half (46 percent) of all countries were not free. By 2011, democratization had advanced substantially, with 45 percent free, 31 percent partly free, and just 24 percent not free.

Democracy has not spread evenly across the glove, however. Western Europe, the birthplace of democracy, has seen the most widespread democratization. By 1973, three-fourths of the region's countries were rated free by Freedom House. In 2011, 96 percent of the region's countries had achieved that laudable status. By contrast, the Middle East and North Africa, extending from Iran in the east to Western Sahara in the west, was the least democratic world region. Only 1 (Israel), or 6 percent, of the region's 18 countries was free, 22 percent (4 countries) were partly free, and the rest (72 percent) were not free.

Then came the so-called Arab Spring, a series of democratic uprisings in the region. People in Tunisia began to protest against the government of Zine El Abidine Ben Ali, who had held power since 1987. Within a month, he was forced to flee into exile in Saudi Arabia. Soon discontent also boiled to the surface in Egypt against its long-time (1981–2011) president, and he was forced from power in February 2011 and subsequently arrested. Libya, flanked by Egypt and Tunisia, followed suit. Protests, rather than a full-scale armed effort, sought the end of Muammar Gadhafi's dictatorship (since 1969). With the help of air and logistics support from European countries and the United States, he was toppled and then killed in October 2011. In addition to these countries, there has been recent progress toward ending authoritarianism in Algeria, Bahrain, Iraq, Jordan, Syria, Yemen, and elsewhere.

For the United States, the Arab Spring created something of a dilemma. Rhetorically and sometimes in action, American foreign policy has traditionally favored democratization. Yet it is also the case that U.S. policy had long supported the authoritarian regimes in the region, such as those in Egypt and Saudi Arabia, because they provided stability and other benefits to U.S. interests in that economically and politically important region. Concerns were raised that the fall of the authoritarian movements in the region could lead to radical Muslim elements hostile to U.S. interests gaining power. Amid this controversy, President Barack Obama signaled support for democracy in a May 2011 speech. He said that providing support to the democracy movement would be "a new chapter in American diplomacy," and, sending a message to the region's people, he declared, "Our message is simple: If you take the risks that reform entails, you will have the full support of the United States." Andrew McCarthy writes in the YES selection that Islamists are adept at seeming to be committed to upholding democracy, human rights, and foreign policy moderation. But once in power, he asserts, they are sure to be anti-American and to contribute materially to the pan-Islamic goal of destroying Israel. In the NO selection, U.S. Secretary of State Hillary Rodham Clinton echoes President Obama's position, contending that it is a "good time for the United States of America to be standing for freedom and democracy."

# YES ⤶

Andrew C. McCarthy

# Islam Is Islam, and That's It

The tumult indelibly dubbed "the Arab Spring" in the West, by the credulous and the calculating alike, is easier to understand once you grasp two basics. First, the most important fact in the Arab world—as well as in Iran, Turkey, Pakistan, Afghanistan, and other neighboring non-Arab territories—is Islam. It is not poverty, illiteracy, or the lack of modern democratic institutions. These, like anti-Semitism, anti-Americanism, and an insular propensity to buy into conspiracy theories featuring infidel villains, are effects of Islam's regional hegemony and supremacist tendency, not causes of it. One need not be led to that which pervades the air one breathes.

The second fact is that Islam constitutes a distinct civilization. It is not merely an exotic splash on the gorgeous global mosaic with a few embarrassing cultural eccentricities; it is an entirely different way of looking at the world. We struggle with this truth, which defies our end-of-history smugness. Enthralled by diversity for its own sake, we have lost the capacity to comprehend a civilization whose idea of diversity is coercing diverse peoples into obedience to its evolution-resistant norms.

So we set about remaking Islam in our own progressive image: the noble, fundamentally tolerant Religion of Peace. We miniaturize the elements of the *ummah* (the notional global Muslim community) that refuse to go along with the program: They are assigned labels that scream "fringe!"—Islamist, fundamentalist, Salafist, Wahhabist, radical, jihadist, extremist, militant, or, of course, "conservative" Muslims adhering to "political Islam."

We consequently pretend that Muslims who accurately invoke Islamic scripture in the course of forcibly imposing the dictates of classical sharia—the Islamic legal and political system—are engaged in "anti-Islamic activity," as Britain's former home secretary Jacqui Smith memorably put it. When the ongoing Islamization campaign is advanced by violence, as inevitably happens, we absurdly insist that this aggression cannot have been ideologically driven, that surely some American policy or Israeli act of self-defense is to blame, as if these could possibly provide rationales for the murderous jihad waged by Boko Haram Muslims against Nigerian Christians and by Egyptian Muslims against the Copts, the persecution of the Ahmadi sect by Indonesian and Pakistani Muslims, or the internecine killing in Iraq of Sunnis by Shiites and vice versa—a tradition nearly as old as Islam itself—which has been predictably renewed upon the recent departure of American troops.

The main lesson of the Arab Spring ought to be that this remaking of Islam has happened only in our own minds, for our own consumption. The Muslims of the Middle East take no note of our reimagining of Islam, being, in the main, either hostile toward or oblivious to Western overtures. Muslims do not measure themselves against Western perceptions, although the shrewdest among them take note of our eagerly accommodating attitude when determining what tactics will best advance the cause.

That cause is nothing less than Islamic dominance.

"The underlying problem for the West is not Islamic fundamentalism," wrote Samuel huntington. "It is Islam, a different civilization whose people are convinced of the superiority of their culture." Not convinced merely in the passive sense of assuming that they will triumph in the end, Muslim leaders are galvanized by what they take to be a divinely ordained mission of proselytism—and proselytism not limited to spiritual principles, but encompassing an all-purpose societal code prescribing rules for everything from warfare and finance to social interaction and personal hygiene. Historian Andrew Bostom notes that in the World War I era, even as the Ottoman empire collapsed and Atatürk symbolically extinguished the caliphate, C. Snouck Hurgronje, then the West's leading scholar of Islam, marveled that Muslims remained broadly confident in what he called the "idea of universal conquest." In Islam's darkest hour, this conviction remained "a central point of union against the unfaithful." It looms more powerful in today's Islamic ascendancy.

Of course, conventional wisdom in the West holds that the Arab Spring spontaneously combusted when Mohamed Bouazizi, a fruit vendor, set himself ablaze outside the offices of the Tunisian klepto-cops who had seized his wares. This suicide protest, the story goes, ignited a sweeping revolt against the corruption and caprices of Arab despots. One by one, the dominos began to fall: Tunisia, Egypt, Yemen, Libya—with rumblings in Saudi Arabia and Jordan as well as teetering Syria and rickety Iran. We are to believe that the mass uprising is an unmistakable manifestation of the "desire for freedom" that, according to Pres. George W. Bush, "resides in every human heart."

That proclamation came in the heady days of 2004, when the democracy project was still a Panglossian dream, not the Pandora's box it proved to be as Islamic parties began to win elections. Like its successor, the Bush administration discouraged all inquiry into Islamic doctrine by anyone seeking to understand Muslim enmity, indulging the fiction that there is something we can do to change it. Inexorably, this has fed President Obama's preferred fiction—that we must have done something to deserve it—as well as the current administration's strident objection to uttering the word "Islam" for any purpose other than hagiography. In this self-imposed ignorance, most Americans still do not know that *hurriya*, Arabic for "freedom," connotes "perfect slavery" or absolute submission to Allah, very nearly the opposite of the Western concept. Even if we grant for argument's sake the dubious proposition that all people crave freedom, Islam and the West have never agreed about what freedom means.

The first count of contemporary Muslims' indictment of Middle Eastern dictators is not that they have denied individual liberty, but that they have repressed Islam. This is not to say that other grievances are irrelevant. Muslims have indeed been outraged by the manner in which their Arafats, Mubaraks, Qaddafis, and Saddams looted the treasuries while the masses lived in squalor. But the agglomerations of wealth and other regime hypocrisies are framed for the masses more as sins against Allah's law than as the inevitable corruptions of absolute power. The most influential figures and institutions in Islamic societies are those revered for their mastery of Islamic law and jurisprudence—such authorities as top Muslim Brotherhood jurist Yusuf al-Qaradawi and Cairo's al-Azhar University, the seat of Sunni learning for over a millennium. In places where Islam is the central fact of life, even Muslims who privately dismiss sharia take pains to honor it publicly. Even regimes that rule by whim nod to sharia as the backbone of their legal systems, lace their rhetoric with scriptural allusions, and seek to rationalize their actions as Islamically appropriate.

If you understand this, you understand why Western beliefs about the Arab Spring—and the Western conceit that the death of one tyranny must herald the birth of liberty—have always been a delusion. There are real democrats, authentically moderate Muslims, and non-Muslims in places such as Egypt and Yemen who long for freedom in the Western sense; but the stubborn fact is that they make up a strikingly small fraction of the population: about 20 percent, a far cry from the Western narrative that posits a sea of Muslim moderates punctuated by the rare radical atoll.

The Muslim Brotherhood is the *ummah's* most important organization, unabashedly proclaiming for nearly 90 years that "the Koran is our law and jihad is our way." Hamas, a terrorist organization, is its Palestinian branch, and leading Brotherhood figures do little to disguise their abhorrence of Israel and Western culture. Thus, when spring fever gripped Tahrir Square, the Obama administration, European governments, and the Western media tirelessly repeated the mantra that the Brothers had been relegated to the sidelines. Time had purportedly passed the Islamists by, just as it was depositing Mubarak in the rear-view mirror. Surely the Tahrir throngs wanted self-determination, not sharia. Never you mind the fanatical chants of *Allahu akbar!* as the dictator fell. Never mind that Sheikh Qaradawi was promptly ushered into the square to deliver a fiery Friday sermon to a congregation of nearly a million Egyptians.

With a transitional military government in place and openly solicitous of the Brotherhood, there occurred the most telling, most tellingly underreported, and most willfully misreported story of the Arab Spring: a national referendum to determine the scheduling of elections that would select a new parliament and president, with a new constitution to follow. It sounds dry, but it was crucial. The most organized and disciplined factions in Egyptian life are the Brotherhood and self-proclaimed Muslim groups even more impatient for Islamization, collectively identified by the media as "Salafists" even though this term does not actually distinguish them from the Brothers, whose founder (Hassan al-Banna) was a leading Salafist thinker. By contrast, secular democratic reformers are in their infancy. Elections on a short schedule would obviously favor the former; the latter need time to take root and grow.

Egypt being Egypt, the election campaign was waged with the rhetoric of religious and cultural solidarity. A vote against a rapid transition was depicted as a vote "against Islam" and in favor of the dreaded Western hands said to be guiding the Christians and secularists. The vote was the perfect test of the Arab Spring narrative. Four-to-one: That's how it went. The democrats were wiped out by the Muslim parties, 78 percent to 22 percent. While Western officials dismissed the vote as involving scheduling arcana, it foretold everything that has followed: the electoral romp in the parliamentary elections, a multi-stage affair in which the Brotherhood and the Salafists are inching close to three-fourths control of the legislature; the ongoing pogrom against the Copts; and the increasing calls for renunciation of the Camp David Accords, which have kept the peace with Israel for more than 30 years.

Four-to-one actually proves to be a reliable ratio in examining Islamic developments. In a 2007 poll conducted by World Public Opinion in conjunction with the University of Maryland, 74 percent of Egyptians favored strict application of sharia in Muslim countries. It was 76 percent in Morocco, 79 percent in Pakistan, and 53 percent in moderate Indonesia. Before American forces vacated Iraq, roughly three-quarters of the people they had liberated regarded them as legitimate jihad targets, and, given the opportunity to vote, Iraqis installed Islamist parties who promised to hasten the end of American "occupation." Three out of four Palestinians deny Israel's right to exist. Even in our own country, a recently completed survey found that 80 percent of American mosques promote literature that endorses violent jihad, and that these same mosques counsel rigorous sharia compliance.

The Arab Spring is an unshackling of Islam, not an outbreak of fervor for freedom in the Western sense. Turkey's third-term prime minister Recep Erdogan, a staunch Brotherhood ally who rejects the notion that there is a "moderate Islam" ("Islam is Islam, and that's it," he says), once declared that "democracy is a train where you can get off when you reach your destination." The destination for Muslim supremacists is the implementation of sharia—the foundation of any Islamized society, and, eventually, of the reestablished caliphate.

The duration of the ride depends on the peculiar circumstances of each society. Erdogan's Turkey has become the model for Islamist gradualism in more challenging environments: Slowly but steadily bend the nation into sharia compliance while denying any intent to do so and singing the obligatory paeans to democracy. Erdogan came to this formula after no shortage of stumbles—it is now rare to hear such outbursts as "The mosques are our barracks, the domes our helmets, the minarets our bayonets, and the faithful our soldiers," the sort of thing he used to say in the late Nineties when he was imprisoned for sedition against Atatürk's secular order. His banned Welfare party eventually reemerged as the new and democracy-ready AKP, the Justice and Development party. Ever since a quirk in Turkish electoral law put these Islamists in power in 2002, Erdogan has cautiously but demonstrably eroded the secular framework Atatürk and his followers spent 80 years building, returning this ostensible NATO ally to the Islamist camp, shifting it from growing friendship to open hostility toward Israel, co-opting the military that was Atatürk's bulwark against Islamization, and salting the country's major institutions with Islamic supremacists. The Turkish model will be the ticket for Brotherhood parties that have just prevailed in Tunisian and Moroccan elections. In Tunisia, Rachid Ghannouchi, a cagey Islamist of the Erdogan stripe, heads the

Ennahda party, convincingly elected in October to control the legislature that will replace ousted ruler Zine el-Abidine Ben Ali. In Morocco, an Islamist party whose namesake is the AKP won the fall elections, but further Islamization is apt to be slower. Far from being driven from power, King Mohammed VI remains popular, having balanced his affinity for the West with deference to sharia norms. Moroccan Islamists are making significant inroads, though, as are their neighbors to the east. Algerian Islamists are poised to accede to power this spring after being thwarted by a military coup that blocked what would have been their certain electoral success in 1991.

Egypt, by contrast, will go quickly. There, the most salient development is not the weakness of secular democrats but the impressive electoral strength of the Salafists. Their numbers are competitive with those of the better-known Brothers, and they will tug their rivals in a more aggressively Islamist direction. Vainly, the West hoped that the country's American-trained and equipped armed forces would serve as a brake. But the Egyptian military, from which several top al-Qaeda operatives have hailed, is a reflection of Egyptian society, especially as one descends to the conscripts of lower rank. The undeniable trend in Egyptian society is toward Islam. That trend is more blatant only in such basket cases as Libya, where each day brings new evidence that today's governing "rebels" include yesterday's al-Qaeda jihadists, and in Yemen, the ancestral home of Osama bin Laden, where even *The New York Times* concedes al-Qaeda's strength.

Led by the Muslim Brotherhood, Islamic parties have become expert at presenting themselves as moderates and telling the West what it wants to hear while they gradually ensnare societies in the sharia web, as slowly or quickly as conditions on the ground permit. They know that when the West says "democracy," it means popular elections, not Western democratic culture. They know the West has so glorified these elections that the victors can steal them (Iran), refuse to relinquish power when later they lose (Iraq), or decline to hold further elections (Gaza) without forfeiting their legitimacy. They know that seizing the mantle of "democracy" casts Islamists as the West's heroes in the dramas still unfolding in Egypt, Libya, and Syria. They know that the Obama administration and the European Union have deluded themselves into believing that Islamists will be tamed by the responsibilities of governance. Once in power, they are sure to make virulent anti-Americanism their official policy and to contribute materially to the pan-Islamic goal of destroying Israel.

We should not be under any illusions about why things are shaking out this way. The Arab Spring has not been hijacked any more than Islam was hijacked by the suicide terrorists of 9/11. Islam is ascendant because that is the way Muslims of the Middle East want it.

Hillary Rodham Clinton

**NO**

# Keynote Address at the National Democratic Institute's 2011 Democracy Awards Dinner

**I** think it's important to recognize that back when the streets of Arab cities were quiet, the National Democratic Institute was already on the ground, building relationships, supporting the voices that would turn a long Arab winter into a new Arab Spring. Now, we may not know where and when brave people will claim their rights next, but it's a safe bet that NDI is there now, because freedom knows no better champion. More than a quarter-century old, NDI and its siblings in the National Endowment for Democracy family have become vital elements of America's engagement with the world. . . .

What a year 2011 has been for freedom in the Middle East and North Africa. We have seen what may well have been the first Arab revolution for democracy, then the second, then the third. And in Yemen, people are demanding a transition to democracy that they deserve to see delivered. And Syrians are refusing to relent until they, too, can decide their own future.

Throughout the Arab world this year, people have given each other courage. Old fears have melted away and men and women have begun making their demands in broad daylight. . . .

Now, in Tunis, Cairo, and a newly free Tripoli, I have met people lifted by a sense that their futures actually do belong to them. In my travels across the region, I have heard joy, purpose, and newfound pride.

But I've also heard questions. I've heard skepticism about American motives and commitments, people wondering if, after decades of working with the governments of the region, America doesn't—in our heart of hearts—actually long for the old days. I've heard from activists who think we aren't pushing hard enough for democratic change, and I've heard from government officials who think we're pushing too hard. I've heard from people asking why our policies vary from country to country, and what would happen if elections bring to power parties we don't agree with or people who just don't like us very much. I've heard people asking America to solve all their problems and others wondering whether we have any role to play at all. And beneath our excitement for the millions who are claiming the rights and freedoms we cherish, many Americans are asking the same questions.

I want to ask and answer a few of these tough questions. . . . As we live this history day by day, we approach these questions with a large dose of

Clinton, Hillary Rodham. From Remarks at the National Democratic Institute, November 7, 2011.

humility, because many of the choices ahead are, honestly, not ours to make. Still, it's worth stepping back and doing our best to speak directly to what is on people's minds.

So let me start with one question I hear often: Do we really believe that democratic change in the Middle East and North Africa is in America's interest? That is a totally fair question. After all, transitions are filled with uncertainty. They can be chaotic, unstable, even violent. And, even if they succeed, they are rarely linear, quick, or easy.

As we saw in the Balkans and again in Iraq, rivalries between members of different religions, sects, and tribes can resurface and explode. Toppling tyrants does not guarantee that democracy will follow, or that it will last. Just ask the Iranians who overthrew a dictator 32 years ago only to have their revolution hijacked by the extremists who have oppressed them ever since. And even where democracy does takes hold, it is a safe bet that some of those elected will not embrace us or agree with our policies.

And yet, as President [Barack] Obama said at the State Department in May, "It will be the policy of the United States to promote reform across the region and to support transitions to democracy." We believe that real democratic change in the Middle East and North Africa is in the national interest of the United States. And here's why.

We begin by rejecting the false choice between progress and stability. For years, dictators told their people they had to accept the autocrats they knew to avoid the extremists they feared. And too often, we accepted that narrative ourselves. Now, America did push for reform, but often not hard enough or publicly enough. And today, we recognize that the real choice is between reform and unrest.

Last January [2011], I told Arab leaders that the region's foundations were sinking into the sand. Even if we didn't know exactly how or when the breaking point would come, it was clear that the status quo was unsustainable because of changes in demography and technology, high unemployment, endemic corruption and a lack of human rights and fundamental freedoms. After a year of revolutions broadcast on Al Jazeera [an Arab-language network headquartered in Qatar] into homes from Rabat [Morocco] to Riyadh [Saudi Arabia], going back to the way things were in December 2010 isn't just undesirable. It's impossible.

The truth is that the greatest single source of instability in today's Middle East is not the demand for change. It is the refusal to change. That is certainly true in Syria, where a crackdown on small, peaceful protests drove thousands into the streets and thousands more over the borders. It is true in Yemen, where President [Ali Abdullah] Saleh has reneged repeatedly on his promises to transition to democracy and suppressed his people's rights and freedoms. And it is true in Egypt. If—over time—the most powerful political force in Egypt remains a roomful of unelected officials, they will have planted the seeds for future unrest, and Egyptians will have missed a historic opportunity.

And so will we, because democracies make for stronger and more stable partners. They trade more, innovate more, and fight less. They help divided societies to air and hopefully resolve their differences. They hold inept leaders accountable at the polls. They channel people's energies away from extremism and toward political and civic engagement. Now, democracies do not always agree with us, and in the Middle East and North Africa they may disagree strongly with some of our policies. But at the end of the day, it is no coincidence that our closest allies—from Britain to South Korea—are democracies.

Now, we do work with many different governments to pursue our interests and to keep Americans safe—and certainly not all of them are democracies. But as the fall of Hosni Mubarak in Egypt made clear, the enduring cooperation we seek will be difficult to sustain without democratic legitimacy and public consent. We cannot have one set of policies to advance security in the here-and-now and another to promote democracy in a long run that never quite arrives.

So for all these reasons, as I said back in March [2011], opening political systems, societies, and economies is not simply a matter of idealism. It is a strategic necessity. But we are not simply acting in our self-interest. Americans believe that the desire for dignity and self-determination is universal—and we do try to act on that belief around the world. Americans have fought and died for these ideals. And when freedom gains ground anywhere, Americans are inspired.

So the risks posed by transitions will not keep us from pursuing positive change. But they do raise the stakes for getting it right. Free, fair, and meaningful elections are essential—but they are not enough if they bring new autocrats to power or disenfranchise minorities. And any democracy that does not include half its population—its women—is a contradiction in terms. Durable democracies depend on strong civil societies, respect for the rule of law, independent institutions, free expression, and a free press. Legitimate political parties cannot have a militia wing and a political wing. Parties have to accept the results of free and fair elections. And this is not just in the Middle East. In Liberia, the leading opposition party is making unsubstantiated charges of fraud and refusing to accept first round voting in which it came in second. And this is already having harmful consequences on the ground. We urge all parties in Liberia to accept the will of the people in the next round of voting tomorrow. That is what democracy anywhere requires.

And that brings me to my second question. Why does America promote democracy one way in some countries and another way in others? Well, the answer starts with a very practical point: situations vary dramatically from country to country. It would be foolish to take a one-size-fits-all approach and barrel forward regardless of circumstances on the ground. Sometimes, as in Libya, we can bring dozens of countries together to protect civilians and help people liberate their country without a single American life lost. In other cases, to achieve that same goal, we would have to act alone, at a much greater cost, with far greater risks, and perhaps even with troops on the ground.

But that's just part of the answer. Our choices also reflect other interests in the region with a real impact on Americans' lives—including our fight against al-Qaeda, defense of our allies, and a secure supply of energy. Over time, a more democratic Middle East and North Africa can provide a more sustainable basis for addressing all three of those challenges. But there will be times when not all of our interests align. We work to align them, but that is just reality.

As a country with many complex interests, we'll always have to walk and chew gum at the same time. That is our challenge in a country like Bahrain, which has been America's close friend and partner for decades. And yet, President Obama and I have been frank, in public and in private, that mass arrests and brute force are at odds with the universal rights of Bahrain's citizens and will not make legitimate calls for reform go away. Meaningful reform and equal treatment for all Bahrainis are in Bahrain's interest, in the region's interest, and in ours—while endless unrest benefits Iran and extremists. The government has recognized the need for dialogue, reconciliation, and concrete reforms. And they have committed to provide access to human rights groups, to allow peaceful protest, and to ensure that those who cross lines in responding to civil unrest are held accountable. King Hamad called for an independent commission of inquiry, which will issue its report soon. And we do intend to hold the Bahraini Government to these commitments and to encourage the opposition to respond constructively to secure lasting reform. We also have candid conversations with others in the neighborhood, like Saudi Arabia—a country that is key to stability and peace—about our view that democratic advancement is not just possible but a necessary part of preparing for the future.

Fundamentally, there is a right side of history. And we want to be on it. And—without exception—we want our partners in the region to reform so that they are on it as well. Now, we don't expect countries to do this overnight, but without reforms, we are convinced their challenges will only grow. So it is in their interest to begin now.

These questions about our interests and consistency merge in a third difficult question: How will America respond if and when democracy brings to power people and parties we disagree with?

We hear these questions most often when it comes to Islamist religious parties. Now, of course, I hasten to add that not all Islamists are alike. Turkey and Iran are both governed by parties with religious roots, but their models and behavior are radically different. There are plenty of political parties with religious affiliations—Hindu, Christian, Jewish, Muslim—that respect the rules of democratic politics. The suggestion that faithful Muslims cannot thrive in a democracy is insulting, dangerous, and wrong. They do it in this country every day.

Now, reasonable people can disagree on a lot, but there are things that all parties, religious and secular, must get right—not just for us to trust them, but most importantly for the people of the region and of the countries themselves to trust them to protect their hard-won rights.

Parties committed to democracy must reject violence; they must abide by the rule of law and respect the freedoms of speech, religion, association, and assembly; they must respect the rights of women and minorities; they must let go of power if defeated at the polls; and in a region with deep divisions within and between religions, they cannot be the spark that starts a conflagration. In other words, what parties call themselves is less important to us than what they actually do. . . .

In Tunisia, an Islamist party has just won a plurality of the votes in an open, competitive election. Its leaders have promised to embrace freedom of religion and full rights for women. To write a constitution and govern, they will have to persuade secular parties to work with them. And as they do, America will work with them, too, because we share the desire to see a Tunisian democracy emerge that delivers for its citizens and because America respects the right of the Tunisian people to choose their own leaders.

And so we move forward with clear convictions. Parties and candidates must respect the rules of democracy, to take part in elections, and hold elective office. And no one has the right to use the trappings of democracy to deny the rights and security of others. People throughout the region worry about this prospect, and so do we. Nobody wants another Iran. Nobody wants to see political parties with military wings and militant foreign policies gain influence. When members of any group seek to oppress their fellow citizens or undermine core democratic principles, we will stand on the side of the people who push back to defend their democracy.

And that brings me to my next question: What is America's role in the Arab Spring? These revolutions are not ours. They are not by us, for us, or against us, but we do have a role. We have the resources, capabilities, and expertise to support those who seek peaceful, meaningful, democratic reform. And with so much that can go wrong, and so much that can go right, support for emerging Arab democracies is an investment we cannot afford not to make.

Now, of course, we have to be smart in how we go about it. For example, as tens of millions of young people enter the job market each year, we recognize that the Arab political awakening must also deliver an economic awakening. And we are working to help societies create jobs to ensure that it does. We are promoting trade, investment, regional integration, entrepreneurship, and economic reforms. We are helping societies fight corruption and replace the old politics of patronage with a new focus on economic empowerment and opportunity. And we are working with Congress on debt relief for Egypt and loan guarantees for Tunisia so that these countries can invest in their own futures.

We also have real expertise to offer as a democracy. . . . Democracies, after all, aren't born knowing how to run themselves. In a country like Libya, [dictator Muammar] Qadhafi spent 42 years hollowing out every part of his government not connected to oil or to keeping him in power. Under the Libyan penal code, simply joining an NGO [international nongovernmental organization] could be punishable by death. When I traveled last month to Libya, the students I met at Tripoli University had all sorts of practical, even technical, questions: How do you form a political party? How do you ensure women's participation in government institutions? What recommendations do you have for citizens in a democracy?

These are questions NDI and its kindred organizations, many of whom are represented here tonight, are uniquely qualified to help new democracies answer. NDI has earned a lot of praise for this work, but also a lot of pushback that stretches far beyond the Arab world. In part, this resistance comes from misconceptions about what our support for democracy does and does not include.

The United States does not fund political candidates or political parties. We do offer training to parties and candidates committed to democracy. We do not try to shift outcomes or impose an American model. We do support election commissions, as well as nongovernmental election monitors, to ensure free and fair balloting. We help watchdog groups learn their trade. We help groups find the tools to exercise their rights to free expression and assembly, online and off. And of course we support civil society, the lifeblood of democratic politics. . . .

We all know a great deal of work lies ahead to help all people, women and men, find justice and opportunity as full participants in new democratic societies. Along with our economic and technical help, America will also use our presence, influence, and global leadership to support change. And later this week, I am issuing new policy guidance to our embassies across the region to structure our efforts.

In Tunisia, Egypt, and Libya, we are working to help citizens safeguard the principles of democracy. That means supporting the forces of reconciliation rather than retribution. It means defending freedom of expression when bloggers are arrested for criticizing public officials. It means standing up for tolerance when state-run television fans sectarian tensions. And it means that when unelected authorities say they want to be out of the business of governing, we will look to them to lay out a clear roadmap and urge them to abide by it.

Where countries are making gradual reforms, we have frank conversations and urge them to move faster. It's good to hold multi-party elections and allow women to take part. It's better when those elections are meaningful and parliaments have real powers to improve people's lives. Change needs to be tangible and real. When autocrats tell us the transition to democracy will take time, we answer, "Well, then let's get started."

And those leaders trying to hold back the future at the point of a gun should know their days are numbered. As Syrians gather to celebrate a sacred holiday, their government continues to shoot people in the streets. In the week since [Syria's President] Bashar al-Asad said he accepted the terms of an Arab League peace plan to protect Syrian civilians, he has systematically violated each of its basic requirements. He has not released all detainees. He has not allowed free and unfettered access to journalists or Arab League monitors. He has not withdrawn all armed forces from populated areas. And he has certainly not stopped all acts of violence. In fact, the regime has increased violence against civilians in places like the city of Homs. Now, Asad may be able to delay change. But he cannot deny his people's legitimate demands indefinitely. He must step down; and until he does, America and the international community will continue to increase pressure on him and his brutal regime.

And for all of Iran's bluster, there is no country in the Middle East where the gulf between rulers and ruled is greater. When Iran claims to support democracy abroad, then kills peaceful protestors in the streets of Tehran, its hypocrisy is breathtaking and plain to the people of the region.

And there is one last question that I'm asked, in one form or another, all the time: What about the rights and aspirations of the Palestinians? Israelis and Palestinians are not immune to the profound changes sweeping the region. And make no mistake, President Obama and I believe that the Palestinian people—just like their Arab neighbors, just like Israelis, just like us—deserve dignity, liberty, and the right to decide their own future. They deserve an independent, democratic Palestinian state of their own, alongside a secure Jewish democracy next door. And we know from decades in the diplomatic trenches that the only way to get there is through a negotiated peace—a peace we work every day to achieve, despite all the setbacks.

Of course, we understand that Israel faces risks in a changing region—just as it did before the Arab Spring began. And it will remain an American priority to ensure that all parties honor the peace treaties they have signed and commitments they have made. And we will always help Israel defend itself. We will address threats to regional peace whether they come from dictatorships or democracies. But it would be shortsighted to think either side can simply put peacemaking on hold until the current upheaval is done. The truth is, the stalemate in the Arab–Israeli conflict is one more status quo in the Middle East that cannot be sustained.

This brings me to my last and perhaps most important point of all. For all the hard questions I've asked and tried to answer on behalf of the United States, the most consequential questions of all are those the people and leaders of the region will have to answer for themselves. Because, ultimately, it is up to them. It is up to them to resist the calls of demagogues, to build coalitions, to keep faith in the system even when they lose at the polls, and to protect the principles and institutions that ultimately will protect them. Every democracy has to guard against those who would hijack its freedoms for ignoble ends. Our founders and every generation since have fought to prevent that from happening here. The founding fathers and mothers of Arab revolutions must do the same. No one bears a greater responsibility for what happens next.

When Deputy Secretary Bill Burns addressed the National Endowment for Democracy over the summer, he recounted the story of an Egyptian teenager who told her father a few years back that she wanted to spend her life bringing democracy to Egypt. "Good," her father said, "because then you will always have a job."

Now, we should never fall prey to the belief that human beings anywhere are not ready for freedom. In the 1970s, people said Latin America and East Asia were not ready. Well, the 1980s began proving them wrong. In the 1980s, it was African soil where democracy supposedly couldn't grow. And the 1990s started proving them wrong. And until this year, some people said Arabs don't really want democracy. Well, starting in 2011, that too is being proved wrong. And funnily enough, it proved that Egyptian father right, because we all still have a job to do.

So we have to keep at it. We have to keep asking the tough questions. We have to be honest with ourselves and with each other about the answers we offer. And we cannot waver in our commitment to help the people of the Middle East and North Africa realize their own God-given potentials and the dreams they risked so much to make real.

And on this journey that they have begun, the United States will be their partner. And of the many tools at our disposal—the National Endowment and NDI and all of the family of organizations that were created three decades ago to help people make this journey successfully—will be right there. . . .

So there are going to be a lot of bumps along this road. But far better that we travel this path, that we do what we can to make sure that our ideals and values, our belief and experience with democracy, are shared widely and well. It's an exciting time. It's an uncertain time. But it's a good time for the United States of America to be standing for freedom and democracy. . . .

# EXPLORING THE ISSUE

## Does the Islamist Movement Threaten the Democracy Gained in the "Arab Spring"?

## Questions for Critical Thinking and Reflection

1. A survey in 2011 that asked "Should the United States try to change a dictatorship to a democracy where it can, or should the United States stay out of other countries' affairs?" found that 15 percent of Americans favored trying to help, while 70 percent favored not taking action. Which position do you hold? Why?
2. Which should be more important in determining the U.S. position on the possible transition of any government or type of government of another country: whether the new government will be democratic or whether it will be friendly toward the United States?
3. If a government is popularly elected and allows opposition, two key requirements of a democracy, but suppresses women's rights, religious freedom, or other civil and political liberties, is that government democratic and deserving of U.S. support?

## Is There Common Ground?

With less than two years having passed since the Arab Spring began in December 2010, it is too early to tell how far it will go. Will the democratization movement topple more of the authoritarian governments in the region? And will the newly democratic governments in Tunisia, Egypt, and Libya survive as democracies or become theocracies or some other form of oppressive regime? A first sign came in the October 2011 parliamentary elections in Tunisia. There the Ennahda party/movement far outdistanced other parties, winning 40 percent of the vote and 89 of the new legislature's 217 seats. Most Ennahda leaders proclaim that while they favor Islam playing a stronger role in Tunisian society and government, they also support civil rights and support democracy. Not everyone is fully reassured. As one Tunisian secularist and liberal told a reporter, Ennahda leaders "say they want to be like [mostly secular] Turkey, but it could turn out like [largely theocratic] Iran."

The next and perhaps most important omen has been Egypt. In parliamentary elections beginning in late November 2011, the Freedom and Justice Party (FJP) of the Islamist Muslim Brotherhood movement, its allies, and other Islamist parties won 64 percent of the seats. In the following presidential election, FJP party candidate Mohamed Morsi was elected with 52 percent of the vote and took office on June 30, 2012. Disturbed by the election, Egypt's top military commanders moved to curb the powers of the president and make him nearly a figurehead, but Morsi outmaneuvered them and eventually replaced them. Which way Egypt will go remains unclear, an uncertainty that is reflected to a degree in the draft constitution that the country is considering as of this writing in late 2012. On the one hand the draft constitution, which was written by an Islamist-dominated commission, seems to ensure democracy and an admirable range of human rights and political rights. But the document also, in the view of some, makes the law subordinate to the *sharia,* Islamic religious law. The NO selection states, "Islam is the state religion, Arabic is the official language, and the principles of Islamic sharia are the main source of legislation." The constitution also recognizes the role of Al-Azhar, the leading center of Islamic thought in Egypt, as the interpreter of the sharia that could trump secular law. With respect to women's rights, for example, the constitution requires the government to "take all measures to establish the equality of women and men," but then adds, "insofar as this does not conflict with the rulings of Islamic sharia."

For the Untied States, the most immediate negative impact of the changes in the Middle East came on September 11, 2012, when Islamist radicals attacked the U.S. consulate in Benghazi, Libya, killing several Americans including U.S. Ambassador Chris Stevens. Libya's weak central government condemned the attack, but has not arrested anyone for it.

## Additional Resources

There are a host of published and web commentaries taking optimistic or pessimistic views of the Arab Spring. A reasonably balanced view is Fouad Ajami, "The Arab Spring at One: A Year of Living Dangerously," *Foreign Affairs* (March/April 2012). Also read Michael J. Totten, "Arab Spring or Islamist Winter?" *World Affairs* (January/February 2012). Insight into the view of the people of the Middle East is available in Mark Tessler, *Public Opinion in the Middle East: Survey Research and the Political Orientations of Ordinary Citizens* (Indiana University Press, 2011).

# Internet References . . .

## IPE NET

The International Political Economy Network, hosted by Indiana University and sponsored by the IPE section of the International Studies Association, is a good starting point to study the intersection of politics and economics globally.

**www.indiana.edu/~ipe/ipesection/**

## United Nations Development Programme (UNDP)

This United Nations Development Programme (UNDP) site offers publications and current information on world poverty, the UNDP's mission statement, information on the UN Development Fund for Women, and more.

**www.undp.org**

## Office of the U.S. Trade Representative

The Office of the U.S. Trade Representative (USTR) is responsible for developing and coordinating U.S. international trade, commodity, and direct investment policy and leading or directing negotiations with other countries on such matters. The U.S. trade representative is a cabinet member who acts as the principal trade adviser, negotiator, and spokesperson for the president on trade and related investment matters.

**www.ustr.gov**

## World Trade Organization (WTO)

The World Trade Organization (WTO) is the only international organization dealing with the global rules of trade between nations. Its main function is to ensure that trade flows as smoothly, predictably, and freely as possible. This site provides extensive information about the organization and international trade today.

**www.wto.org**

## Third World Network

The Third World Network (TWN) is an independent, nonprofit international network of organizations and individuals involved in economic, social, and environmental issues relating to development, the developing countries of the world, and the North–South divide. At the Network's website you will find recent news, TWN position papers, action alerts, and other resources on a variety of topics, including economics, trade, and health.

**www.twnside.org.sg**

# Economic Issues

*I*nternational economic and trade issues have an immediate and personal effect on individuals in ways that few other international issues do.
They influence the jobs we hold and the prices of the products we buy—
in short, our lifestyles. In the worldwide competition for resources and
markets, tensions arise between allies and adversaries alike. This section
examines some of the prevailing economic tensions.

- Is Economic Globalization Good for Both Rich and Poor?

- Does China's Currency Manipulation Warrant International and National
  Action?

# ISSUE 8

# Is Economic Globalization Good for Both Rich and Poor?

**YES: International Monetary Fund Staff**, from "Globalization: A Brief Overview," *Issues Brief* (May 2008)

**NO: Ravinder Rena**, from "Globalization Still Hurting Poor Nations," *Africa Economic Analysis* (January 2008)

### ISSUE SUMMARY

**YES:** Staff members of the International Monetary Fund conclude on the basis of experiences across the world that unhindered international economic interchange, the core principle of globalization, seems to underpin greater prosperity.

**NO:** Ravinder Rena, an associate professor of economics at the Eritrea Institute of Technology, contends that globalization creates losers as well as winners and the losers are disproportionately found among the world's poorer countries.

**G**lobalization is a process that is diminishing many of the factors that divide the world. Advances in travel and communication have made geographical distances less important; people around the world increasingly resemble one another culturally; and the United Nations and other international organizations have increased the level of global governance. Another aspect, economic integration, is the most advanced of any of the strands of globalization. Tariffs and other barriers to trade have decreased significantly since the end of World War II. As a result, all aspects of international economic exchange have grown rapidly. For example, global trade, measured in the value of exported goods and services, has grown about 2000 percent since the mid-twentieth century and now comes to over $15 trillion annually. International investment in real estate and stocks and bonds in other countries, and in total, now exceeds $25 trillion. The flow of currencies is so massive that there is no accurate measure, but it certainly is more than $1.5 trillion a day.

In this liberalized atmosphere, huge multinational corporations (MNCs) have come to dominate global commerce. Just the top 500 MNCs have combined annual sales of over $15 trillion. The impact of all these changes is that the economic prosperity of almost all countries and the individuals within them is heavily dependent on what they import and export, the flow of investment in and out of each country, and the exchange rates of the currency of each country against the currencies of other countries.

The issue here is whether this economic globalization and integration is a positive or negative trend. For more than 60 years, the United States has been at the center of the drive to open international commerce. The push to reduce trade barriers that occurred during and after World War II was designed to prevent a recurrence of the global economic collapse of the 1930s and the war of the 1940s. Policymakers believed that protectionism caused the Great Depression, that the ensuing human desperation provided fertile ground for the rise of dictators who blamed scapegoats for what had occurred and who promised national salvation, and that these fascist dictators had set off World War II. In sum, policymakers thought that protectionism caused economic depression, which caused dictators, which caused war. They believed that free trade, by contrast, would promote prosperity, democracy, and peace.

Based on these political and economic theories, American policymakers took the lead in establishing a new international economic system, including helping to found such leading global economic organizations as the International Monetary Fund (IMF), the World Bank, and the World Trade Organization (WTO). During the entire latter half of the twentieth century, the movement toward economic globalization was strong, and there were few influential voices opposing it.

In the following selection, members of the IMF staff contend that there is substantial evidence, from countries of different sizes and with different regions, that suggests that as nations globalize, their citizens benefit because they gain "access to a wider variety of goods and services, lower prices, more and more better-paying jobs, improved health, and higher overall living standards." Not everyone agrees, though, and in recent years the idea that globalization is necessarily beneficial has come under increasing scrutiny and has met with increasing resistance. Within countries, globalization has benefited some, whereas others have lost jobs to imports and suffered other negative consequences. Similarly, some countries, notably those in sub-Saharan Africa, have not prospered. Reflecting this uneven impact, one line of criticism of globalization comes from those who believe that the way global politics work is a function of how the world is organized economically. These critics contend that people within countries are divided into "haves" and "have-nots" and that the world is similarly divided into have and have-not countries. Moreover, these critics believe that, both domestically and internationally, the wealthy haves are using globalization to keep the have-nots weak and poor in order to exploit them. Representing this view, Ravinder Rena argues in the second selection that globalization is not a panacea for world economic development because it broadens the gap between rich and poor and creates other distortions in the global economy.

# YES ↵

IMF Staff

# Globalization: A Brief Overview

A perennial challenge facing all of the world's countries, regardless of their level of economic development, is achieving financial stability, economic growth, and higher living standards. There are many different paths that can be taken to achieve these objectives, and every country's path will be different given the distinctive nature of national economies and political systems. The ingredients contributing to China's high growth rate over the past two decades have, for example, been very different from those that have contributed to high growth in countries as varied as Malaysia and Malta.

Yet, based on experiences throughout the world, several basic principles seem to underpin greater prosperity. These include investment (particularly foreign direct investment) [owning foreign companies or real estate], the spread of technology, strong institutions, sound macroeconomic policies, an educated workforce, and the existence of a market economy. Furthermore, a common denominator which appears to link nearly all high-growth countries together is their participation in, and integration with, the global economy.

There is substantial evidence, from countries of different sizes and different regions, that as countries "globalize" their citizens benefit, in the form of access to a wider variety of goods and services, lower prices, more and better-paying jobs, improved health, and higher overall living standards. It is probably no mere coincidence that over the past 20 years, as a number of countries have become more open to global economic forces, the percentage of the developing world living in extreme poverty—defined as living on less than $1 per day—has been cut in half.

As much as has been achieved in connection with globalization, there is much more to be done. Regional disparities persist: while poverty fell in East and South Asia, it actually rose in sub-Saharan Africa. The UN's Human Development Report notes there are still around 1 billion people surviving on less than $1 per day—with 2.6 billion living on less than $2 per day. Proponents of globalization argue that this is not because of too much globalization, but rather too little. And the biggest threat to continuing to raise living standards throughout the world is not that globalization will succeed but that it will fail. It is the people of developing economies who have the greatest need for globalization, as it provides them with the opportunities that come with being part of the world economy.

These opportunities are not without risks—such as those arising from volatile capital movements. The International Monetary Fund works to help economies manage or reduce these risks, through economic analysis and policy advice and through technical assistance in areas such as macroeconomic policy, financial sector sustainability, and the exchange-rate system.

The risks are not a reason to reverse direction, but for all concerned—in developing and advanced countries, among both investors and recipients—to embrace policy changes to build strong economies and a stronger world financial system that will produce more rapid growth and ensure that poverty is reduced.

The following is a brief overview to help guide anyone interested in gaining a better understanding of the many issues associated with globalization.

# What Is Globalization?

Economic "globalization" is a historical process, the result of human innovation and technological progress. It refers to the increasing integration of economies around the world, particularly through the movement of goods, services, and capital across borders. The term sometimes also refers to the movement of people (labor) and knowledge (technology) across international borders. There are also broader cultural, political, and environmental dimensions of globalization.

The term "globalization" began to be used more commonly in the 1980s, reflecting technological advances that made it easier and quicker to complete international transactions—both trade and financial flows. It refers to an extension beyond national borders of the same market forces that have operated for centuries at all levels of human economic activity—village markets, urban industries, or financial centers.

There are countless indicators that illustrate how goods, capital, and people have become more globalized.

- The value of trade (goods and services) as a percentage of world GDP [gross domestic product: the value of all goods and services produced within an economic unit] increased from 42.1 percent in 1980 to 62.1 percent in 2007.
- Foreign direct investment increased from 6.5 percent of world GDP in 1980 to 31.8 percent in 2006.
- The stock of international claims (primarily bank loans), as a percentage of world GDP, increased from roughly 10 percent in 1980 to 48 percent in 2006.
- The number of minutes spent on cross-border telephone calls, on a per-capita basis, increased from 7.3 in 1991 to 28.8 in 2006.
- The number of foreign workers has increased from 78 million people (2.4 percent of the world population) in 1965 to 191 million people (3.0 percent of the world population) in 2005.

The growth in global markets has helped to promote efficiency through competition and the division of labor—the specialization that allows people and economies to focus on what they do best. Global markets also offer greater opportunity for people to tap into more diversified and larger markets around the world. It means that they can have access to more capital, technology, cheaper imports, and larger export markets. But markets do not necessarily ensure that the benefits of increased efficiency are shared by all. Countries must be prepared to embrace the policies needed, and, in the case of the poorest countries, may need the support of the international community as they do so. The broad reach of globalization easily extends to daily choices of personal, economic, and political life. For example, greater access to modern technologies, in the world of health care, could make the difference between life and death. In the world of communications, it would facilitate commerce and education, and allow access to independent media. Globalization can also create a framework for cooperation among nations on a range of non-economic issues that have cross-border implications, such as immigration, the environment, and legal issues. At the same time, the influx of foreign goods, services, and capital into a country can create incentives and demands for strengthening the education system, as a country's citizens recognize the competitive challenge before them.

Perhaps more importantly, globalization implies that information and knowledge get dispersed and shared.

Innovators—be they in business or government—can draw on ideas that have been successfully implemented in one jurisdiction and tailor them to suit their own jurisdiction. Just as important, they can avoid the ideas that have a clear track record of failure. Joseph Stiglitz, a Nobel laureate and frequent critic of globalization, has nonetheless observed that globalization "has reduced the sense of isolation felt in much of the developing world and has given many people in the developing world access to knowledge well beyond the reach of even the wealthiest in any country a century ago."

## International Trade

A core element of globalization is the expansion of world trade through the elimination or reduction of trade barriers, such as import tariffs. Greater imports offer consumers a wider variety of goods at lower prices, while providing strong incentives for domestic industries to remain competitive. Exports, often a source of economic growth for developing nations, stimulate job creation as industries sell beyond their borders. More generally, trade enhances national competitiveness by driving workers to focus on those vocations where they, and their country, have a competitive advantage. Trade promotes economic resilience and flexibility, as higher imports help to offset adverse domestic supply shocks. Greater openness can also stimulate foreign investment, which would be a source of employment for the local workforce and could bring along new technologies—thus promoting higher productivity.

Restricting international trade—that is, engaging in protectionism—generates adverse consequences for a country that undertakes such a policy. For example, tariffs raise the prices of imported goods, harming consumers, many of which may be poor. Protectionism also tends to reward concentrated, well-organized and politically-connected groups, at the expense of those whose interests may be more diffuse (such as consumers). It also reduces the variety of goods available and generates inefficiency by reducing competition and encouraging resources to flow into protected sectors.

Developing countries can benefit from an expansion in international trade. Ernesto Zedillo, the former president of Mexico, has observed that, "In every case where a poor nation has significantly overcome its poverty, this has been achieved while engaging in production for export markets and opening itself to the influx of foreign goods, investment, and technology."

And the trend is clear. In the late 1980s, many developing countries began to dismantle their barriers to international trade, as a result of poor economic performance under protectionist polices and various economic crises. In the 1990s, many former Eastern bloc countries integrated into the global trading system and developing Asia—one of the most closed regions to trade in 1980—progressively dismantled barriers to trade. Overall, while the average tariff rate applied by developing countries is higher than that applied by advanced countries, it has declined significantly over the last several decades.

# The Implications of Globalized Financial Markets

The world's financial markets have experienced a dramatic increase in globalization in recent years. Global capital flows fluctuated between 2 and 6 percent of world GDP during the period 1980–95, but since then they have risen to 14.8 percent of GDP, and in 2006 they totaled $7.2 trillion, more than tripling since 1995. The most rapid increase has been experienced by advanced economies, but emerging markets and developing countries have also become more financially integrated. As countries have strengthened their capital markets they have attracted more investment capital, which can enable a broader entrepreneurial class to develop, facilitate a more efficient allocation of capital, encourage international risk sharing, and foster economic growth. Yet there is an energetic debate underway, among leading academics and policy experts, on the precise impact of financial globalization. Some see it as a catalyst for economic growth and stability. Others see it as injecting dangerous—and often costly—volatility into the economies of growing middle-income countries.

A recent paper by the IMF's Research Department takes stock of what is known about the effects of financial globalization. The analysis of the past 30 years of data reveals two main lessons for countries to consider.

First, the findings support the view that countries must carefully weigh the risks and benefits of unfettered capital flows. The evidence points to largely unambiguous gains from financial integration for advanced economies. In emerging and developing countries, certain factors are likely to influence the effect of financial globalization on economic volatility and growth: countries with well-developed financial sectors, strong institutions, sound macroeconomic policies, and substantial trade openness are more likely to gain from financial liberalization and less likely to risk increased macroeconomic volatility and to experience financial crises. For example, well-developed financial markets help moderate boom-bust cycles that can be triggered by surges and sudden stops in international capital flows, while strong domestic institutions and sound macroeconomic policies help attract "good" capital, such as portfolio equity flows and FDI.

The second lesson to be drawn from the study is that there are also costs associated with being overly cautious about opening to capital flows. These costs include lower international trade, higher investment costs for firms, poorer economic incentives, and additional administrative/monitoring costs. Opening up to foreign investment may encourage changes in the domestic economy that eliminate these distortions and help foster growth.

Looking forward, the main policy lesson that can be drawn from these results is that capital account liberalization should be pursued as part of a broader reform package encompassing a country's macroeconomic policy framework, domestic financial system, and prudential regulation. Moreover, long-term, non-debt-creating flows, such as FDI, should be liberalized before short-term, debt-creating inflows. Countries should still weigh the possible risks involved in opening up to capital flows against the efficiency costs associated with controls, but under certain conditions (such as good institutions, sound domestic and foreign policies, and developed financial markets) the benefits from financial globalization are likely to outweigh the risks.

## Globalization, Income Inequality, and Poverty

As some countries have embraced globalization, and experienced significant income increases, other countries that have rejected globalization, or embraced it only tepidly, have fallen behind. A similar phenomenon is at work within countries—some people have, inevitably, been bigger beneficiaries of globalization than others.

Over the past two decades, income inequality has risen in most regions and countries. At the same time, per capita incomes have risen across virtually all regions for even the poorest segments of populations, indicating that the poor are better off in an absolute sense during this phase of globalization, although incomes for the relatively well off have increased at a faster pace. Consumption data from groups of developing countries reveal the striking inequality that exists between the richest and the poorest in populations across different regions.

As discussed in the October 2007 issue of the *World Economic Outlook*, one must keep in mind that there are many sources of inequality. Contrary to popular belief, increased trade globalization is associated with a decline in inequality. The spread of technological advances and increased financial globalization—and foreign direct investment in particular—have instead contributed more to the recent rise in inequality by raising the demand for skilled labor and increasing the returns to skills in both developed and developing countries. Hence, while everyone benefits, those with skills benefit more.

It is important to ensure that the gains from globalization are more broadly shared across the population. To this effect, reforms to strengthen education and training would help ensure that workers have the appropriate skills for the evolving global economy. Policies that broaden the access of finance to the poor would also help, as would further trade liberalization that boosts agricultural exports from developing countries. Additional programs may include providing adequate income support to cushion, but not obstruct, the process of change, and also making health care less dependent on continued employment and increasing the portability of pension benefits in some countries.

Equally important, globalization should not be rejected because its impact has left some people unemployed. The dislocation may be a function of forces that have little to do with globalization and more to do with inevitable technological progress. And, the number of people who "lose" under globalization is likely to be outweighed by the number of people who "win."

Martin Wolf, the *Financial Times* columnist, highlights one of the fundamental contradictions inherent in those who bemoan inequality, pointing out that this charge amounts to arguing "that it would be better for everybody to be equally poor than for some to become significantly better off, even if, in the long run, this will almost certainly lead to advances for everybody."

Indeed, globalization has helped to deliver extraordinary progress for people living in developing nations. One of the most authoritative studies of the subject has been carried out by World Bank economists David Dollar and Aart Kraay. They concluded that since 1980, globalization has contributed to a reduction in poverty as well as a reduction in global income inequality. They found that in "globalizing" countries in the developing world, income per person grew three-and-a-half times faster than in "non-globalizing" countries, during the 1990s. In general, they noted, "higher growth rates in globalizing developing countries have translated into higher incomes for the poor." Dollar and Kraay also found that in virtually all events in which a country experienced growth at a rate of two percent or more, the income of the poor rose.

Critics point to those parts of the world that have achieved few gains during this period and highlight it as a failure of globalization. But that is to misdiagnose the problem. While serving as Secretary-General of the United Nations, Kofi Annan pointed out that "the main losers in today's very unequal world are not those who are too much exposed to globalization. They are those who have been left out."

A recent BBC World Service poll found that on average 64 percent of those polled—in 27 out of 34 countries—held the view that the benefits and burdens of "the economic developments of the last few years" have not been shared fairly. In developed countries, those who have this view of unfairness are more likely to say that globalization is growing too quickly. In contrast, in some developing countries, those who perceive such unfairness are more likely to say globalization is proceeding too slowly. As individuals and institutions work to raise living standards throughout the world, it will be critically important to create a climate that enables these countries to realize maximum benefits from globalization. That means focusing on macroeconomic stability, transparency in government, a sound legal system, modern infrastructure, quality education, and a deregulated economy.

# Myths about Globalization

No discussion of globalization would be complete without dispelling some of the myths that have been built up around it.

*Downward pressure on wages:* Globalization is rarely the primary factor that fosters wage moderation in low-skilled work conducted in developed countries. As discussed in a recent issue of the *World Economic Outlook,* a more significant factor is technology. As more work can be mechanized, and as fewer people are needed to do a given job than in the past, the demand for that labor will fall, and as a result the prevailing wages for that labor will be affected as well.

*The "race to the bottom":* Globalization has not caused the world's multinational corporations to simply scour the globe in search of the lowest-paid laborers. There are numerous factors that enter into corporate decisions on where to source products, including the supply of skilled labor, economic and political stability, the local infrastructure, the quality of institutions, and the overall business climate. In an open global market, while jurisdictions do compete with each other to attract investment, this competition incorporates factors well beyond just the hourly wage rate.

According to the UN Information Service, the developed world hosts two-thirds of the world's inward foreign direct investment. The 49 least developed countries—the poorest of the developing countries—account for around 2 percent of the total inward FDI stock of developing countries. Nor is it true that multinational corporations make a consistent practice of operating sweatshops in low-wage countries, with poor working conditions and substandard wages. While isolated examples of this can surely be uncovered, it is well established that multinationals, on average, pay higher wages than what is standard in developing nations, and offer higher labor standards.

*Globalization is irreversible:* In the long run, globalization is likely to be an unrelenting phenomenon. But for significant periods of time, its momentum can be hindered by a variety of factors, ranging from political will to availability of infrastructure. Indeed, the world was thought to be on an irreversible path toward peace and prosperity in the early 20th century, until the outbreak of Word War I. That war, coupled with the Great Depression, and then World War II, dramatically set back global economic integration. And in many ways, we are still trying to recover the momentum we lost over the past 90 years or so.

That fragility of nearly a century ago still exists today—as we saw in the aftermath of September 11th, when U.S. air travel came to a halt, financial markets shut down, and the economy weakened. The current turmoil in financial markets also poses great difficulty for the stability and reliability of those markets, as well as for the global economy. Credit market strains have intensified and spread across asset classes and banks, precipitating a financial shock that many have characterized as the most serious since the 1930s.

These episodes are reminders that a breakdown in globalization—meaning a slowdown in the global flows of goods, services, capital, and people—can have extremely adverse consequences.

*Openness to globalization will, on its own, deliver economic growth:* Integrating with the global economy is, as economists like to say, a necessary, but not sufficient, condition for economic growth. For globalization to be able to work, a country cannot be saddled with problems endemic to many developing countries, from a corrupt political class, to poor infrastructure, and macroeconomic instability.

*The shrinking state:* Technologies that facilitate communication and commerce have curbed the power of some despots throughout the world, but in a globalized world governments take on new importance in one critical respect, namely, setting, and enforcing, rules with respect to contracts and property rights. The potential of globalization can never be realized unless there are rules and regulations in place, and individuals to enforce them. This gives economic actors confidence to engage in business transactions. Further undermining the idea of globalization shrinking states is that states are not, in fact, shrinking. Public expenditures are, on average, as high or higher today as they have been at any point in recent memory. And among OECD [Organization of Economic Cooperation and Development is composed of 30 mostly high-income countries] countries, government tax revenue as a percentage of GDP increased from 25.5 percent in 1965 to 36.6 percent in 2006.

# The Future of Globalization

Like a snowball rolling down a steep mountain, globalization seems to be gathering more and more momentum. And the question frequently asked about globalization is not whether it will continue, but at what pace.

A disparate set of factors will dictate the future direction of globalization, but one important entity—sovereign governments—should not be overlooked. They still have the power to erect significant obstacles to globalization, ranging from tariffs to immigration restrictions to military hostilities.

Nearly a century ago, the global economy operated in a very open environment, with goods, services, and people able to move across borders with little if any difficulty. That openness began to wither away with the onset of World War I in 1914, and recovering what was lost is a process that is still underway. Along the process, governments recognized the importance of international cooperation and coordination, which led to the emergence of numerous international organizations and financial institutions (among which the IMF and the World Bank, in 1944).

Indeed, the lessons included avoiding fragmentation and the breakdown of cooperation among nations. The world is still made up of nation states and a global marketplace. We need to get the right rules in place so the global system is more resilient, more beneficial, and more legitimate. International institutions have a difficult but indispensable role in helping to bring more of globalization's benefits to more people throughout the world. By helping to break down barriers—ranging from the regulatory to the cultural—more countries can be integrated into the global economy, and more people can seize more of the benefits of globalization.

Ravinder Rena　　　　　　　　　　　　　　➜ **NO**

# Globalization Still Hurting Poor Nations

**G**lobalization is a buzzword gaining increasing importance all over the world. Today, the world appears radically altered. A very significant feature of the global economy is the integration of the emerging economies in world markets and the expansion of economic activities across state borders. Other dimensions include the international movement of ideas, information, legal systems, organizations, people, popular globetrotting cuisine, cultural exchanges, and so forth.

However, the movement of people, even in this post-1970s era of globalization, is restricted and strictly regulated in the aftermath of the 9/11 attacks. More countries are now integrated into a global economic system in which trade and capital flow across borders with unprecedented energy. Nonetheless, globalization has become painful, rather than controversial, to the developing world. It has produced increasing global economic interdependence through the growing volume and variety of cross-border flows of finance, investment, goods, and services, and the rapid and widespread diffusion of technology.

A World Bank study, "Global Economic Prospects: Managing the Next Wave of Globalization," succinctly discusses the advantages of globalization. Driven by 1974-onward globalization, exports have doubled, as a proportion of world economic output, to over 25 percent, and, based on existing trends, will rise to 34 percent by 2030.

World income has doubled since 1980, and almost half-a-billion people have climbed out of poverty since 1990. According to current trends, the number of people living on less than 1-purchasing power-dollar-a-day will halve from today's 1 billion by 2030. This will take place as a result of growth in Southeast Asia, whose share of the poor will halve from 60 percent, while Africa's will rise from 30 percent to 55 percent.

The scale, benefits, and criticism of globalization are often exaggerated. On the contrary, compared to the immediate post-war period, the average rate of growth has steadily slowed during the age of globalization, from 3.5 percent per annum in the 1960s to 2.1 percent, 1.3 percent, and 1.0 percent in the 1970s, 1980s, and 1990s, respectively.

The growing economic interdependence is highly asymmetrical. The benefits of linking and the costs of de-linking are not equally distributed.

Industrialized countries—the European Union, Japan, and the United States—are genuinely and highly interdependent in their relations with one another. The developing countries, on the other hand, are largely independent from one another in terms of economic relations, while being highly dependent on industrialized countries. Indeed, globalization creates losers as well as winners, and entails risks as well as opportunities. An International Labor Organization blue-ribbon panel noted in 2005 that the problems lie not in globalization per se but in the deficiencies in its governance.

Some globalization nay-sayers have vouched that there has been a growing divergence, not convergence, in income levels, both between countries and peoples. Inequality among, and within, nations has widened. Assets and incomes are more concentrated. Wage shares have fallen while profit shares have risen. Capital mobility alongside labor immobility has reduced the bargaining power of organized labor. The rise in unemployment and the accompanying "casualization" of the workforce, with more and more people working in the informal sector, have generated an excess supply of labor and depressed real wages.

Globalization has spurred inequality—both in the wealthiest countries as well as the developing world. China and India compete globally, yet only a fraction of their citizens prosper. Increasing inequality between rural and urban populations, and between coastal and inland areas in China, could have disastrous consequences in the event of political transition. Forty of the poorest nations, many in Africa, have had zero growth during the past 20 years. Their governments followed advice from wealthy nations and World Bank consultants on issues ranging from privatization to development, but millions of people suffer from poverty. Ironically, the wealthiest people benefit from the source of cheap labor. Western policies reinforce the growing divide between rich and poor.

Nearly three-quarters of Africa's population live in rural areas in contrast with less-than-10-percent in the developed world. Globalization has driven a wedge between social classes in the rich countries, while among the world's poor, the main divide is between countries—those that adapted well to globalization and, in many areas, prospered, and those that maladjusted and, in many cases, collapsed.

As the Second World [the Soviet Union and the communist countries of Eastern Europe] collapsed and globalization took off, the latter rationale evaporated and a few countries, notably India and China, accelerated their growth rates significantly, enjoying the fruits of freer trade and larger capital flows. Although the two countries adapted well to globalization, there is little doubt that their newfound relative prosperity opened many new fissure lines. Inequality between coastal and inland provinces, as well as between urban and rural areas, skyrocketed in China.

Another large group of Third World countries in Latin America, Africa, and former Communist countries experienced a quarter-century of decline, or stagnation, punctuated by civil wars, international conflicts, and the onslaught of AIDS. While rich countries grew on average by almost 2 percent per capita annually from 1980 to 2002, the world's poorest 40 countries had a combined growth rate of zero. For large swaths of Africa, the income level today is less than 1-dollar-per-day.

For these latter countries, the promised benefits of globalization never arrived. Social services were often taken over by foreigners. Western experts and technocrats arrived on their jets, stayed in luxury hotels, and hailed the obvious worsening of economic and social conditions as a step toward better lives and international integration.

Indeed, for many people in Latin America and Africa, globalization was merely a new, more attractive label, for the old imperialism, or worse—for a form of re-colonization. The left-wing reaction sweeping Latin America, from Mexico to Argentina, is a direct consequence of the fault lines opened by policies designed to benefit Wall Street, not the people in the streets of Asmara [capital of Eritrea] or Kampala [capital of Uganda].

The rapid growth of global markets has not seen the parallel development of social and economic institutions to ensure their smooth and efficient functioning; labor rights have been less diligently protected than capital and property rights; and the global rules on trade and finance are unfair to the extent that they produce asymmetric effects on rich and poor countries.

The deepening of poverty and inequality has implications for the social and political stability among, and within, nations. It is in this context that the plight and hopes of developing countries have to be understood in the Doha Round of trade talks. Having commenced in 2001, the Doha Round was supposed to be about the trade-led and trade-facilitated development of the world's poor countries. After five years of negotiations, the talks collapsed because of unbridgeable differences among the EU [European Union], the US, and developing countries led by India, Brazil, and China. [The Doha Round is the latest and continuing series of negotiations under the aegis of the World Trade Organization to reduce restrictions on trade and other forms of international economic interchange. The Doha Round began in 2001 and is at a virtual standstill because of, among other things, disagreements between the wealthier and poorer countries.]

From the developing world's perspective, the problem is that the rich countries want access to poor countries' resources, markets, and labor forces at the lowest possible price. Some rich countries were open to implementing deep cuts in agricultural subsidies, but resisted opening their markets, others wanted the reverse. Developing countries like India, China, and Eritrea, among other[s], are determined to protect the livelihood of their farmers. In countries like India, farmer suicide has been a terrible human cost and a political problem for India's state and central governments for some time, as well as a threat to rural development. Protecting farmers' needs, therefore, is essential for social stability as well as the political survival of governments in the developing world.

The rich countries' pledges of flexibility failed to translate into concrete proposals during the Doha negotiations. Instead, they effectively protected the interests of tiny agricultural minorities. By contrast, in developing countries, farming accounts for 30 to 60 percent of the Gross Domestic Product [GDP] and up to 70 percent of the labor force. This is why labor rights protection is at least as critical for developing countries as intellectual property rights protection is for the rich.

Developing countries were promised a new regime that would allow them to sell their goods and trade their way out of poverty through undistorted market openness. This required generous market access by the rich for the products of the poor, and also reduction-cum-elimination of market-distorting producer and export subsidies, with the resulting dumping of the rich world's produce on world markets.

Thus, Europe launched its "Everything but Arms" initiative whereby it would open its markets to the world's poorest countries. The initiative foundered on too many non-tariff barriers, for example in the technical rules of origin. The US seemed to offer so-called EBP—Everything But what they Produce. Under its proposals, developing countries would have been free to export jet engines and supercomputers to the US, but not textiles, agricultural products, or processed foods.

Elimination of rich country production and export subsidies, and the opening of markets, while necessary, would not be sufficient for developing countries to trade their way out of underdevelopment. They also have a desperate need to institute market-friendly incentives and regulatory regimes and increase their farmers' productivity, and may require technical assistance from international donors to achieve this through investment in training, infrastructure, and research.

The failure of the Doha Round is also, finally, symptomatic of a much bigger malaise, namely the crisis of multilateral governance in security and environmental matters, as well as in trade. In agriculture, as in other sectors, problems-without-passports require solutions-without-borders.

To convince Africans about the benefits of globalization, we must take a more enlightened view of liberalizing trade, services, and labor-intensive manufacturing in which African countries are competitive. Trade is not only a means to prosperity, but also a means of peace-building. We need to devise an enlightened approach in negotiations over the reduction of harmful gas emissions, intellectual property rights, lifesaving drugs, and the transfer of technologies toward combating poverty. Ultimately, globalization broadens the gap between rich and poor. It also creates distortions in the global economy. Therefore, it is not a panacea for world economic development.

# EXPLORING THE ISSUE

## Is Economic Globalization Good for Both Rich and Poor?

## Questions for Critical Thinking and Reflection

1. Are the poor being harmed by globalization or modernization—with robotics, the high value of technology, the importance of education, and related factors?
2. Would it be better to reform or reduce globalization?
3. Is it possible to significantly reform and regulate globalization without creating binding international law and authoritative international enforcement agencies that will diminish national sovereignty?

## Is There Common Ground?

Globalization is both old and new. It is old in that the efforts of humans to overcome distance and other barriers to increased interchange have long existed. The first canoes and signal fires are part of the history of globalization. The first event in true globalization occurred between 1519 and 1522, when Ferdinand Magellan circumnavigated the globe. MNCs have existed at least since 1600 when a group of British merchants formed the East India Company. In the main, though, globalization is mostly a modern phenomenon. The progress of globalization until the latter half of the 1800s might be termed "creeping globalization." There were changes, but they occurred very slowly. Since then, the pace of globalization has increased exponentially. A brief introduction to globalization is available in Jürgen Osterhammel, Niels P. Petersson, and Dona Geyer, *Globalization: A Short History* (Princeton University Press, 2005). A contemporary look at globalization is Thomas L. Friedman's updated and expanded *The World Is Flat: A Brief History of the Twenty-First Century* (Picador, 2007).

The recent rapid pace of globalization has sparked an increasing chorus of criticism against many of its aspects including economic interdependence. Now it is not uncommon for massive protests to occur when the leaders of the world countries meet to discuss global or regional economics or when the WTO, IMF, or World Bank holds important conferences. One of the oddities about globalization, economic or otherwise, is that it often creates a common cause between those of marked conservative and marked liberal views. More than anything, conservatives worry that their respective countries are losing control of their economies and, thus, a degree of their independence. Echoing this view, archconservative political commentator Patrick J. Buchanan has warned that unchecked globalization threatens to turn the United States into a "North American province of what some call The New World Order."

Some liberals share the conservatives' negative views of globalization but for different reasons. This perspective is less concerned with sovereignty and security; it is more concerned with workers and countries being exploited and the environment being damaged by MNCs that shift their operations to other countries to find cheap labor and to escape environmental regulations. During the 2008 campaign for the Democratic presidential nomination, both Barack Obama and Hillary Clinton expressed concern about the impact that U.S. free trade agreements were having both on American and foreign workers and on their environments.

## Additional Resources

One widely read critique of economic globalization is Joseph E. Stiglitz, *Making Globalization Work* (W. W. Norton, 2006). Taking the opposite view is Jagdish N. Bhagwati, *In Defense of Globalization* (Oxford University Press, 2007).

# ISSUE 9

## Does China's Currency Manipulation Warrant International and National Action?

**YES: Gordon G. Chang,** from Testimony during Hearings on "China and U.S. Interests" before the Committee on Foreign Affairs, U.S. House of Representatives (January 19, 2011)

**NO: Pieter Bottelier and Uri Dadush,** from "The RMB: Myths and Tougher-To-Deal-With Realities," Testimony during Hearings on "China's Exchange Rate Policy" before the Committee on Ways and Means, U.S. House of Representatives (March 24, 2010)

### ISSUE SUMMARY

**YES:** Gordon Chang, a columnist at *Forbes*, the financial magazine, argues that China is manipulating the value of its currency in a way that is harming the U.S. international economic position and that it is time to use international and, if necessary, national pressure to remedy the situation.

**NO:** Pieter Bottelier, the senior adjunct professor of China studies at the School of Advanced International Studies at Johns Hopkins University and the former chief of the World Bank's resident mission in Beijing, and Uri Dadush, the director of the International Economics Program at the Carnegie Endowment for International Peace and former (2002–2008) World Bank's director of international trade, contend that dangerous myths about China's currency may unwisely touch off a strong U.S. reaction while more effective solutions will be overlooked.

To follow this debate, it is essential to understand three facts about money. First, money has no inherent value. Domestically, the value of the U.S. dollar and every other currency decreases during inflation or, more rarely, increases during deflation. Internationally, the "exchange rate" between two countries' currencies normally varies based on supply of and demand for each currency. Comparing the dollar to China's renminbi (RMB, people's currency, also yuan), one dollar could be exchanged for 8.28 RMB in 2000. In mid-2010, when the testimony that makes up the second reading was given, you would only get 6.78 RMB for a dollar.

The second key point is that the comparative values of two currencies have major impact on the flow of trade and investment between those countries and, therefore, on each country's economy. If, as occurred in our example, the dollar loses value (weakens) versus the RMB, then it should be easier (cheaper) for China to buy products imported from the United States and harder (costlier) for Americans to buy products exported by China. Third, fair trade and global economic rules require that countries generally allow their currencies to "float" against one another, that is, to have their value determined by market forces rather than by government intervention. This third point is the core of this debate.

During the 1980s, as the cold war eased and trade between China and the West grew, China moved to artificially lower the value of its currency in order to promote exports. Among other things, from 1997 through 2004, China "pegged" the exchange rate at 8.62 RMB = $1 by making any other rate of exchange in China illegal. Virtually all experts agreed the RMB was far overvalued, with some putting the disparity as much as 50 percent. Partly as a result of the artificial exchange rate, Chinese exports to the United States boomed, while U.S. exports to China lagged. In 1995, China sold $46 billion in goods to the United States but bought only $12 billion in U.S. products. Thus, China's exports to the United States exceeded its imports 3.8 times (3.8:1) over, or by $34 billion. By 2005, China was selling $244 billion in goods to the United States but buying only $42 billion in U.S. products. Thus, the U.S. trade deficit with China worsened between 1995 and 2005 both in terms of the ratio (from 3.8:1 to 5.8:1) and the amount (from $34 billion to $202 billion).

As the U.S. deficit grew amid charges of unfair practices on China's part, pressure to retaliate mounted. Among other things, legislation was introduced to impose a 27.5 percent increase in the U.S. tariff on goods from China unless it devalued its currency. Perhaps in response, in July 2005, China "unpegged" its currency from the dollar in July 2005. However, China continued to use other methods to keep the RMB from changing too fast against the dollar, and in mid-2008, amid global economic turmoil, Beijing once again pegged the RMB to the dollar.

Overall between 2005 and 2011, when the testimony in the first reading was given, China let the RMB weaken some, with the exchange rate per dollar dropping from an average of 8.19 RMB in 2005 to 6.63 RMB in January 2011, or about 19 percent for the period. This drop had a positive impact on the trade deficit, with the ratio declining from 5.8:1 in 2005 to 4.0:1 in 2010. While this was better, the gaping U.S. trade deficit with China ($273 billion in 2010) remained, and in the view of some analysts the fair RMB–dollar ratio should have been about 5 RMB = $1. Gordon Chang in the second reading tells Congress that it is time to intensify the pressure on China to let the RMB truly float and find a fair exchange rate. Pieter Bottelier and Uri Dadush take a very different view, arguing, among other things, that China is not artificially manipulating the value of the RMB and that weakening the RMB versus the dollar will not help the U.S. economy overall.

# YES ↩

**Gordon G. Chang**

# China and U.S. Interests

**M**ost Americans fundamentally misunderstand the economic relationship between the United States and China. I want to comment on three of these misunderstandings: China's dependency on the American market, America's dependency on China buying American debt, and the effect of Beijing's currency manipulation.

## China's Dependency on America

First, most of us believe that the Chinese economy has become less dependent on ours. The generally accepted narrative is that, as the American economy tumbled during the Great Recession, China's exporters looked to other markets.

In 2008 and 2009, every China analyst—including me—believed Chinese exporters were successful in diversifying away from the U.S. This storyline seemed true because it made so much sense. Trade numbers, however, tell a different story.

In 2008, 90.1% of China's overall trade surplus related to sales to the United States. So what happened in 2009, the first full year of the downturn? That percentage increased to 115.7%.

And what happened last year? China's trade surplus last year was $183.1 billion, according to the official Xinhua News Agency. Through the first 11 months of last year, U.S. Commerce Department figures show China's trade surplus against the United States was $252.4 billion. That's up from $208.7 billion for the same period in 2009, a 20.9% increase. The Commerce Department has not released the December trade number yet. China's surplus for that month should end up somewhere around $22 billion. Yet let's assume, purely for the sake of argument, that China's December surplus was zero. If December's surplus was zero—not very likely—137.8% of China's overall trade surplus last year related to sales to the United States.

China's increasing trade dependence on the United States gives Washington enormous leverage over Beijing, especially because a large portion of the Chinese surplus is attributable to violations of its World Trade Organization obligations. China has an increasingly turbulent economy, heavily dependent on exports. And its exporters, despite all the talk about their "diversification," increasingly need the American market.

U.S. House of Representatives, January 19, 2011.

# Beijing's Holding of U.S. Debt

Second, just about everybody says that Beijing's holding of American debt gives China a hold over the United States.

They are right—but only because we think it does. China's holding of Treasury debt—$906.8 billion as of October 2010—would not be a weapon if we properly understood how global markets work.

Because of China's increasing dependence on exports to America, Beijing has to buy American debt as a practical matter. It receives dollars from its export sales and has to invest those dollars somewhere. The Chinese could convert their dollars into other currencies, but no other currency has a deep-enough market. Furthermore, the euro, an alternative to the dollar, may not exist, say, two years from now, complicating Beijing's diversification plans. China is stuck with the dollar for as long as it is stuck with the American market.

Chinese officials periodically threaten to diversify their holdings and to stop buying U.S. Treasury obligations. It seems there has been some diversification of China's foreign exchange reserves but not enough to make a difference to the Treasury Department's fund-raising plans. Even when Beijing sells Treasuries from accounts analysts watch, it appears the Chinese buy through nominee accounts—in other words, they try to hide their purchases.

Chinese officials have publicly threatened to dump our debt in global markets since August 2007. They call this tactic, appropriately enough, the "nuclear option." China's officials have not nuked us because they know their attack plan won't work. Let's suppose the worst case scenario of Beijing trying to dump all its dollars at one time. What would happen? The Chinese would have to buy something, as a practical matter, pounds, euros, and yen. The values of those currencies would then shoot up through the ceiling. London, Brussels, and Tokyo, to bring down the values of their currencies, would then have to go into global markets to buy . . . dollars. In short, there would be a great circular flow of cash in the world's currency markets.

There would be turmoil in those markets, but it would not last long, perhaps just a few weeks. And we would end up in just the same place that we are now, except that our friends would be holding our debt instead of our adversary. Global markets are deep and flexible and can handle just about anything.

Hillary Clinton, in 2005, famously said we can't argue with our Chinese bankers. I think we can. I hasten to add that I do not want China to hold a single cent of our debt, but, because it does, we need to understand the limits of the power that such holding confers on Beijing.

# China's Manipulation of the Renminbi

Third, you hear many commentators say that changing China's currency practices will not solve America's trade deficit. Of course that's true—but only because Beijing's currency manipulation is not the sole reason for the plight of

American manufacturers and workers. Yet Chinese manipulation is an important factor.

China has, during various periods, pegged its currency and allowed a "dirty float." Throughout all these times, the yuan, as the renminbi is informally know, has been kept at an artificially low level. Today, Beijing continues to intervene in its market so that the currency hits a target in the middle of a moving band, and it does so to give an advantage to its exporters. Due to this active intervention, no one knows the true value of the renminbi, but the discount to market value is thought to be somewhere in the vicinity of 30 percent.

A discount of that magnitude is, of course, significant. I practiced law for more than two decades, much of it in Asia. I represented parties involved in trade between China and the United States and often saw them haggling for days over pennies when negotiating unit prices. A swing either way of a few cents had a disproportionate effect on the success of the business of my clients. So it is counterintuitive to think that currency manipulation, which can change the price of a product by thirty or forty percent, would have no affect on our country's trade deficit.

But don't take my word for it. Listen to China's top economic official. Premier Wen Jiabao, last September, raised the possibility of "countless Chinese enterprises going bankrupt and countless Chinese workers becoming unemployed" if the renminbi were to appreciate substantially. If China's enterprises and workers would suffer if he did not manipulate the renminbi, then how can anyone maintain that our manufacturers and our workers are not disadvantaged by his currency policy?

Nonetheless, economists and analysts tell us we shouldn't complain about China's predatory currency policies. For instance, they maintained that the China currency bill the House passed late last September—H.R. 2378, the Currency Reform for Fair Trade Act—was the result of misguided protectionism.

It is a mystery to me why trying to do something about protectionism is itself considered protectionist. In my view, the United States should do all it can to bring Chinese currency practices in line with those of China's trading partners. The real risk for us—America and the rest of the global community— is that Beijing will take too long to do so. Asian nations are already depressing the value of their currencies to make their exports more competitive with China's. In the 1930s, tariff walls deepened the Great Depression and prolonged it. This time, more subtle—but probably as destructive—measures look like they will produce the same effect.

China won't change its destructive currency policies if we merely appeal to its self-interest—the approach of the current administration and the preceding one. China will change its currency policies only when the United States acts to defend its manufacturers and workers. If the administration won't act, Congress should.

Pieter Bottelier and
Uri Dadush

→ **NO**

# The RMB: Myths and Tougher-To-Deal-With Realities

**C**hina fever will again grip Washington as the U.S. Treasury nears its mid-April deadline for pronouncing whether China manipulates its currency. Dangerous myths about the RMB will again be propagated, feeding China bashers and protectionist lobbies. Meanwhile, more important and politically tougher reforms in both the United States and China will be conveniently overlooked.

Most economists would agree that the RMB is undervalued and that it is in China's interest to allow appreciation. By pegging its exchange rate to the dollar, China abdicates a large measure of control over its monetary policy. In addition, an undervalued currency increases prices for Chinese consumers and contributes to inflationary pressures and excessive accumulation of low-yielding reserves.

However, the benefits of RMB appreciation for the United States are mixed at best and—whether net positive or negative—are certainly exaggerated. U.S. policy makers should prioritize maintaining a collaborative relationship with China, now the world's largest trading nation, over staging another fruitless debate on the RMB.

## The Myths

### China's Growth Has Depended Primarily on Exports

While integration into world markets has been vital for China's development, domestic demand has always been the country's primary growth driver. During the decade before the crisis, net-exports accounted for only about 1 percentage point of China's 9.5 percent average annual growth, as imports grew almost as fast as exports.

### China Did Not Contribute Enough to Global Demand during the Crisis

Chinese demand was integral to Asia's early emergence from the recession, and the rest of the world benefited as well. In 2008, China accounted for over 50 percent of world growth; last year, China expanded rapidly while the world economy contracted.

U.S. House of Representatives, March 24, 2010.

Domestic demand in China expanded 12.3 percent in 2009, while domestic demand in the United States and industrialized countries contracted 2.6 percent and 2.7 percent, respectively. China's output was able to grow nearly 9 percent even as exports plummeted 16 percent. Imports held up much better than exports, and China's current account surplus declined from 9.6 percent of GDP in 2008 to 5.8 percent in 2009. Data till February this year suggests that the surplus is still shrinking.

Furthermore, during the most acute phase of the crisis—the fourth quarter of 2008 to the first quarter of 2009, when the dollar appreciated against nearly all currencies—China maintained the RMB's peg to the dollar. This helped other countries weather the demand collapse.

## China's Consumption Is Not Growing Fast Enough

Private consumption in China grew by an average of about 7.5 percent over the ten years prior to the crisis, faster than in any other large economy. In the United States, private consumption grew at an annual rate of 3.6 percent over the same period. Nonetheless, consumption's share of China's national income fell over that period as investment grew even faster. In 2009, however, consumption's share rose, another hopeful sign that the economy may be rebalancing toward domestic demand at the expense of exports.

## The United States Depends on China to Buy Its Government Debt

At the end of 2009, China held only about 7 percent of U.S. federal government debt outstanding. Sold at a high price (low yield), U.S. government debt is a popular security. At the same time, the United States is benefiting China: China has few good alternatives to hold its reserves and U.S. firms are large investors and employers in China. In the investment arena, as in others, the United States and China are mutually dependent.

## China Has Been Manipulating Its Currency to Get an Unfair Advantage in Trade for Years

About 60 countries peg their exchange rates to the dollar today, and they are not all currency manipulators. The real question is whether a country systematically pegs its currency at an artificially low rate in order to gain competitive advantage—a violation of IMF [International Monetary Fund] and WTO [World Trade Organization] rules.

The evidence against the RMB is mixed at best. China pegged the RMB to the dollar at the end of 1997, in the midst of the Asian crisis. At that time, the United States and other countries applauded the peg as a generous act that promoted stability in the region. Serious complaints did not emerge until 2003, when China's trade surplus and America's trade deficit (with the world and with China) began to rise sharply.

However, the RMB/dollar rate, which had not changed, was not the primary reason for the growing imbalance. Rather, in the United States, the fiscal surpluses of the final Clinton years had shifted to large deficits and the Greenspan Fed [the US Federal Reserve Board under the chairmanship Alan Greenspan from 1987 to 2006] was pursuing very loose monetary policies while the financial sector generated additional liquidity as a result of inadequate oversight and regulation. In China, aggressive domestic reforms had prompted exceptional productivity growth in manufacturing, while the government promoted both exports and import substitution.

Recognizing these shifts, China adopted a policy of gradual RMB appreciation in July 2005. Three years later, the RMB had risen 21 percent against the dollar. Because of the sharp, crisis-induced drop in export orders, however, China suspended the policy. China's central bank governor recently confirmed that the suspension is a special, crisis-related measure, implying that gradual appreciation will resume as the crisis abates.

## Revaluation of the RMB Will Help the U.S. Economy

The immediate effect of RMB appreciation would be to raise prices for U.S. consumers. A 25 percent revaluation of the RMB, which some economists have said is needed, would—if not offset by a reduction in China's prices—add $75 billion to the U.S. import bill. Since the United States imports three times as much from China as it exports there, higher U.S. exports to China would not nearly offset the welfare loss to U.S. consumers from higher Chinese prices.

It would take years for adjustment to a higher RMB to occur, but in the end, though some U.S. firms would gain and some export jobs would be created, the U.S. consumer would be the loser, and the net welfare effect on U.S. workers would probably be negative.

## Revaluation of the RMB Is Critical for Reducing Global Trade Imbalances

A revaluation of the RMB by itself would do little to redress global imbalances, and could, as mentioned, initially lead to a wider U.S.–China trade deficit. Most likely, unless U.S. domestic demand falls for other reasons, the overall U.S. trade deficit would hardly budge in the end as the United States would simply import more from other countries that would resist following China's lead in allowing currency appreciation.

# The (Tougher-To-Deal-With) Realities

## China's Policies Artificially Promote Investment, Exports, and Import Substitution at the Expense of Consumption

Many leaders in China acknowledge the need to address the country's pervasive export and import-substitution policies, as well as the suppressed interest rates, which lower the cost of capital for Chinese firms. However, tough internal policy battles lie ahead as powerful vested interests resist change. International pressure on these issues would strengthen the hand of reformers.

## China Needs to Improve Its Safety Nets

Although budget outlays for health and education have increased significantly in recent years, much more needs to be done. Further improvements would probably prompt households to reduce savings and increase consumption. However, the impact on China's trade balance would depend on how the safety nets were financed. If social security contributions to the de-facto pay-as-you-go system were simply raised, national savings would change little. If, on the other hand, these outlays increased government deficits and borrowing, national savings and China's trade surplus might decline.

## Overwhelmingly, U.S. External Deficits Are Determined by U.S. Policies

All fair-minded economists recognize that measures to reduce the U.S. fiscal deficit and encourage household savings will do infinitely more to correct U.S. current account deficits than any conceivable policy change in China. Though the needed measures are well known, and include raising consumption and energy taxes, increasing competition and efficiency in healthcare, and establishing a needs-tested social security system, these changes are politically complicated to say the least.

# Conclusion

China's economy has become so large and globally integrated that its exchange rate policy is a matter of international concern. But, more than an international issue, it is crucial for China. Given the realities outlined above, it makes little sense for the United States to point to China's exchange rate as a major bilateral issue. Designating China a currency "manipulator" will only impair a crucial relationship. In addition, the debate diverts attention from the politically difficult, but much more significant, domestic reforms that are needed in both the United States and China.

# EXPLORING THE ISSUE

## Does China's Currency Manipulation Warrant International and National Action?

## Questions for Critical Thinking and Reflection

1. What should be the single most important goal of U.S. relations with China?
2. Trade sanctions on China would mean higher prices for some goods and also retaliatory sanctions by China that would limit some U.S. exports and therefore also harm the U.S. economy. Are the costs to Americans worth the fight?
3. Should the United States pressure China solely through multilateral avenues as the World Trade Organization or should Washington also pressure unilateral action by such means as imposing trade sanctions on Beijing?

## Is There Common Ground?

In June 2010, about three months after the congressional hearings from which the second reading in this debate was taken, China announced that it would once again unpeg its currency from the dollar. From that point when the exchange rate was 6.63 to 1, the RMB fell to 6.31 in late October 2012. That is an overall drop of 23 percent since 2005, but it is still about 26 percent higher than the 5 to 1 exchange rate some analysts think is fair. The impact of the continuing narrowing of the exchange rate to trade was uncertain. On the one hand, the ratio of the U.S. trade deficit narrowed from 4.0 to 1 in 2010 to 3.9 to 1 in 2011. But the dollar amount of the trade deficit for the two years increased from $273 billion to $295 billion because of the larger volume of trade.

Although the two readings focus on the economic consequences of confronting China on its currency, it is important to remember that issues between countries are often not treated in isolation. The two countries have a complex strategic relationship, and the United States needs China's help in many areas. For example, China is one of the few countries with any influence in North Korea, and Chinese participation is important to the effort to resolve the ongoing confrontation with North Korea over its nuclear weapons program. China also has a veto in the UN Security Council and could block U.S. efforts there on such matters as getting sanctions or even military action authorized against Iran in response to its nuclear program (see Issue 5). At the least, strong U.S. pressure on China would hurt short-term political relations and could even promote long-term animosity (see Issue 3). Therefore, the costs of a trade war with China cannot be calculated only in dollars and cents. None of this means, however, that the United States should do nothing.

## Additional Resources

A book that puts the exchange rate controversy within the context of U.S.–China trade relations is Imad Moosa, *US-China Trade Dispute: Facts, Figures and Myths* (Edward Elgar, 2012). Also valuable is Gary Clyde Hufbauer and Jared C. Woollacott, "Trade Disputes Between China and the United States: Growing Pains So Far, Worse Ahead," *European Yearbook of International Economic Law,* 2012. The U.S. perspective is provided on the website of the U.S. Trade Representative at www.ustr.gov/countries-regions/china. China's very different view can be found in Zhou Shijian, "China-U.S. Economic Relations: Accords and Discords," *China Today* (February 27, 2012), on the Internet at www.china.org.cn/opinion/2012-02/27/content_24744473.htm. Former U.S. Secretary of the Treasury Henry M. Paulson, Jr. makes some recommendations for the future in *Framework for US-China Economic Relations* (July 17, 2012), which is on the website of the Atlantic Council at www.acus.org/publication/new-framework-us-china-economic-relation.

# *Internet References . . .*

## Disarmament Diplomacy

This site, maintained by the Acronym Institute for Disarmament Diplomacy, provides up-to-date news and analysis of disarmament activity, with a particular focus on weapons of mass destruction.

**www.acronym.org.uk**

## The Center for Security Policy

The website of this Washington, DC–centered "think tank" provides a wide range of links to sites dealing with national and international security issues.

**www.centerforsecuritypolicy.org**

## National Defense University

This leading center for joint professional military education is under the direction of the chairman of the U.S. Joint Chiefs of Staff. Its website is valuable for general military thinking and for material on terrorism.

**www.ndu.edu/**

## Centre for the Study of Terrorism and Political Violence

The primary aims of the Centre for the Study of Terrorism and Political Violence are to investigate the roots of political violence; to develop a body of theory spanning the various and disparate elements of terrorism; and to recommend policy and organizational initiatives that governments and private sectors might adopt to better predict, detect, and respond to terrorism and terrorist threats.

**www.st-ANDREWS.ac.uk/academic/intrel/research/cstpv/**

# Armaments and Violence Issues

*W*hatever we may wish, war, terrorism, and other forms of physical coercion are still important elements of international politics. Countries calculate both how to use the instruments of force and how to implement national security. There can be little doubt, however, that significant changes are under way in this realm as part of the changing world system. Strong pressures exist to expand the mission and strengthen the security capabilities of international organizations and to gauge the threat of terrorism. This section examines how countries in the international system are addressing these issues.

- Should the United States Ratify the Comprehensive Nuclear Test Ban Treaty?

- Should U.S. Forces Continue to Fight in Afghanistan?

- Does Using Drones to Attack Terrorists Globally Violate International Law?

- Is the Use and Threat of Force Necessary in International Relations?

# ISSUE 10

## Should the United States Ratify the Comprehensive Nuclear Test Ban Treaty?

**YES: Ellen Tauscher,** from "The Case for the Comprehensive Nuclear Test Ban Treaty," Remarks at the Arms Control Association Annual Meeting at the Carnegie Endowment for International Peace, U.S. Department of State (May 10, 2011)

**NO: Baker Spring,** from "U.S. Should Reject Ratification of the Comprehensive Test Ban Treaty," *The Heritage Foundation Web Memo* #3272 (May 26, 2011)

### ISSUE SUMMARY

**YES:** U.S. Under Secretary of State for Arms Control and International Security Ellen Tauscher expresses the view that the United States will lose nothing and gains much by ratifying the Comprehensive Test Ban Treaty.

**NO:** Baker Spring, the F. M. Kirby Research Fellow in National Security Policy at The Heritage Foundation, asserts that the problems with the Comprehensive Test Ban Treaty that led the U.S. Senate to reject it in 1999 have, if anything, worsened in the intervening years.

**A** blinding flash, doomsday roar, and destructive pressure wave announced the first atomic weapons blast, the U.S. test near Alamogordo, New Mexico, on July 16, 1945. Following this first atomic test, the annual number of tests mushroomed to 178 in 1962. Then testing began to ebb in response to a number of arms control treaties beginning with the 1963 U.S.–U.S.S.R. Limited Test Ban Treaty prohibiting nuclear weapons tests in the atmosphere, in outer space, or under water; a declining need to test; and increasing international condemnation of those tests that did occur. The number of annual tests dipped into single numbers in 1992 for the first time in 35 years, and since 1996 there have been no American, British, Chinese, French, or Russian tests. Then in 1998 a series of tests marked India and Pakistan's acquisition of nuclear weapons. The last two tests as of the beginning of 2012 were conducted by North Korea in 2006 and 2009, signaling its becoming the eighth country with an acknowledged nuclear arsenal (Israel has an unacknowledged arsenal). Because of the frequent secrecy of tests, there are disputes about the exact number of tests that have occurred, but the reputable Stockholm International Peace Research Institute (SIPRI) puts the total at 2,054.

One of the major efforts in arms control has been to ensure that no further nuclear weapons tests will ever occur. The centerpiece of that goal is the Comprehensive Test Ban Treaty (CTBT), which bans all such tests. The treaty was concluded in 1996, and 155 countries (79 percent of all countries) have ratified it as of early 2012). Nevertheless, the CTBT remains in limbo because it will not become operational until all the 44 countries that had nuclear reactors in 1996 ratify it. Several such countries, including the United States and China, have not ratified it. With President Bill Clinton in the White House, the United States signed the treaty in 1996, but the Senate rejected it in 1999. The vote of 48 yeas to 51 nays fell far short of the two-thirds vote necessary to ratify a treaty.

The Senate action has not meant new U.S. tests, however. The last of these 1,032 tests conducted occurred in 1992, and in the first selection U.S. Under Secretary of State for Arms Control and International Security Ellen Tauscher argues that the United States no longer needs to conduct nuclear explosive tests and, therefore, the Senate should reconsider its 1999 vote and ratify the CTBT. In the second selection, Baker Spring, a national security expert at the Heritage Foundation, disagrees. He contends that the reasons that the Senate rejected the CTBT remain relevant and that the effort to revive the treaty is an attack on the Senate's integrity.

# YES ↵

Ellen Tauscher

# The Case for the Comprehensive Nuclear Test Ban Treaty

**M**any of you have heard me speak many times about what this Administration intended to accomplish and what we have accomplished. In the two years since President [Barack] Obama's speech in Prague, the Administration has taken significant steps and dedicated unprecedented financial, political, and technical resources to prevent proliferation, live up to our commitments, and to move toward a world without nuclear weapons. [In an April 2009 speech in Prague, the Czech Republic, President Obama said, "To put an end to Cold War thinking, we will reduce the role of nuclear weapons in our national security strategy and urge others to do the same."]

Under the President's leadership, we have achieved the entry into force of the New START agreement, adopted a Nuclear Posture Review that promotes nonproliferation and reduces the role of nuclear weapons in our national security policy, and helped to achieve a consensus Action Plan at the 2010 Nuclear Nonproliferation Treaty Review Conference.

The Administration also convened the successful 2010 Nuclear Security Summit, helped secure and relocate vulnerable nuclear materials, led efforts to establish an international nuclear fuel bank, and increased effective multilateral sanctions against both Iran and North Korea. As for what's next, our goal is to move our relationship with Russia from one based on Mutually Assured Destruction to one on Mutually Assured Stability. We want Russia inside the missile defense tent so that it understands that missile defense is not about undermining Russia's deterrent.

Even though this is a bipartisan goal—President [Ronald] Reagan and President [George H. W.] Bush both supported missile defense cooperation—it will not be easy. I know that many of you have opposed missile defenses. I have as well when the plans were not technically sound or the mission was wrong. But this Administration is seeking to turn what has been an irritant to U.S.–Russian relations into a shared interest. Cooperation between our militaries, scientists, diplomats, and engineers will be more enduring and build greater confidence than any type of assurances. We are also preparing for the next steps in nuclear arms reductions, including—as the President has directed—reductions in strategic, non-strategic, and non-deployed weapons. We are fully engaged with our allies in this process.

Tauscher, Ellen. Remarks at Arms Control Association Annual Meeting, Washington, DC, May 10, 2011.

But let me turn to the Comprehensive Test Ban Treaty. President Obama vowed to pursue ratification and entry into force of the CTBT in his speech in Prague. In so doing the United States is once again taking a leading role in supporting a test ban treaty just as it had when discussions first began more than 50 years ago.

As you know, in the aftermath of the Cuban Missile Crisis, the United States ratified the Limited Test Ban Treaty, which banned all nuclear tests except those conducted underground. The Cuban Missile Crisis, which was about as close as the world has ever come to a nuclear exchange, highlighted the instability of the arms race. Even though scholars have concluded that the United States acted rationally, the Soviet Union acted rationally, and even [Cuba's President] Fidel Castro acted rationally, we came perilously close to nuclear war. Luck certainly played a role in helping us avoid nuclear catastrophe.

In the months after the crisis, President [John F.] Kennedy used his new found political capital and his political skill to persuade the military and the Senate to support a test ban treaty in the hopes of curbing a dangerous arms race. He achieved a Limited Test Ban Treaty, but aspired to do more. Yet, today, with more than 40 years of experience, wisdom, and knowledge about global nuclear dangers, a legally binding ban on all nuclear explosive testing still eludes us. This being Washington, everything is seen through a political lens. So before discussing the merits of the Treaty, let me talk about this in a political sense for a moment. I know that the conventional wisdom is that the ratification of New START [Strategic Arms Reduction Treaty] has delayed or pushed aside consideration of the CTBT. I take the opposite view.

The New START debate, in many ways, opened the door for the CTBT. Months of hearings and debate and nine long days of floor deliberations engaged the Senate, especially its newer Members, in an extended seminar on the composition of our nuclear arsenal, the health of our stockpile, and the relationship between nuclear weapons and our national security. When the Senate voted for the Treaty, it inherently affirmed that our stockpile is safe, secure, and effective, and can be kept so without nuclear testing.

More importantly, the New START debate helped cultivate emerging new arms control champions, such as Senator [Jeanne] Shaheen [D-NH] and Senator [Bob] Casey [D-PA], who are here today. Before the debate, there was not a lot of muscle memory on treaties, especially nuclear treaties in the Senate. Now, there is. So we are in a stronger position to make the case for the CTBT on its merits. To maintain and enhance that momentum, the Obama Administration is preparing to engage the Senate and the public on an education campaign that we expect will lead to ratification of the CTBT.

In our engagement with the Senate, we want to leave aside the politics and explain why the CTBT will enhance our national security. Our case for Treaty ratification consists of three primary arguments.

One, the United States no longer needs to conduct nuclear explosive tests, plain and simple. Two, a CTBT that has entered into force will obligate other states not to test and provide a disincentive for states to conduct such tests. And three, we now have a greater ability to catch those who cheat.

Let me take these points one by one.

From 1945 to 1992, the United States conducted more than 1,000 nuclear explosive tests—more than all other nations combined. The cumulative data gathered from these tests have provided an impressive foundation of knowledge for us to base the continuing effectiveness of our arsenal. But historical test data alone is insufficient.

Well over a decade ago, we launched an extensive and rigorous Stockpile Stewardship program that has enabled our nuclear weapons laboratories to carry out the essential surveillance and warhead life extension programs to ensure the credibility of our deterrent.

Every year for the past 15 years, the Secretaries of Defense and Energy from Democratic and Republican Administrations, and the directors of the nuclear weapons laboratories have certified that our arsenal is safe, secure, and effective. And each year they have affirmed that we do not need to conduct explosive nuclear tests.

The lab directors tell us that Stockpile Stewardship has provided a deeper understanding of our arsenal than they ever had when testing was commonplace. Think about that for a moment. Our current efforts go a step beyond explosive testing by enabling the labs to anticipate problems in advance and reduce their potential impact on our arsenal—something that nuclear testing could not do. I, for one, would not trade our successful approach based on world-class science and technology for a return to explosive testing.

This Administration has demonstrated an unprecedented commitment to a safe, secure, and effective arsenal so long as nuclear weapons exist. Despite the narrative put forward by some, this Administration inherited an underfunded and underappreciated nuclear complex. We have worked tirelessly to fix that situation and ensure our complex has every asset needed to achieve its mission.

The President has committed $88 billion in funding over the next decade to maintain a modern nuclear arsenal, retain a modern nuclear weapons production complex, and nurture a highly trained workforce. At a time when every part of the budget is under the microscope, this pledge demonstrates our commitment and should not be discounted. To those who doubt our commitment, I ask them to put their doubts aside and invest the hard work to support our budget requests in the Congress.

When it comes to the CTBT, the United States is in a curious position. We abide by the core prohibition of the Treaty because we don't need to test nuclear weapons. And we have contributed to the development of the International Monitoring System. But the principal benefit of ratifying the Treaty, constraining other states from testing, still eludes us. That doesn't make any sense to me and it shouldn't make any sense to the Members of the Senate.

I do not believe that even the most vocal critics of the CTBT want to resume explosive nuclear testing. What they have chosen instead is a status quo where the United States refrains from testing without using that fact to lock in a legally binding global ban that would significantly benefit the United States.

Second, a CTBT that has entered into force will hinder other states from advancing their nuclear weapons capabilities. Were the CTBT to enter into force, states interested in pursuing or advancing a nuclear weapons program would risk either deploying weapons that might not work or incur international condemnation and sanctions for testing.

While states can build a crude first generation nuclear weapon without conducting nuclear explosive tests, they would have trouble going further, and they probably wouldn't even know for certain the yield of the weapon they built. More established nuclear weapons states could not, with any confidence, deploy advanced nuclear weapon capabilities that deviated significantly from previously tested designs without explosive testing.

Nowhere would these constraints be more relevant than in Asia, where you see states building up and modernizing their forces. A legally binding prohibition on all nuclear explosive testing would help reduce the chances of a potential regional arms race in the years and decades to come.

Finally, we have become very good at detecting potential cheaters. If you test, there is a very high risk of getting caught. Upon the Treaty's entry into force, the United States would use the International Monitoring System [IMS] to complement our own state of the art national technical means to verify the Treaty.

In 1999, not a single certified IMS station or facility existed. We understand why some senators had doubts about its future, untested capabilities. But today the IMS is more than 75 percent complete. Two hundred fifty-four of the planned 321 monitoring stations are in place and functioning. And 10 of 16 projected radio-nuclide laboratories have been completed. The IMS detected both of North Korea's two announced nuclear tests.

While the IMS did not detect trace radioactive isotopes confirming that the 2009 event was in fact a nuclear explosive test, there was sufficient evidence to support an on-site inspection. On-site inspections are only permissible once the Treaty enters into force. An on-site inspection could have clarified the ambiguity of the 2009 test.

While the IMS continues to prove its value, our national technical means remain second to none and we continue to improve them. Last week, our colleagues at the NNSA conducted the first of a series of Source Physics Experiments at the Nevada Nuclear Security Site. These experiments will allow the United States to validate and improve seismic models and the use of new generation technology to further monitor compliance with the CTBT. Senators can judge our overall capabilities for themselves by consulting the National Intelligence Estimate released last year.

Taken together, these verification tools would make it difficult for any state to conduct nuclear tests that escape detection. In other words, a robust verification regime carries an important deterrent value in and of itself. Could we imagine a far-fetched scenario where a country might conduct a test so low that it would not be detected? Perhaps. But could a country be certain that it would not be caught? That is unclear. Would a country be willing to risk being caught cheating? Doubtful, because there would be a significant cost to pay for those countries that test.

We have a strong case for Treaty ratification. In the coming months, we will build upon and flesh out these core arguments. We look forward to objective voices providing their opinions on this important issue. Soon, the National Academy of Sciences, a trusted and unbiased voice on scientific issues, will release an unclassified report examining the Treaty from a technical perspective. The report will look at how U.S. ratification would impact our ability to maintain our nuclear arsenal and our ability to detect and verify explosive nuclear tests.

Let me conclude by saying that successful U.S. ratification of the CTBT will help facilitate greater international cooperation on the other elements of the President's Prague Agenda. It will strengthen our leverage with the international community to pressure defiant regimes like those in Iran and North Korea as they engage in illicit nuclear activities. We will have greater credibility when encouraging other states to pursue nonproliferation objectives, including universality of the Additional Protocol.

In short, ratification helps us get more of what we want. We give up nothing by ratifying the CTBT. We recognize that a Senate debate over ratification will be spirited, vigorous, and likely contentious. The debate in 1999, unfortunately, was too short and too politicized. The Treaty was brought to the floor without the benefit of extensive Committee hearings or significant input from Administration officials and outside experts.

We will not repeat those mistakes.

But we will make a more forceful case when we are certain the facts have been carefully examined and reviewed in a thoughtful process. We are committed to taking a bipartisan and fact-based approach with the Senate.

For my Republican friends who voted against the Treaty and might feel bound by that vote, I have one message: Don't be. The times have changed. Stockpile Stewardship works. We have made significant advances in our ability to detect nuclear testing. As my good friend George Shultz [U.S. Secretary of State, 1982–1989 in the Reagan adminstration] likes to say, those who opposed the Treaty in 1999 can say they were right, but they would be right to vote for the Treaty today.

We have a lot of work to do to build the political will needed to ratify the CTBT. Nuclear testing is not a front-burner issue in the minds of most Americans, in part, because we have not tested in nearly 20 years. To understand the gap in public awareness, just think that in 1961 some 10,000 women walked off their job as mothers and housewives to protest the arms race and nuclear testing. Now, that strike did not have the same impact as the nonviolent marches and protests to further the cause of Civil Rights.

But the actions of mothers taking a symbolic and dramatic step to recognize global nuclear dangers showed that the issue has resonance beyond "the Beltway," beyond the think tank world and beyond the Ivory Tower. That level of concern is there today and we need your energy, your organizational skills, and your creativity to tap into it.

If we are to move safely and securely to a world without nuclear weapons, then we need to build the requisite political support and that can only be done by people like you.

# U.S. Should Reject Ratification of the Comprehensive Test Ban Treaty

The United States Senate voted to reject ratification of the 1996 Comprehensive Test Ban Treaty (CTBT) on October 13, 1999 [by a vote of 48 in favor to 51 opposed]. This determinate action by the Senate should have marked the end of consideration of the treaty by the U.S. Nevertheless, Under Secretary of State for Arms Control and International Security Ellen Tauscher recently told an audience that the Administration is preparing to engage the Senate and the public on an education campaign that is designed to lead to U.S. ratification of the CTBT.

The substantive problems that led to the Senate's considered judgment in 1999 remain relevant today. If anything, they have worsened in the intervening years. But procedurally, there is no justification for reconsideration of the treaty today. The institutional integrity of the Senate is now at stake.

## Substantive Problems with the CTBT Persist

According to Tauscher, Senate consent to the ratification of the CTBT may be justified on the basis that "times have changed." In reality, the substantive problems with the CTBT that led to its rejection in 1999 are still present. In fact, the problems regarding the maintenance of a safe, reliable, and militarily effective nuclear arsenal have grown worse over the intervening years:

- **The CTBT does not define what it purports to ban.** The text of the treaty remains identical to that which the Senate rejected in 1999. Its central provision, as well as its object and purpose, is to ban explosive nuclear testing. The treaty does not, however, define the term. The U.S. interpretation is that it means a "zero-yield" ban, but other states may not share that interpretation.
- **The U.S. nuclear weapons complex has grown weaker during the intervening years.** After considerable pressure from a number of senators, chief among them Jon Kyl (R-AZ), about the alarming decline in the U.S.'s nuclear weapons, the [President Barack] Obama Administration committed to invest more money in the complex in order to pressure the Senate into granting consent to the badly flawed New START [Strategic Arms Reduction Treaty] arms control treaty with Russia. [The New START agreement was ratified by the U.S. Senate in December

Spring, Baker From *The Heritage Foundation Web Memo*, May 26, 2011. Copyright © 2011 by The Heritage Foundation. Reprinted by permission.

2010.] But this investment program is only just getting started, and its success is far from guaranteed.

- **A zero-yield ban on nuclear explosive tests remains unverifiable.** If the U.S. interpretation of the CTBT as a zero-yield ban is accurate, it was impossible to verify the ban in 1999, and it remains so today. The International Monitoring System (IMS) being put in place to detect violations depends largely on seismic evidence. The fact is that extremely low-yield tests are not likely to be detected by the IMS. Even Tauscher acknowledged that it is possible that a "country might conduct a test so low [in yield] that it would not be detected." At the same time, she dismissed this possibility as "far-fetched." In reality, it is not at all far-fetched.

- **The Obama Administration has imposed self-defeating output limits on the nuclear weapons modernization program.** While the Obama Administration has pledged to increase the investment level in the nuclear weapons complex and stockpile stewardship programs, it is also imposing limits on what the complex and program may do. Specifically, the April 2010 Nuclear Posture Review Report [by the U.S. Department of Defense] states: "The United States will not develop new nuclear warheads. . . . Life Extension Programs will use only nuclear components based on previously tested designs, and will not support new military missions or provide for new military capabilities."

- **Nuclear proliferation trends are pointing in the wrong direction.** The Obama Administration sees its nuclear disarmament agenda, of which CTBT ratification is a part, as necessary to giving the U.S. the moral standing to combat nuclear proliferation. The fact that countries such as Iran, North Korea, and Pakistan are continuing to pursue or expand their nuclear weapons capabilities suggests that the Obama Administration's moral suasion argument is ineffective and that Iran and North Korea view the U.S. commitment to nuclear disarmament as a sign of weakness to be exploited.

## Undermining the Senate's Institutional Integrity

Tauscher charged that the debate in the Senate in 1999 was too politicized and too short. Contrary to her assertion, the Senate's opponents of CTBT ratification did not fail to exercise due diligence in their review of CTBT at that time. They reviewed the treaty carefully and made considered arguments against ratification. Their arguments proved convincing to the Senate as a whole, and they prevailed overwhelmingly in the subsequent vote.

Regarding the time for consideration, it was CTBT proponents in the Senate that insisted on its immediate consideration in 1999. They effectively charged Senator Jesse Helms (R-NC), a leading opponent of ratification, with engaging in obstructionism over the matter. Further, the debate and vote on the CTBT in the Senate was conducted under a painstakingly worked out *unanimous* consent agreement. This is a far cry from the recent procedure for the consideration of New START, where proponents, having failed to achieve a unanimous consent agreement, simply rammed the treaty through by invoking cloture [thereby ending a filibuster by the treaty's opponents]. Clearly, the proponents of the CTBT now view the Senate's 1999 vote to reject CTBT as procedurally illegitimate only because they lost.

The Senate should not take such an attack on its integrity lightly. Members of the Senate, therefore, would be justified in sending a letter to President Obama making the following two requests:

1. **That President Obama ask the Senate to return the CTBT to the executive branch.** On the basis that the 1999 Senate vote to reject ratification of the CTBT was the Senate's considered and institutional judgment on the matter, President Obama should ask the Senate to terminate any further domestic consideration of the treaty's ratification by returning it to the executive branch. If President Obama fails to respond, the Senate may wish to consider returning the treaty to the executive branch on its own volition.

2. **That President Obama announce that the U.S. has no intention of ratifying the CTBT.** Senators may also ask President Obama to act in a manner consistent with Article 18 of the Vienna Convention on the Law of Treaties and announce that the U.S. has no intention of ratifying the CTBT. Not only would this relieve the U.S. of the obligation not to take actions contrary to the object and purpose of the treaty, but it would resolve the entire matter of CTBT entry into force. This is because Article XIV of the treaty requires that the U.S., among other states, become a party before it may enter into force. Senators, by making this request, would help bring the entire matter of the CTBT's entry into force to an appropriate conclusion.

## Stand Up

The Senate's action to reject ratification in 1999 should be recognized and honored by its current members. Nothing has changed in the past 12 years to make the treaty any more palatable. Moreover, the integrity of the Senate as an institution is now being attacked. The Senate should not take this attack lying down.

# POSTSCRIPT

## Should the United States Ratify the Comprehensive Nuclear Test Ban Treaty?

It is unlikely that the Senate will reverse its 1999 rejection of the CTBT, whatever the merits of the arguments presented by Ellen Tauscher and Baker Spring. In the vote against the CTBT, all but 4 of the Senate's 55 Republicans voted against it, with those 4 joining the 44 Democrats (1 did not vote) in favor. Still, that left the treaty well below the two-thirds required vote, and that remains 67 votes. Achieving it would require a vote in which 14 of the Senate's 47 Republicans (in 2012) join all 53 Democrats and Independents to support the treaty. Even if the 2012 Senate elections result in Democratic gains, there will almost certainly be enough Republicans opposed to the treaty to block it. If reelected, President Barack Obama could publicly pledge to not test nuclear weapons, but that would not fulfill the CTBT's self-imposed requirement that has prevented the treaty from becoming operational without ratification by the United States and some other countries. Still, the debate over the CTBT has been going on at least since 1999, and it will certainly continue no matter what the Senate does or does not do in the immediate future.

For more on the treaty, the status of its ratification, and other matters, go to the website of the Preparatory Commission for the Comprehensive Nuclear-Test-Ban Treaty Organization at www.ctbto.org. The United Nations Office of Disarmament Affairs also has an informative site at www.un.org/disarmament/WMD/Nuclear/CTBT.shtml. Another site, one that has changed from negative about the treaty under President George W. Bush to positive under President Barack Obama, is at the U.S. State Department at www.state.gov/t/avc/c45942.htm. For additional reading opposing the treaty, see "Reconsidering the Comprehensive Test Ban Treaty," *National Review Online*, September 8, 2011, at www.nationalreview.com. A look at the current U.S. political climate related to ratification is found in Liviu Horovitz, "A Detour Strategy for the Test Ban Treaty," *Washington Quarterly* (September 2011).

## Questions for Critical Thinking and Reflection

1. Given the huge U.S. lead in the number and quality of its nuclear weapons compared to any other country except, perhaps, Russia, does it make a difference to the debate over ratifying the CTBT that smaller nuclear weapons–capable countries such as North Korea may refuse to do so?

2. Does the fact that the last U.S. nuclear test occurred in 1992 probably mean that testing is overdue or that tests are not necessary to maintain a reliable nuclear weapons capability?
3. A survey taken in 1999 after the Senate rejected the CTBT found that a plurality of Americans (46 percent) disagreed with the Senate, 28 percent agreed, and 26 percent were unsure. Did the Senate err by ignoring the view of a plurality or did the combined opposition and uncertainty of a majority of Americans mean that the Senate was wise in its caution?

# ISSUE 11

# Should U.S. Forces Continue to Fight in Afghanistan?

**YES: Ileana Ros-Lehtinen, Howard Berman, Adam Smith, and Buck McKeon,** from "Continue to Fight," remarks on the floor of the U.S. House of Representatives on House Concurrent Resolution 28, "Directing the President . . . to Remove the United States Armed Forces from Afghanistan" (March 17, 2011)

**NO: Dennis Kucinich, Barbara Lee, Walter B. Jones, Jason Chaffetz, and Ron Paul,** from "Withdraw Immediately," remarks on the floor of the U.S. House of Representatives on House Concurrent Resolution 28, "Directing the President . . . to Remove the United States Armed Forces from Afghanistan" (March 17, 2011)

## ISSUE SUMMARY

**YES:** Representatives Ileana Ros-Lehtinen (R-FL), Howard Berman (D-CA), Adam Smith (D-WA), and Buck McKeon (D-CA) oppose a resolution before the U.S. House of Representatives calling for the immediate withdrawal of U.S. military forces from Afghanistan, arguing that it is important that American troops remain until the U.S. goal of providing Afghanistan with the ability to defend itself against being once again taken over by the Taliban and al Qaeda is complete.

**NO:** Representatives Dennis Kucinich (D-OH), Barbara Lee (D-CA), Walter Jones (D-NC), Jason Chaffez (R-UT), and Ron Paul (R-TX) support a resolution before the U.S. House of Representatives calling for the withdrawal of all U.S. troops from Afghanistan no later than December 31, 2011, and argue that there is no good reason to continue the loss of American lives and the expense that the war entails.

**W**ith the rubble still smoldering at the site of the World Trade Center in New York City and the Pentagon outside of Washington, DC, in the aftermath of the 9/11 terrorist attacks, an angry President George W. Bush told Vice President Richard Cheney, "We're at war, Dick. We're going to find out who did this and kick their ass." Americans overwhelmingly agreed with that sentiment. After the al Qaeda terrorist group and its supporter, the Taliban government of

Afghanistan, were identified as the culprits, 82 percent of Americans favored military action to destroy al Qaeda and topple the Taliban. This level of support made the war in Afghanistan the second most popular in U.S. history, trailing only support (97 percent) of the declaration of war against Japan following its attack on Pearl Harbor, Hawaii, on December 7, 1941.

Soon, U.S. troops, aided by a much smaller number of allied, mostly British, troops ousted the Taliban from power and put them and al Qaeda to flight. Then began the much more difficult task of fully securing rural areas from continuing Taliban control, of creating a functioning government, and of uniting a historically fractious population. This daunting task was made even more challenging when the war with and occupation of Iraq that began in March 2003 diverted U.S. troops, funds, and attention away from Afghanistan. This persisted for about five years until the following two changes occurred in 2008. One was that the U.S. combat role in Iraq began to wind down. In 2007, 914 American troops died in Iraq; only 314 perished in 2008. Second, part of Barack Obama's presidential campaign attack on the Bush administration and the Republicans was to charge that the ill-conceived Iraq war had diverted attention from the justified, antiterrorism war in Afghanistan. As Obama put it during a campaign speech, "What President Bush and Senator [John] McCain don't understand is that the central front in the war on terror is not in Iraq, and it never was—the central front is in Afghanistan . . . where the terrorists who hit us on 9/11 are still plotting attacks seven years later."

Two other factors also promoted the shift in American's attention to Afghanistan once Obama was in the White House. During his first year in office, Obama nearly doubled the number of U.S. troops in Afghanistan to about 68,000. Also in 2009, the number of American deaths in Afghanistan (317) exceeded those in Iraq (149). These rising human and budgetary costs accompanied by an unpromising military and political situation in Afghanistan undermined Americans' support of the war. The share of Americans thinking that the war was worth fighting dropped from 56 percent in February 2009 to 52 percent that December. As 2010 dawned, President Obama was faced with a situation in Afghanistan much like President Bush had faced in 2007 in Iraq. Bush responded by sending a "surge" of more than 20,000 troops into Iraq. Taking the same route, Obama announced in December 2009 that he would send more than 30,000 additional U.S. troops to Afghanistan. Americans supported Obama's move, but only by a less than overwhelming 57 percent. By then the war was in its ninth year, the second longest in U.S. history after Vietnam. The additional troops had some initial positive impact, but at best progress was marginal and the long-term success of the U.S. effort remained seriously in doubt. Moreover, the war continued to cost American lives and to cost billions of dollars at a time of severe economic distress in the United States and a mounting budget deficit crisis. This set the stage for the March 2011 debate in the two following readings between those opposed and those in favor of a House resolution to rapidly get all U.S. troops out of the country.

# YES ⟵     Ileana Ros-Lehtinen et al.

# Continue to Fight

## Representative Ros-Lehtinen

I rise in strong opposition to this resolution [in favor of the immediate withdrawal of U.S. combat troops from Afghanistan], as it would undermine the efforts of our military and our international partners in Afghanistan and would gravely harm our Nation's security. Insanity has been described as doing the same thing over and over again and expecting different results. Three thousand people died on September 11 because we walked away once from Afghanistan, thinking that it didn't matter who controlled that country. We were wrong then. Let us not make the same mistake twice. Completing our mission in Afghanistan is essential to keeping our homeland safe.

As Under Secretary of Defense Michele Flournoy stated in testimony to the Senate Armed Services Committee earlier this week, "The threat to our national security and the security of our friends and allies that emanates from the borderland of Afghanistan and Pakistan is not hypothetical. There is simply no other place in the world that contains such a concentration of al Qaeda senior leaders and operational commanders. To allow these hostile organizations to flourish in this region is to put the security of the United States and our friends and allies at grave risk."

To quit the area before we have routed out the terrorists would not only hand al Qaeda a propaganda victory of immeasurable value, it would cede them a sanctuary from which they could mount fresh strikes at the west with virtual immunity. To withdraw from Afghanistan at this point, before we finish the job, is to pave the way for the next 9/11.

Therefore, the question that we must consider is, Can we afford to abandon our mission in Afghanistan? General David Petraeus, commander, International Security Assistance Force, ISAF, commander, U.S. Forces Afghanistan, stated, "I can understand the frustration. We have been at this for 10 years. We have spent an enormous amount of money. We have sustained very tough losses and difficult, life-changing wounds. But I think it is important to remember why we are there."

This is about our vital national security interests. It is about doing what is necessary to ensure that al Qaeda and other extremists cannot reestablish safe havens such as the ones they had in Afghanistan when the 9/11 attacks were planned against our Nation and our people. The enemy, indeed, is on

U.S. House of Representatives, March 17, 2011.

the run. It is demoralized and divided. Let us not give up now. Let us not betray the sacrifices of our men and women serving in harm's way, and they ask for nothing in return, except our full support. Dedicated servants such as my stepson Douglas and daughter-in-law Lindsay, who served in Iraq—and Lindsay also served in Afghanistan. Dedicated servants such as Matt Zweig and Greg McCarthy of our Foreign Affairs Committee majority staff, who just returned from serving a year in Kandahar and Kabul. And we thank them for their service. Let us follow the lead of our wounded warriors who, after long and arduous recoveries, volunteer to return to the battlefield to finish their mission. I urge our colleagues to oppose this dangerous resolution.

# Representative Smith

I [also] rise in opposition to this resolution, and I do so as one who does firmly believe that we need to, as soon as we responsibly can, end our military engagement in Afghanistan. The cost is very real. I represent Joint Base Lewis-McChord, which includes Fort Lewis Army Base, and we have lost many soldiers in Afghanistan. The families understand the cost. We need to wind down this war as quickly and as responsibly as we can. Unfortunately, this resolution does not give us the opportunity to do that. And we have clear national security interests in Afghanistan.

While I may agree with many of the statements about the troubles and challenges that we face in that region, the one thing that you will hear today that I cannot agree with is the idea that we have no national security interests in Afghanistan and Pakistan, or that we somehow do not have a clear mission. We have a clear mission. We do not want the Taliban and their al Qaeda allies back in charge of Afghanistan or any significant part of Afghanistan from which they could plot attacks against us, as they are still trying to do in the parts of Pakistan that they are in.

We need to get an Afghanistan Government that can stand up, and they are going to need our help to get there. Now there are many who have argued—and I am sure some on both sides of the aisle would be sympathetic with the notion that we need to reduce our commitment there—that a full-scale counterinsurgency effort, or 100,000 U.S. troops and 150,000 NATO and U.S. troops combined, is too much. Let's go with a much lighter footprint [that] focuses on counterterrorism, focuses on going after the terrorists, and allows the Afghans to take the lead on everything else. And there is a plausible argument for that.

This resolution does not allow that. I want the members of this chamber to understand this resolution requires complete withdrawal of all U.S. forces by the end of this year. And I can tell you, as the ranking member on the Armed Services Committee, that [doing so] is not in the national security interest of this country.

We may have a legitimate debate about what our presence should be, how we should change it, but the notion that we can simply walk away from this problem, as [Representative] Ros-Lehtinen pointed out, is simply not true. And it is a problem that, believe me, I, as much as anyone in this body, would love to be able to walk away from. It is an enormous challenge. And what Mr. Friedman has to say about the governments of Afghanistan and Pakistan is spot on. But the problem is, we can't simply walk away from them and let them fall because of the national security implications that that has for us right here at home, given what the Taliban and al Qaeda would plan. I am all in favor of a more reasonable plan for how we go forward in Afghanistan, but simply heading for the hills and leaving is not a responsible plan. It's not even really a plan for how to deal with the very difficult challenges that we face in that region, and I urge this body to oppose this resolution.

# Representative McKeon

I join with my colleagues from the Foreign Services Committee, Foreign Affairs Committee, and my colleagues from the Armed Services Committee in opposition to this resolution. This resolution would undermine the efforts of our military commanders and troops as they work side by side with their Afghan and coalition partners.

Yesterday, in his testimony before the House Armed Services Committee, General Petraeus, commander of the U.S. and allied forces in Afghanistan, described significant progress made by our troops and Afghan forces. But while the United States is on track to accomplish our objectives by 2014, the general also warned that this hard fought progress is fragile and reversible; and he urged that continued support from this Congress for our mission in Afghanistan is vital to success.

When asked specifically how our troops and enemies would view the resolution before us today, General Petraeus stated: The Taliban and al Qaeda obviously would trumpet this as a victory. Needless to say, it would completely undermine everything our troopers have fought so much and sacrificed so much for.

When the President [Barack Obama] authorized a surge of 30,000 additional troops, he reminded us of why we are in Afghanistan. It's the epicenter of where al Qaeda planned and launched the 9/11 attacks against innocent Americans. It remains vital to the national security of this country to prohibit the Taliban from once again providing sanctuary to al Qaeda leaders. Moreover, withdrawing before completing our mission would reinforce extremist propaganda that Americans are weak and unreliable allies and could facilitate extremist recruiting and future attacks.

Like most Republicans, I supported the President's decision to surge in Afghanistan. I believe that with additional forces, combined with giving General Petraeus the time, space and resources he needs, we can win this conflict.

During a visit last week with our troops in Afghanistan, Secretary Gates observed the closer you get to this fight, the better it looks. Having just returned myself from Afghanistan a few weeks ago, I couldn't agree more. Our delegation to Afghanistan met with senior military commanders and diplomats, talked to airmen at Bagram [air base], marines in Helmand [Province], and soldiers in Kandahar [the second largest city in Afghanistan]. It was clear to our delegation that our forces have made significant gains and have reversed the Taliban's momentum.

Our forces and their Afghan partners have cleared enemy strongholds, swept up significant weapons caches, and given more Afghans the confidence to defy the Taliban. We have made considerable progress in growing and professionalizing Afghanistan's army and police so these forces are more capable and reliable partners to our own troops.

As significant as our troops' achievements in the fields are, they can easily be undone by poor decisions made here in Washington. Today's debate is not being conducted in a vacuum. Our troops are listening. Our allies are listening. The Taliban and al Qaeda are also listening. And, finally, the Afghan people are listening. We want to send a clear message to the Afghan people and government, our coalition partners, our military men and women that this Congress will stand firm in our commitment to free us from the problems that the Taliban created for us on 9/11. We will not have this sanctuary ever happen again.

I urge my colleagues to vote "no" on this resolution.

I completely agree with [the proponents of the resolution to immediately withdraw from Afghanistan] that as we are moving into the 10th year of this conflict, it is critical—not just nice, it is really critical for the House to have an open and honest debate on the merits of our ongoing military operations in Afghanistan, and that debate should be outside of the context of a defense spending bill.

But what I also do is take strong issue with the invocation of section 5(c) of the War Powers Act as the basis for this debate. If we are here to respect the law and the procedures, you have to remember that it is that section which authorizes a privileged resolution, like the one we have before us today, to require the withdrawal of U.S. Forces when they are engaged in hostilities and Congress has not authorized the use of military force.

There may be aspects of our operations around the world that people can claim under section 5(c) have not been authorized. No one can make a contention that what we are now doing in Afghanistan was not authorized by the Congress. There can be no doubt this military action in Afghanistan was authorized. It was authorized in 2001, soon after 9/11.

But let's set aside the procedure and the specific dictates of the statute. I do think and share my concerns, well articulated by the ranking member of the House Armed Services Committee, that it is not responsible to demand a complete withdrawal of our troops from Afghanistan by the end of the year without regard to the consequence of our withdrawal, without regard to the situation on the ground, including efforts to promote economic development and expand the rule of law, and without any measurement of whether the current strategy is indeed working.

I am very sensitive to the arguments posed by [those who want to rapidly withdraw]. The cost of human life due to the war and the heavy costs incurred by our country at a time of great economic hardship should give any Member of Congress pause.

I am also keenly aware of the concerns regarding our overall U.S. strategy in Afghanistan. It remains to be seen whether a counterinsurgency strategy will succeed there and, equally important, whether the Afghans are taking sufficient responsibility for this war. I am troubled that the war very much remains an American-led effort and that the U.S. presence has created a culture of dependency in Afghanistan. Notwithstanding all that, I won't support a call for a full withdrawal until we give the President's strategy additional time, at least through the spring, to show results or, without a responsible withdrawal strategy, to ensure gains made thus far will not be lost.

A number of positive developments make me unwilling to throw in the towel just yet. For example, as noted by General Petraeus in testimony yesterday, coalition forces have been making some progress against Taliban forces in southern Afghanistan. In addition, the training of Afghan security forces has exceeded targets, and we are inching slowly toward the point at which they may be able to secure their own borders.

A final plea to my colleagues, and that is to some of my colleagues who are joining me in opposing this resolution. I am sure we are not going to succeed in Afghanistan unless our civilian efforts are fully resourced. When I traveled to Afghanistan last April, I was encouraged to see our military forces, diplomats, and development experts working closely together in the field.

General Petraeus couldn't have been more clear in his testimony: We are setting ourselves up for failure if we fully fund the clear part of the President's counterinsurgency strategy, the part carried out by the military, but short-change the hold-and-build portions of the strategy, like economic development and building good governance. These are the keys to lasting success in Afghanistan. These are the keys to a successful counterinsurgency strategy. And when we meet those tests and do those works, we may be able to create the environment that will allow our troops to return home. For all these reasons, I oppose the resolution.

## Representative Berman

I just want to take a couple of minutes to talk about one point. That part of the majority party that is urging the same position I am on this resolution, which is a "no" vote, has made when you're dealing with fundamental issues of national security, you spend money, even under difficult times, a point that I have no disagreement with. And they argue the issue of what the alternatives will be and the potential for providing new safe havens for terrorists or more safe havens for terrorists or a return of Afghanistan as a safe haven for terrorists if we pass this resolution, and I don't disagree with that point.

What I find upsetting about the majority's position is their denial of the fundamental point. They quote General Petraeus for every position that they find philosophically and factually satisfying and ignore General Petraeus and Secretary Gates on the fundamental concept of how we hope to change the course of what is happening in Afghanistan. Because if we don't change it, then we have to come and address the fundamental question of what we're doing there through a counterinsurgency strategy.

So we talk about clear and hold and build. And it is the military's job to clear and, for a time, to hold, but build is fundamentally a civilian program. General Petraeus over and over again has said this conflict in Afghanistan cannot be won unless we strengthen the governance of a very flawed government in Afghanistan, unless we provide economic opportunities for that society to progress and win the hearts and minds of the people of Afghanistan to the cause for which we are fighting. It's also a view of Afghanistan as if it's isolated from the rest of the world. I can go through countries around the world—failed states, nearly failing states, terrible problems—which are certainly becoming safe harbors for terrorism.

So when the same party that makes a strong case for our national security interests here at the same time passes legislation which slashes every aspect of efforts to strengthen governance and development assistance and to provide the kinds of opportunities that serve our national security interests, I find it a strange kind of logic and a flaw in their approach to this.

I understand the economic hardships we have. If one wanted to look at the foreign assistance budget and take specific things that aren't working and get rid of them, I understand that, and if one wanted to make proportional cuts in the foreign assistance budget. But to come with the argument of, "We're broke; we've got to cut spending," and then disproportionately focus on that aspect of our national security strategy which will do a tremendous amount and will be fundamental to any effort to stop them from being safe harbors for terrorism, and that is to massively slash disproportionately foreign assistance, it's a terrible mistake. It terribly undermines the national security strategy that we're trying to achieve through our operations and our presence and the money we're spending in Afghanistan. It's not thinking, I think, as clearly as needs to be thought. And I urge those in the majority to think again about how much the cuts that we need to make should be coming from that part of the budget that constitutes 1 percent of the Federal budget.

Dennis Kucinich et al.

→ **NO**

# Withdraw Immediately

## Representative Kucinich

In the next 2 hours [of debate on the floor of the House of Representatives], we are going to demonstrate that the American people oppose this war by a margin of two to one. I will enter into the [*Congressonal*] *Record* this *Washington Post* poll that was published on March 15, which says that nearly two-thirds of Americans say the war isn't worth fighting. In the next 2 hours, we are going to demonstrate that we are spending $100 billion per year on this war. There are those who are saying the war could last at least another 10 years. Are we willing to spend another $1 trillion on a war that doesn't have any exit plan, for which there is no timeframe to get out, no endgame, where we haven't defined our mission? The question is not whether we can afford to leave. The question is, can we afford to stay? And I submit we cannot afford to stay. In the next 2 hours, we are going to demonstrate that the counterintelligence strategy of General Petraeus is an abysmal failure, and it needs to be called as such. So I want to conclude this part of my presentation with an article by Thomas Friedman in *The New York Times,* which says, "What are we doing spending $110 billion this year supporting corrupt and unpopular regimes in Afghanistan and Pakistan that are almost identical to the governments we are applauding the Arab people for overthrowing?"

Members have been very concerned about out-of-control spending. They are calling for a reduction in the Federal budget. Cutting spending on the war in Afghanistan would solve their concerns. Spending on the war is greater than the minimum amount of Federal spending certain Members believe must be cut from the budget for fiscal responsibility.

In the fiscal year 2012 budget request, the President has requested $113.4 billion to continue the war. In fact, congressional appropriations of over $100 billion for the Afghanistan war has been the rule in recent years; and as we've seen, there is talk of extending this war for another 10 years. $1 trillion, perhaps?

Spending on the Afghanistan war has increased much faster than overall government spending in recent years. Consider a comparison of the average annual rates of growth of government spending versus the Afghanistan war spending from 2008 through 2011. Overall government spending has increased 9 percent from 2008 through 2011, but Afghanistan war spending has increased 25 percent. If you want to save $100 billion, then vote for this

U.S. House of Representatives, March 17, 2011.

resolution. . . . I had a hearing last year before the Veterans' Affairs Committee in which Nobel Prize-winning economist Joseph Stigleitz testified. He said these wars in Iraq and Afghanistan will be $5 trillion to $7 trillion wars over their whole course. Let us not forget—and that's not calculated in your costs.

The veterans, those who have served in this war with great courage, with great professionalism. Treating these veterans costs hundreds of billions of dollars more, and we're not considering that when we talk about ending this war. We've been told that there have been about 45,000 casualties in these two wars in the last 10 years. Then why have almost 1 million people shown up at the Veterans Administration hospitals for war-related injuries? One million. This is not a rounding error. This is a deliberate attempt to misguide us on the cost of this war. This war is costing, in addition to what the budget says, hundreds of billions more for treating our veterans. We must calculate that into the cost of this war. . . . We keep coming back to 9/11. We're near the eighth anniversary of the invasion of Iraq, which had nothing to do with 9/11, and which was predicated on a lie, no weapons of mass destruction. The war in Afghanistan is based on a misreading of history. The Soviet Union understood that at hard cost.

The occupation is fueling an insurgency. Now, Jeremy Scahill in the *Nation* points out that Taliban leaders have said they've seen a swelling in Taliban ranks since 9/11 in part attributed to the widely held perception that the Karzai government is corrupt and illegitimate, and that Afghans, primarily ethnic Pashtuns, want foreign occupation forces out. They're only fighting to make foreigners leave Afghanistan. Occupation fuels insurgency. That is an ironclad fact. . . .

The 2001 authorization of military force and the justification for our continued military presence in Afghanistan is that the Taliban in the past provided a safe haven for al Qaeda or could do so again in the future. General Petraeus has already admitted that al Qaeda has little or no presence in Afghanistan. Al Qaeda is an international organization, and, yes, they are a threat to America. The Taliban is only a threat to us as long as we continue our military occupation in Afghanistan.

After more than 9 years of military occupation of Afghanistan, can we really continue to claim to be acting in self-defense? The premise that the presence of our troops on the ground keeps us safer at home has been repudiated by recent terrorist attacks on the United States, all done by people other than Afghans outraged at continuing U.S. military occupation of predominantly predominantly Muslim countries. That is not to justify what they do, but it is to clarify the condition that we have in Afghanistan.

For how long are we going to continue to dedicate hundreds of billions of dollars and thousands of lives before we realize we can't win Afghanistan militarily?

At the end of the year, the administration and U.S. military leaders were touting peace talks to end the war with high-level Taliban leaders. These Taliban leaders turned out to be fake. A November 2010 article in *The New York Times* detailed joint U.S. and Afghan negotiations with Mullah Akhtar Muhammad Mansour, a man the U.S. claimed was one of the most senior commanders in the Taliban. According to *The New York Times*, "the episode underscores the uncertain and even bizarre nature of the atmosphere in which Afghan and American leaders search for ways to bring the American-led war to an end. The leaders of the Taliban are believed to be hiding in Pakistan, possibly with assistance of the Pakistani government, which receives billions of dollars in U.S. aid."

How can we claim that a cornerstone of our counterinsurgency strategy is to take out Taliban strongholds across the country while at the same time conducting negotiations with the Taliban in an effort to end the war? This episode further underlies the significant weakness in our strategy. We think we can separate the Taliban from the rest the Afghan population. Our counterinsurgency strategy fails to recognize a basic principle: Occupations fuel insurgencies. Occupations fuel insurgencies. Occupations fuel insurgencies.

The Taliban is a local resistance movement that is part and parcel of the indigenous population. We lost the Vietnam war because we failed to win the hearts and minds of the local population. Without providing them with a competent government that provided them with basic security and a decent living, we're committing the same mistake in Afghanistan.

News reports indicate the Taliban is regaining momentum. The increase in civilian casualties due to higher levels of violence by insurgents further undermines the assurances of progress. As we send more troops into the country and kill innocent civilians with errant air strikes, the Taliban gains more support as resistors of foreign occupation. If we accept the premise that we can never leave Afghanistan until the Taliban is eradicated, we'll be there forever.

## Representative Lee

Thank you very much. Mr. Speaker, I rise today in strong support of this resolution, of which I'm proud to be an original cosponsor, and I'd like to thank Representative KUCINICH for his work on this resolution and also mainly for his continued and passioned defense of congressional war powers authority. Also, I, too, want to commend Congressman JONES for his leadership on this issue and so many other issues.

This resolution is simple and straightforward. It directs the President to end the near decade-long war in Afghanistan and to redeploy United States Armed Forces from Afghanistan by the end of this year. Al Qaeda is not in Afghanistan, and Osama bin Laden still has not been found. This resolution comes at a time when a growing number of Members of Congress, military and foreign policy experts, and, in particular, the American people, are calling for an immediate end to this war. Enough is enough.

Let me just say something. First of all, we've heard that polls are showing that nearly three-quarters of the American public favors action to speed up U.S. withdrawal from Afghanistan. Yes, the Congress authorized the use of force in 2001, which I voted against because it gave the President, any President, a blank check to use force, anytime, anyplace, anywhere in the world for any period of time. It was not a declaration of war, yet this has been the longest war in American history, the longest war in American history. As the daughter of a 25-year Army officer who served in two wars, let me salute our troops, let me honor our troops and just say our servicemen and women have performed with incredible courage and commitment in Afghanistan. But they have been put in an impossible situation. It's time to bring them home. There is no military solution in Afghanistan.

As we fight here in Congress to protect investments in education, health care, public health and safety, the war in Afghanistan will cost more than $100 billion in 2011 alone. No one can deny that the increasing costs of the war in Afghanistan are constraining our efforts to invest in job creation and jump-start the economy.

Yesterday, I joined a bipartisan group of 80 Members of Congress in sending a letter to President Obama calling for a significant and sizeable reduction in United States troop levels in Afghanistan no later than July of this year.

This debate that we're having today here should have occurred in 2001 when Congress authorized this blank check. It was barely debated. It was barely debated, and the rush to war has created not less anger towards the United States but more hostilities, and it's not in our national security nor economic interests to continue. . . .

# Representative Jones

We are debating how long we are going to be in Afghanistan. Recently, Secretary Gates testified before the Armed Services Committee, which I serve on, and said that he thought by 2014 we could start substantial reduction in our troop strength in Afghanistan, 2014, that it might be 2015, 2016.

That's why this debate and this resolution is so important, not important for those of us in the House, but important for our military and the American people. And [Representative] Kucinich did make reference to The Washington Post-ABC poll that was taken a couple of days ago that said 73 percent of the American people said it's time, this year, to bring our troops home.

In addition, I would like to share a quote from the leader of Afghanistan, Mr. Karzai. He's our man in Afghanistan. All right, now, he's our man. This was his quote 3 days ago: "I request that NATO and America should stop these operations on our soil," Karzai said. "This war is not on our soil. If this war is against terror, then this war is not here. Terror is not here." The number of al Qaeda and their presence in Afghanistan is about 20 or 30. Most of them are in Pakistan. I would agree with that. But this debate is critical.

I want to share very quickly a letter from a retired colonel who's a marine that lives in my district: "I am writing this letter to express my concern over the current Afghanistan war. I am a retired marine officer with 31-plus years of active duty. I retired in 2004 due to service limitations, or I am sure I would have been on my third or fourth deployment by now to a war that has gone on too long."

And I'll go to the bottom of this: "It makes no sense if we're there 4 years or 40. The results will be the same." And he closed his letter this way: "This war is costing the United States billions of dollars a month to wage, and we still continue to get more young Americans killed. The Afghan war has no end state for us. I urge you to make contact with all the current and newly elected men and women in Congress and ask them to end this war and bring our young men and women home. If any of my comments will assist in this effort, you are welcome to use them and my name. Respectfully, Dennis G. Adams, Lieutenant Colonel retired, United States Marine Corps."

I am grateful that we are having this debate from both sides, those that want to stay there for another 4 or 5 years versus those of us who would like to bring our troops home. I want to put a face on this debate if I may.

This young man's name is Tyler Jordan from Cincinnati, Ohio. He is attending his father's funeral. He was a gunnery sergeant, Phillip Jordan, who was killed for this country. . . . How many more moms and dads and wives and husbands are going to be at Dover Air Force Base to receive the remains of their loved ones? That is why this debate is so important, and why we need to have a date and a time to start bringing them home. My last poster: this absolutely handsome couple. The marine went out with PTSD [post-traumatic stress disorder]. His beautiful wife, Katie, and his little boy. Last year at [Marine Corps] Camp Lejeune, McHugh Boulevard, he pulls his car over in the middle of the day, and he shoots himself in the head and kills himself.

How many more Tom Bagosys will commit suicide? How many Tyler Jordans will not have their daddies coming home? How many moms and dads, wives and husbands will be at Dover to see those in a flag-draped coffin?

## Representative Chaffetz

I am going to be voting in favor of this resolution. The United States military is the greatest fighting force on the face of the planet. I could not be more proud of our troops who have served our country with such valor and such vigor.

This is the longest war in the history of the United States of America. And let there be no mistake, the global war on terror is real. It is very real.

I reject the notion that polls should matter in any way, shape, or form in this debate. That is not how the United States operates. This is not how we decide whether or not we go to war or we bring our troops home.

I reject the notion that bringing our troops home at some point, which I consider to be victory, is somehow a pathway or paving a pathway to another 9/11. I think that is offensive, and I think it is inaccurate.

Now, in many ways we have had success over the course of the years. Let's understand that according to the National Intelligence Estimate, which has been printed in many newspapers, that the Taliban poses no clear and present danger to the current Afghan Government, nor do they pose a danger to the United States of America. Further, we have had our CIA Director state that there are less than 50 al-Qaeda in the entire boundaries of Afghanistan. I believe it should be the policy of the United States of America that if we send our troops to war, we go with everything we have. We do not hold back. A politically correct war is a lost war, and at the present time we are playing politics. We aren't going with everything everything we have. If we are serious about doing it, Mr. President, you go with everything. And until this President attends more funerals than he does rounds of golf, this person will be highly offended.

We have to define the mission. The President of the United States has failed to define success in Afghanistan. We are participating in the business of nation building, and I reject that. We are propping up a government that is fundamentally corrupt, and we all know it. It will not get us to where we want to go.

We must redefine the rules of engagement. Even when I was in Afghanistan visiting with General Petraeus, he admitted that we are using smaller caliber rounds. Again, we are trying to be more politically correct instead of actually protecting American lives.

Let me also say again that terrorism is a global threat. We must use our forces around the world when there is a direct threat on the United States of America. That is not confined to just the boundaries of Afghanistan. It is happening globally, and it is real. We have to deal with the threats in Iran and not take our eye off the ball. Finally, I would say that our national debt is a clear and present danger to the United States of America, and we must pay attention to that.

# Representative Paul

The question we are facing today is, should we leave Afghanistan? I think the answer is very clear, and it's not complicated. Of course we should, as soon as we can. This suggests that we can leave by the end of the year. If we don't, we'll be there for another decade, would be my prediction.

The American people are now with us. A group of us here in the Congress, a bipartisan group, for nearly a decade have been talking about this, arguing not to expand the war, not to be over there, not to be in nation building. And the American people didn't pay much attention. Now they are. The large majority of the American people now say it's time to get out of Afghanistan. It's a fruitless venture. Too much has been lost. The chance of winning, since we don't even know what we are going to win, doesn't exist. So they are tired of it. Financially, there's a good reason to come home as well.

Some argue we have to be there because if we leave under these circumstances we'll lose face; it will look embarrassing to leave. So how many more men and women have to die, how many more dollars have to be spent to save face? That is one of the worst arguments possible.

We are not there under legal conditions. This is a war. Who says it isn't a war? Everybody talks about the Afghan war. Was the war declared? Of course not. It wasn't declared. There was a resolution passed that said that the President at that time, under the emergency of 9/11, could go and deal with al Qaeda, those who brought upon the 9/11 bombings. But al Qaeda is not there anymore. So we are fighting the Taliban.

The Taliban used to be our allies at one time when the Soviets were there. The Taliban's main goal is to keep the foreign occupation out. They want foreigners out of their country. They are not al Qaeda. But the argument here on the floor is we have got to go after al Qaeda. This is not a war against al Qaeda. If anything, it gives the incentive for al Qaeda to grow in numbers rather than dealing with them.

The money issue, we are talking about a lot of money. How much do we spend a year? Probably about $130 billion, up to $1 trillion now in this past decade. Later on in the day, we are going to have two votes. We are going to have a vote on doing something sensible, making sense out of our foreign policy, bringing our troops home and saving hundreds of billions of dollars. Then we also will have a vote against NPR [National Public Radio], to cut the funding of NPR. There is a serious question about whether that will even cut one penny. But at least the fiscal conservatives are going to be overwhelmingly in support of slashing NPR, and then go home and brag about how they are such great fiscal conservatives. And the very most they might save is $10 million, and that's their claim to fame for slashing the budget. At the same time, they won't consider for a minute cutting a real significant amount of money. All empires end for fiscal reasons because they spread themselves too far around the world, and that's what we are facing. We are in the midst of a military conflict that is contributing to this inevitable crisis and it's financial. And you would think there would be a message there.

The process that we are going through is following the War Powers Resolution. This is a proper procedure. It calls attention to how we slip into these wars. I have always claimed that it's the way we get into the wars that is the problem. If we would be precise and only go to war with a declaration of war, with the people behind us, knowing who the enemy is, and fight, win, and get it over with, that would be more legitimate. They don't do it now because the American people wouldn't support it. Nobody is going to declare war against Afghanistan or Iraq or Libya. We now have been so careless for the past 50 or 60 years that, as a Congress and especially as a House, we have reneged on our responsibilities. We have avoided our prerogatives of saying that we have the control. We have control of the purse. We have control of when we are supposed to go to war. Yet the wars continue. They never stop. And we are going to be completely brought down to our knees.

We can't change Afghanistan. The people who are bragging about these changes, even if you could, you are not supposed to. You don't have the moral authority. You don't have the constitutional authority. . . . So I would say, the sooner, the better, we can come home. This process says come home. Under the [resolution], it says you should start bringing troops home within 30 days. This allows up to the end of the year after this would be passed. But this needs to be done. A message needs to be sent.

# EXPLORING THE ISSUE

## Should U.S. Forces Continue to Fight in Afghanistan?

## Questions for Critical Thinking and Reflection

1. If the war in Afghanistan was worth undertaking in 2001, why is it still not worth "winning"?
2. How, in a situation such as the one in Afghanistan, does one determine when one has won enough to begin to bring troops home?
3. What, if anything, do you think the United States should do if, after all U.S troops are out of Afghanistan, the Taliban regain control of the country? What if the Taliban also allow al Qaeda or other terrorist groups to reestablish a base in the country?

## Is There Common Ground?

The resolution in the House calling for an immediate withdrawal from Afghanistan was overwhelmingly defeated, drawing only 93 yes votes, compared to 321 no votes. That lopsided defeat did not accurately reflect sentiments in the House about the war, though, because many members who noted no did not want to seem to be undercutting U.S. troops in the field or, among Democrats, did not want to add to President Obama's travails. Even more clearly, the House vote did not coincide with Americans' opinion. A CBS poll taken one day after the March 17, 2011, vote found that when Americans were asked, "Do you think the US [United States] is doing the right thing by fighting the war in Afghanistan now, or should the US not be involved in Afghanistan now?" only 39 percent replied "right thing" compared to 53 percent who said the U.S. should no longer be involved.

Almost certainly responding at least in part to Americans' declining support for the war, President Obama in June 2011 announced a series of troop withdrawals and an end to combat missions by U.S. troops in Afghanistan by the end of 2014. There have been several occasions, including during the presidential debates during the 2012 election, that Obama said that U.S. troops would be out of Afghanistan by the end of 2014, but that is not quite what he said in June 2011. The difference could be that some troops would remain in Afghanistan to provide training for the Afghans and some defensive security positions. Subsequently, the White House indicated that the earlier, more limited version of the withdrawal remained U.S. policy. Thus, the debate here is not limited by what happens by 2015, but also whether any U.S. military personnel should be in Afghanistan. A poll taken in October 2012 shows that a plurality of Americans (46 percent) thought troops were being withdrawn at about the right speed, 28 percent want a faster withdrawal, and 17 percent said the withdrawals were moving too quickly.

## Additional Resources

To find out more about Afghanistan, go to the website of the government of Afghanistan at www.afghangovernment.com/ or to www.afghanweb.com/. A source for U.S. policy is the White House's web page at www.whitehouse. gov. Keyboard "Afghanistan" into the search window. Using the search window at the Department of Defense site, www.defenselink.mil/, will yield more on the military side. Casualty data for Afghanistan, and Iraq also, are at http://icasualties.org/. For a general background, read David Loyn, *In Afghanistan: Two Hundred Years of British, Russian and American Occupation* (Palgrave Macmillan, 2009). For an analysis of the long-term impact of the U.S. interventions in and withdrawals from Iraq and Afghanistan on the terrorist threat to the United States, read Mark N. Katz, *Leaving without Losing: The War on Terror after Iraq and Afghanistan* (Johns Hopkins University Press, 2012).

# ISSUE 12

# Does Using Drones to Attack Terrorists Globally Violate International Law?

**YES: Mary Ellen O'Connell,** from "Lawful Use of Combat Drones," Testimony during Hearings on "Rise of the Drones II: Examining the Legality of Unmanned Targeting," before the Subcommittee on National Security and Foreign Affairs, Committee on Oversight and Government Reform, U.S. House of Representatives (April 28, 2010)

**NO: Michael W. Lewis,** from "Examining the Legality of Unmanned Targeting," Testimony during Hearings on "Rise of the Drones II: Examining the Legality of Unmanned Targeting," before the Subcommittee on National Security and Foreign Affairs, Committee on Oversight and Government Reform, U.S. House of Representatives (April 28, 2010)

## ISSUE SUMMARY

**YES:** Mary Ellen O'Connell, a research professor at the Kroc Institute, University of Notre Dame, and the Robert and Marion Short Professor of Law at the School of Law, University of Notre Dame, tells a congressional committee that the United States is failing more often than not to follow the most important single rule governing drones: restricting their use to the battlefield.

**NO:** Michael W. Lewis, a professor of law at Ohio Northern University's Pettit College of Law, disagrees, contending that there is nothing inherently illegal about using drones to target specific terrorists or groups of terrorists on or away from the battlefield.

**D**uring March and April 2010, the Subcommittee on National Security and Foreign Affairs of the Committee on Oversight and Government Reform in the U.S. House of Representatives held a series of hearings to look into the military use of unmanned aerial vehicles (UAVs, drones). These remotely piloted aircraft are capable of launching missiles and otherwise attacking targets, of using cameras and other sensors to gather intelligence, of facilitating communications, and of performing other tasks. The characteristics of the numerous types of UAVs in the U.S. military inventory vary considerably by mission, but one of the best known is the Predator. It is propeller driven, has a top speed of 135 mph, has a 450-mile range, is 27 feet long, has a 48-foot wingspan, can stay aloft for 20 hours, and is armed with two air-to-surface Hellfire missiles, each tipped with a warhead carrying 20 pounds of high explosives. Relative to piloted warplanes, UAVs are inexpensive, costing about one-tenth as much each. There are also great differences in the time and money spent creating pilots.

During the first session of the hearings on March 23, 2010, the subcommittee's chair, Representative John F. Tierney (D-MA), opened the inquiry by outlining its purpose. As Tierney put it with regard to the subject of this debate:

> . . . Over the last decade, the number of unmanned systems and their applications has grown rapidly. So too has the number of operational, political, and legal questions associated with this technology. The growing demand for and reliance on unmanned systems has serious implications, . . . As the United States is engaged in two wars abroad, unmanned systems, particularly unmanned aerial vehicles, have become a centerpiece of that war effort. In recent years, the Department of Defense's UAV inventory has rapidly grown in size, from 167 in 2002 to over 7000 today. Last year, for the first time, the U.S. Air Force trained more unmanned pilots than traditional fighter pilots.
>
> Some express no doubt that unmanned systems have been a boost to U.S. war efforts in the Middle East and South Asia. CIA Director Leon Panetta said last May that "drone strikes are the only game in town in terms of confronting or trying to disrupt the al Qaeda leadership." Media reports over the last year that the top two leaders of the Pakistani Taliban were killed by drone strikes also support this argument.
>
> But some critics argue that drone strikes are unethical at best and counter-productive at worst. They point to the reportedly high rate of civilian casualties . . . and argue that the strikes do more to stoke anti-Americanism than they do to weaken our enemies. . . . This is particularly relevant in the era of counter-insurgency doctrine, a central tenet of which is, "first, do no harm."
>
> It also may be the case that we are fighting wars with modern technology under an antiquated set of laws. For example, if the United States uses unmanned weapons systems, does that require an official declaration of war or an authorization for the use of force? . . .
>
> These trends are already forcing us to ask new questions about domestic airspace regulation: who is allowed to own unmanned systems, and where are they allowed to operate them?
>
> These are some of the questions that we will begin to answer in this hearing. Surely we will not conclude this conversation in one afternoon, . . .

In the following readings, two experts on international law relating to war take up the use of UAVs to attack targets away from an immediate war zone or "battlefield." Ellen O'Connell argues that such attacks violate international law. Michael Lewis disagrees.

# YES ↵

**Mary Ellen O'Connell**

# Lawful Use of Combat Drones

Combat drones are battlefield weapons. They fire missiles or drop bombs capable of inflicting very serious damage. Drones are not lawful for use outside combat zones. Outside such zones, police are the proper law enforcement agents and police are generally required to warn before using lethal force. Restricting drones to the battlefield is the most important single rule governing their use. Yet, the United States is failing to follow it more often than not. At the very time we are trying to win hearts and minds to respect the rule of law, we are ourselves failing to respect a very basic rule: remote weapons systems belong on the battlefield.

## I. A Lawful Battlefield Weapon

The United States first used weaponized drones during the combat in Afghanistan that began on October 7, 2001. We requested permission from Uzbekistan, which was then hosting the U.S. air base where drones were kept. We also used combat drones in the battles with Iraq's armed forces in the effort to topple Saddam Hussein's government that began in March 2003. We are still using drones lawfully in the ongoing combat in Afghanistan. Drones spare the lives of pilots, since the unmanned aerial vehicle is flown from a site far from the attack zone. If a drone is shot down, there is no loss of human life. Moreover, on the battlefield drones can be more protective of civilian lives than high aerial bombing or long-range artillery. Their cameras can pick up details about the presence of civilians. Drones can fly low and target more precisely using this information. [The U.S. commander in Afghanistan] General [Stanley] McChrystal has wisely insisted on zero-tolerance for civilian deaths in Afghanistan. The use of drones can help us achieve that. What drones cannot do is comply with police rules for the use of lethal force away from the battlefield. In law enforcement it must be possible to warn before using lethal force, in war-fighting this is not necessary, making the use of bombs and missiles lawful. The United Nations Basic Principles for the Use of Force and Firearms by Law Enforcement Officials (*UN Basic Principles*) set out the international legal standard for the use of force by police:

> Law enforcement officials shall not use firearms against persons except in self-defense or defense of others against the imminent threat of death or serious injury, to prevent the perpetration of a particularly

U.S. House of Representatives, April 28, 2010.

serious crime involving grave threat to life, to arrest a person presenting such a danger and resisting their authority, or to prevent his or her
escape, and only when less extreme means are insufficient to achieve
these objectives. In any event, intentional lethal use of firearms may
only be made when strictly unavoidable in order to protect life.

The United States has failed to follow these rules by using combat drones
in places where no actual armed conflict was occurring or where the U.S. was
not involved in the armed conflict. On November 3, 2002, the CIA used a
drone to fire laser-guided Hellfire missiles at a passenger vehicle traveling in a
thinly populated region of Yemen. At that time, the Air Force controlled the
entire drone fleet, but the Air Force rightly raised concerns about the legality
of attacking in a place where there was no armed conflict. CIA agents based in
Djibouti carried out the killing. All six passengers in the vehicle were killed,
including an American. In January 2003, the United Nations Commission on
Human Rights received a report on the Yemen strike from its special rapporteur on extrajudicial, summary, or arbitrary killing. The rapporteur concluded
that the strike constituted "a clear case of extrajudicial killing."

Apparently, Yemen gave tacit consent for the strike. States [countries]
cannot, however, give consent to a right they do not have. States may not
use military force against individuals on their territory when law enforcement
measures are appropriate. At the time of the strike, Yemen was not using military force anywhere on its territory. More recently, Yemen has been using military force to suppress militants in two parts of the country. The U.S.'s ongoing
drone use, however, has not been part of those campaigns.

The United States has also used combat drones in Somalia probably starting in late 2006 during the Ethiopian invasion when the U.S. assisted Ethiopia
in its attempt to install a new government in that volatile country. Ethiopia's
effort had some support from the UN and the African Union. To the extent that
the U.S. was assisting Ethiopia, our actions had some justification. It is clear,
however, that the U.S. has used drone strikes independently of the attempt to
restore order in Somalia. The U.S. has continued to target and kill individuals
in Somalia following Ethiopia's pullout from the country.

The U.S. use of drones in Pakistan has similar problems to the uses in
Yemen and Somalia. Where military force *is* warranted to address internal violence, governments have widely resorted to the practice of inviting in another
state to assist. This is the legal justification the U.S. cites for its use of military
force today in Afghanistan and Iraq. Yet, the U.S. cannot point to invitations
from Pakistan for most of its drone attacks. Indeed, for much of the period
that the United States has used drones on the territory of Pakistan, there has
been no armed conflict. Therefore, even express consent by Pakistan would
not justify their use.

The United States has been carrying out drone attacks in Pakistan since
2004. Pakistani authorities only began to use major military force to suppress
militancy in May 2009, in Buner Province. Some U.S. drone strikes have been
coordinated with Islamabad's efforts, but some have not. Some strikes have
apparently even targeted groups allied with Islamabad.

# II. The Battlefield Defined

The Bush administration justified the 2002 Yemen strike and others as justified under the law of armed conflict in the "Global War on Terror." The current State Department Legal Adviser, Harold Koh, has rejected the term "Global War on Terror," preferring to base our actions on the view that the U.S. is in an "armed conflict with al-Qaeda, the Taliban and associated forces." Under the new label, the U.S. is carrying out many of the same actions as the Bush administration under the old one: using lethal force without warning, far from any actual battlefield.

Armed conflict, however, is a real thing. The United States is currently engaged in an armed conflict in Afghanistan. The United States has tens of thousands of highly trained troops fighting a well-organized opponent that is able to hold territory. The situation in Afghanistan today conforms to the definition of armed conflict in international law. The International Law Association's Committee on the Use of Force issued a report in 2008 confirming the basic characteristics of all armed conflict: (1) the presence of organized armed groups that are (2) engaged in intense inter-group fighting. The fighting or hostilities of an armed conflict occur within limited zones, referred to as combat or conflict zones. It is only in such zones that killing enemy combatants or those taking a direct part in hostilities is permissible.

Because armed conflict requires a certain intensity of fighting, the isolated terrorist attack, regardless of how serious the consequences, is not an armed conflict. Terrorism is crime. Members of al Qaeda or other terrorist groups are active in Canada, France, Germany, Indonesia, Morocco, Saudi Arabia, Spain, the United Kingdom, Yemen and elsewhere. Still, these countries do not consider themselves in a war with al Qaeda. In the words of a leading expert on the law of armed conflict, the British Judge on the International Court of Justice, Sir Christopher Greenwood:

> In the language of international law there is no basis for speaking of a war on Al-Qaeda or any other terrorist group, for such a group cannot be a belligerent, it is merely a band of criminals, and to treat it as anything else risks distorting the law while giving that group a status which to some implies a degree of legitimacy.

To label terrorists "enemy combatants" lifts them out of the status of *criminal* to that of *combatant,* the same category as America's own troops on the battlefield. This move to label terrorists combatants is contrary to strong historic trends. From earliest times, governments have struggled to prevent their enemies from approaching a status of equality. Even governments on the verge of collapse due to the pressure of a rebel advance have vehemently denied that the violence inflicted by their enemies was anything but criminal violence. Governments fear the psychological and legal advantages to opponents of calling them "combatants" and their struggle a "war."

President Ronald Reagan strongly opposed labeling terrorists combatants. He said that to "grant combatant status to irregular forces even if they do not satisfy the traditional requirements . . . would endanger civilians among whom terrorists and other irregulars attempt to conceal themselves."

The United Kingdom and other allies take the same position as President Reagan: "It is the understanding of the United Kingdom that the term 'armed conflict' of itself and in its context denotes a situation of a kind which is not constituted by the commission of ordinary crimes including acts of terrorism whether concerted or in isolation."

In the United States and other countries plagued by al Qaeda, institutions are functioning normally. No one has declared martial law. The International Committee of the Red Cross is not active. Criminal trials of suspected terrorists are being held in regular criminal courts. The police use lethal force only in situations of necessity. The U.S.'s actions today are generally consistent with its long-term policy of separating acts of terrorism from armed conflict—except when it comes to drones.

## III. Battlefield Restraints

Even when the U.S. is using drones at the request of Pakistan in battles it is waging, we are failing to follow important battlefield rules. The U.S. must respect the principles of necessity, proportionality and humanity in carrying out drone attacks. "Necessity" refers to military necessity, and the obligation that force is used only if necessary to accomplish a reasonable military objective. "Proportionality" prohibits that "which may be expected to cause incidental loss of civilian life, injury to civilians, damage to civilian objects, or a combination thereof, which would be excessive in relation to concrete and direct military advantage anticipated." These limitations on permissible force extend to both the quantity of force used and the geographic scope of its use.

Far from suppressing militancy in Pakistan, drone attacks are fueling the interest in fighting against the United States. This impact makes the use of drones difficult to justify under the terms of military necessity. Most serious of all, perhaps, is the disproportionate impact of drone attacks. A principle that provides context for all decisions in armed conflict is the principle of humanity. The principle of humanity supports decisions in favor of sparing life and avoiding destruction in close cases under either the principles of necessity or proportionality. According to the International Committee of the Red Cross, the principles of necessity and humanity are particularly important in situations such as Pakistan:

> In classic large-scale confrontations between well-equipped and organized armed forces or groups, the principles of military necessity and of humanity are unlikely to restrict the use of force against legitimate military targets beyond what is already required by specific provisions of IHL [international humanitarian law]. The practical importance of their restraining function will increase with the ability of the conflict to control the circumstances and area in which its military operations are conducted, may become decisive where armed forces operate against selected individuals in situations comparable to peacetime policing. In practice, such considerations are likely to become particularly relevant where a party to the conflict exercises effective territorial control, most notably in occupied territories and non-international armed conflicts.

Another issue in drone use is the fact that strikes are carried out in Pakistan by the CIA and civilian contractors. Only members of the United States armed forces have the combatant's privilege to use lethal force without facing prosecution. CIA operatives are not trained in the law of armed conflict. They are not bound by the Uniform Code of Military Justice to respect the laws and customs of war. They are not subject to the military chain of command. This fact became abundantly clear during the revelation of U.S. use of harsh interrogation tactics. Given the negative impact of that unlawful conduct on America's standing in the world and our ability to promote the rule of law, it is difficult to fathom why the Obama administration is using the CIA to carry out drone attacks, let alone civilian contractors.

# Conclusion

The use of military force in counter-terrorism operations has been counter-productive. Military force is a blunt instrument. Inevitably unintended victims are the result of almost any military action. Drone attacks in Pakistan have resulted in large numbers of deaths and are generally seen as fueling terrorism, not abating it. In congressional testimony in March 2009, counter-terrorism expert, David Kilcullen, said drones in Pakistan are giving "rise to a feeling of anger that coalesces the population around the extremists and leads to spikes of extremism well outside the parts of the country where we are mounting those attacks." Another expert told the *New York Times*, "The more the drone campaign works, the more it fails—as increased attacks only make the Pakistanis angrier at the collateral damage and sustained violation of their sovereignty." A National Public Radio Report on April 26, 2010, pointed out that al Qaeda is losing support in the Muslim world because of its violent, lawless tactics. We can help eliminate the last of that support by distinguishing ourselves through commitment to the rule of law, especially by strict compliance with the rules governing lethal force.

Michael W. Lewis

➜ **NO**

# Examining the Legality of Unmanned Targeting

## Introduction

I am a professor of law at Ohio Northern University's Pettit College of Law where I teach International Law and the Law of Armed Conflict. I spent over 7 years in the U.S. Navy as a Naval Flight Officer flying F-14s. I flew missions over the Persian Gulf and Iraq as part of Operations Desert Shield/Desert Storm and I graduated from Top Gun [the U.S. Navy Fighter Weapons School] in 1992. After my military service I attended Harvard Law School and graduated *cum laude* in 1998. Subsequently I have lectured on a variety of aspects of the laws of war, with an emphasis on aerial bombardment, at dozens of institutions including Harvard, NYU, Columbia and the University of Chicago. I have published several articles and co-authored a book on the laws of war relating to the war on terror. My prior experience as a combat pilot and strike planner provides me with a different perspective from most other legal scholars on the interaction between law and combat.

## The Current Laws of War Are Sufficient to Address the Drone Question

There is nothing inherently illegal about using drones to target specific individuals. Nor is there anything legally unique about the use of unmanned drones as a weapons delivery platform that requires the creation of new or different laws to govern their use.

As with any other attack launched against enemy forces during an armed conflict, the use of drones is governed by International Humanitarian Law (IHL). Compliance with current IHL that governs aerial bombardment and requires that all attacks demonstrate military necessity and comply with the principle of proportionality is sufficient to ensure the legality of drone strikes. In circumstances where a strike by a helicopter or an F-16 [a U.S. warplane] would be legal, the use of a drone would be equally legitimate. However, this legal parity does not answer three fundamental questions that have been raised by these hearings. Who may be targeted? Where may they be targeted? And finally who is allowed to pilot the drones and determine which targets are legally appropriate?

U.S. House of Representatives, April 28, 2010.

# Who May Be Targeted?

In order to understand the rules governing the targeting of individuals, it is necessary to understand the various categories that IHL assigns to individuals. To best understand how they relate to one another it is useful to start from the beginning.

All people are civilians and are not subjected to targeting unless they take affirmative steps to either become combatants or to otherwise lose their civilian immunity. It is important to recognize that a civilian does not become a combatant by merely picking up a weapon. In order to become a combatant an individual must be a member of the "armed forces of a Party to a conflict." This definition is found in Article 43 of Additional Protocol I to the Geneva Conventions. It goes on to define the term "armed forces" as:

> The armed forces of a Party to a conflict consist of all organized armed forces, groups and units which are under a command responsible to that Party for the conduct of its subordinates, even if that Party is represented by a government or an authority not recognized by an adverse Party. Such armed forces shall be subject to an internal disciplinary system which, *inter alia,* shall enforce compliance with the rules of international law applicable in armed conflict.

The status of combatant is important because combatants "have the right to participate directly in hostilities." This "combatants' privilege" allows privileged individuals to participate in an armed conflict without violating domestic laws prohibiting the destruction of property, assault, murder, etc. The combatant's conduct is therefore regulated by IHL rather than [by] domestic law.

Combatant status is something of a double-edged sword, however. While it bestows the combatant privilege on the individual, it also subjects that individual to attack at any time by other parties to the conflict. A combatant may be lawfully targeted whether or not they pose a current threat to their opponents, whether or not they are armed, or even awake. The only occasion on which IHL prohibits attacking a combatant is when that combatant has surrendered or been rendered *hors de combat.* Professor Geoff Corn has argued compellingly that this ability to target based upon status, rather than on the threat posed by an individual, is the defining feature of an armed conflict.

After examining the definition of combatant, it becomes apparent that combatant status is based upon group conduct, not individual conduct. Members of al Qaeda are not combatants because as a group they are not "subject to an internal disciplinary system which [enforces] compliance with the rules of international law applicable in armed conflict." It does not matter whether an individual al Qaeda member may have behaved properly; he can never obtain the combatants' privilege because the group he belongs to does not meet IHL's requirements. Professor [David] Glazier's testimony [before this committee] that al Qaeda and the Taliban could possess "the basic right to engage in combat against us" is mistaken. These groups have clearly and unequivocally forfeited any "right" to be treated as combatants by choosing to employ means and methods of warfare that violate the laws of armed conflict, such as deliberately targeting civilians.

If al Qaeda members are not combatants, then what are they? They must be civilians, and civilians as a general rule are immune from targeting. However, civilians lose this immunity "for such time as they take a direct part in hostilities." The question of what constitutes direct participation in hostilities (DPH) has been much debated. While DOD [the U.S. Department of Defense] has yet to offer its definition of DPH, the International Committee of the Red Cross (ICRC) recently completed a six-year study on the matter and has offered interpretive guidance that, while not binding on the United States, provides a useful starting point. The ICRC guidance states that "members of organized armed groups [which do not qualify as combatants] belonging to a party to the conflict lose protection against direct attack for the duration of their membership (i.e., for as long as they assume a continuous combat function)."

The concept of a "continuous combat function" within DPH is a reaction to the "farmer by day, fighter by night" tactic that a number of organized armed terrorist groups have employed to retain their civilian immunity from attack for as long as possible. Because such individuals (be they fighters, bomb makers, planners or leaders) perform a continuous combat function, they may be directly targeted for as long as they remain members of the group. The only way for such individuals to reacquire their civilian immunity is to disavow membership in the group.

So the answer to "Who may be targeted?" is any member of al Qaeda or the Taliban, or any other individuals that have directly participated in hostilities against the United States. This would certainly include individuals that directly or indirectly (e.g. by planting IEDs) [improvised explosive devices] attacked Coalition forces as well as any leadership within these organizations. Significantly, the targeting of these individuals does not involve their elevation to combatant status as Professor O'Connell implied in her testimony [found in the first reading]. These individuals are civilians who have forfeited their civilian immunity by directly participating in hostilities. They are not, and cannot become, combatants until they join an organized armed group that complies with the laws of armed conflict, but they nevertheless remain legitimate targets until they clearly disassociate themselves from al Qaeda or the Taliban.

# Where May Attacks Take Place?

Some witnesses have testified to this subcommittee that the law of armed conflict only applies to our ongoing conflict with al Qaeda in certain defined geographic areas. Professor O'Connell states that the geographic limit of the armed conflict is within the borders of Afghanistan while others include the border areas of Pakistan and Iraq. They take the position that any operations against al Qaeda outside of this defined geography are solely the province of law enforcement, which requires that the target be warned before lethal force is employed. Because drones cannot meet this requirement they conclude that drone strikes outside of this geographical area should be prohibited. The geographical boundaries proposed are based upon the infrequency of armed assaults that take place outside of Afghanistan, Iraq and the border region of Pakistan. Because IHL does not specifically address the geographic scope of armed conflicts, to assess these proposed requirements it is necessary to step back and consider the law of armed conflict as a whole and the realities of warfare as they apply to this conflict.

One of the principal goals of IHL is to protect the civilian population from harm during an armed conflict. To further this goal IHL prohibits direct attacks on civilians and requires that parties to the conflict distinguish themselves from the civilian population. As a result, it would seem anomalous for IHL to be read in such a way as to reward a party that regularly targets civilians, and yet that is what is being proposed. As discussed above, a civilian member of al Qaeda who is performing a continuous combat function may be legitimately targeted with lethal force without any warning. But the proposed geographic limitations on IHL's application offer this individual a renewed immunity from attack. Rather than disavowing an organization that targets civilians, IHL's preferred result, the proposed geographic restrictions allow the individual to obtain the same immunity by crossing an international border and avoiding law enforcement while remaining active in an organization that targets civilians. When law enforcement's logistical limitations are considered, along with the host state's ambivalence for actively pursuing al Qaeda within its borders, it becomes clear that the proposed geographical limitations on IHL are tantamount to the creation of a safe haven for al Qaeda.

More importantly these proposed limitations would hand the initiative in this conflict over to al Qaeda. Militarily the ability to establish and maintain the initiative during a conflict is one of the most important strategic and operational advantages that a party can possess. To the extent that one side's forces are able to decide when, where and how a conflict is conducted, the likelihood of a favorable outcome is greatly increased. If IHL is interpreted to allow al Qaeda's leadership to marshal its forces in Yemen or the Sudan, or any number of other places that are effectively beyond the reach of law enforcement and to then strike at its next target of choice, whether it be New York, Madrid, London, Bali, Washington, DC or Detroit, then IHL is being read to hand the initiative in the conflict to al Qaeda. IHL should not be read to reward a party that consistently violates IHL's core principles and as Professor Glazier points out in his reference to the Cambodian incursion, it was not read that way in the past.

Those opposed to the position that IHL governs the conflict with al Qaeda regardless of geography, and therefore allows strikes like the one conducted in Yemen in 2002, have voiced three main concerns. The first concern is that the United States may be violating the sovereignty of other nations by conducting drone strikes on their territory. It is true that such attacks may only be conducted with the permission of the state on whose territory the attack takes place and questions have been raised about whether Pakistan, Yemen and other states have consented to this use of force. This is a legitimate concern that must be satisfactorily answered while accounting for the obvious sensitivity associated with granting such permission. The fact that Harold Koh, the State Department's Legal Advisor, specifically mentioned [in his testimony] the "sovereignty of the other states involved" in his discussion of drone strikes is evidence that the Administration takes this requirement seriously.

The second concern is that such a geographically unbounded conflict could lead to drone strikes in Paris or London, or to setting the precedent for other nations to employ lethal force in the United States against its enemies that have taken refuge here. These concerns are overstated. The existence of the permission requirement mentioned above means that any strikes conducted in London or Paris could only take place with the approval of the British or French governments. Further, any such strike would have to meet the requirements of military necessity and proportionality and it is difficult to imagine how these requirements could be satisfactorily met in such a congested urban setting.

Lastly, there is a legitimate concern that mistakes could be made. An individual could be inappropriately placed on the list and killed without being given any opportunity to challenge his placement on the list. Again, Mr. Koh's assurances that the procedures for identifying lawful targets "are extremely robust" are in some measure reassuring, particularly given his stature in the international legal community. However, some oversight of these procedures is clearly warranted. While *ex ante* [before the fact/event] review must obviously be balanced against secrecy and national security concerns, *ex post* review can be more thorough. When the Israeli Supreme Court approved the use of targeted killings, one of its requirements was for transparency after the fact coupled with an independent investigation of the precision of the identification and the circumstances of the attack. A similar *ex post* transparency would be appropriate here to ensure that "extremely robust" means something.

## Who May Do the Targeting?

Another question raised in the hearings was the propriety of allowing the CIA to control drone strikes. Professor Glazier opined that CIA drone pilots conducting strikes are civilians directly participating in hostilities and suggested that they might be committing war crimes by engaging in such conduct. Even if these are not considered war crimes, if the CIA members are civilians performing a continuous combat function then they are not entitled to the combatants' privilege and could potentially be liable for domestic law violations.

Therefore, if CIA members are going to continue piloting drones and planning strikes, then they must obtain combatant status. Article 43(3) of Protocol I [to the Geneva Convention of 1949] allows a party to "incorporate a paramilitary or armed law enforcement agency into its armed forces" after notifying other parties to the conflict. For such an incorporation to be effective a clear chain of command would have to be established (if it does not already exist) that enforces compliance with the laws of armed conflict. Without this incorporation or some other measure clearly establishing the CIA's accountability for law of armed conflict violations, the continued use of CIA drone pilots and strike planners will be legally problematic.

## Conclusion

Drones are legitimate weapons platforms whose use is effectively governed by current IHL applicable to aerial bombardment. Like other forms of aircraft they may be used to target enemy forces, whether specifically identifiable individuals or armed formations.

IHL permits the targeting of both combatants and civilians that are directly participating in hostilities. Because of the means and methods of warfare that they employ, al Qaeda and Taliban forces are not combatants and are not entitled to the combatants' privilege. They are instead civilians that have forfeited their immunity because of their participation in hostilities. Members of al Qaeda and the Taliban that perform continuous combat functions may be targeted at any time, subject to the standard requirements of distinction and proportionality.

Placing blanket geographical restrictions on the use of drone strikes turns IHL on its head by allowing individuals an alternative means for reacquiring effective immunity from attack without disavowing al Qaeda and its methods of warfare. It further bolsters al Qaeda by providing them with a safe haven that allows them to regain the initiative in their conflict with the United States. The geographical limitations on drone strikes imposed by sovereignty requirements, along with the ubiquitous requirements of distinction and proportionality, are sufficient to prevent these strikes from violating international law. However, some form of *ex post* [after the fact/event] transparency and oversight is necessary to review the identification criteria and strike circumstances to ensure that they remain "extremely robust."

# EXPLORING THE ISSUE

## Does Using Drones to Attack Terrorists Globally Violate International Law?

## Questions for Critical Thinking and Reflection

1. If al Qaeda were able to attack the White House using a small airplane with suicide bombers that killed Barack, Michelle, Sasha, and Melia Obama, would that strike be different in terms of *jus in bello* than the missile strike that specifically targeted Mustafa Abu al-Yazid and also killed his family members?
2. What do you think of the implication in the remarks of UN investigator Philip Alston that the ability to kill from a far distance, including now using robotic weapons system, is causing a "disconnect" from the death and suffering caused?
3. In April 2010, President Obama reportedly authorized a drone attack, if possible, on an American citizen living in Yemen. The individual, Muslim cleric Anwar al-Aulaqi, is alleged, but not proven, to have been involved in several terrorist plots against the United States. Do you support President Obama's decision, and, if so, are there other circumstances in which the president can justifiably authorize the *de facto* execution of an American without judicial sanction?

## Is There Common Ground?

A UAV attack on May 31, 2010, illustrates a number of issues involved in this debate. The strike killed Mustafa Abu al-Yazid, a founding member of al Qaeda and its third-ranking leader after Osama bin Laden and Ayman al-Zawahiri. However, the attack also killed Yazid's wife, three of his daughters, and a granddaughter. Moreover, the attack occurred in the area of Miramshah, Pakistan, close to the border with, but not in, Afghanistan.

Drone attacks undoubtedly often kill and wound noncombatants and/or destroy their property. But how much this occurs is open to debate. One study (Brookings Institution, 2009) of U.S. drone attacks in Pakistan estimated that they killed 10 noncombatants for every Taliban or al Qaeda combatant, but another study (New America Foundation, 2010) estimated only one civilian died for every two combatants killed. Inasmuch as zero collateral damage in all military operations is neither an achievable standard nor required under *jus in bello* (just conduct of war) by international law, the issue of collateral damage remains highly debatable. So do the boundaries of the battlefield.

214

President Obama has authorized several increases in the geographic use of drones and permissible targets, and State Department legal adviser Harold Koh has defended those extensions, arguing that the war of terrorism is global, not confined to Afghanistan or any other battle zone and that the United States has a right of self-defense to attack terrorists and their supporters anywhere. Koh also described U.S. procedures for identifying and hitting legal targets as "extremely robust" and becoming "even more precise." A different view was given to the United Nations Human Rights Council in a June 2010 report by UN special investigator Philip Alston. He criticized U.S. UAV attacks as having displaced "clear legal standards with a vaguely defined license to kill," and also for creating a "risk of developing a 'Playstation' mentality to killing."

## Additional Resources

For a background on drones and other unmanned weapons systems, read Peter W. Singer, *Wired for War: The Robotics Revolution and Conflict in the 21st Century* (Penguin Press, 2009). Details on part of the U.S. arsenal of drones can be found at www.airforce-technology.com/projects/predator/. Two recent looks at how terrorism has impacted the law of war are Myra Williamson, *Terrorism, War and International Law* (Ashgate, 2009) and Michael Lewis et al., *The War on Terror and the Laws of War: A Military Perspective* (Oxford University Press, 2009).

# ISSUE 13

# Is the Use and Threat of Force Necessary in International Relations?

**YES: Peter Van Uhm**, from "Why I Chose a Gun," address delivered at TEDxAmerstam, Amsterdam, The Netherlands (November 25, 2011)

**NO: Peace Pledge Union**, from *What Is Pacifism?* www.ppu.org.uk/

## ISSUE SUMMARY

**YES:** Peter Van Uhm, a general in the Royal Netherlands Army and chief of the Netherlands Defense Staff (the equivalent of the U.S. Joint Chiefs of Staff), explains that he became a soldier because sometimes only the gun stands between good and evil.

**NO:** The Peace Pledge Union, a pacifist organization in Great Britain that has been campaigning for a warless world since 1934, argues on its website that war is indefensible, that it is wrong for people to kill each other in large numbers.

**W**ar has existed throughout recorded history and probably before that. The last 1,000 years has seen about 1,000 international and civil wars, and, indeed it is possible to estimate that throughout history at least one war has been underway during 11 of every 12 years. Thus, peace is the exception, not the rule. The world has been totally free of significant interstate, colonial, or civil war in only about 1 out of every 12 years in all of recorded human history.

Of the wars during the last millennium, about 30 percent have been fought since 1800. Even more alarming is the fact that of the estimated 150 million people who have died in wars over the last 1,000 years, about three-quarters have perished in wars since 1900. Even worse, the advent of nuclear weapons and the missile technology to deliver them over long distances mean that the death toll on the first day of the next war could far exceed that of the 150 million dead since the year 1000. This potential was behind President John F. Kennedy's warning in 1961 that "mankind must put an end to war, or war will put an end to mankind."

Americans have not been spared the costs of war. About 850,000 Americans have died in war between the beginning of the Revolutionary War in 1775 and the current war in Afghanistan through 2011. The most recent wars in Iraq (2003–2010) and Afghanistan (since 2001) have claimed 6,628 American lives as of late 2012. Moreover, the U.S. casualties are only a small fraction of the nearly 300,000 people, military and civilians, that the Cost of War Project estimates have died during these two conflicts.

War is also very expensive. Military spending is one measure. Global military spending over the past 20 years has averaged about 2.5 percent of the world gross domestic product (GDP), a measure of global economic activity. According to the Stockholm International Peace Research Institute, world military spending in 2011 was $1.7 trillion. At $711 billon, U.S. military spending was by far the highest of any country. Indeed, U.S. military spending was greater than the military spending of the combined military budgets of the next 15 highest spending countries. From another perspective, the U.S. military spending accounted for 41 percent of the world total and 4.7 percent of the U.S. GDP.

Estimating the cost of war is complicated and controversial, but the U.S. military involvements in Iraq and Afghanistan have cost at least $1 trillion when including only direct military costs, and potentially four times that when indirect costs such as the interest paid on financing the war through deficit spending and the long-term costs of caring for the wounded and providing other veterans' benefits are factored in.

The devastating human and financial costs of fighting wars and being ready to fight them naturally raises the question, Why war? There have been many answers to that question advanced by philosophers, world leaders, and social scientists, but none has explained the general phenomenon. A likely reason for the lack of consensus is that there is no one reason why people fight. Is it possible not to have wars and militaries? In the YES selection, General Van Uhm does not directly answer that question, but tells an audience that until the day comes when we can do away with having a military, peace and stability will not come free of charge and that countries must maintain a capable military and be willing to use it if necessary. The Peace Pledge Union argues in the NO selection that human beings invented war, and human beings should make it obsolete.

# YES ↵

# Why I Chose a Gun

As the highest military commander of the Netherlands, with troops stationed around the world, I am honored to be here today. When I look around, I see a very special audience. I see people who want to make a contribution. I see people who want to make a better world. By doing groundbreaking scientific work. By creating impressive works of art. By writing critical articles or inspiring books. By starting up sustainable businesses. You all have chosen your own instruments to fulfill this mission of creating a better world.

Some chose the microscope as their instrument. Others chose dancing or painting or making music. Some chose the pen. Others work through the instrument of money. I share your goals. I too want to make a better world. I did not choose to take up the pen, the brush, [or] the camera. I chose this instrument [Uhm is holding up a machine gun]. I chose . . . the gun. For you, being so close to this gun, may make you feel uneasy. It may even feel scary. A real gun. At a few feet's distance.

Let us stop for a moment and feel this uneasiness. Let us cherish this feeling. Let us cherish the fact that probably most of you have never been close to a gun. It means the Netherlands is a peaceful country. The Netherlands is not at war. It means soldiers are not needed to patrol our streets. Guns are not a part of our lives.

In many countries, it is a different story. In many countries, people are confronted with guns. They are oppressed, they are intimidated. By war-lords. By terrorists. By criminals. Weapons can do a lot of harm. They are the cause of much distress.

Why then, am I standing before you, with this weapon? Why did I choose the gun as my instrument? Today I want to tell you why. Today I want to tell you why I chose the gun to create a better world.

And I want to tell you how this gun can help. My story starts in Nijmegen, in the east of the Netherlands, the city where I was born. My father was a hard-working baker. But when he had finished work in the bakery, he told me and my brother stories.

And most of the time, he told us this story. . . . The story of what happened when he was a conscript soldier in the Dutch armed forces at the beginning of the Second World War. The Nazis invaded the Netherlands. Their grim plans were evident. They meant to rule by means of repression. Diplomacy had failed to stop the Germans. Only brute force remained. It was our last resort.

My father was there to provide it. As the son of a farmer, who knew how to hunt, he was an excellent marksman. When he aimed, he never missed. At

Van Uhm, Peter. From address delivered at TEDxAmsterdam, Amsterdam, The Netherlands, November 25, 2011. Copyright © 2011 by TEDxAmsterdam Foundation. Reprinted by permission.

this decisive moment in Dutch history, my father was positioned on the bank of the river Waal, near the city of Nijmegen. He had a clear shot at the German soldiers who came to occupy a free country. He fired. Nothing happened. He fired again. No German soldier fell to the ground.

My father had been given an old gun that could not reach the opposite river bank. Hitler's troops marched on and there was nothing my father could do about it. Until the day my father died, he was frustrated about missing these shots. He could have done something. But with an old gun, not even the best marksman in the army could have hit the mark.

This story stayed with me. Then, in high school, I was gripped by the stories of the Allied soldiers. Soldiers who left the safety of their own homes and risked their lives to liberate a country and a people they did not know. It was then, that I decided I would take up the gun. Out of respect and gratitude for those men who came to liberate us. From the awareness that, sometimes, only the gun stands between good and evil.

That is why I took up the gun. Not to shoot. Not to kill. Not to destroy. But to stop those who would do evil. To protect the vulnerable. To defend democratic values. To stand up for the freedom we have, to talk here today in Amsterdam, about how we can make the world a better place.

I do not stand here today to tell you about the glory of weapons. I do not like guns. And once you have been under fire yourself, it brings home even more clearly, the notion that a gun is not some macho instrument to brag about. I stand here today to tell you about the use of the gun as an instrument of peace and stability.

The gun may be one of the most important instruments of peace and stability that we have in this world.

Now this may sound contradictory to you. But not only have I seen this with my own eyes, during my deployments in the Lebanon and Sarajevo, and as the Netherlands Chief of Defense. This is also supported by cold, hard statistics. Violence has declined dramatically over the last 500 years. Despite the pictures we are shown daily in the news. Wars between developed countries are no longer commonplace, the murder rate in Europe has dropped by a factor of thirty since the Middle Ages . . . and occurrences of civil war and repression have declined since the end of the Cold War. Statistics show that we are living in a relatively peaceful era. Why? Why has violence decreased? Has the human mind changed? Did we simply lose our beastly impulses for revenge, for violent rituals, for pure rage? Or is there something else? In his latest book, Harvard professor Steven Pinker, and many other thinkers before him, concludes that one of the main drivers behind less violent societies is the spread of the constitutional state. And the introduction on a large scale of the state monopoly on the legitimized use of violence.

Legitimized by a democratically elected government. Legitimized by checks and balances and an independent judicial system. In other words, a state monopoly that has the use of violence well under control. Such a state monopoly on violence first of all serves as a reassurance. It removes the incentive for an arms race between potentially hostile groups in our societies. Secondly, the presence of penalties that outweigh the benefits of using violence, tips the balance even further.

Abstaining from violence becomes more profitable than starting a war. Now, non-violence starts to work like a fly wheel. It enhances peace even further. Where there is no conflict, trade will flourish. And trade is another important incentive against violence. With trade, there is mutual interdependency and mutual gain between parties. And where there is mutual gain, both sides stand to lose more than they would gain if they started a war. War is simply no longer the best option. That is why violence has decreased.

This is the rationale behind the existence of my armed forces. The armed forces implement the state monopoly on violence. We do this in a legitimized way, only after our democracy has asked us to do so. It is this legitimate, controlled use of the gun that has contributed greatly to reducing the statistics of war, conflict and violence around the globe.

It is this participation in peacekeeping missions that has led to the resolution of many civil wars. My soldiers use the gun as an instrument of peace. And this is exactly why failed states are so dangerous. Failed states have no legitimized, democratically controlled use of force. Failed states do not know of the gun as an instrument of peace and stability. That is why failed states can drag down a whole region into chaos and conflict.

That is why spreading the concept of the constitutional state is such an important aspect of our foreign missions.

That is why we are trying to build a judicial system right now in Afghanistan. That is why we train police officers, judges and public prosecutors around the world. And that is why the Dutch Constitution states that one of the main tasks of the armed forces is to uphold and promote the international rule of law.

Looking at this gun, we are confronted with the ugly side of the human mind. We are confronted with the horrible things humans do to other humans. Every day, I hope that politicians, diplomats and development workers can turn conflict into peace and threat into hope.

I hope that one day, armies can be disbanded and humans will find a way of living together without violence and oppression. But until that day comes, we will have to make ideals and human failure meet somewhere in the middle.

Until that day comes, I stand for my father, who tried to shoot the Nazis with that old gun. I stand for my men and women, who are prepared to risk their lives for a less violent world for all of us. I stand for this soldier who suffered partial hearing-loss and sustained permanent injuries to her leg when she was hit by a rocket on her mission in Afghanistan.

Ladies and gentlemen, until the day comes when we can do away with the gun, I hope we all agree that peace and stability do not come free of charge. It takes hard work, often behind the scenes. It takes good equipment and well-trained, dedicated soldiers.

I hope you will support the efforts of our armed forces to train soldiers like this young captain and provide her with a good gun instead of the bad gun my father was given. I hope you will support our soldiers when they are out there. When they come home. When they are injured and need our care. They put their lives on the line for us and we cannot let them down.

I hope you will respect this soldier with this gun. Because she wants a better world. Because she makes an active contribution to that better world.

# What Is Pacifism?

## Why is War Wrong?

Disasters make news. Television and newspapers show us the pictures: the destruction, the injured survivors, the dead. What we don't see, unless we're the victims of an earthquake or flood or volcano ourselves, is what life is like afterwards. We rarely get glimpses of survivors struggling to cope with grief and illness or disability, in makeshift conditions and facing years maybe even a lifetime—of deprivation and loss. There is another kind of disaster: war. Pictures from war zones show the same tragic scenes, the same dreadful aftermath. But war is worse. When war is going on, help for its victims may be slow in coming, or never arrive at all. The victims can themselves become pawns of war: deliberately driven from their homes, abused or tortured, their towns and villages bombed or burned. Large areas of land become uninhabitable, poisoned by dangerous chemicals and littered with unexploded weapons that go on killing for years to come. Some people—often children—are forced by governments or self-appointed leaders to join in the fighting and commit brutal acts and killings themselves. In war zones law and order disappear, and no-one is safe.

Unlike earthquakes, floods and volcanic eruptions, war is a disaster created entirely by people, against people. It is never an accident: making war is always somebody's decision. Nations spend vast amounts of money on training soldiers to fight and kill. They spend even more on devising and manufacturing weapons and machinery for fighting and killing. That is not the only expense. Huge sums are also needed for dealing with the damage when a war is officially over. ('Officially', because the effects of war continue long after the truce has been signed.) From this evidence alone, it ought to be clear to everyone that there's little to be said for war. But little has been done to liberate the world from it. War still fascinates and excites some people, though it fills many others with revulsion and horror. Too many people—and too many of their leaders—still think that war is defensible, and that it's not actually wrong for people to learn how to kill each other in large numbers. For all these reasons, and more, the invention of war is one of humankind's greatest blunders. It needs to be put right.

The bottom line of pacifism is simply this: human beings invented war, and human beings should make it obsolete. War, like a disease, can in time be eradicated; and that's what we should be working to achieve. It means learning to overcome the conditioned belief that armed force is an acceptable way of dealing with disputes. It's a human weakness, not a strength, to solve problems with cruelty, brutality and murder. As a species we have already matured enough for modern societies to decide that wartime atrocities are crimes; people can be arrested for them, tried and punished. Now we should realize that war is itself a crime against humanity, and grow wise enough to solve our problems another way.

## Aggression and Revenge

Some people want to believe that human beings are naturally aggressive, and that war is a natural way of showing it. Regrettable, they say, 'but it's in our genes'. In fact, scientists have proved that aggression is not inborn, and said so publicly in 1989. Of course many people do feel and show aggressiveness. But this is the result of circumstances, not biology.

There is always a traceable reason for aggressive behavior. (It often has to do with social and economic problems which war may have created and defense budgets could be diverted to resolve.) But there is no good reason, innate or acquired, for human beings to plan aggression on a large scale, teach people how to put it into practice, and encourage them to carry it to lethal extremes. The road to devastation begins long before war does: it begins when nations and groups equip themselves for war. Preparing for war ensures that it will happen (though it may not be the war that's being prepared for). You might as well try preventing a forest fire by pouring petrol over the trees and then standing by with a box of matches. In fact aggression and revenge are deliberately incited to fuel war. Every war is backed by political and military propaganda, which fires anger, hatred and impulses to attack and retaliate. This serves at least two purposes: it allows armies to believe in what they're doing, and seduces people into supporting their leaders' war policies. But however solid the reasons for aggression or revenge may seem, war is never the only way to handle them. It is certainly the worst and most dangerous way; and it isn't even practical. Aggression and violence set up a sequence of violent attacks and reprisals that, like a forest fire, is easy to start but very hard to stop, and leaves destruction and death wherever it occurs.

Put it another way: if you are aggressive and vengeful, then you bring aggression and revenge on yourself. As the pacifist civil rights activist Martin Luther King said, an-eye-for-an-eye leaves everyone blind. In the grisly competitiveness of war it's more often two-eyes-for-an-eye. People who actually want war often put their case for it by saying it's a form of defense, needed to protect a community, a land, an idea. But this sort of defense is really a form of aggression, a threat permanently ready to be carried out. In fact there's compelling evidence to show that armed defense is no kind of protection. The use of force doesn't solve problems; it may alter them, but it inevitably creates new ones at the same time. It also breeds further violence. The causes of human conflict are too subtle and complex to be dealt with by brute force, which is no more than a crude short-term response that sets up a load of long-term trouble.

# The Right to Live

In 1948, shortly after the horrors of the Second World War, forty-eight countries signed the Universal Declaration of Human Rights [UDHR]. It begins [in Article I]: "All human beings are born free and equal in dignity and rights. They are endowed with reason and conscience and should act towards one another in a spirit of brotherhood." Furthermore, [the UDHR says in Article II], "no distinction shall be made on the basis of the political, jurisdictional or international status of the country or territory to which a person belongs, whether it be independent, trust, non-self-governing or under any other limitation of sovereignty." [Article III states] "Everyone has the right to life, liberty and security of person." Our common humanity demands that we make friends, not enemies, of each other. Nor should belonging to a country or state be a reason for being the enemy of other nations and states. 'Everyone'—everyone—'has the right to life'.

Rights such as these are not only human, they are also humane. War, killing and violence are never humane, whatever excuses may be put up by people who want to justify them. Yet human societies are so entangled in the web of war that the Universal Declaration, a commendably sane and reasonable agreement, soon began to be eroded. First, an additional clause was signed allowing 'the State' to 'take measures' (in what it judged to be a 'public emergency') that break the terms of the Declaration. Then the European Convention on Human Rights (1950), which aims to 'guarantee the fundamental civil and political rights of Man' by making human rights a legal obligation, provided warmongers with a loophole. This Convention allows that a State may authorize killing as a response to 'unlawful violence' or to suppress an uprising; and also 'in time of war or other public emergency'. The proviso? Such killing must only result from 'the use of force which is no more than absolutely necessary'—an impossible decision to make in the midst of the chaos of war, and an immoral dilemma at any time.

What does this loophole mean? It means that governments have the legal power to decide that in some circumstances people can and should be killed: that is to say, they have the legal power to strip us of our most fundamental human right. Is this the sort of power we really want our government, or any other government, to have? It's quite clear that war is an abuse of human rights. But we have not yet developed a society that is prepared to acknowledge that and entirely reject war as an option. Since most people are peaceable and peace-loving, and no-one wants to be killed, you'd think that war would be universally regarded as the human race's greatest shame. It's extraordinary that any modern and civilized society can still take armed force for granted. Yet in the last century up to 200 million people were killed in wars, the majority of them civilians, many of them children. Why ever hasn't war been abolished?

# The Web of War

One of the reasons why it's so difficult to outlaw war is that it's built into the fabric of most societies, installed there by their pasts. As it happens, the earliest archaeological discoveries show that human beings used their evolving brains to make tools, not weapons. But as populations grew, so did problems we know today: quarrels over land, property, resources and power. It was an easy step, though not an intelligent one, to turn a two-person squabble into a group brawl, and so descend into mass violence and bloodshed. From there it was easy, though not far-sighted, to learn how to organize that violence and use it as a threat.

War became a part of human society a long time ago, but for many centuries it was a relatively small part. It dominates historical records, because documenting the everyday lives of ordinary people did not seem important. Men became warriors because it went with the job of being a prince or lord, and foot soldiers because it went with the job of being a lord's servant; some took up soldiering when it became a profession, or joined in as amateurs to support a particular cause. But most men were farmers, laborers, craft workers, or employed by the church. Sadly, as people came to understand science better, some of them applied their intelligence and learning to the machinery of war. By the 20th century weapons had been devised that could kill many people at once, and not just soldiers; and war had become a multi-billion dollar industry.

Studying world history (with eyes and minds open) in tandem with the history of people who have worked to abolish war gives a fascinating insight into the way our species behaves. The human race went blindly ahead with the advancement of warfare—brutal, brutalizing and corrupt—without stopping to think of the consequences for succeeding generations, or for the planet itself, and without listening to enlightened warnings and advice against it. War got a grip on people's minds, societies and ways of life with the strength (and many of the strategies) of a virus. And, not least because of the huge cost of its needs, war now in one way or another touches almost every aspect of life.

Take taxes, for example. In democracies, theoretically people elect governments to budget on their behalf to keep them healthy, educated and comfortable. But huge amounts of taxpayers' money are hived off to pay for 'defense'—which means 'equipment for killing'—and welfare is under-supported as a result. Taxpayers aren't consulted about this; decisions about war are never put to the people. In the UK income tax was originally invented to meet the costs of war. In some countries, especially developing ones, expenditure on arms and armies leaves the general population enduring poverty, disease and deprivation. (And it's often those countries that are most vulnerable to natural disasters.) A major cause of concern is that many people, caught in the historic web of war, find it hard to believe that all war is always wrong. They may agree that it should be avoided if at all possible, but not, they say, at all costs: it should remain a worst-case scenario. But war is worse than that. Think of the terrible events of the First World War—the first to be conducted on an industrial scale. Think of the Second World War's saturation bombing, atomic weapons and, with the Holocaust, organized racism—all of which caused the widespread murder of civilians and made such actions an 'acceptable' part of war. Think of what the Vietnam War did to both civilians and soldiers, and the effects of massacres and 'ethnic cleansing' round the world. Think of the appalling kinds of warfare, global and local, which modern technology has made possible.

If nothing else, think of the growing number of books and films praised for carrying an anti-war message in their depictions of the true horror and futility of war. Indeed, the world-wide movement in favor of peace has grown substantially over the last half-century; its varied voices and actions have been heard and noticed. In some places they've been so successful that some governments have been obliged to try to sell war with claims that it's morally sound! Arms trade fairs promote 'weapons that save lives', and in 1999 the British were encouraged to support what the government called a 'humanitarian war'—contradictions in terms that would be absurd if they weren't so dangerous. But even where the pursuit of peace is encouraged and applauded, the web of war still clings. Driven by the lawless pursuit of power and wealth, private and public interests both local and world-wide have so far kept war and its machinery going.

## Changing the Way We Think

Disentangling any society from the web of war not only needs hard work, imagination, resourcefulness and persistence; it also needs a change of attitude. Attitudes in societies can and do change—there are examples of such changes throughout history. Not all changes are for the better, but people can develop a social and political will to alter that too. In particular, we have the ability to change our society so that war is no longer an option. It's tempting to think that when no fighting is going on there is peace—but beneath the peace-talking, war-thinking continues. The systems that sustain war-thinking have to be dismantled. To make this possible we need to develop a social climate in which violence is no longer used to counter violence. It means questioning attitudes we have taken for granted until now. It means rethinking the way we work, the way we play, the way we think about money, the way we think about other people, and the way we think about government.

Such a fresh look at our values may be unsettling, but it can be absorbing and stimulating too. One of pacifism's many virtues is that it can be practiced in a diversity of ways—and it thrives on new approaches. What they have in common is nonviolence, and nonviolence is a powerful and exciting instrument of change. Another article on this site looks at nonviolence, its history and meaning. Here, it needs to be stressed that nonviolence doesn't mean inaction. It means action, aimed at constructive problem-solving without the use of weapons or war. This doesn't mean there's no place for violent feelings. Most human beings have them—and most human beings learn how to control them, too.

## Pacifism in Action

Pacifists are vocal about what they think, and look for ways of expressing it in all aspects of life. Some ways of bringing pacifism to public attention demand courage and stamina, especially in places where it is regarded as a threat to the vested interests of war. Some people disobey the law by withholding part of their income tax (and paying the money into peace trusts instead) proportional to the percentage of the national budget spent on war. Others risk arrest and imprisonment by making 'direct action' protests: entering prohibited areas occupied by military installations, setting up peace camps on or beside military sites, or disabling machinery intended for use in war. Others learn and teach techniques of defusing conflict, and seek out danger areas where these skills can be applied. But being a pacifist is not in itself dangerous or even particularly difficult: it's only a step beyond being the peaceable, peace-seeking person most of us naturally are. Many find ways to demonstrate their principles in ordinary life, being up-front about never responding to violence with violence. Everyday life, after all, is where social change begins.

Some people have been working for a long time on what is called conversion: practical ways for transforming the world's vast military complexes into organizations benefiting the civilian world. Military expertise can be turned to civilian use (as demonstrated by military assistance in dealing with natural catastrophes). Energy and intelligence devoted to devising modern weapons systems can be diverted to life technologies. Military sites and installations can become parks, business complexes, civilian science centers (and museums that warn future generations against a return to violence). The aim is to 'turn swords into ploughshares' without, for example, damaging economies or depriving people of employment. Some of these changes are already being tried out experimentally: the learning curve has begun.

Other people are studying the nature and dynamics of conflict, and how it too can be transformed to the good. They promote the learning of skills in resolving conflicts—skills now being refined by many peace research organizations as well as out in the field. Nonviolent techniques of mediation and negotiation, for example, are increasingly practiced in many areas of life, such as schools and workplaces. Processes of reconciliation are also being initiated—famously in South Africa after apartheid, and in Rwanda after civil war. Also being studied are the real causes of war. These aren't the flashpoints that seem to start wars off—such as an assassination, a border infringement, an incitement to riot, or even an invasion.

The real causes lie deeper, in earlier history; in human psychology; in social and economic injustices; in political discontent and power-seeking. It means looking, too, at what these tensions are nurtured by. Maybe there's a political motive, war used as a deliberately planned diversion of people's attention from other problems; or maybe there's a disaffected sector of society (often, in the past, a country's army) interested in violent rebellion; or feuds, vendettas, tribal conflict; or disputes over trade, land, water, oil; or the lucrative arms business itself, which depends on war for its existence. These are the real reasons for war, hidden by cosmetic ones of patriotism or a stance against insult or injustice. The better the real reasons are understood, the better they can be predicted, detected, diagnosed, and defused.

Pain, fear, distress and conflict are part of the human condition. Selfishness, cruelty, vengeance, and all the other aspects of aggression, aren't likely to disappear (though they can be better controlled, especially in a society that finds them repellent). Pacifism doesn't imagine, or ask for, a world of visionary bliss. But it does mean rejecting absolutely the great wrong that we have done ourselves: organized killing, or war. It does mean that, at last, we will stop deliberately imposing suffering on other people and ourselves.

# EXPLORING THE ISSUE

## Is the Use and Threat of Force Necessary in International Relations?

## Questions for Critical Thinking and Reflection

1. Is peace possible? Can humans learn not to wage war on one another?
2. Does having a strong military promote peace by deterring others or does a strong military promote war by creating the ability and temptation to use force to settle disputes?
3. In domestic societies, people have sought to curb violence by giving up most of their weapons, by agreeing to abide by laws, and by creating governments to provide protection, enforce the laws, and settle disputes through police and judicial agencies. Should countries try to increase peace by surrendering some or all of their independence and their weapons to international organizations such as the United Nations and empowering them to provide protection and enforce the law through UN forces and to settle disputes and punish law-breakers through judicial agencies such as the International Court of Justice and the International Criminal Court?

## Is There Common Ground?

No obvious progress has been made toward abolishing war, and the need for military forces has been made in the short time between the time General Van Uhm gave his speech and the Peach Pledge Union posted its views and this writing. Indeed, new conflicts such as the ghastly civil war in Syria have broken out or intensified.

One step toward lessening or eliminating war is to study its causes, frequency, intensivity, and other factors. A leading effort to do that is the Correlates of War Project. It has existed since 1963 and its findings and current research efforts can be found on its website at www.correlatesofwar.org/.

## Additional Resources

For more on the cost of the wars in Afghanistan and Iraq, go to the website of the Cost of War Project at http://costsofwar.org/. Although it is almost 20 years old, a fine book on the history of the conduct of war is John Keegan, *A History of Warfare* (Vintage, 1994). On the various theories about why wars occur, read Jack S. Levy and William R. Thompson, *Causes of War* (Wiley-Blackwell, 2010). On current efforts to increase peace through conflict resolution, turn to Peter Wallensteen, *Understanding Conflict*

*Resolution: War, Peace and the Global System* (Sage, 2011). A study of the history of pacifism is David Cortright, *Peace: A History of Movements and Ideas* (Cambridge University Press, 2008). Also worthwhile is Duane Cady, *From Warism to Pacifism: A Moral Continuum* (Temple University Press, 2010).

# *Internet References . . .*

## United Nations Department of Peacekeeping Operations

This UN site is the gateway to all the peacekeeping functions of the United Nations.

**www.un.org/en/peacekeeping/**

## International Law Association

The International Law Association, which is currently headquartered in London, was founded in Brussels in 1873. Its objectives, under its constitution, include the "study, elucidation and advancement of international law, public and private, the study of comparative law, the making of proposals for the solution of conflicts of law and for the unification of law, and the furthering of international understanding and goodwill."

**www.ila-hq.org**

## United Nations Treaty Collection

The United Nations Treaty Collection is a collection of 30,000 treaties, addenda, and other items related to treaties and international agreements that have been filed with the UN Secretariat since 1946. The collection includes the texts of treaties in their original language(s) and English and French translations.

**http://untreaty.un.org**

# International Law and Organization Issues

*P*art of the process of globalization is the increase in scope and importance of both international law and international organizations. The issues in this unit represent some of the controversies involved with the expansion of international law and organizations into the realm of military security. Issues here relate to increasing international organizations' responsibility for security, the effectiveness of international financial organizations, and the proposal to authorize international courts to judge those who are accused of war crimes.

- Is the UN a Worthwhile Organization?
- Is U.S. Refusal to Join the International Criminal Court Wise?
- Should the United States Ratify the Convention to Eliminate All Forms of Discrimination Against Women?

# ISSUE 14

# Is the UN a Worthwhile Organization?

**YES: Susan E. Rice**, from "Six Reasons the United Nations Is Indispensable," address delivered at the World Affairs Council of Oregon, Portland, Oregon (February 11, 2011)

**NO: Bruce S. Thornton**, from "The U.N.: So Bad It's Almost Beautiful," *Hoover Digest* (January 2012)

## ISSUE SUMMARY

**YES:** Susan E. Rice, U.S. ambassador to the United Nations, tells an audience that the United States is much better off—much stronger, much safer, and more secure—in a world with the United Nations than the United States would be in a world without the UN.

**NO:** Bruce S. Thornton, a research fellow at the Hoover Institution at Stanford University in California, writes that the United Nations is fatally flawed by not having consistent, unifying moral and political principles shared by member nations that can justify UN policies or legitimize the use of force to deter and punish aggression.

T he United Nations was established in 1945 as a reaction to the failure of its predecessor, the League of Nations, to prevent World War II and its horrendous destruction of life and property. From this perspective, founding the UN in 1945 represented something akin to a sinner resolving to reform. In this case, a world that had just barely survived a ghastly experience pledged to organize itself to preserve the peace and improve humanity. Now, nearly 70 years later, international violence continues, global justice and respect for international law remain goals rather than reality, and grievous economic and social ills still afflict the world.

It is also the case that the UN has been and remains principally a political organization in which the countries of the world maneuver to advance their political agendas rather than an international organization in which the world's countries work together in the spirit of cooperation to solve global problems. Moving forward is often particularly difficult because most peacekeeping activity using UN forces and many other key UN functions need the approval of the Security Council. But in a scheme that dates to the power realities in 1945 when the UN was organized, the Council is dominated by five permanent members, each of which can veto almost anything the Council does. These members are China, France, Great Britain, Russia, and the United States. In recent times, for example, efforts to put strong UN-backed sanctions on Iran in response to its alleged nuclear weapons program have been blocked in the Security Council by the unwillingness of China and Russia to support tough sanctions.

The United States also often finds itself outvoted in the other main UN legislative body, the General Assembly. For a quarter century most UN members were U.S. allies, and Washington was usually able to dominate the General Assembly, where each country has one vote. However, the UN's membership changed during the 1960s and 1970s when dozens of former colonies in Africa, Asia, and elsewhere gained independence and joined the UN. These new member countries often saw things differently than the United States, and by the 1980s the United States' ability to almost always muster a majority in the UN General Assembly had waned.

There have also been widespread charges that the UN's bureaucracy is excessive and inefficient. Partly in reaction to that, Congress in 2002 mandated a 12 percent reduction in the percentage of the basic UN budget funded by the United States and has rarely appropriated enough money to even meet the new, lower figure. Even more recently, several scandals have rocked the UN. From 1996 to 2003, it ran an "oil-for-food" program that permitted Iraq to sell oil and use the receipts to buy food, medicine, and other humanitarian supplies under UN supervision. Persistent rumors about corruption in the $67 billion program led to an investigation in 2004 that found substantial corruption, including the program administrator taking brides to ignore the fact that Iraq was diverting huge sums to the purchase of munitions and for other banned uses. The UN's image was further sullied in 2004 when evidence came to light of UN peacekeeping troops and personnel trading food and other necessities of life to obtain sex from those they were supposedly protecting.

Yet for all the flaws and frustrations, the UN has made many contributions. Since the UN was founded, it has fielded 67 peacekeeping operations using hundreds of thousands of military personnel, tens of thousands of UN police offices, and many support personnel from 120 countries. More than 3,000 of these peacekeepers have died while serving under the UN flag. The UN has also helped shelter and fed millions of refugees, has supplied agricultural and other developmental assistance to more than half the world's countries, and has made many other contributions. Are these enough to offset the UN's limits and flaws? In the YES selection, Susan Rice answers yes. She contends that while the UN is not perfect, it plays an indispensable role in promoting U.S. interests and values. Bruce Thornton disagrees in the NO selection. He criticizes Americans who believe in the usefulness of the UN. He contends that the UN is a collection of unaccountable functionaries of tyrannous regimes—regimes that undermine the legitimacy of UN policy.

# YES ⤶

Susan E. Rice

# Six Reasons the United Nations Is Indispensable

**W**e're meeting at the end of an extraordinary day—a rare moment in our lives when we have had the privilege to witness history in the making. Egyptians have just overthrown long-time, authoritarian president Hosni Mubarak. The proud people of Egypt have reminded the world of the power of human dignity and the universal longing for liberty. The American people have been deeply inspired by the scenes in Cairo and across that great ancient land. President Obama today recalled the words of Dr. Martin Luther King Jr., who said, "There is something in the soul that cries out for freedom." As those cries came from Tahrir Square [in Cairo], they moved the entire world. The United States will fully support a credible and irreversible transition to genuine democracy in Egypt.

February 11 [2011] is turning out to be one of those dates that echoes in history. How many of you remember that 21 years ago today, Nelson Mandela walked out of prison? [Mandela was a leader of the effort to end the white-dominated racist government of South Africa. He became the country's first president under the new, reformed government.] There were those who said that South Africa could not handle democracy, that it would set off a wave of instability and violence. Instead it set off a wave of liberty for South Africans. Many people thought South Africa couldn't do it. South Africa proved the naysayers wrong. I'm very confident the people of Egypt can do the same. Now, let me turn from a day of astonishing change to some of the changes we have made in America's approach to the wider world.

We're now two years into the Obama Administration. At a time of economic trial and sweeping change, we've made America stronger and more secure by pursuing a strategy of national renewal and energetic global leadership. Tonight, I want to discuss how the United Nations fits into that strategy—why we need the UN, how it makes us all safer, and what we're doing to fix its shortcomings and help fulfill its potential.

In these tough economic times, we're focused on getting our economy growing and providing jobs to Americans who're hurting. Yet even as we get our own house in order, we cannot afford to ignore problems beyond our borders. When nuclear weapons materials remain unsecured in many countries around the world, all our children are at risk. When states are wracked by conflict or ravaged by poverty, they can incubate threats that spread across borders—from terrorism to pandemic disease, from criminal networks to

Rice, Susan E. From remarks delivered at World Affairs Council of Oregon, Portland, OR, February 11, 2011.

environmental degradation. Like it or not, we live in a new era of challenges that cross borders as freely as a storm—challenges that even the world's most powerful country often cannot tackle alone. In the 21st century, indifference is not an option. It's not just immoral. It's dangerous.

Now more than ever, Americans' security and wellbeing are inextricably linked to those of people everywhere. Now more than ever, we need common responses to global problems. And that is why America is so much better off— so much stronger, so much safer and more secure—in a world with the United Nations than we would be in a world without it.

Main Street America needs the United Nations, and so do you and I, especially in these tough economic times. America can't police every conflict, end every crisis, and shelter every refugee. The UN provides a real return on our tax dollars by bringing 192 countries together to share the cost of providing stability, vital aid, and hope in the world's most broken places. Because of the UN, the world doesn't look to America to solve every problem alone. And the UN offers our troops in places like Afghanistan the international legitimacy and support that comes only from a Security Council mandate—which, in turn, is a force multiplier for our soldiers on the frontlines. It is all too easy to find cases where the UN could be more efficient and effective. I spend plenty of time pointing them out and trying to fix them—and not always diplomatically. But judging the UN solely by isolated cases of mismanagement or corruption misses the forest for the trees. We're far better off working to strengthen the UN than trying to starve it—and then having to choose between filling the void ourselves or leaving real threats untended.

The American public—you get it. An October 2010 survey . . . found that 72 percent of Americans support paying our UN peacekeeping dues in full and on time. The American people are fundamentally pragmatic. They know, after all, that America created the UN. In 1942, during World War II, Franklin Delano Roosevelt summoned 26 allies to Washington to sign the Declaration of the United Nations and pledged "to defend life, liberty, independence and religious freedom." As President Truman subsequently boasted, "We started the United Nations. It was our idea." Years later, President Reagan affirmed: "We are determined that the United Nations shall succeed and serve the cause of peace for humankind.

Roosevelt and Truman were practical men who wanted common action to halt aggression and prevent another world war. As one of the UN's greatest Secretaries-General, Dag Hammarskjöld [in office, 1953–1961], put it, the UN was designed "not to bring humanity to heaven but to save it from hell." Over the years, we've learned the price of letting global problems go unaddressed. So the UN has taken on huge responsibilities for keeping the peace—and for saving innocent civilians not just from the hell of conflict but also from the hell of displacement, disease, and despair.

The truth is: the UN has also picked up some bad habits along the way, and we must continue to be clear about its shortcomings. You hear a lot of criticism of the UN from some quarters—and, I confess, I agree with some of it. But we must not lose sight of the many burdens the UN helps shoulder and the many benefits it provides to every American.

Some critics argue that we should withhold our UN dues to try to force certain reforms, or that we should just pay for those UN programs we like the most. This is short-sighted, and it plain just doesn't work. The United States tried this tactic during parts of the 1980s and 1990s, and the result was that we were more isolated and less potent. That is because great and proud nations like ours are judged by their example. They are expected to keep their treaty commitments and pay their bills. When we shirk our responsibilities, our influence wanes, and our standing is diminished. Imagine going to a restaurant, getting a pretty good steak that could have been cooked a little better, and then skipping out on the check. We just cannot lead from a position of strength when we're awash in unpaid bills. We cannot depend on UN missions in Iraq and Afghanistan to help our troops return home safely and in success—and then decimate the budgets that fund them. And, if we treat our legally binding financial obligations like some kind of a la carte menu, we invite others to do the same. So, instead of paying just 22 percent of the nearly half a billion dollar annual cost of crucial UN support operations in Iraq and Afghanistan, we'd be stuck with almost the whole tab ourselves.

Yet paying our bills in full and on time doesn't mean giving the UN a pass. As we work with Congress in a bipartisan spirit to meet our responsibilities, we continue to lead the charge for serious and comprehensive reform. The UN has far more to do to create a culture of economy, ethics, and excellence. The UN must be more lean, more nimble, and more cost-effective. In recent years, the United States has spurred important changes, including revitalizing the UN Ethics Office, now headed by a respected American. The newly appointed UN inspector-general is a tough Canadian auditor committed to whipping into shape an atrophied investigations division. And no one has pushed harder than the U.S. to protect whistleblowers, impose budget discipline, and promote transparency. But the UN still has much to do to reduce bureaucracy, reap savings, reward talent, and retire underperformers.

Some Americans believe the UN infringes on American sovereignty. Frankly, I am baffled by this concern. The fact is: the UN can't tax us. It can't override U.S. law. The UN can't order our soldiers into battle. It can't take away our Second Amendment rights. The UN can't impose social norms on us. And it doesn't begin to have any much-hyped fleet of secret black helicopters. The truth is: the UN Security Council can't even issue a press release without America's blessing. The UN depends entirely on its member states, not the other way around. When the UN stumbles, it's usually because its members stumble—because big powers duck tough issues in the Security Council or spoilers grandstand in the General Assembly. As one of my predecessors, the late Richard Holbrooke, was fond of saying, "Blaming the UN when things go wrong is like blaming Madison Square Garden when the Knicks play badly."

Others charge that UN peacekeepers haven't done enough to stop rape and sexual abuse on their watch and occasionally even perpetrate abuses. Indeed, the epidemic of rape in conflict zones is shocking and horrific. That's why the United States has consistently led Security Council efforts to strengthen the mandates and means to protect civilians. That's why we pushed to create a high-level office to combat sexual violence against women and girls in conflict zones. And that's why we consistently champion account-ability for genocide and justice for war criminals, whoever they are. But let's not forget the practical limitations on what peacekeepers can do. The Demo-cratic Republic of Congo is a country the size of the United States east of the Mississippi River, with few roads, few cops, and far too many marauders. Some 20,000 peacekeepers with only a couple dozen helicopters can hardly be everywhere they may be needed all the time. Even as we demand that the UN do more and do better, we must focus our attention on the main problem: thugs with guns who deliberately use rape as a weapon of war.

Many others lament that the UN is too focused on singling out Israel. On that, they're right. UN members devote disproportionate attention to Israel and consistently adopt biased resolutions, which too often divert attention from the world's most egregious human rights abuses. I spend a good deal of time working to ensure that Israel's legitimacy is beyond dispute and its security is never in doubt. The tough issues between Israelis and Palestinians can only be solved by direct negotiations between the two parties, not in New York. We've been blunt about the deep flaws of the Goldstone Report and the Human Rights Council's inquiry into the tragic flotilla episode. We'll keep fighting to ensure that Israel has the same rights and responsibilities as all states—including membership in all appropriate regional groupings at the UN. Efforts to chip away at Israel's legitimacy will continue to be met by the frontal opposition of the United States.

Some people have criticized the Obama Administration for having sought and won a seat on the UN Human Rights Council in 2009. We have no illusions about the Human Rights Council, and we get why some people think of it as a symbol for what ails the UN. But, let me tell you this: the results were worse when America sat on the sidelines. Dictators frequently weren't called to account; abused citizens couldn't count on their voices being heard; and Israel was still bashed. We've got a long way to go to transform the Human Rights Council, but we've already gotten important results by working for real change from within. We helped set up the first-ever Special Rapporteur to monitor crackdowns on civil society groups and protect the right to free assembly and association. We twice renewed the term of the UN's Independent Expert on Sudan—the only international mechanism tracking human rights violations throughout the country. We shone the spotlight on abuses in Kyrgyzstan, Guinea, and the Democratic Republic of Congo. And, instead of abandoning Israel, we've been there to contest moves to single it out unfairly.

Put simply, some of the criticisms of the UN are overdone, and some are right on the money. Despite the UN's flaws, it's indispensable to our security in this age of tighter bonds and tighter belts. Let me provide a bit of perspective. Out of every tax dollar you pay, 34 cents goes to Social Security and Medicare, 22 cents to national security and our amazing military, and a nickel to paying interest on the national debt. Just one-tenth of a single penny goes to pay our UN dues. And here's what that buys you.

First, the UN helps prevent conflict and keep the peace around the globe. Since 1948, UN missions have saved lives, averted wars, and helped bring democracy to dozens of countries. More than 120,000 military, police, and civilian peacekeepers are now deployed in 14 operations around the world, from Haiti to Darfur to East Timor. Of those 120,000 peacekeepers, just 87 are Americans in uniform. Every peacekeeping mission must be approved by the Security Council—where America has a final say over all decisions. In Iraq and Afghanistan, UN civilian missions are mediating local disputes, coordinating international aid, and helping advance democracy—all of which helps us bring our soldiers home responsibly. UN "peacebuilding" efforts help rebuild shattered societies and prevent yesterday's hatreds from sparking tomorrow's infernos. And UN mediation has helped broker the end of conflicts, from Cambodia to Guatemala. Each UN peacekeeper costs a fraction of what it would cost to field a U.S. soldier to do the same job. So what's better, for America to bear the entire burden, or to share the burden for UN peacekeepers and pay a little more than a quarter of the cost? I don't know about you, but personally, I like places where I get 75 percent off. This is burden-sharing for a reasonable price—a lifesaving way to enable others to join us in preventing the conflict and chaos that can breed terrorism, pandemics, and other 21st-century threats. It's a whole lot more responsible to work together and share responsibility than to let threats multiply and innocents suffer.

Second, the UN helps halt the proliferation of nuclear weapons. In 2009, President Obama presided over a historic Security Council summit that unanimously adopted robust, binding steps to reduce nuclear dangers. The International Atomic Energy Agency, a key UN agency, has exposed Iran and North Korea's nuclear violations. And in the past two years, with U.S. leadership, the Security Council imposed the toughest sanctions that Iran and North Korea have ever faced. Strong Security Council resolutions have provided a foundation for others—from the European Union to Canada to South Korea—to levy additional sanctions of their own. And they warn governments that would defy their international obligations that they too will face isolation and consequences.

Third, UN humanitarian agencies go where nobody else will go to provide desperately needed food, shelter, and medicine. When polio erupted in Central Asia last year, health ministries were caught off-guard—but the World Health Organization vaccinated 6 million kids in Tajikistan and Uzbekistan, at a cost of less than $2 million. Where young people are at risk from deadly disease, UNICEF [United Nations Children's Fund] provides vaccines to fully 40 percent of the world's children and supplies millions of insecticide-treated mosquito nets in 48 countries to prevent malaria. When 125,000 Iraqi refugees were huddled in the winter chill, the UN High Commissioner for Refugees provided cash grants to buy heating fuel and warm clothes. When floods devastated Pakistan last year, the World Food Program helped feed 6.9 million people. UN humanitarian assistance doesn't just save lives. It also helps break the devastating downward spiral of chronic desperation that fuels violence and threatens international peace and security.

Fourth, the UN helps countries combat poverty, including by championing the lifesaving Millennium Development Goals. These goals include cutting extreme poverty in half and slashing the mortality rate of children under 5 by two-thirds by the year 2015. We're all more secure when people around the world have a shot at the better future we insist on for our own kids. It should trouble us deeply that half of humanity lives on less than $2.50 a day. Desperate poverty and the lack of basic services can fuel war and turmoil, creating ready havens for terrorists, criminals, and drug traffickers. Fortunately, UN development efforts afford millions the opportunity for a more dignified future. By investing in our common humanity, we simultaneously strengthen our common security.

Fifth, the UN helps foster democracy by providing expertise and oversight to strengthen fragile state institutions and support elections worldwide. Through the UN, when the people of South Sudan vote for their own freedom, the world can lend a vital hand. And when a strongman like Laurent Gbagbo of the Ivory Coast tries to steal an election, the UN, on behalf of the world, can blow the whistle.

Finally [sixth], the UN is a place where countries can come together to advance universal human rights and condemn the world's worst indignities. U.S. leadership has helped produce important results in the UN General Assembly, where we have condemned Iran, Burma, and North Korea's human rights abuses by unprecedented vote margins. We have fought and won protection for gay rights, and created UN Women, a new agency dedicated to advancing women's rights. Those steps and many more help rally the world to support bedrock U.S. and universal values: liberty, equality, and human dignity.

In the 21st century, we need the UN more than ever—to help bridge the gaps between war and reconciliation, between division and cooperation, and between misery and hope. Those of us—Democrats, Republicans, and independents alike—who support the United Nations owe it to American taxpayers to ensure that their dollars are well and cleanly spent. But, equally, those who push to curtail U.S. support to the United Nations owe it to U.S. soldiers to explain why they should perform missions now handled by United Nations peacekeepers, and they owe it to parents around the world to explain why their children should suffer without the medicine, food, and shelter that only the United Nations provides.

The United Nations plays an indispensable role in advancing our interests and defending our values. It provides a real return to the American taxpayer on our investment. The United Nations isn't perfect—far from it. The United Nations isn't the sum of our strategy—not even close. But it's an essential piece of it.

As my friend and mentor, former Secretary of State Madeleine Albright, has said, "There is a vast, sensible middle ground between those who see the United Nations as the only hope for the world and those who see in it the end of the world." A wise and deep bipartisan tradition has long seen the United Nations as essential to spurring the common actions that make Americans safer. That tradition recognizes that, if the United Nations didn't exist, we would have to invent it. Thankfully, we did help invent it. Our challenge today is to strengthen it—and in doing so, to make America more secure.

Bruce S. Thornton

→ **NO**

# The U.N.: So Bad It's Almost Beautiful

A bill introduced in Congress would allow the United States—which pays 22 percent of the United Nations' core budget and 25 percent of its peacekeeping expenses—to keep better track of how the money is spent and make sure that spending serves policies and programs consistent with American interests and principles. Yet tinkering with the United Nations' funding mechanisms will never correct the fatal flaw with the organization itself. To think otherwise is to assume that glasnost and perestroika could have saved the Soviet Union.

That flaw is the lack of consistent, unifying moral and political principles shared by member nations that can justify U.N. policies or legitimize the use of force to deter and punish aggression. Because of that absence, authoritarian, totalitarian, and even gangster regimes have seats in the U.N. General Assembly and its various councils and commissions. Of course, lip service is paid to Western ideals like universal human rights, political freedom, and liberal democracy, but these are nominally recognized not because all other nations believe in them but because of the West's economic and military dominance.

As a result, these ideals are simply redefined beyond recognition by non-Western cultures. In the Cairo Declaration on Human Rights in Islam [1990], for example, pleasing lists of "human rights" are in effect canceled out by Article 24, which says, "All the rights and freedoms stipulated in this Declaration are subject to the Islamic sharia." Or, taking their cue from Western cultural relativism, other nations dismiss such ideals as specific to the West. They argue that trying to impose Western ideals on non-Western cultures is stealth imperialism, if not outright racism.

The vacuum created by a lack of unified principles has been filled by national, political, and ideological self-interests. Thus the United Nations becomes the vehicle for pursuing those interests, as when the Soviet bloc in 1986 engineered a resolution that in effect forbade using human rights abuses as a rationale for U.N. intervention. In 1993 a U.N. conference on human rights wrote a declaration that left out any reference to individual rights such as freedom of speech. As Israeli statesman and diplomat Dore Gold writes in *Tower of Babble [: How the United Nations Has Fueled Global Chaos]*, "The new

U.N. majority had emptied the term 'human rights' of its original meaning and hijacked it to serve its authoritarian political agenda."

## Rewarding Terrorism

As the sorry history of the United Nations has shown, the various non-democratic regimes use the organization to pursue their interests at the expense of those of the United States. But then, so do American allies, as when France and Germany labored mightily in 2002 to thwart a U.N. resolution authorizing the war against Saddam Hussein, despite the fact that he had flouted seventeen previous U.N. resolutions.

*The fundamental problem: member nations don't share consistent, unifying moral and political principles.* Examples of such unprincipled behavior in pursuit of national interests are legion. The most egregious are the various resolutions that legitimize and reward terrorism. For example, [Palestinian leader] Yasser Arafat addressed the General Assembly wearing a holster on his hip in November 1974, a mere six months after his terrorist Palestine Liberation Organization had murdered scores of Israeli schoolchildren and three American diplomats. Arafat's visit was inevitable after the United Nations in 1970 passed Resolution 2708, which states that the United Nations "reaffirms its recognition of the legitimacy of the struggle of the colonial peoples and peoples under alien domination to exercise self-determination and independence by all the necessary means at their disposal." This free pass for terrorists was reaffirmed in 1982 when the U.N. General Assembly approved the "legitimacy of the struggle of peoples . . . from colonial and foreign domination and foreign occupation by all available means, including armed struggle."

*In April 2005, the Commission on Human Rights refused to condemn killing in the name of religion.* Even more despicable, in 1975—on the thirty-seventh anniversary of Kristallnacht, the Nazi pogrom against German Jews—the United Nations passed Resolution 3379, which defined Zionism as a form of racism. This odious resolution was revoked sixteen years later, but only because Israel had made its repeal a condition of participating in the Madrid peace conference. That this repeal reflected expediency rather than principle was obvious in April 2002, when the U.N. Commission on Human Rights affirmed "the legitimate right of the Palestinian people to resist Israeli occupation," just after a Hamas suicide bomber had killed thirty Israelis celebrating Passover.

The Commission on Human Rights and its allegedly improved successor, the Human Rights Council, may be the best representatives of the United Nations' Orwellian hypocrisy [a reference to George Owell's *1984*, a novel in which the government Ministry of Truth changes historical records to reflect the doctrine of the government]. Thug states like Iran, Sudan, Cuba, China, Zimbabwe, Saudi Arabia, and North Korea, which support terrorism and violate human rights as a matter of policy, have been allowed to sit on the council, where terrorist and state violence is never censured, even as Israel faces serial condemnation. Indeed, in April 2005, the commission refused to condemn killing in the name of religion. At the same time, it asserted that criticizing Muslim terrorists was "defamation of religion."

In March 2007, the council's response to the killings and riots that followed the publication of cartoons depicting Muhammad was to call for a ban on the defamation of religion—even as it ignored the threat to the human right to free speech. Neither the genocidal charter of Hamas [a Palestinian political organization considered to be terrorist by the United States and many other countreis] nor the widespread, state-sanctioned anti-Semitism in the Middle East has ever been condemned, while thirty-three resolutions through 2010 have criticized Israel. The animus of the Human Rights Council against the only liberal democracy in the Middle East was evident recently in its wildly inaccurate and biased Goldstone Report, an investigation into Israel's actions in Gaza. [The Goldstone Report is 575-page document, *Report of the United Nations Fact Finding Mission on the Gaza Conflict* submitted in 2009 to the Human Rights Council by a UN investigative commission headed by South African Judge Richard Goldstone.] Even the report's author was compelled to disavow it because of inaccuracies and obvious bias. Like the United Nations, the council is an instrument of member states' interests, not the presumed principles and rights enshrined in its charter and rhetoric.

## "Harmony of Interests" a Cruel Illusion

Given its purpose as a means for weak or autocratic states to pursue their interests, the United Nations has evolved into a bloated, corrupt, ineffective bureaucracy. Its budget has doubled since 2000. The most famous U.N. scandal is the 1995–2003 oil-for-food program that operated in Saddam Hussein's Iraq, overseeing $15 billion a year supposedly meant to feed the Iraqi people. Instead it was "an open bazaar of payoffs, favoritism, and kickbacks," as *The New York Times* put it, generating over $10 billion in illicit funds for Saddam's regime and billions more for Russian and French politicians and businessmen.

Worse than these financial scandals, however, is the utter impotence of the United Nations in stopping violence in places like Sudan, Bosnia, and Rwanda, where horrific violence occurred a stone's throw away from U.N. "peacekeeping" forces. In fact, in Bosnia, U.N. "safe areas" simply made it easier for the Serbs to round up and slaughter seven thousand Bosnian Muslims.

*Even worse than its financial scandals is the U.N.'s utter impotence in stopping violence in places like Sudan, Bosnia, and Rwanda.* The United Nations is a relic of the same Enlightenment idealism that has driven internationalism for almost two centuries and which has failed dismally to stop the violence of the twentieth century and beyond. That idealism assumes that all humanity is progressing beyond the use of force, tyrannical regimes, and parochial nationalist interests to a transnational "harmony of interests" created by communication technologies, global trade, and the spread of liberal democracy. These shared interests, moreover, can be institutionalized in international laws, courts, treaties, and supranational organizations that will substitute diplomacy and negotiation for force.

This vision created the League of Nations, which in the Twenties and Thirties completely failed to stop the state violence of Japan, Italy, and Germany. Its successor, the United Nations, has done no better for the simple reason that such a "harmony of interests" does not exist and never will. States and peoples have different values, beliefs, and aims. They pursue interests that conflict with the interests and aims of other states. And the melancholy lesson of history is that these conflicts usually are resolved by force or the credible threat of force, not by diplomatic chatter in a "cockpit in the Tower of Babel," to use the phrase conjured up by Winston Churchill when the United Nations was born.

The question, then, is not how we fix the United Nations, as the U.N. Transparency, Accountability, and Reform Act, introduced in August [2011] by Florida Republican Ileana Ros-Lehtinen [chairwoman of the Committee on Foreign Affairs, U.S. House of Representatives], attempts to do. Instead it is why we continue to spend U.S. taxpayer dollars—$7.7 billion in 2010—on an institution filled with states hostile to us and working against our own foreign policy interests. Herein lies the greatest flaw in the thinking of those Americans who still believe in the usefulness of the United Nations: they believe that unelected, unaccountable functionaries of tyrannous regimes—regimes not only pursuing their own interests but frequently working against our interests—are more capable of determining the legitimacy of the United States' foreign policy and behavior than are the American people.

In contrast to the United Nations, the legitimacy of American actions is conferred by the democratic process: the free, open debate on the part of citizens who can hold their leaders accountable and have a sense of the ideals and principles that animate foreign policy and provide its goals. Subjecting those decisions to the corrupt deliberations of the United Nations merely hampers our own interests and endangers our national security. We need to get out of the United Nations, not fix it.

# EXPLORING THE ISSUE

## Is the UN a Worthwhile Organization?

## Questions for Critical Thinking and Reflection

1. Both Susan Rice and Bruce Thornton in the YES and NO selections evaluate the UN in terms of how well it advances U.S. policy and interests. Is that a correct standard, even for Americans, or should the UN be evaluated from the point of view of how well it promotes the goals of its Charter including maintain and promoting peace, protecting human rights, and improving the conditions of less fortunate people and countries?

2. To fund its operations, the UN assesses countries based on their wealth. The United States pays the greatest share, which came to about $3 billion or general operations and peacekeeping in 2012. The U.S. also contributes about another $5 billion to various UN-associated agencies like the World Health Organization. These funds total about two-tenths of 1 percent of the U.S. budget. Some say these amounts to the UN are too high. Do you agree?

3. Would you favor or oppose abolishing the veto in the UN Security Council?

## Is There Common Ground?

Evaluating the value of the UN has a great deal to do with what standard of evaluation you adopt. One standard is akin to asking whether a glass is half full or half empty. Undoubtedly, the UN has not come anywhere near achieving the lofty goals set out in its Charter. Thus, the evaluative glass is at least half empty. However, it is also true that the UN has accomplished a great deal. Many UN peacekeeping operations have been fielded, and some of them have made an important contribution. In late 2012, there were over 97,000 troops, police, and other personnel from 116 countries trying to provide security through 18 different UN peacekeeping operations. For all the human abuse and poverty that remain, there is greater justice and better living conditions in the world now than that existed a few decades ago. Again, the UN can legitimately claim some of the credit. So from this perspective, the glass is at least fuller than it once was.

Yet another standard of measurement has to do with the old adage about being careful when throwing stones in glass houses. The UN has sometimes wasted money, its workers have not always performed admirably, and even Secretary General Kofi Annan (1997–2006) conceded that to some degree the UN's administration had "become fragmented, duplicative, and rigid."

Yet every government, including the U.S. government, is subject to the same accusation. Annan was able to implement many changes, and his successor beginning in 2006, Secretary General Ban Ki-moon, has said continued reform will be a top priority. It is also the case that a small number of UN troops and personnel have behaved immorally, but the equally if not more abominable performance of a few American soldiers at Abu Ghraib Prison and elsewhere show how the actions of the reprehensive few can besmirch the reputations of the honorable many.

The ultimate question is if not the UN, then what. Calls to "fix" the UN are many and varied, and debating what should be done and what is possible are worthwhile. Perhaps creating a successor organization would be a good idea. Then there is the suggestion of doing without a central global organization. Ask yourself whether that would open the way to a safer, more prosperous, more just world or even further your country's national interests.

## Additional Resources

Karen A. Mingst and Margaret P. Karns, *The United Nations in the 21st Century* (Westview Press, 2011), provide a good introduction to the UN. A book suggesting reforms from a relatively friendly perspective regarding the UN is Thomas G. Weis, *What's Wrong with the United Nations and How to Fix It* (Polity, 2012). A much less positive take on reform is provided by Brett D. Schaefer, ed., *ConUNdrum: The Limits of the United Nations and the Search for Alternatives* (Rowman & Littlefield, 2009). For more on the pivotal Security Council, read David L. Bosco, *Five to Rule Them All: The UN Security Council and the Making of the Modern World* (Oxford University Press, 2009).

# ISSUE 15

# Is U.S. Refusal to Join the International Criminal Court Wise?

**YES: Brett Schaefer and Steven Groves**, from "The U.S. Should Not Join the International Criminal Court," Backgrounder on International Organization, The Heritage Foundation (August 18, 2009)

**NO: Jonathan F. Fanton**, from "The Challenge of International Justice," Remarks to the U.S. Military Academy at West Point, New York (May 5, 2008)

### ISSUE SUMMARY

**YES:** Brett Schaefer, the Jay Kingham fellow in international regulatory affairs at the Heritage Foundation, and Steven Groves, the Bernard and Barbara Lomas fellow in the Margaret Thatcher Center for Freedom, a division of the Kathryn and Shelby Cullom Davis Institute for International Studies at the Heritage Foundation, contend that although the court's supporters have a noble purpose, there are a number of reasons to be cautious and concerned about how ratification of the Rome Statute would affect U.S. sovereignty and how ICC action could affect politically precarious situations around the world.

**NO:** Jonathan F. Fanton, president of the John D. and Catherine T. MacArthur Foundation, which is headquartered in Chicago, Illinois, and is among the world's largest independent foundations, maintains that creation of the International Court of Justice is an important step toward creating a more just world, and that the fear that many Americans have expressed about the court has not materialized.

**H**istorically, international law has focused primarily on countries. More recently, individuals have increasingly become subject to international law. The first major step in this direction was the convening of the Nuremberg and Tokyo war crimes trials after World War II to try German and Japanese military and civilian leaders charged with various war crimes. There were no subsequent war crimes tribunals until the 1990s when the United Nations (UN) established two of them. One sits in The Hague, the Netherlands, and deals with the horrific events in Bosnia. The other tribunal is in Arusha, Tanzania, and provides justice for the genocidal massacres in Rwanda. These tribunals have indicted numerous people for war crimes and have convicted and imprisoned many of them. Nevertheless, there was a widespread feeling that such ad hoc tribunals needed to be replaced by a permanent international criminal tribunal.

In 1996, the UN convened a conference in Rome to do just that. At first the United States was supportive, but it favored a very limited court that could only prosecute and hear cases referred to it by the UN Security Council (where the United States had a veto) and, even then, could only try individuals with the permission of the defendant's home government. Most countries disagreed, but in 1998 the Rome conference voted overwhelmingly to create a relatively strong court. The Rome Statute of the International Criminal Court (ICC) gives the ICC jurisdiction over wars of aggression, genocide, and other crimes, but only if the home country of an alleged perpetrator fails to act.

Although the ICC treaty was open for signature in July 1998, President Bill Clinton showed either ambivalence or a desire not to have it injected as an issue into the 2000 presidential election by waiting until December 31, 2000, to have a U.S. official sign the treaty. If Clinton had his doubts, his successor, George W. Bush, did not. He was adamantly opposed to the treaty. As directed by the White House, State Department official John R. Bolton sent a letter dated May 6, 2002, to UN Secretary General Kofi Annan informing him that "in connection with the Rome Statute of the International Criminal Court . . . , the United States does not intend to become a party to the treaty . . . [and] has no legal obligations arising from its signature on December 31, 2000." The Bush administration also launched an effort to persuade other countries to sign "Article 98" agreements by which countries agree not to surrender U.S. citizens to the ICC.

The letter formally notifying the UN that the United States does not intend to become a party to the Rome Statute also ended any U.S. participation in the workings of the court. In the YES selection Brett Schaefer and Steven Groves review the ICC's legal implications and assess its operation so far. As a result, they conclude that although the court reflects an admirable desire to hold war criminals accountable for their terrible crimes, the ICC is so flawed that it would be unwise for the United States to join it. In the NO selection Jonathan F. Fanton also reviews the evolution of the ICC and comes to a different conclusion. He says he is convinced that the United States and its armed forces have nothing to fear from the ICC and much to both offer to and gain from its success.

# YES ↵

Brett Schaefer and
Steven Groves

# The U.S. Should Not Join the International Criminal Court

The idea of establishing an international court to prosecute serious international crimes—war crimes, crimes against humanity, and genocide—has long held a special place in the hearts of human rights activists and those hoping to hold perpetrators of terrible crimes to account. In 1998, that idea became reality when the Rome Statute of the International Criminal Court was adopted at a diplomatic conference convened by the U.N. General Assembly. The International Criminal Court (ICC) was formally established in 2002 after 60 countries ratified the statute. The ICC was created to prosecute war crimes, crimes against humanity, genocide, and the as yet undefined crime of aggression. Regrettably, although the court's supporters have a noble purpose, there are a number of reasons to be cautious and concerned about how ratification of the Rome Statute would affect U.S. sovereignty and how ICC action could affect politically precarious situations around the world.

Among other concerns, past U.S. Administrations concluded that the Rome Statute created a seriously flawed institution that lacks prudent safeguards against political manipulation, possesses sweeping authority without accountability to the U.N. Security Council, and violates national sovereignty by claiming jurisdiction over the nationals and military personnel of non-party states in some circumstances. These concerns led President Bill Clinton to urge President George W. Bush not to submit the treaty to the Senate for advice and consent necessary for ratification. After extensive efforts to change the statute to address key U.S. concerns failed, President Bush felt it necessary to "un-sign" the Rome Statute by formally notifying the U.N. Secretary-General that the U.S. did not intend to ratify the treaty and was no longer bound under international law to avoid actions that would run counter to the intent and purpose of the treaty. Subsequently, the U.S. took a number of steps to protect its military personnel, officials, and nationals from ICC claims of jurisdiction.

Until these and other concerns are fully addressed, the Obama Administration should resist pressure to "re-sign" the Rome Statute, eschew cooperation with the ICC except when U.S. interests are affected, and maintain the existing policy of protecting U.S. military personnel, officials, and nationals from the court's illegitimate claims of jurisdiction. Nor should the Obama Administration seek ratification of the Rome Statute prior to the 2010 review, and then only if the Rome Statute and the ICC and its procedures are amended to address all of the serious concerns that led past U.S. Administrations to oppose ratification of the Rome Statute.

# Background

The United States has long championed human rights and supported the ideal that those who commit serious human rights violations should be held accountable. Indeed, it was the United States that insisted—over Soviet objections—that promoting basic human rights and fundamental freedoms be included among the purposes of the United Nations. The United States also played a lead role in championing major international efforts in international humanitarian law, such as the Geneva Conventions.

The U.S. has supported the creation of international courts to prosecute gross human rights abuses. It pioneered the Nuremburg and Tokyo tribunals to prosecute atrocities committed during World War II. Since then, the U.S. was a key supporter of establishing the ad hoc International Criminal Tribunal for the former Yugoslavia (ICTY) and International Criminal Tribunal for Rwanda (ICTR), which were both approved by the Security Council.

Continuing its long support for these efforts, the U.S. initially was an eager participant in the effort to create an International Criminal Court in the 1990s. However, once negotiations began [in 1998] on the final version of the Rome Statute, America's support waned because many of its concerns were ignored or opposed outright. According to David J. Scheffer, chief U.S. negotiator at the 1998 Rome conference:

> In Rome, we indicated our willingness to be flexible. . . . Unfortunately, a small group of countries, meeting behind closed doors in the final days of the Rome conference, produced a seriously flawed take-it-or-leave-it text, one that provides a recipe for politicization of the court and risks deterring responsible international action to promote peace and security.

In the end, despite persistent efforts to amend the Rome Statute to alleviate U.S. concerns, the conference rejected most of the changes proposed by the U.S., and the final document was approved over U.S. opposition.

Since the approval of the Rome Statute in 1998, U.S. policy toward the ICC has been clear and consistent: The U.S. has refused to join the ICC because it lacks prudent safeguards against political manipulation, possesses sweeping authority without accountability to the U.N. Security Council, and violates national sovereignty by claiming jurisdiction over the nationals and military personnel of non-party states in some circumstances.

The United States is not alone in its concerns about the ICC. As of August 6, 2009, only 110 of the 192 U.N. member states had ratified the Rome Statute. In fact, China, India, and Russia are among the other major powers that have refused to ratify the Rome Statute out of concern that it unduly infringes on their foreign and security policy decisions—issues rightly reserved to sovereign governments and over which the ICC should not claim authority.

# The ICC's Record

The International Criminal Court has a clear legal lineage extending back to the Nuremburg and Tokyo trials and ad hoc tribunals, such as the ICTY and the ICTR, which were established by the U.N. Security Council in 1993 and 1994, respectively. However, the ICC is much broader and more independent than these limited precedents. Its authority is not limited to disputes between governments as is the case with the International Court of Justice (ICJ) or to a particular jurisdiction as is the case with national judiciaries. Nor is its authority limited to particular crimes committed in a certain place or period of time as was the case with the post-World War II trials and the Yugoslavian and Rwandan tribunals.

Instead, the ICC claims jurisdiction over individuals committing genocide, crimes against humanity, war crimes, and the undefined crime of aggression. This jurisdiction extends from the entry into force of the Rome Statute in July 2002 and applies to all citizens of states that have ratified the Rome Statute. However, it also extends to individuals from countries that are not party to the Rome Statute if the alleged crimes occur on the territory of an ICC party state, the non-party government invites ICC jurisdiction, or the U.N. Security Council refers the case to the ICC.

International lawyers Lee Casey and David Rivkin point out that the ICC is a radical departure from previous international courts [because] "It has jurisdiction over individuals, including elected or appointed government officials, and its judgments may be directly enforced against them, regardless of their own national constitutions or court systems."

> Moreover, the court's structure establishes few, if any, practical external checks on the ICC's authority. Among the judges' responsibilities are determining whether the prosecutor may proceed with a case and whether a member state has been "unwilling or unable genuinely to carry out the investigation or prosecution," which would trigger the ICC's jurisdiction under the principle of "complementarity," which is designed to limit the court's power and avoid political abuse of its authority. Thus, the various arms of the ICC are themselves the only real check on its authority.

Even though the Rome Statute entered into force in July 2002, there is little concrete basis for judging the ICC's performance. Shortly after its formal establishment, the ICC began receiving its first referrals. Currently, the ICC has opened four cases, involving situations in the Democratic Republic of Congo (DRC), Uganda, the Central African Republic, and Darfur, Sudan.

As an institution, the ICC has performed little, if any, better than the ad hoc tribunals that it was created to replace. Like the Rwandan and Yugoslavian tribunals, the ICC is slow to act. The ICC prosecutor took six months to open an investigation in Uganda, two months with the DRC, over a year with Darfur, and nearly two years with the Central African Republic. It has yet to conclude a full trial cycle more than seven years after being created. Moreover, like the ad hoc tribunals, the ICC can investigate and prosecute crimes only after the fact. The alleged deterrent effect of a standing international criminal court has not ended atrocities in the DRC, Uganda, the Central African Republic, or Darfur, where cases are ongoing. Nor has it deterred atrocities by Burma against its own people, crimes committed during Russia's 2008 invasion of Georgia (an ICC party), ICC party Venezuela's support of leftist guerillas in Colombia, or any of a number of other situations around the world where war crimes or crimes against humanity may be occurring.

Another problem is that the ICC lacks a mechanism to enforce its rulings and is, therefore, entirely dependent on governments to arrest and transfer perpetrators to the court. However, such arrests can have significant diplomatic consequences, which can greatly inhibit the efficacy of the court in pursuing its warrants and prosecuting outstanding cases. The most prominent example is Sudanese President Bashir's willingness to travel to other countries on official visits—thus far only to non-ICC states—despite the ICC arrest warrant. This flaw was also present with the ICTY and the ICTR, although they could at least rely on a Security Council resolution mandating international cooperation in enforcing their arrest warrants. In contrast, the Nuremburg and Tokyo tribunals were established where the authority of the judicial proceedings could rely on Allied occupation forces to search out, arrest, and detain the accused.

# The Myth of Bush Administration Intransigence

The U.S. refusal to ratify the Rome Statute has been mischaracterized by ICC proponents as solely a Bush Administration policy. In fact, the Clinton Administration initiated the U.S. policy of distancing itself from the ICC. According to David J. Scheffer, Ambassador-at-Large for War Crimes Issues under the Clinton Administration:

> Foreign officials and representatives of non-governmental organizations tried to assure us in Rome that procedural safeguards built into the treaty—many sought successfully by the United States—meant that there would be no plausible risk to U.S. soldiers. We could not share in such an optimistic view of the infallibility of an untried institution. . . .

President Clinton himself acknowledged the treaty's "significant flaws" and recommended that President Bush not submit the treaty to the Senate for advice and consent. When President Clinton authorized the U.S. delegation to sign the Rome Statute on December 31, 2000, it was not to pave the way for U.S. ratification, but solely to give the U.S. an opportunity to address American concerns about the ICC. As Clinton said at the time in his signing statement:

> In signing, however, we are not abandoning our concerns about significant flaws in the treaty. In particular, we are concerned that when the court comes into existence, it will not only exercise authority over personnel of states that have ratified the treaty but also claim jurisdiction over personnel of states that have not. With signature, however, we will be in a position to influence the evolution of the court. Without signature, we will not.

After adoption of the Rome Statute in 1998, both the Clinton and Bush Administrations sought to rectify the parts of the statute that precluded U.S. participation. Specifically, the U.S. actively participated in the post-Rome preparatory commissions, hoping to address its concerns. As former U.S. Under Secretary for Political Affairs Marc Grossman noted:

> After the United States voted against the treaty in Rome, the U.S. remained committed and engaged—working for two years to help shape the court and to seek the necessary safeguards to prevent a politicization of the process. While we were able to make some improvements during our active participation in the UN Preparatory Commission meetings in New York, we were ultimately unable [to] obtain the remedies necessary to overcome our fundamental concerns. . . .

The consequences of failing to change the objectionable provisions of the Rome Statute became acute when the 60th country ratified the treaty, causing the statute to enter into force in July 2002. Faced with the prospect of a functioning International Criminal Court that could assert jurisdiction over U.S. soldiers and officials in certain circumstances, the Bush Administration and Congress took steps to protect Americans from the court's jurisdiction, which the U.S. did not recognize. For instance, Congress passed the American Service-Members' Protection Act of 2002 (ASPA), which restricts U.S. interaction with the ICC and its state parties by:

- Prohibiting cooperation with the ICC by any official U.S. entity, including providing support or funds to the ICC, extraditing or transferring U.S. citizens or permanent resident aliens to the ICC, or permitting ICC investigations on U.S. territory.
- Prohibiting participation by U.S. military or officials in U.N. peacekeeping operations unless they are shielded from the ICC's jurisdiction.
- Prohibiting the sharing of classified national security information or other law enforcement information with the ICC.
- Constraining military assistance to ICC member states, except NATO countries and major non-NATO allies and Taiwan, unless they entered into an agreement with the U.S. not to surrender U.S. persons to the ICC without U.S. permission.
- Authorizing the President to use "all means necessary and appropriate" to free U.S. military personnel or officials detained by the ICC.

Congress also approved the Nethercutt Amendment to the foreign operations appropriations bill for fiscal year 2005, which prohibited disbursement of selected U.S. assistance to an ICC party unless the country has entered into a bilateral agreement not to surrender U.S. persons to the ICC (commonly known as an Article 98 agreement) or is specifically exempted in the legislation. Both ASPA and the Nethercutt Amendment contained waiver provisions allowing the President to ignore these restrictions with notification to Congress. In recent years, Congress has repealed or loosened restrictions on providing assistance to ICC state parties that have not entered into Article 98 agreements with the U.S. However, other ASPA restrictions remain in effect.

The Bush Administration signed these legislative measures and undertook several specific efforts to fulfill the mandates of the legislation and to protect U.S. military personnel and officials from potential ICC prosecution.

## Possible Legal Obligations from Signing the Rome Statute

Under Article 18 of the Vienna Convention on the Law of Treaties, the Bush Administration determined that its efforts to protect U.S. persons from the ICC could be construed as "acts which would defeat the object and purpose of a treaty." To resolve this potential conflict, the U.S. sent a letter to U.N. Secretary-General Kofi Annan, the depositor for the Rome Statute, stating that it did not intend to become a party to the Rome Statute and declaring that "the United States has no legal obligations arising from its signature" of the Rome Statute. This act has been described as "un-signing" the Rome Statute. As John Bellinger, former Legal Advisor to Secretary of State Condoleezza Rice, made clear in a 2008 speech, "the central motivation was to resolve any confusion whether, as a matter of treaty law, the United States had residual legal obligations arising from its signature of the Rome Statute."

## Article 98 Agreements

Because the ICC could claim jurisdiction over non-parties to the Rome Statute—an assertion unprecedented in international legal jurisdiction—the Bush Administration sought legal protections to preclude nations from surrendering, extraditing, or transferring U.S. persons to the ICC or third countries for that purpose without U.S. consent. Under an Article 98 agreement, a country agrees not to turn U.S. persons over to the ICC without U.S. consent.

Contrary to the claims of the more strident critics, who label the Article 98 agreements as "bilateral immunity agreements" or "impunity agreements," the agreements neither absolve the U.S. of its obligation to investigate and prosecute alleged crimes, constrain the other nation's ability to investigate and prosecute crimes committed by an American person within its jurisdiction, nor constrain an international tribunal established by the Security Council from investigating or prosecuting crimes committed by U.S. persons. The agreements simply prevent other countries from turning U.S. persons over to an international court that does not have jurisdiction recognized by the United States.

The limited nature of the agreements is entirely consistent with international law, which supports the principle that a state cannot be bound by a treaty to which it is not a party. The agreements are also consistent with customary international law because the issue of ICC jurisdiction is very much in dispute. Moreover, they are consistent with the Rome Statute itself, which contemplates such agreements in Article 98:

> The Court may not proceed with a request for surrender which would require the requested State to act inconsistently with its obligations under international agreements pursuant to which the consent of a sending State is required to surrender a person of that State to the Court, unless the Court can first obtain the cooperation of the sending State for the giving of consent for the surrender.

Although the U.S. is not currently seeking to negotiate additional Article 98 agreements, there are no known plans to terminate existing agreements. Reportedly, 104 countries have signed Article 98 agreements with the U.S., of which 97 agreements remain in effect.

## Language to Protect U.S. Persons

In 2002, the U.S. sought a Security Council resolution to indefinitely exempt from ICC jurisdiction U.S. troops and officials participating in U.N. peacekeeping operations. The effort failed in the face of arguments that the Security Council lacked the authority to rewrite the terms of the Rome Statute, but the Security Council did adopt Resolution 1422, which deferred ICC prosecution of U.N. peacekeeping personnel for one year under Article 16 of the Rome Statute. The deferral was renewed once and expired in June 2004. The U.S. also successfully included language in Resolution 1497 on the U.N. Mission to Liberia granting exclusive jurisdiction over "current or former officials or personnel from a contributing State" to the contributing state if it is not a party to the Rome Statute.

# Persistent Barriers to U.S. Ratification

ICC supporters have called for the Obama Administration to re-sign the Rome Statute, reverse protective measures secured during the Bush Administration (Article 98 agreements), and fully embrace the ICC. Indeed, the Obama Administration may be considering some or all of those actions. However, the ICC's flaws advise caution and concern, particularly in how the ICC could affect national sovereignty and politically precarious situations around the globe.

When it decided to un-sign the Rome Statute, the Bush Administration voiced five concerns regarding the Rome Statute. These critical concerns have not been addressed.

## The ICC's Unchecked Power

The U.S. system of government is based on the principle that power must be checked by other power or it will be abused and misused. With this in mind, the Founding Fathers divided the national government into three branches, giving each the means to influence and restrain excesses of the other branches. For instance, Congress confirms and can impeach federal judges and has the sole authority to authorize spending, the President nominates judges and can veto legislation, and the courts can nullify laws passed by Congress and overturn presidential actions if it judges them unconstitutional.

> The ICC lacks robust checks on its authority, despite strong efforts by U.S. delegates to insert them during the treaty negotiations. The court is an independent treaty body. In theory, the states that have ratified the Rome Statute and accepted the court's authority control the ICC. In practice, the role of the Assembly of State Parties is limited. The judges themselves settle any dispute over the court's "judicial functions." The

prosecutor can initiate an investigation on his own authority, and the ICC judges determine whether the investigation may proceed. The U.N. Security Council can delay an investigation for a year—a delay that can be renewed—but it cannot stop an investigation.

## The Challenges to the Security Council's Authority

The Rome Statute empowers the ICC to investigate, prosecute, and punish individuals for the as yet undefined crime of "aggression." This directly challenges the authority and prerogatives of the U.N. Security Council, which the U.N. Charter gives "primary responsibility for the maintenance of international peace and security" and which is the only U.N. institution empowered to determine when a nation has committed an act of aggression. Yet, the Rome Statute "empowers the court to decide on this matter and lets the prosecutor investigate and prosecute this undefined crime" free of any oversight from the Security Council.

## A Threat to National Sovereignty

A bedrock principle of the international system is that treaties and the judgments and decisions of treaty organizations cannot be imposed on states without their consent. In certain circumstances, the ICC claims the authority to detain and try U.S. military personnel, U.S. officials, and other U.S. nationals even though the U.S. has not ratified the Rome Statute and has declared that it does not consider itself bound by its signature on the treaty. As Grossman noted, "While sovereign nations have the authority to try non-citizens who have committed crimes against their citizens or in their territory, the United States has never recognized the right of an international organization to do so absent consent or a U.N. Security Council mandate."

As such, the Rome Statute violates international law as it has been traditionally understood by empowering the ICC to prosecute and punish the nationals of countries that are not party to it. In fact, Article 34 of the Vienna Convention on the Law of Treaties unequivocally states: "A treaty does not create either obligations or rights for a third State without its consent."

> Protestations by ICC proponents that the court would seek such prosecutions only if a country is unwilling or unable to prosecute those accused of crimes within the court's jurisdiction—the principle of complementarity—are insufficient to alleviate sovereignty concerns.

For example, the Obama Administration recently declared that no employee of the Central Intelligence Agency (CIA) who engaged in the use of "enhanced interrogation techniques" on detainees would be criminally prosecuted. That decision was presumably the result of an analysis of U.S. law, legal advice provided to the CIA by Justice Department lawyers, and the particular actions of the interrogators. Yet if the U.S. were a party to the Rome Statute, the Administration's announced decision not to prosecute would fulfill a prerequisite for possible prosecution by the ICC under the principle of complementarity. That is, because the U.S. has no plans to prosecute its operatives for acts that many in the international community consider torture, the ICC prosecutor would be empowered (and possibly compelled) to pursue charges against the interrogators.

## Erosion of Fundamental Elements of the U.N. Charter

The ICC's jurisdiction over war crimes, crimes against humanity, genocide, and aggression directly involves the court in fundamental issues traditionally reserved to sovereign states, such as when a state can lawfully use armed force to defend itself, its citizens, or its interests; how and to what extent armed force may be applied; and the point at which particular actions constitute serious crimes. Blurring the lines of authority and responsibility in these decisions has serious consequences. As Grossman notes, "with the ICC prosecutor and judges presuming to sit in judgment of the security decisions of States without their assent, the ICC could have a chilling effect on the willingness of States to project power in defense of their moral and security interests." The ability to project power must be protected, not only for America's own national security interests, but also for those individuals threatened by genocide and despotism who can only be protected through the use of force.

## Complications to Military Cooperation Between the U.S. and Its Allies

The treaty creates an obligation to hand over U.S. nationals to the court, regardless of U.S. objections, absent a competing obligation such as that created through an Article 98 agreement. The United States has a unique role and responsibility in preserving international peace and security. At any given time, U.S. forces are located in approximately 100 nations around the world, standing ready to defend the interests of the U.S. and its allies, engaging in peacekeeping and humanitarian operations, conducting military exercises, or protecting U.S. interests through military intervention. The worldwide extension of U.S. armed forces is internationally unique. The U.S. must ensure that its soldiers and government officials are not exposed to politically motivated investigations and prosecutions.

# Ongoing Causes for Concern

Supporters of U.S. ratification of the Rome Statute often dismiss these concerns as unjustified, disproved by the ICC's conduct during its first seven years in operation, or as insufficient to overcome the need for an international court to hold perpetrators of serious crimes to account. Considering the other options that exist or could be created to fill the ICC's role of holding perpetrators of war crimes, crimes against humanity, genocide, and aggression to account, the benefits from joining such a flawed institution do not justify the risks.

Furthermore, based on the ICC's record and the trend in international legal norms, they are being disingenuous in dismissing concerns about over-politicization of the ICC, its impact on diplomatic initiatives and sovereign decisions on the use of force, its expansive claim of jurisdiction over the citizens of non-states parties, and incompatibility with U.S. legal norms and traditions. A number of specific risks are obvious.

## Politicization of the Court

Unscrupulous individuals and groups and nations seeking to influence foreign policy and security decisions of other nations have and will continue to seek to misuse the ICC for politically motivated purposes. Without appropriate checks and balances to prevent its misuse, the ICC represents a dangerous temptation for those with political axes to grind. The prosecutor's *proprio motu* authority to initiate an investigation based solely on his own authority or on information provided by a government, a nongovernmental organization (NGO), or individuals is an open invitation for political manipulation.

One example is the multitude of complaints submitted to the ICC urging the court to indict Bush Administration officials for alleged crimes in Iraq and Afghanistan. The Office of the Prosecutor received more than 240 communications alleging crimes related to the situation in Iraq. Thus far, the prosecutor has demonstrated considerable restraint, declining to pursue these cases for various reasons, including that the ICC does not have "jurisdiction with respect to actions of non-State Party nationals on the territory of Iraq," which is also not a party to the Rome Statute.

All current ICC cases were referred to the ICC by the governments of the territories in which the alleged crimes occurred or by the Security Council. Comparatively speaking, these cases are low-hanging fruit—situations clearly envisioned to be within the authority of the court by all states. Even so, they have not been without controversy, as demonstrated by the AU reaction to the arrest warrant for President Bashir and attempts to have the Security Council defer the case.

However, the ICC's brief track record is no assurance that future cases will be similarly resolved, especially given the increasing appetite for lodging charges with the ICC. A far more significant test will arise if the prosecutor decides to investigate (and the court's pre-trial chamber authorizes) a case involving a non-ICC party without a Security Council referral or against the objections of the government of the involved territory.

This could arise from the prosecutor's monitoring of the situation in Palestine. Even though Israel is not a party to the Rome Statute, the ICC prosecutor is exploring a request by the Palestinian National Authority to prosecute Israeli commanders for alleged war crimes committed during the recent actions in Gaza. The request is supported by 200 complaints from individuals and NGOs alleging war crimes by the Israeli military and civilian leaders related to military actions in Gaza.

Palestinian lawyers maintain that the Palestinian National Authority can request ICC jurisdiction as the de facto sovereign even though it is not an internationally recognized state. By countenancing Palestine's claims, the ICC prosecutor has enabled pressure to be applied to Israel over alleged war crimes, while ignoring Hamas's incitement of the military action and its commission of war crimes against Israeli civilians. Furthermore, by seemingly recognizing

Palestine as a sovereign entity, the prosecutor's action has arguably created a pathway for Palestinian statehood without first reaching a comprehensive peace deal with Israel. This determination is an inherently political issue beyond the ICC's authority, yet the prosecutor has yet to reject the possibility that the ICC may open a case on the situation.

Alternatively, the prosecutor could raise ire by making a legal judgment call on a crime under the court's jurisdiction that lacks a firm, universal interpretation, such as:

- "Committing outrages upon personal dignity, in particular humiliating and degrading treatment";
- "Intentionally launching an attack in the knowledge that such attack will cause incidental loss of life or injury to civilians or damage to civilian objects or widespread, long-term and severe damage to the natural environment which would be clearly excessive in relation to the concrete and direct overall military advantage anticipated"; or
- Using weapons "which are of a nature to cause superfluous injury or unnecessary suffering or which are inherently indiscriminate in violation of the international law of armed conflict."

In each of these cases, a reasonable conclusion could be made to determine whether a crime was committed. For instance, many human rights groups allege outrages on personal dignity and "humiliating and degrading treatment" were committed at the detention facility at Guantanamo Bay, Cuba. The U.S. disputes these claims. Excessive use of force has been alleged in Israel's attacks in Gaza, while others insist Israel demonstrated forbearance and consideration in trying to prevent civilian casualties. There is also an ongoing international effort to ban landmines and cluster munitions. If the ICC member states agree to add them to the annex of banned weapons, it could lead to a confrontation over their use by non-party states, such as the U.S., which opposes banning these weapons. These are merely some scenarios in which politicization could become an issue for the ICC.

## The Undefined Crime of Aggression

It would be irresponsible for the U.S. to expose its military personnel and civilian officials to a court that has yet to define the very crimes over which it claims jurisdiction. Yet that is the situation the U.S. would face if it ratified the Rome Statute. The Statute includes the crime of aggression as one of its enumerated crimes, but the crime has yet to be defined, despite a special working group that has been debating the issue for more than five years.

For instance, some argue that any military action conducted without Security Council authorization violates international law and is, therefore, an act of aggression that could warrant an ICC indictment. The U.S. has been the aggressor in several recent military actions, including military invasions of the sovereign territories of Afghanistan and Iraq, albeit with the U.N. Security Council's blessing in the case of Afghanistan. U.S. forces bombed Serbia in 1999 and launched dozens of cruise missiles at targets in Afghanistan and the Sudan in

1998 without explicit Security Council authorization. While charges of aggression are unlikely to be brought against U.S. officials *ex post facto* for military actions in Iraq and elsewhere—certainly not for actions before July 2002 as limited by the Rome Statute—submitting to the jurisdiction of an international court that judges undefined crimes would be highly irresponsible and an open invitation to levy such charges against U.S. officials in future conflicts.

If the U.S. becomes an ICC party, every decision by the U.S. to use force, every civilian death resulting from U.S. military action and every allegedly abused detainee could conceivably give cause to America's enemies to file charges against U.S. soldiers and officials. Indeed, any U.S. "failure" to prosecute a high-ranking U.S. official in such instances would give a cause of action at the ICC. For example, the principle of complementarity will not prevent a politicized prosecutor from bringing charges against a sitting U.S. President or Secretary of Defense. That is, the U.S. Department of Justice is unlikely to file criminal charges against such officials for their decisions involving the use of military force. This decision not to prosecute would be a prerequisite for the ICC taking up the case.

At best, the U.S. would find itself defending its military and civilian officials against frivolous and politically motivated charges submitted to the ICC prosecutor. At worst, international political pressure could compel the ICC's prosecutor to file charges against current or former U.S. officials. Until the crime of aggression is defined, U.S. membership in the ICC is premature.

# What the U.S. Should Do

The serious flaws that existed when President Clinton signed the Rome Statute in December 2000 continue to exist today. The Bush Administration's policy toward the ICC was prudent and in the best interests of the U.S., its officials, and particularly its armed forces. Since the ICC came into existence, the U.S. has treaded carefully by supporting the ICC on an ad hoc basis without backing away from its long-standing objections to the court. The U.S. has simultaneously taken the necessary steps to protect U.S. persons from the court's illegitimate claims of jurisdiction.

Despite intense pressure to overturn U.S. policies toward the ICC, the Obama Administration appears to appreciate the possible ramifications of joining the court. Indeed, as a candidate, Obama expressed the need to ensure that U.S. troops have "maximum protection" from politically motivated indictments by the ICC and did not openly support ratification of the Rome Statute. However, the Obama Administration has expressed less caution than either the Bush or Clinton Administrations did about the ICC. Specifically, during her confirmation hearing as Secretary of State Hillary Clinton stated:

> The President-Elect believes as I do that we should support the ICC's investigations. . . .
> But at the same time, we must also keep in mind that the U.S. has more troops deployed overseas than any nation. As Commander-in-Chief, the President-Elect will want to make sure they continue to

have the maximum protection. . . . Whether we work toward joining or not, we will end hostility towards the ICC, and look for opportunities to encourage effective ICC action in ways that promote U.S. interests by bringing war criminals to justice.

News reports indicate that the Obama Administration is close to announcing a change in U.S. policy toward the ICC, including affirming the 2000 signature on the Rome Statute and increasing U.S. cooperation with the court. On her recent trip to Africa, Secretary of State Clinton stated that it was "a great regret but it is a fact that we are not yet a signatory [to the Rome Statute]. But we have supported the court and continue to do so."

These steps are premature if the Administration seriously wishes to provide "maximum protection" for U.S. troops. Instead, to protect U.S. military personnel and other U.S. persons and to encourage other member states to support reforms to the Rome Statute that would address U.S. concerns, the Obama Administration should:

- *Not re-sign the Rome Statute.* The Obama Administration is under pressure to "re-sign" the Rome Statute, reversing the Bush Administration's decision. In critical ways, this would be tantamount to signing a blank check. The Rome Statute is up for review by the Assembly of States Parties in 2010, and key crimes within the court's jurisdiction have yet to be defined and long-standing U.S. objections to the treaty have yet to be addressed. The Obama Administration should use the possibility of U.S. membership as an incentive to encourage the state parties to remedy the key flaws in the Rome Statute.
- *Maintain existing Article 98 agreements.* Until the Rome Statute is reformed to address all of the U.S. concerns, the Obama Administration should confirm and endorse all existing Article 98 agreements. The U.S. is militarily engaged in Iraq and Afghanistan, has troops stationed and in transit around the globe, and in all likelihood will be involved in anti-terror activities around the world for many years. Now is not the time to terminate the legal protections enjoyed by U.S. military personnel and officials deployed in foreign nations. Even if the U.S. joins the ICC at some future date, the U.S. should not terminate the Article 98 agreements because they are consistent with the Rome Statute and would serve as a useful protection if the court overreaches.
- *Establish clear objectives for changes to the Rome Statute for the 2010 review conference that would help to reduce current and potential problems posed by the ICC.* In 2010, the Assembly of States Parties is scheduled to hold the first review conference to consider amendments to the Rome Statute. A key issue on the agenda is agreeing to a definition of the crime of aggression, which is technically under the ICC's jurisdiction, but remains latent due to the states parties' inability to agree to a definition. Rather than accede to an anodyne definition, the U.S. should either seek an explicit, narrow definition to prevent politicization of this crime or, even better, seek to excise the crime from the Rome Statute entirely, on the grounds that it infringes on the Security Council's authority. Moreover, the review conference should reverse the

Rome Statute's violation of customary international law by explicitly limiting the ICC's jurisdiction only to nationals of those states that have ratified or acceded to the Rome Statute and to nationals of non-party states when the U.N. Security Council has explicitly referred a situation to the ICC.

* *Approach Security Council recommendations to the ICC on their merits and oppose those deemed detrimental to U.S. interests.* The U.S. abstentions on Security Council resolutions on Darfur indicate only that it is not U.S. policy to block all mentions of the ICC. However, accepting the reality of the ICC does not mean that the U.S. should acquiesce on substantive issues when they may directly or indirectly affect U.S. interests, U.S. troops, U.S. officials, or other U.S. nationals. Many concerns about the Rome Statute have not yet been adequately addressed. The U.S. should abstain if the resolution addresses issues critical to U.S. interests and would not directly or indirectly undermine the U.S. policy of opposing ICC claims of jurisdiction over U.S. military personnel and its nationals. Moreover, the U.S. should insist that all resolutions include language protecting military and officials from non-ICC states participating in U.N. peacekeeping operations.

# Conclusion

While the International Criminal Court represents an admirable desire to hold war criminals accountable for their terrible crimes, the court is flawed notionally and operationally. The ICC has not overcome many of the problems plaguing the ad hoc tribunals established for Yugoslavia and Rwanda. It remains slow and inefficient. Worse, unlike ad hoc tribunals, it includes a drive to justify its budget and existence in perpetuity rather than simply completing a finite mission.

Its broad autonomy and jurisdiction invite politically motivated indictments. Its inflexibility can impede political resolution of problems, and its insulation from political considerations can complicate diplomatic efforts. Efforts to use the court to apply pressure to inherently political issues and supersede the foreign policy prerogatives of sovereign nations—such as the prosecutor's decision to consider Israel's actions in Gaza—undermine the court's credibility and threaten its future as a useful tool for holding accountable the perpetrators of genocide, war crimes, and crimes against humanity.

President Clinton considered the ICC's flaws serious enough to recommend against U.S. ratification of the Rome Statute unless they were resolved, and President Bush concurred. These issues remain unresolved and continue to pose serious challenges to U.S. sovereignty and its national interests. Unless the serious flaws are addressed fully, President Obama should similarly hold the ICC at arm's length. To protect its own interests and to advance the notion of a properly instituted international criminal court, the U.S. should continue to insist that it is not bound by the Rome Statute and does not recognize the ICC's authority over U.S. persons and should exercise great care when deciding to support the court's actions.

Jonathan F. Fanton

# The Challenge of International Justice

I am glad to be here at the U.S. Military Academy, an institution deeply woven into the fabric of this country's history. In 1902, President Theodore Roosevelt said, "No other educational institution in the land has contributed as many names as West Point to the honor roll of the nation's greatest citizens." After more than a century, that statement remains true – a compelling testimony to the enduring value of the Academy and its high ideals.

The John D. and Catherine T. MacArthur Foundation, has a shorter tradition: we were established in 1978. . . . With an endowment of $6.5 billion, MacArthur will give $300 million in grants and program-related investments to individuals and organizations in the U.S. and abroad this year. . . . The Foundation aims to help build a more just, peaceful, and sustainable world. We do so through sponsoring research, educating the public, and supporting organizations that work in fields that range from conservation to international nuclear disarmament, from renewing America's cities to creating high-quality documentaries for public television. In 2006, we made a grant that was unusual for us – $750,000 to West Point's Program in Conflict and Human Security Studies to support coursework and overseas cadet internships with non-governmental organizations (or NGOs).

I have been impressed by the content and quality of the courses offered in Conflict and Human Security Studies – such as "International Conflict and Negotiation," "Winning the Peace," and "International Security Strategy." The breadth of their approach, their awareness of the human dimension of conflict and restoring peace are impressive and encouraging. . . .

There is no shortage of NGOs with which to work – by one count, there are already five million of them, and new organizations are founded each year. The vision and engagement of these groups – together, called "civil society" – is helping to change the world for the better. Many of them concentrate on issues of human rights, justice for all citizens, and the rule of law – causes MacArthur has supported from our very first grant, which went to Amnesty International.

We fund large organizations that monitor abuses around the world, like Human Rights Watch, and small local institutions that tackle issues like child marriage in India, police abuse in Russia, and the rights of prisoners in Nigeria.

MacArthur holds passionately that individuals everywhere have intrinsic rights that should be enshrined in law and defended by due process. The U.S.

Fanton, Jonathan. Remarks to the U.S. Military Academy at West Point, New York, May 5, 2008. Copyright © 2007 by John D. and Catherine T. MacArthur Foundation. Reprinted by permission. http://www.macfound.org

262

has a Bill of Rights and courts that are responsive to wronged individuals, other countries have similarly clear and effective justice systems – but many nations do not.

Where are individuals to turn when they are denied freedom of speech, beaten by the police, subjected to harsh discrimination, or forcibly conscripted into rebel armies and there are no independent national courts to hear them? And how is the world to deal with genocide, war crimes, and the brutal acts called "crimes against humanity"?

MacArthur believes that the answer lies in an international system of justice that will supplement unresponsive local courts and provide a forum for those who have suffered the worst abuses. The international community has courts for other purposes, for example the International Court of Justice, International Tribunal for the Law of the Sea, or Dispute Settlement System of the World Trade Organization. These bodies have been functioning over many decades and are central to international relations.

But the time has come to develop an international system of justice with the International Criminal Court as the centerpiece. Let me describe the evolution and objectives of this movement.

The first Geneva Conventions of 1864 and the Hague Conventions of 1899 serve as the foundations for modern attempts to stop wartime atrocities. Tribunals for war crimes were proposed, but not effectively implemented, after WWI. The Nuremberg and Far East tribunals after WWII tried and convicted the most prominent Axis leaders, at last holding individuals accountable for their criminal acts – even when following orders.

The WWII tribunals were possible because there was international consensus among the Allied powers. The Cold War ended that consensus. Only when the Soviet Union had collapsed was there a new impetus toward establishing an international system of criminal justice, prompted by the disintegration of Yugoslavia and the infamous "ethnic cleansing" that followed.

NGOs, human rights activists, and diplomats called for a forum to deal specifically with such crimes against humanity when national systems failed to do so. The UN Security Council responded, establishing an ad hoc Criminal Tribunal for Yugoslavia in 1993 and another in response to the Rwandan genocide in 1994.

The results were encouraging. [President] Slobodan Milosovic of Serbia was the first sitting head of state ever indicted; Jean Kambanda, former prime minister of Rwanda, faced charges of genocide, pled guilty, and is now serving a life sentence in Mali. With trials and appeals continuing, 239 people have been indicted and 78 convicted so far. New tribunals are now at work dealing with the atrocities committed in Sierra Leone's civil war and Cambodia's "killing fields."

The early tribunals helped establish the feasibility of a permanent International Criminal Court (ICC). In 1989, preparation and drafting had begun for a Statute that would establish such a Court; it was completed in 1998 and is commonly called "the Rome Statute." States were asked to ratify the Statute individually; by 2002 the required 60 had done so, allowing the Court to have jurisdiction. To date, 106 countries have ratified and joined the Court; the United States has not.

The Court, based in The Hague, is permanent and independent, dedicated to prosecuting only the most serious crimes against humanity. It has jurisdiction over acts committed on the territory, or by nationals, of States Party to the Statute. Also, the UN Security Council may refer a situation to the Court, regardless of the nationality of the accused or the location of their crimes.

The ICC is a "court of last resort," which means that it has authority only when national courts are unable or unwilling to act. All member nations retain the primary right and responsibility to investigate their own citizens – the principle of complementarity, which the U.S. helped embed in the Treaty.

How is the Court performing so far? It issued warrants, beginning in 2005, against Joseph Kony, head of the Lord's Resistance Army in Uganda, for the murder and torture of civilians; against Thomas Lubanga, leader of the UPF militia in the Democratic Republic of the Congo, for kidnapping children to become soldiers; and against Ahmad Mohammad Harun, formerly Sudan's Minister of State for the Interior, and Ali Kushayb, leader of the Janjaweed militia, for their crimes in Darfur – the forced displacement of millions, and a campaign of terror including abduction, rape, and murder.

Lubanga is in custody and his trial expected to begin in June. It will be the first in the Court's history. Two other militia leaders from the Congo are also in The Hague awaiting trial.

The two other cases exemplify the problems of international justice in practice. Joseph Kony of Uganda is still at large and his rebel movement active. The government of Sudan has no incentive to turn over either Kushayb or Harun. Indeed, it has appointed Harun Minister of Humanitarian Affairs, responsible for hearing human rights complaints from the victims of Darfur.

Unless the international community is prepared to act on the Court's warrants, it cannot be effective. More needs to be done to establish responsibility for apprehending and arresting those charged.

There has been debate about whether the threat of prosecution will be an obstacle in negotiating settlements to violent situations. Leaders who fear indictment, it is argued, will be less likely to relinquish power or end conflicts. This is a valid concern. A 2006 peace accord between the Lord's Resistance Army and the Ugandan government rejected the LRA's demand for amnesty. This may explain why Joseph Kony did not appear to sign the treaty earlier this month. But peace and justice, I believe, complement and reinforce one another. Societies that have been torn apart by atrocities are unlikely to heal unless there is resolution for those who have been harmed and some penalty for the perpetrators.

There is evidence also that the Court has a deterrent effect. In late 2004, there was a wave of violence in Côte d'Ivoire, accompanied by radio broadcasts of hate speech reminiscent of the Rwandan genocide. Juan Mendez, the UN's Special Adviser on the Prevention of Genocide, wrote to remind the Security Council that the ICC has jurisdiction over acts that may lead to crimes against humanity. His intervention was widely reported, and the message was heard in Côte d'Ivoire: the hate speech and threats subsided.

I should note that, while the ICC is the centerpiece of the system of international justice, there are other venues for ordinary people to seek redress when they have exhausted remedies in their own countries.

Regional human rights courts and commissions for Africa, Latin America, and Europe deal with cases that range from freedom of speech to discrimination to police brutality. Often, the courts' decisions have the effect of compelling countries to recognize rights that exist under their own laws or in international treaties they have signed. At present, 80,000 such cases from 70 nations are pending. Perhaps the most significant contribution of the regional courts and the ICC will be strengthening national courts and bringing national laws up to international standards.

So far, MacArthur's staff has been impressed with the early record of the ICC, but the Court is not without its critics. The U.S., as I have noted, is not party to the Rome Statute. This broke with America's record of leading the way in international justice since the Nuremberg and Far East tribunals. The U.S. actively supported the tribunals for the former Yugoslavia, Rwanda, and Sierra Leone and assisted in drafting the Rome Statute. But fears that membership in the ICC would expose Americans to politically-motivated cases have persuaded two successive administrations not to ratify.

Opponents of the Court also object that the Rome Statute impinges on U.S. sovereignty, that it overrides the Constitutional due-process protections afforded to U.S. citizens, and that it would limit America's ability to operate abroad – even in joint humanitarian operations.

So far, those fears have not materialized. And I do not believe they are likely to. ICC procedures have all the same due-process protections as U.S. courts, except that of trial by jury. And the Court has been rigorous in pursuing only those cases that are sufficiently grave and over which it clearly has jurisdiction. The Court has received almost 3,000 communications from 140 nations. The vast majority has been rejected outright, only four investigations have been opened by the Prosecutor, and all charges involving Americans have been dismissed.

The Court would certainly be stronger if the U.S. were a member. American legal expertise would strengthen the early cases and shape the Court's future jurisprudence; American intelligence agencies could provide evidence to ensure successful prosecutions.

Many in the U.S. military have concerns about the ICC. In 2006, MacArthur sponsored the Stimson Center to survey and assess how professional officers, some from the military justice system, perceived the Court and its impact.

Stimson found a range of opinion – much of it positive, some strongly negative – but also that many officers knew little about the Court or the Rome Statute. The most common objections were that the Court "second-guessed" decisions taken in action that were thought to fall within the rules of combat, that American service personnel would be unfairly targeted when abroad, that ignorance of the provisions of the Rome Statute would lead to inadvertent infractions, and that field operations and military alliances would be hampered by further layers of legal restrictions. Others felt the Court would simply be ineffective, unable to bring criminals to justice.

Specific problems were cited: Would the U.S.'s deployment of cluster bombs and landmines, outlawed by the 140 countries party to the Ottawa Convention, give grounds for prosecution? Would decisions taken on faulty intelligence, such as the accidental bombing of the Chinese Embassy in Belgrade in 1999, make officers liable?

Officers with legal expertise pointed out gaps between U.S. domestic law and the Uniform Code of Military Justice and the Rome Statute, which they saw opening the possibility of prosecution for offences that were unclearly defined, or not addressed at all, in American legislation.

These are cogent objections, but I believe they are not insurmountable. Most of the acts prohibited by the Rome Statute are already illegal under U.S. military and civilian codes; where there are gaps or more clarity is needed, further legal work could harmonize the legislation and sharpen definitions. A simple program of education would give service personnel adequate working knowledge of the Statute. As there are few areas in which the Statute differs from existing U.S. codes, there would be little practical difference in field operations.

The specific objections may be met by noting that the use of certain weapons and specific operational decisions do not come under the remit of the Court, whose role is to deal with only the most egregious crimes. If the U.S. joined the Court, the principle of complementarity requires that its military personnel charged with misconduct would be subject to existing U.S. laws and procedures, which are robust and high-functioning.

It is worth noting that, between 2003 and 2006, the Prosecutor received almost 250 submissions related to the conflict in Iraq, the majority concerned with military operations by U.S. and allied troops. In his 2006 response, Prosecutor Luis Moreno Ocampo declined to pursue any of them further, ruling that the Court had no jurisdiction in most cases, that the individual instances did not rise to the level of gravity required, and that there were adequate national judicial systems in place to deal with the alleged offences.

Most of those who participated in the Stimson project supported the overall goals of the Court as being consistent with fundamental American values and the legal standards to which U.S. military personnel are already held. Some also saw the advantages for U.S. personnel of an international court that would strengthen the rule of law within countries that, in the past, would have ignored international standards altogether.

The ICC is arguably the most important new international institution since the founding of the United Nations itself. It is destined to have a considerable and lasting impact on how justice and human rights are defined and enforced. I urge you to acquaint yourselves with the Court, to investigate how it works, and to debate its future. How do you, as citizens, evaluate America's relationship to the ICC? How should your training, and your conduct in operations, take account of the Court's mission to protect the world's most vulnerable people and bring perpetrators of atrocities to justice?

MacArthur will continue to educate the public about the Court, fund groups that further its work, and support an integrated system of international justice. We are convinced that America and its armed forces have nothing to fear from such a system, and much to offer to its success. And we are sure that lively and free-ranging discussion of the issues involved will help build a consensus that the world needs clear, universal, and humane standards of justice for all.

# EXPLORING THE ISSUE

## Is U.S. Refusal to Join the International Criminal Court Wise?

## Questions for Critical Thinking and Reflection

1. If you are opposed to the United States being subject to the ICC, what changes in the ICC's procedures and jurisdiction would change your mind?
2. What do you make of the following results of two surveys taken just a few months apart in 2002–2003 In the first survey, 71 percent of Americans said the United States should agree to the ICC as a court that could try individuals for war crimes "if their own country won't try them." The second survey asked about support of the ICC given that it could try U.S. soldiers accused of war crimes "if the United States government refuses to try them." Only 37 percent supported the ICC on this question.
3. Small, weak countries sometimes criticize the ICC because all its investigations and indictments have so far involved small, weak countries. Is this a valid criticism or does the blame property rest with powerful countries that would block access by the ICC?

## Is There Common Ground?

With the ICC treaty in effect, the countries that were a party to it met in 2003 and elected the court's 18 judges and its chief prosecutor. The following year the ICC began operations at its seat in The Hague, the Netherlands. Soon thereafter, the ICC prosecutor launched several investigations, mostly focusing on conflicts in central Africa and in the Darfur region of Sudan in northeast Africa. As of late 2012, the ICC was conducting investigations in seven countries (Central African Republic, Uganda, Kenya, Sudan, Ivory Coast, and Libya), had indicted 29 individuals, and had five in custody awaiting trial. Most significantly, the ICC has indicted President Omar al-Bashir of Sudan for 10 counts of genocide, war crimes, and crimes against humanity, and in July 2009 issued an instrumental warrant for his arrest. As of late 2012, Bashir remains in power in Sudan and for now beyond the reach of the ICC. In other activity, the court's first trial was held. The defendant, Thomas Lubanga, a former rebel leader in the Democratic Republic of the Congo (DRC), was charged with forcibly conscripting and using "child soldiers" (under age 15). In 2012 the ICC convicted Lubanga and sentenced him to 14 years in prison.

As of October 2012, 121 countries had formally agreed to the Rome Statute and joined the Assembly of State Parties that constitutes the ICC's governing board. Most of the major countries of Western Europe, Africa, and South and Central America are now parties to the ICC, as are Canada and Japan. China, Russia, India, Iran, Israel, and most of the Arab countries are among the prominent nonadherents. The United States has also remained among the absent. It is unlikely that will change. Barack Obama has taken a more positive approach to the ICC than President Bush did but still has made no move to ask the Senate to ratify the Treaty of Rome. Even if Obama did so, ratification would be unlikely without, at the least, much greater protections for U.S. troops abroad against possible ICC indictments.

## Additional Resources

A way to begin learning more about the evolution of the ICC is by reading William A. Schabas, *An Introduction to the International Criminal Court* (Cambridge University Press, 2011). Also excellent is Erna Paris, *The Sun Climbs Slow: The International Criminal Court and the Struggle for Justice* (Steven Stories Press, 2009). Excellent as a general resource is the *Journal of International Criminal Justice*, published quarterly. Americans' concern with diminishing U.S. sovereignty is one barrier to U.S. ratification of the Treaty of Rome. A study that explains why most countries in Europe have chosen to support the ICC and the United States has not is Lisa Aronsson, "Europe and America: Still Worlds Apart on the International Criminal Court," *European Political Science* (2011).

# ISSUE 16

## Should the United States Ratify the Convention to Eliminate All Forms of Discrimination Against Women?

**YES: Melanne Verveer,** from Testimony during Hearings on "Ratify the CEDAW," before the Subcommittee on Human Rights and the Law, the Committee on the Judiciary, U.S. Senate (November 18, 2010)

**NO: Steven Groves,** from Testimony during Hearings on "Reject CEDAW," before the Subcommittee on Human Rights and the Law, the Committee on the Judiciary, U.S. Senate (November 18, 2010)

### ISSUE SUMMARY

**YES:** Melanne Verveer, ambassador-at-large, Office of Global Women's Issues, U.S. Department of State, tells a congressional committee that the U.S. Senate should ratify the Convention on the Elimination of All Forms of Discrimination Against Women (CEDAW) because doing so would send a powerful message about the U.S. commitment to equality for women across the globe.

**NO:** Steven Groves, the Bernard and Barbara Lomas Fellow in the Margaret Thatcher Center for Freedom, a division of the Kathryn and Shelby Cullom Davis Institute for International Studies at the Heritage Foundation, headquartered in Washington, DC, contends that ratifying CEDAW would neither advance U.S. international interests nor enhance the rights of women in the United States.

Females constitute about half the world population, but they are a distinct economic–political–social minority because of the wide gap in societal power and resources between women and men. Women constitute 70 percent of the world's poor and two-thirds of its literates. They occupy only 14 percent of the managerial jobs, are less than 40 percent of the world's professional and technical workers, and garner only 35 percent of the earned income in the world. Women are also disadvantaged politically. In late 2012, only 14 women were serving as the top political leader in their countries; women make up just 8 percent of all national cabinet officers; and only one of every five national legislators is a woman. On average, life for women is not only harder and more poorly compensated than it is for men, but also more dangerous. "The most painful devaluation of women," the United Nations reports, "is the physical and psychological violence that stalks them from cradle to grave." Signs of violence against women include the fact that about 80 percent of the world's refugees are women and their children. Other assaults on women arguably constitute a form of genocide. According to the UN Children's Fund, "In many countries, boys get better care and better food than girls. As a result, an estimated one million girls die each year because they were born female." None of these economic, social, and political inequities are new. Indeed, the global pattern of discrimination against women is ancient. What is new is the global effort to recognize the abuses that occur and to ameliorate and someday end them. To help accomplish that goal, the U.N. General Assembly in 1979 voted by 130 to 0 to put the Convention on the Elimination of All Forms of Discrimination Against Women (CEDAW) before the world's countries for adoption. Supporters hailed the treaty as a path-breaking step on behalf of advancing the status of women. Many countries agreed, and by September 1981 enough countries had signed and ratified CEDAW to put it into effect. This set a record for the speed with which any human rights convention had gone into force.

CEDAW is a women's international bill of rights. Most of these rights are enumerated in various other treaties as applicable to all humans, but women's rights had not been specifically and fully addressed in any other treaty before CEDAW. Countries that legally adhere to the convention agree to undertake measures to end all the various forms of discrimination against women. Doing so entails accepting legal gender equality and ensuring the practice of gender equality by abolishing all discriminatory laws, enacting laws that prohibit discrimination against women, and establishing agencies to protect women's rights.

President Jimmy Carter signed CEDAW in 1980 and submitted it to the Senate for ratification. However, he was soon thereafter defeated for reelection, and the treaty languished in legislative limbo ever since. President Bill Clinton did make an effort to move CEDAW forward, but he was unsuccessful. Hope among those who support ratifying CEDAW rose anew when President Barack Obama was elected president and he appointed Hillary Clinton as secretary of state. Both supported CEDAW. Additionally, the Democrats controlled Congress. This led to hearings before a Senate committee in 2010. The testimony that constitutes the YES and NO selections comes from those hearings. In the YES selection, Melanne Verveer urges the adoption of CEDAW and tells the Senate that it is long overdue for the United States to stand with the women of the world in their effort to obtain the basic rights that women in this country enjoy. Steven Groves disagrees, telling the committee that U.S. ratification of CEDAW would have little or no impact on women's rights globally and that it would unnecessarily and unwisely subject the United States to interference by the United Nations and international courts.

# YES ↩          Melanne Verveer

# Ratify the CEDAW

Thank you for this opportunity to discuss with you the United Nations Convention on the Elimination of All Forms of Discrimination Against Women, commonly known as CEDAW, or the Women's Treaty. . . . Today, I would like to talk about what the Women's Treaty represents and why U.S. ratification is critical to our efforts to promote and defend the rights of women across the globe.

This hearing could not come at a more critical time for the world's women. Gender inequality and oppression of women are rampant across the globe. The scale and savagery of human rights violations committed against women and girls is nothing short of a humanitarian tragedy. Today, violence against women is a global pandemic. In some parts of the world, such as the Democratic Republic of Congo, Burma, and Sudan, women are attacked as part of a deliberate and coordinated strategy of armed conflict where rape is used as a tool of war. In others, like Afghanistan, girls are attacked with acid and disfigured simply because they dare attend school. Girl infanticide and neglect has contributed to the absence from school of an estimated 100 million girls worldwide. In places where girls are not as valued and there is a strong preference for sons, practices ranging from female genital mutilation, to child marriage, to so-called "honor killings," to the trafficking of women and girls into modern-day slavery highlight the low status of females around the globe.

In far too many places, women's participation in parliaments, village councils and peace negotiations is circumscribed or prevented altogether. Policies instructing that "women need not apply" continue to limit employment opportunities and pay. The majority of the world's illiterate are women and, according to the World Bank, girls constitute 55 percent of all out-of-school children. This has devastating consequences on the health and well-being of families and communities. And today, the HIV-AIDS pandemic has a woman's face, with the number of infections rising at alarming rates among adolescent girls in many places who face the threat of violence, including sexual violence, in their lives.

Women's equality has rightly been called the moral imperative of the 21st century. Where women cannot participate fully and equally in their societies, democracy is a contradiction in terms, economic prosperity is hampered, and stability is at risk. Standing up against the appalling violations of women's human rights around the globe, and standing with the women of the world, is what ratifying the Women's Treaty is about.

U.S. Senate, November 18, 2010.

# Why the United States Should Ratify the Women's Treaty

In my time at the State Department, I have visited scores of countries and met with women from all walks of life, from human rights activists in Russia, to microcredit recipients and small-business entrepreneurs in rural South Asia, to survivors of rape and conflict in the Democratic Republic of the Congo. In my travels, the number-one question I am asked time and time again is, "Why hasn't the United States ratified CEDAW?"

It is understandable that I continue to receive this question everywhere I go. The United States has long stood for the principles of equal justice, the rule of law, respect for women, and the defense of human dignity. We know that women around the world look to the United States as a moral leader on human rights. And yet when it comes to the Women's Treaty, which reflects the fundamental principle that women's rights are human rights, we stand with only a handful of countries that have not ratified, including Somalia, Iran, and Sudan—countries with some of the worst human rights records in the world. We stand alone as the only industrialized democracy in the world that has not ratified the Women's Treaty. And we stand on the sidelines, un-able to use the Women's Treaty to join with champions of human rights who seek to use it as a means to protect and defend women's basic human rights.

U.S. ratification of the Women's Treaty matters because the moral leader-ship of our country on human rights matters. Some governments use the fact that the U.S. has not ratified the treaty as a pretext for not living up to their own obligations under it. Our failure to ratify also deprives us of a powerful tool to combat discrimination against women around the world, because as a non-party, it makes it more difficult for us to press other parties to live up to their commitments under the treaty.

The United States is firmly committed to the principles of women's equal-ity as enshrined in the U.S. Constitution. Our ratification will send a powerful and unequivocal message about our commitment to equality for women across the globe. It will lend much needed validation and support to advocates fight-ing the brutal oppression of women and girls everywhere, who seek to replicate in their own countries the strong protections against discrimination that we have in the United States. And it will signal that the United States stands with the women of the world. Importantly, ratification will also advance U.S. foreign policy and national security interests. As the Obama Administration has made clear, women's equality is critical to our national security. President Obama's National Security Strategy recognizes that "countries are more peaceful and prosperous when women are accorded full and equal rights and opportunity. When those rights and opportunities are denied, countries lag behind." And as Secretary [Hillary] Clinton has stated, "the subjugation of women is a threat to the national security of the United States. It is also a threat to the common security of our world, because the suffering and denial of the rights of women and the instability of nations go hand in hand." Ratification of this treaty, which enshrines the rights of women in international law, is not only in the interest of oppressed women around the world—it is in our interest as well.

In fact, my office has been working closely with the Office of the Under Secretary of Defense for Policy at the Department of Defense to highlight issues related to women, peace and security. We as a U.S. government recognize the interconnection of women's progress and the advancement of U.S. objectives across the world. And Admiral Mullen, Chairman of the Joint Chiefs of Staff, recently stated, "Secretary of State Hillary Clinton wisely summed it up last week when she said, 'If we want to make progress towards settling the world's most intractable conflicts, let's enlist women.' I couldn't agree more—and I would only add: The time to act is now so we don't have to ask, yet again, why did this take so long? But as we think about how far we've come, we must also consider how far we have still to go."

## How the Women's Treaty Helps Eliminate Discrimination Against Women

I would like to briefly describe what the Women's Treaty is, the principles it enshrines, and how it can be used to challenge discrimination against women around the world. The Women's Treaty was adopted by the United Nations nearly 31 years ago and is the first treaty to comprehensively address women's rights and fundamental freedoms. The treaty builds on several previous international human rights instruments, including the UN Universal Declaration of Human Rights, and the International Covenant on Civil and Political Rights (ICCPR). It obliges parties to end discrimination against women and addresses areas that are crucial to women's equality, from citizenship rights and political participation to inheritance and property rights to freedom from domestic violence and sex trafficking. It is consistent with the approach that we have already taken on these issues domestically. To date, 186 out of 192 UN member states are party to the treaty.

Around the world, women are using the Women's Treaty as an instrument for progress and empowerment. There are countless stories of women who have used their countries' commitments to the treaty to bring constitutions, laws, and policies in line with the principle of nondiscrimination against women. Over the course of my travels, I have seen firsthand its incredible influence in helping women change their societies. Today, I would like to highlight just a few examples that illuminate the treaty's ability to help women push for equal treatment in their communities.

**Morocco:**   The Women's Treaty has been used to fight discrimination against women in family law. For example, in Morocco, for nearly a century, family law was largely determined by differing interpretations of Islamic law, which resulted in oppression and unequal treatment for wives. Brides were not asked to give their consent to marriage during the wedding ceremony. Polygamy was widespread, and husbands had the power to "repudiate" a marriage without court proceedings or their wives' consent. Women in Moroccan civil society worked tirelessly and even faced imprisonment in their effort to end discrimination against women in family law, but they did not back down. In 1993, Morocco ratified the Women's Treaty with a set of reservations, and in 2004, a new Morocco Family Code was enacted that protected women's rights in matters of marriage and family relations. Today, women no longer need a matrimonial guardian to determine whom they will marry. In addition, a woman can now initiate divorce proceedings, which are now determined in a court of law, and there are a series of restrictions in place making polygamy far more difficult to practice.

**Afghanistan:**   The Women's Treaty has also been used to combat discrimination against women even in countries that fall far short of their commitment to women's equality under the treaty, such as Afghanistan. As we know, under the brutal Taliban regime, Afghan women and girls suffered untold deprivations of their basic human rights, including the right to attend school, thereby penalizing an entire generation. The fact that Afghanistan is party to agreements like the ICCPR and the Women's Treaty has helped to provide legitimacy for women's rights advocates seeking to improve conditions for women and girls. Indeed, Afghan activists recently pushed for a new law to eliminate violence against women. And several Afghan women's organizations have banded together to release their own "shadow report" detailing the government's actions to prevent and respond to violence against women. Thanks to the efforts of women's advocates, the Afghan government—for the first time since ratifying the Women's Treaty—is working to prepare a public report on its implementation of the treaty.

**Mexico:**   The Women's Treaty has also been used to combat violence against women and sexual assault. In Mexico, for example, the treaty was deployed as a tool against violence in some of the country's most dangerous areas. An estimated 450 girls and women have been killed in Ciudad Juárez and Chihuahua City since 1993. According to Mexican authorities, most of these women were sexually assaulted before their murders. Local human rights groups report that few cases have been investigated and in even fewer have perpetrators been brought to justice. But in 2007, human rights groups won a major victory with the enactment of a national law inspired, in large part, by the Women's Treaty. The new Mexican law requires federal, state and local authorities to coordinate activities to prevent and respond to violence against women, and authorizes the Interior Minister to declare a state of alert if he or she determines there is an outbreak of widespread gender-based violence.

**Philippines:**   The Women's Treaty has provided activists around the world with a useful framework for women's human rights that has advanced and improved laws prohibiting discrimination against women. For instance, in the Philippines, the treaty was heavily relied upon as a blueprint for framing the first Magna Carta of Women, a comprehensive equal-rights statute that provides political, civil, and economic rights for all Filipino women, with special protections for those who are members of marginalized groups. Women's groups, working in coordination with international organizations, used the Women's Treaty to help develop a definition of gender discrimination and outline the responsibilities of the government to protect its citizens. This historic and far-reaching law was signed into law by President Gloria Arroyo in 2009. Among its several provisions, the Magna Carta affirms Filipino women's rights to education, political participation and representation, and equal treatment before the law.

**Uganda:**   The Women's Treaty has also been used to achieve equal treatment for women in the critical area of land rights. In some parts of the world, women produce 70 percent of the food and yet earn only 10 percent of the income and own only 1 percent of the land—a situation that is not only unfair, but also relegates women to lives of poverty. In Uganda, a robust women's movement has made efforts to tackle this problem by relying on both the Women's Treaty and national legislation to pursue land ownership rights and challenge customary land tenure practices. Empowered by the Women's Treaty and the enactment of the country's Land Act in 1998, women's groups and activists began a tireless campaign to ensure that women were protected in the tenure, ownership and administration of land. In their fight for equal treatment, these activists continue to rely on the Women's Treaty.

# Conclusion

Fifteen years ago, as First Lady of the United States, Hillary Clinton addressed the UN Fourth World Conference on Women in Beijing and proclaimed that women's rights are human rights. Today, the litany of abuses against women that she described in her address—from violence against women to trafficking to female genital mutilation to girl infanticide—persists. We cannot stand by while girls and women continue to be fed less, fed last, overworked, underpaid, subjected to violence both in and out of their homes—in short, while discrimination against women and girls remains commonplace around the globe. For as long as the oppression of women continues, the peaceful, prosperous world we all seek will not be realized. It has been over 30 years since the Women's Treaty was first adopted by the United Nations. Since that time, as I have described, the treaty has been used to advocate for and realize equal treatment for women and girls around the world. But much work remains to be done. And it is long overdue for the United States to stand with the women of the world in their effort to obtain the basic rights that women in this country enjoy.

As Secretary Clinton has said, "the United States must remain an unambiguous and unequivocal voice in support of women's rights in every country, every region, on every continent." By ratifying the Women's Treaty, we will speak with this clarity of voice and purpose. We will strengthen the efforts of those who toil for women's rights, for equal treatment, and for human dignity. And we will make clear our belief that human rights are women's rights and women's rights are human rights, once and for all.

# Reject CEDAW

**T**hank you for inviting me to testify before you today regarding the Convention on the Elimination of All Forms of Discrimination Against Women (CEDAW). Ratification of CEDAW would neither advance U.S. national interests within the international community nor enhance the rights of women in the United States. Domestically, CEDAW membership would not improve our existing comprehensive statutory framework or strengthen our enforcement system for the protection of women's rights.

Within the international sphere, the United States need not become party to the Convention to demonstrate to the rest of the world its commitment to women's rights at home or abroad. Becoming a member of CEDAW would produce, at best, an intangible and dubious public diplomacy benefit.

Moreover, it does not serve the interests of the United States to periodically submit its record on women's rights to scrutiny by a committee of gender experts that has established a record of promoting policies that do not comport with existing American norms and that encourages national governments to engage in social engineering on a massive scale.

The United States should become party to a treaty only if membership would advance U.S. national interests. For a human rights treaty such as CEDAW, national interests may be characterized in both domestic and international terms. Only if U.S. membership in CEDAW would advance the cause of women's rights domestically and further U.S. national interests in the world should the United States consider ratification of the treaty.

Domestically, ratification of CEDAW is not needed to end gender discrimination or advance women's rights. The United States already has effective avenues of enforcement in place to combat discrimination based on sex. Specifically, in addition to the Equal Protection Clause of the Fourteenth Amendment to the U.S. Constitution, the United States has in place a wide range of state and federal laws to protect and advance women's rights concerning their employment, compensation, housing, education, and other areas. Federal laws include, but are not limited to:

- Title VII of the Civil Rights Act of 1964, which prohibits discrimination in employment on the basis of, *inter alia*, sex and has been interpreted to prohibit sexual harassment or the creation of a hostile working environment;
- The Pregnancy Discrimination Act, enacted in 1978, which prohibits discrimination on the basis of pregnancy and childbirth;

U.S. Senate, November 18, 2010.

- The Equal Pay Act of 1963, which prohibits discrimination on the basis of sex in regard to the compensation paid to men and women for substantially equal work performed in the same establishment;
- The Fair Housing Act of 1968, which prohibits discrimination in the sale or rental of housing on the basis of, *inter alia*, sex;
- Title IX of the Education Amendments of 1972, which prohibits discrimination on the basis of sex in federally funded education programs or activities;
- The Equal Credit Opportunity Act, enacted in 1974, which prohibits discrimination against credit applicants on the basis of, *inter alia*, sex;
- The Violence Against Women Act of 1994, which was intended to improve criminal justice and community responses to acts of domestic violence, dating violence, sexual assault, and stalking; and
- The Lilly Ledbetter Fair Pay Act of 2009, which revised the statute of limitations requirements in equal-pay lawsuits to assist women in recovering wages lost due to discrimination.

Taking this extensive legal framework into consideration, it is difficult to imagine how membership in CEDAW will further advance the protections provided to women in the United States. In fact, the protections provided by the U.S. Constitution and existing U.S. law exceed the provisions in the treaty. This legal framework serves as a foundation that can be modified or expanded as necessary through the democratic process.

Some of this federal legislation remains controversial and will continue to be debated in Congress and litigated in U.S. courts. Differences of opinion regarding these laws and the extent of constitutional protections based on gender are likely to persist for years to come. The resolution of these issues should be sought through domestic legislative and judicial avenues rather than through the judgment of gender experts sitting on the CEDAW Committee who may possess inadequate specific knowledge or understanding of U.S. laws and practices. Robust debate regarding these issues continues in the United States despite the fact that it is not a party to CEDAW. For instance, the existence of pending federal legislation on the "pay equity" issue—such as the Paycheck Fairness Act—indicates an ongoing effort in Congress to resolve gender and compensation issues through the traditional democratic process.

Unlike the expansive provisions of CEDAW and the overly broad recommendations of the CEDAW Committee, these federal laws were crafted to address specific issues of gender discrimination in the United States, not to address the general policy opinions of the international community.

Measuring whether U.S. membership in CEDAW would actually improve the image of the United States abroad may be impossible.

Those who say that ratification would allow the United States to claim the moral high ground within the international community—at least in regard to women's rights—imply that the United States is deficient in protecting those rights, when in truth the United States has been a leader and standard bearer for empowering women. It already holds the moral high ground. Ratifying a treaty merely to score points overseas is not a sound justification for a decision that could have unforeseen or negative domestic ramifications.

The United States amply demonstrated to the international community that it is committed to the protection of women's rights when, in 1992, it ratified the International Covenant on Civil and Political Rights (ICCPR). By ratifying the ICCPR, the United States made an international political commitment to guarantee the individual liberties, political rights, and physical integrity of its citizens "without distinction of any kind, such as race, colour, sex, language, religion, political or other opinion, national or social origin, property, birth or other status." Indeed, Article 3 of the ICCPR requires that the United States "undertake to ensure the equal right of men and women to the enjoyment of all civil and political rights set forth in the present Covenant."

Moreover, the United States has demonstrated in the past and continues to demonstrate its commitment to women's rights not just in the U.S., but around the world as well, regardless of the fact that it is not a member of CEDAW. The presence at this very hearing of Ambassador Melanne Verveer, the first Ambassador-at-Large for Global Women's Issues, is only the latest indication that the U.S. is committed to the political, economic, and social empowerment of women around the globe. Secretary Clinton's establishment of the International Fund for Women further indicates that the U.S. government is continually formulating programs for the advancement of women's causes outside of the United States.

While everyone may not agree with the policy aims of these programs, these acts by the United States are far more relevant to women in need around the world than U.S. membership in an international convention.

In short, to assert that the United States lacks credibility on the issue of international women's rights due to its non-membership in CEDAW is simply specious.

Beyond the dubious public diplomacy benefit that would allegedly be enjoyed by the United States upon ratification of CEDAW, it is difficult to determine how U.S. national interests would otherwise be advanced by participating in the central activity required by the treaty—reporting to the CEDAW Committee every four years regarding the U.S. record on women's rights. The CEDAW Committee has for 30 years established a consistent record of promoting gender-related policies that do not comport with existing American legal and cultural norms and has encouraged the national governments of CEDAW members to engage in social engineering on a massive scale.

For instance, Article 5 of CEDAW compels members of the treaty to "modify the social and cultural patterns of conduct of men and women, with a view to achieving the elimination of prejudices and customary and all other practices which are based on . . . stereotyped roles for men and women." The CEDAW Committee has cited this provision over the years to oblige member states to seek the modification of the roles of men and women as husbands, wives, caregivers, and breadwinners.

The Committee appears to be particularly contemptuous of the role of women as mothers and caregivers. For example, in 1999 it determined that "the persistence of the emphasis on the role of women as mothers and caregivers [in Ireland] tends to perpetuate sex role stereotypes and constitutes a serious impediment to the full implementation of the Convention." In its report on Georgia, the

Committee expressed concern over "the stereotyped roles of women . . . based on patterns of behaviour and attitudes that overemphasize the role of women as mothers." In 2000, the Committee issued its now famous concluding observation to Belarus in which it referred to Mothers' Day as a stereotypical symbol and chided Belarus for "encouraging women's traditional roles."

The CEDAW Committee has made other policy choices that are inconsistent with U.S. societal norms. Prostitution, in particular, has been treated by the Committee not as a crime that should be discouraged, but rather as a reality that should be tolerated and regulated. Indeed, the Committee appears to have little or no regard for the moral choices made by member states concerning whether they consider prostitution to be a criminal act that should be prohibited. For instance, in 2001, a representative from Guinea told the Committee that prostitution was "one of the social scourges" in Guinea and was illegal and "rejected and condemned by society." Undaunted, the Committee ignored Guinea's social and cultural norms and urged the government not to "penaliz[e] women who provide sexual services." Similarly, in 1999, the Committee instructed Liechtenstein to "review . . . the law relating to prostitution to ensure that prostitutes are not penalized." Also in 1999, the Committee told China that it was "concerned that prostitution . . . is illegal in China." Rather than recommending that China take steps to reduce poverty and enhance economic freedom to alleviate the problem, the Committee "recommend[ed] decriminalization of prostitution."

Many of the policy choices prescribed by the CEDAW Committee are at odds with other social, political, cultural, legal, and democratic norms in the United States. The Committee supports the concept of "comparable worth" to address allegations of gender discrimination in compensation. It advocates the use of quota systems to achieve de facto equality in various fields including education, politics, and employment—a policy that demands equal outcomes rather than equal opportunity. Finally, and controversially, the Committee regularly instructs member states to amend their laws to ease restrictions on abortion.

In short, it does not advance U.S. national interests to submit itself to scrutiny every four years by a committee of gender experts that has already demonstrated its divergence with U.S. policy choices, including on highly controversial issues regarding American social and cultural norms. In the eyes of the CEDAW Committee, the current laws and norms of the United States place it in direct and flagrant violation of CEDAW's provisions, even though those provisions arguably seek to dictate women's roles in a manner that may not be welcomed by all women or, in the case of prostitution, may be antithetical to their welfare.

The United States should not make international political commitments that it cannot keep due to its own legal, social, and cultural traditions, and joining CEDAW will unfairly place it in an untenable position.

An objective analysis of CEDAW indicates that ratifying it would not advance U.S. national interests either at home or abroad.

U.S. ratification of CEDAW would produce, at best, an intangible and fleeting public diplomacy benefit in the international community. The United

States need not become party to the convention to demonstrate its commitment to women's rights or to advance the cause of women in other nations. Any nation that questions U.S. dedication to protecting the rights of American women need only review the architecture of our laws and the network of state and federal agencies that enforce those laws.

Instead of seeking membership in CEDAW, the U.S. Congress and American civil society should continually review the implementation of existing laws barring gender discrimination in all spheres of domestic life. Those entities are far better positioned to conduct such a review than a committee of supposed gender experts from 23 foreign nations.

# EXPLORING THE ISSUE

## Should the United States Ratify the Convention to Eliminate All Forms of Discrimination Against Women?

## Questions for Critical Thinking and Reflection

1. Start by reading the text of CEDAW at www.un.org/womenwatch/daw/cedaw/cedaw.htm. Then ask yourself whether it protects any rights that American women should not have. If it does so, which ones?
2. Those who worry about U.S. sovereignty argue that if U.S. law and the U.S. courts refused to uphold the rights women have under CEDAW, the women could appeal to international courts for justice. Is that ability to appeal good or bad?
3. Is U.S. ratification of CEDAW superfluous given the extensive range of rights American women already have?

## Is There Common Ground?

The concentrated effort to promote women's rights internationally within the context of advancing globalism dates back only to 1975, which the UN declared the International Women's Year. There have been many changes that benefit women since that time, but those changes have only begun to ease the problems that advocates of women's rights argue need to be addressed. CEDAW has been a keystone of the international effort to promote women's rights. As of late 2012, 187 countries had adhered to CEDAW, leaving only seven countries (the United States, Iran, Sudan, Somalia, Palau, newly formed South Somalia, and Tonga) that have not formally adhered to CEDAW. The only other country, the Holy See (the Vatican) has also not agreed to CEDAW.

The hearings held by the Senate Judiciary Committee in 2010 were more a symbolic show of support than portending any real chance the Senate would ratify the treaty. Indicative of that is the Senate Foreign Relations Committee, which has jurisdiction over treaties and would under most circumstances have to hold hearings prior to a treaty moving for debate and decision on the Senate floor. That did not happen in 2010 at least in part, analysts conclude, because the Obama administration, while supporting CEDAW, has not made a concerted effort to get the Senate to ratify it.

# Additional Resources

An article about using CEDAW to measure women's rights in countries is available in Lisa Baldez, "The UN Convention to Eliminate All Forms of Discrimination Against Women (CEDAW): A New Way to Measure Women's Interests," *Politics & Gender* (September 2011). For a review of the effect of CEDAW, read Andrew Byrnes and Jane Connors, *The International Bill of Rights for Women: The impact of the CEDAW Convention* (Oxford University Press, 2012). A briefing report for the Senate is contained in Congressional Research Service, *The U.N. Convention on the Elimination of All Forms of Discrimination Against Women (CEDAW): Issues in the U.S. Ratification Debate*, CRS report to Congress R40750, June 28, 2011. The main UN website for women's issues is www.un.org/womenwatch/daw/cedaw/. Websites for opposing views of CEDAW are those of the CEDAW Task Force of the Leadership Conference on Civil and Human Rights at www.cedaw2011.org/ and We're Concerned Women for America Legislative Action Committee (CWALAC) at www.cwalac.org/.

# *Internet References . . .*

## Center for International Earth Science Information Network

Located at Columbia University, the site provides excellent information on global environmental change. See especially their very useful Socioeconomic Data and Applications Center, with datasets, interactive maps, and links designed to integrate social and natural science data for better decision making on environmental issues.

**http://ciesin.columbia.edu/**

## National Oceanic and Atmospheric Administration

The National Oceanic and Atmospheric Administration (NOAA) is a division of the U.S. Department of Commerce involved with the cimate, environment, oceanography, and weather. It has some great graphics.

**www.noaa.gov/**

## National Geographic Society

News and other information, blogs, great photography, and other resources about all aspects of the environment are available on this "nonacademic" site.

**http://environment.nationalgeographic.com/environment/**

# Environmental Issues

*W*hen all is said and done, policy is, or at least ought to be, about values. That is, how do we want our world to be? There are choices to make about what to do (and what not to do). It would be easy if these choices were clearly good versus evil. But things are not usually that simple, and the issue in this part shows the disparity of opinions regarding the current state of the environment.

• Are International Negotiations to Control Global Warming Useful?

# ISSUE 17

# Are International Negotiations to Control Global Warming Useful?

**YES: Elliot Diringer**, from "The Threats of Climate Change," Testimony during Hearings on "UN Climate Talks and Power Politics—It's Not about the Temperature" before the Subcommittee on Oversight and Investigations, Committee on Foreign Affairs, U.S. House of Representatives (May 25, 2011)

**NO: Steven F. Hayward**, from "Climate Change Negotiations: Implausible and Unpromising," Testimony during Hearings on "UN Climate Talks and Power Politics—It's Not about the Temperature" before the Subcommittee on Oversight and Investigations, Committee on Foreign Affairs, U.S. House of Representatives (May 25, 2011)

## ISSUE SUMMARY

**YES:** Elliot Diringer, the vice president for international strategies at the Pew Center on Global Climate Change (now renamed the Center for Climate and Energy Solutions, located in Arlington, VA) contends that global warming seriously threatens U.S. prosperity and national security and that it is imperative to seek a global solution to climate change.

**NO:** Steven F. Hayward, the F. K. Weyerhaeuser Fellow at the American Enterprise Institute in Washington, DC, says that the current diplomatic effort to curb global warming has failed so far and is unlikely to improve, and that the best way to address global warming is through a revised national energy policy.

The past few centuries have witnessed rapid increases in human prosperity driven in substantial part by industrialization, electrification, the burgeoning of private and commercial vehicles, and a host of other inventions and improvements that, in order to work, consume massive amounts of fossil fuel (mostly coal, petroleum, and natural gas). The burning of fossil fuels gives off carbon dioxide ($CO_2$) into the atmosphere. The discharge of $CO_2$ from burning wood, animals exhaling, and some other sources is nearly as old as Earth itself, but the last century's advances have rapidly increased the level of discharge. Since 1950 alone, annual global $CO_2$ emissions have more than tripled. Much of this is retained in the atmosphere because the ability of nature to cleanse the atmosphere of the $CO_2$ through plant photosynthesis has been overwhelmed by the vast increases in fossil fuel burning and the simultaneous cutting of vast areas of the world's forests for habitation and agriculture.

It is clear to almost all scientists that human-generated $CO_2$ has at least accelerated global warming. The reason, they contend, is the greenhouse effect. As $CO_2$ accumulates in the upper atmosphere, it creates a blanket effect, trapping heat and preventing the nightly cooling of the Earth. Other gases, such as methane, also contribute to creating the thermal blanket. How much human-generated $CO_2$ is responsible for global warming is a bit less certain. Over the Earth's history during the last 400 million years, there have been cycles of rising and declining temperature, each of which has lasted 150,000 years or so. The last high peak was about 125,000 years ago; the following low was about 10,000 years ago, after which temperatures began to rise again. Some argue that the current global warming trend is partly an extension of the long-term trend that has been accelerated since the beginning of the industrial revolution in the 1700s. Others attributed most of increasing concentrations of $CO_2$ and global temperatures to global warming gasses generated by the surge of fossil fuel burning in recent centuries. What is clear is that over the last century Earth's average temperature has risen about 1.1 degree Fahrenheit and that the last decade has been the warmest since temperature records were first kept in 1856. Most scientists also believe that global warming will have a dramatic and in some cases catastrophic impact on rainfall, wind currents, and other climatic patterns. Among other impacts, the polar ice caps are already melting more quickly. As a result, sea levels will rise, displacing perhaps over 100 million people on the continents' coasts during the coming century. Some weather experts also project an increase in the number and intensity of hurricanes and other catastrophic weather events. Droughts will also dry once fertile lands. It may also be the case, though, that warming will turn once marginal lands in the north into more productive areas.

Analyzing the problems is much more difficult than coming up with a solution. There have been long international negotiations, and, as a result, some countries have reduced their $CO_2$ emissions, but overall they have continued to grow rapidly. A major cause has been the economic development of China, India, and other less developed countries and the steep increases in their emissions. These argue they cannot be asked to abandon their development and cannot afford costly processes to develop alternative energy sources and to clean up coal and emissions from other traditional fossil fuels. The United States and some other industrialized nations have balked at giving aid to these countries or at imposing strict and, arguably, economically costly limits on their own emission unless the less developed countries also adopt restrictions.

There is also tremendous debate how costly restrictions on $CO_2$ emissions will be. Some argue that developing alternative energy and other activities will offset the cost of restrictions. Others argue that higher energy prices and other costs will cause serious economic damage. Whatever the correct answer, the global economic downturn since 2008 and the weak recovery have made most countries unwilling to risk their economies.

In the readings for this debate, neither of the authors dismisses global warming as a problem. Instead, they differ on the path to a solution. Elliot Diringer argues that since global warming is a globally generated phenomenon that has global impacts, the solution must involve global negotiations. Stephen Hayward favors abandoning what he sees as fruitless international negotiations and on imposing economically damaging emissions restrictions and instead launching a massive U.S. effort to develop and employ energy that will generate fewer or no emissions. This includes nuclear energy.

# YES ↵

**Elliot Diringer**

# The Threats of Climate Change

**C**limate change poses a serious long-term threat to our nation's resources, our economic well-being, and our national security. While action to address climate change must begin at home, this is a quintessentially global challenge, which therefore requires a global solution. I would like to focus my testimony today on three topics: (1) the status of the international climate negotiations, and the objectives that should guide U.S. climate diplomacy; (2) the policies being implemented in other countries—including our major trading partners—to reduce greenhouse gas emissions; and (3) the environmental, economic, and security rationales for stronger climate action.

My principal points are as follows:

- The past two years have seen the emergence of a more realistic and balanced approach in the international climate negotiations, thanks in large measure to the efforts of U.S. negotiators. The United States must remain fully engaged in the talks with the aim of strengthening multilateral support and transparency, thereby promoting action while laying the groundwork for a future binding agreement.
- A growing number of countries are pursuing policies that help reduce greenhouse gas emissions. Many see the challenge as an important opportunity as well. Some of our major trading partners are moving aggressively to grow their clean energy technology industries, which create domestic jobs and high-value exports. Without stronger policies creating similar incentives here, the United States risks falling further behind in the rapidly expanding clean energy market.
- U.S. inaction on climate change exposes our nation to real and rising risks. The longer we delay action, the harder it will be to avert the worst consequences of warming, the higher the cost of coping with those that cannot be avoided, and the further we fall behind in the clean energy race. Taking steps now to expand clean energy and reduce greenhouse gas emissions is squarely in our strong national interest.

## Moving the Negotiations Forward

Multilateral regimes do not generally spring forth fully formed—rather, they evolve over time. The international climate effort is no different. It began with the 1992 United Nations Framework Convention on Climate Change (UNFCCC), which was signed by the President George H. W. Bush and

U.S. House of Representatives, May 25, 2011.

unanimously ratified by the U.S. Senate. The UNFCCC, now ratified by 195 parties, established a long-term objective of preventing "dangerous anthropogenic interference with the climate system" and a framework within which countries can work together to achieve it. To be certain, countries' positions in the climate negotiations are heavily conditioned by their respective national interests. But underlying the Framework Convention is a clear recognition that countries share a common interest in averting dangerous climate change. And a fundamental principle of the Convention is that while our respective responsibilities are differentiated, depending on nations' circumstances, we all share a common responsibility for meeting this common challenge.

Since the signing of the Framework Convention, the climate regime has evolved in fits and starts. While the Convention is largely voluntary in nature, countries resolved shortly after its entry into force that stronger action was needed, and initiated a new round of negotiations aimed at establishing binding emission targets for developed countries. This led in 1997 to the Kyoto Protocol. Although the United States chose not to participate, Kyoto entered into force in 2005, and most other industrialized countries are on track to meeting their obligations. For many countries, the principal aim since 2005 has been to extend this legally binding regime through a second round of targets. But many of the countries with targets have made clear that they will not assume new binding obligations without commensurate commitments by the United States and the major developing economies. Through this prolonged stalemate, the negotiations were stuck in a mode of binding-or-nothing, and consequently produced virtually nothing.

Over the past two years, however, we have seen the emergence of a more realistic, more balanced and more constructive approach, in large measure through the efforts of the United States. Many viewed the Copenhagen summit in 2009 as a major failure because they had hoped—unrealistically—that it would produce a binding agreement. In our view, the Copenhagen Accord, negotiated personally by President Obama and other world leaders, represented genuine progress. Among other things, the Accord set an aspirational goal of limiting global temperature increase to 2 degrees Celsius; set goals for mobilizing financial support to help developing countries reduce emissions, preserve forests, and adapt to climate change; and established the broad parameters of a system to ensure transparency and accountability. What's more, it provided for mitigation pledges from both developed and developing countries. As a result, for the first time ever, all of the world's major economies—including China and India—have now made explicit pledges to reduce or limit their greenhouse gas emissions.

In the chaotic final hours in Copenhagen, the Accord was not formally adopted by the UNFCCC Conference of the Parties. However, at the 16th Conference of the Parties last year in Cancún, parties adopted a package of decisions incorporating the essential elements of the Copenhagen Accord into the UNFCCC framework, and taking initial steps to implement them. The Cancún Agreements represent the most tangible progress within the UNFCCC negotiations in nearly a decade. First, they memorialize the pledges taken under the Copenhagen Accord by more than 80 countries accounting for more than

80 percent of global emissions. Second, the Agreements establish the fundamentals of a stronger support system for developing countries, and a stronger transparency system enabling countries to verify whether others are fulfilling their pledges.

The Agreements also reflect a more flexible and realistic framework for enshrining countries' actions. Unlike the Kyoto Protocol, which allows only one type of commitment (a binding emissions target with a prescribed, common base year), the Agreements allow for a diversity of approaches. In the case of developed countries, pledges take the form of economy-wide emission targets, but with flexibility on base year and accounting. Developing countries have even broader discretion in defining their "nationally appropriate mitigation actions." China and India, for instance, have pledged reductions in emissions intensity (emissions per unit of GDP), while Brazil, South Africa, Mexico and the Republic of Korea have pledged to reduce emissions below "business as usual." This more realistic and balanced approach reflected in the Cancún Agreements, as well as the movement toward greater transparency for all major economies, are direct consequences of U.S. engagement and leadership in the climate negotiations.

It is important to emphasize that the pledges countries have made at this stage are voluntary in nature. We continue to believe that the global response to climate change should ultimately be enshrined in fair, effective and binding commitments among all of the world's major economies. Countries will deliver their strongest possible efforts only if they are confident that others are also contributing their fair share, and this confidence is best maintained through mutual and binding commitments. We also recognize, however, that it will be a number of years before the United States, China, and other key countries are prepared to assume binding commitments. Under these circumstances, we believe the United States must remain fully engaged in the climate negotiations with the aim of strengthening the UNFCCC as a means of delivering support and transparency, thereby promoting near-term action while laying the groundwork for a future legal agreement.

At the Conference of the Parties later this year in Durban, we believe the aim should be further progress on the operational issues addressed in the Cancún Agreements, including the launch of a new Green Climate Fund to support developing country efforts and significant progress in strengthening transparency through new "measurement, reporting and verification" practices; and a clear declaration by parties of their intent to work toward legally binding outcomes. This outcome would build on the achievements of the past two years and continue the incremental progress needed to strengthen confidence in the regime and among parties.

# Efforts in Other Countries

While international agreements and commitments are critical to our success in addressing global climate change, a more important measure of efforts to date are the policies and actions countries are undertaking domestically. A growing number of countries are developing or implementing policies contributing in one way or another to reducing greenhouse gas emissions. Many see the challenge as an important opportunity as well. A number of our major trading partners are moving aggressively to grow their clean energy technology industries, which create domestic jobs and high-value exports. Without stronger policies creating similar incentives here, the United States risks falling further behind our competitors in the rapidly expanding clean energy market.

The European Union is a clear leader in the development, manufacture, and deployment of clean technologies. The EU has set mandatory targets to reduce greenhouse gas emissions 20 percent below 1990 levels, and to increase renewables to 20 percent of its energy mix, by 2020. The centerpiece of EU climate policy is the Emissions Trading System (ETS) launched in 2005, which regulates carbon dioxide emissions ($CO_2$) in the power and major industrial sectors generating about half of the EU's $CO_2$ emissions. Having overcome the early complications typical of a new compliance market, the system is set to expand in 2012 to cover other gases and the aviation sector. Europe's clean energy investments, the world's largest, doubled from 2009 to 2010, reaching nearly $81 billion. From 2004, the year before the ETS began, through 2008, the year before the global financial crisis, the European Union reduced its emissions 4.1 percent, while its GDP grew 9.8 percent.

China also has taken major steps towards increasing its manufacture and use of clean energy technologies. Under the Cancún Agreements, China pledged that by 2020 it will reduce the $CO_2$ intensity of its economy 40 to 45 percent below 2005 levels; increase the share of nonfossil fuels in primary energy consumption to 15 percent by 2020; and increase forest coverage by 40 million hectares and forest stock volume by 1.3 billion cubic meters. These targets are reflected in domestic policy as well. Additional policies include a national target for renewables to provide 15 percent of primary energy by 2020, with specific targets for wind, solar, biomass, and hydropower; feed-in tariffs for onshore wind power; and proposed fuel efficiency standards requiring urban cars and light trucks to achieve an average of 36.9 miles per gallon by 2015. The Five-Year Plan adopted by the Chinese leadership in March devotes considerable attention to energy and climate, establishing a series of targets and policies for 2011–2015.

These include a suite of policies to promote innovation in new strategic and emerging technologies, including nuclear, solar, wind, biomass, and hybrid and electric vehicles. The plan also includes a goal to "gradually establish a carbon trade market."

To be certain, China continues to build coal-fired power plants as well, and its emissions continue to rise. A recent analysis by the Lawrence Berkeley National Laboratory projects that on the present path China's emissions will peak between 2030 and 2035. But the climate and energy provisions of the new Five-Year Plan show how China is moving forward with domestic policies in line with the pledge it offered in Copenhagen and formalized in the Cancún Agreements. Many of the policies also are clearly calculated to help ensure that China—which recently surpassed the United States and other countries to become the leading manufacturer of wind turbines and solar panels—retains a strong competitive edge going forward.

Other major developing countries are also stepping up their efforts to limit emissions growth and transition to cleaner energy. India, which pledged to reduce its emissions intensity (excluding the agricultural sector) 20 to 25 percent below 2005 levels by 2020, is pursuing a range of policies under its 2008 National Action Plan on Climate Change, including a renewable energy target; a feed-in tariff for renewable energy; a market-based system of tradable energy savings certificates in industrial sectors; and a coal levy generating finance for clean energy research and innovation. Brazil and Indonesia have set goals to reduce deforestation. South Africa has set national renewable energy and energy efficiency targets and established a renewable energy feed-in tariff. Meanwhile, the governments of Mexico and South Korea have proposed establishing emissions trading systems.

While the global picture is uneven, these examples demonstrate a growing will among countries to undertake a wide variety of measures to promote clean energy and to reduce greenhouse gas emissions.

# Addressing Climate Change Is in Our National Interest

Earlier I emphasized that all nations share a common interest in averting dangerous climate change. It is important to understand why stronger efforts to address climate change and pursue clean energy are in our direct national interest as well. There are many reasons, whether from an environmental, national security, or economic perspective.

## Environmental Risks

The scientific and environmental rationale for lowering our greenhouse gas emissions is clear and compelling. As again underscored two weeks ago in America's Climate Choices, a report produced by the U.S. National Academy of Sciences at the request of Congress, "Climate change is occurring, is very likely caused by human activities, and poses significant risks for a broad range of human and natural systems."

On these fundamental points, there is very strong consensus within the scientific community. Due largely to the combustion of fossil fuels, atmospheric concentrations of carbon dioxide are at their highest level in at least 800,000 years. Over the last century, average global temperatures rose more than 1 degree Fahrenheit and in some places, including parts of the United States, temperatures rose more than 4 degrees.

If greenhouse gas emissions continue to grow, average global temperatures are projected to reach 2.0°F to 11.5°F (1.1°C to 6.4°C) above pre-industrial levels by 2100, with warming in the U.S. expected to be even higher. We are already witnessing the impacts of climate change here in the United States; the widespread flooding now afflicting communities along the Mississippi River vividly illustrates how vulnerable we are to the rising risks associated with climate change. Most of North America is experiencing increasing numbers of unusually warm days and nights and a decreasing number of unusually cool ones. At the same time, droughts are occurring more frequently while snow-packs are melting earlier in the year. Sea-level rise of 8 inches or more has been recorded in some coastal areas of the country.

Continued warming will mean further sea-level rise, elevating storm surges and gradually inundating low-lying coastal areas along all U.S. coast-lines; increased frequency and severity of extreme weather events; increased risk of droughts and floods; significant threats to ecosystems and biodiversity; and increased public health risks. Beyond such readily foreseeable impacts, the longer warming persists and the greater its magnitude, the greater the risk of abrupt or catastrophic changes in the global climate.

Actions to reduce the risks of climate change by lowering greenhouse gas emissions have other environmental co-benefits as well. Lower-carbon tech-nologies such as natural gas and renewable energy also emit less of other pol-lutants including nitrogen dioxide, particulates, sulfur dioxide, lead, carbon monoxide, mercury, and other hazardous pollutants that have a wide range of harmful health effects, from asthma to cancer and premature death. Past regulatory efforts to reduce these pollutants have proven highly successful and cost-effective. The Office of Management and Budget (OMB) found that from 1992 to 2002 "major rules" enacted under the Clean Air Act produced benefits of between $145 billion and $218 billion a year, far exceeding the annual costs $22 billion to $25 billion. A study by researchers at MIT found total annual benefits rising from $50 billion in 1975 to $400 billion in 2000. We can expand these benefits by moving towards cleaner energy sources.

## Security Risks

America's military leaders recognize that climate change also poses increas-ing risks to our national security and new demands on our military resources. According to the Pentagon's latest Quadrennial Defense Review, climate change may act as "an accelerant of instability or conflict, placing a burden to respond on civilian institutions and militaries around the world."

Indeed, climate change will be a threat multiplier, further destabilizing regions of the world already burdened with countless other problems. Chronic drought, rising seas, extreme weather and other climate impacts could under-mine weak governments, induce mass migrations, and trigger or heighten resource competition, contributing to social instability and, potentially, armed conflict. Rising seas could displace as many as 30 million people in Bangladesh, creating additional tensions on the Indian subcontinent. Reced-ing glaciers could leave millions across Asia facing chronic water shortages. A distinguished group of retired three- and four-star U.S. military officers warns that drought, thirst, and hunger are already exacerbating the conflicts and humanitarian disasters in Darfur and Somalia, and climate change portends more situations like these.

Within the past year, devastating floods in Pakistan have strained the resources and stability of a key U.S. ally in the battle against international terrorism, and an intense drought and heat wave has diminished food produc-tion in Eastern Europe and Central Asia, causing a spike in global wheat prices.

Yemen, where the CIA says Al Qaeda is of greatest concern today, is running out of groundwater for its under-employed population.

While these events cannot be directly attributed to climate change, scientists are very clear that these types of events will occur more frequently in a warming world.

Other security issues are arising closer to home. The Arctic has long been a place where defense issues were minimized because the waterways were largely frozen over year-round. With warming now occurring there at twice the average global rate, the Arctic Ocean is opening to military and civilian transportation, and the potential security implications are already apparent. Receding sea ice is creating increased competition over territory and resources in a region where the United States is currently unprepared to address potential military situations. Protecting our nation's security necessarily involves being prepared to deal with an uncertain future. Indeed, planning under uncertainty is business as usual for the defense community. The fact that military and security experts are increasingly concerned about the risks associated with climate change should serve as an important wake-up call to us all.

## Economic Risks

Finally, addressing climate change is very much in our economic interest. The United States is the world's leading manufacturer, producing 21 percent of global output while supporting 18.6 million domestic jobs. Yet in the growing clean energy sector, we risk falling further behind our competitors because the demand for these goods is not as strong at home as it is overseas. China and other countries are investing heavily in clean energy technologies, positioning themselves to compete in a growing global market projected to reach $106 billion to $230 billion a year in 2020, and as much as $424 billion a year in 2030. In order for the United States to develop a successful, profitable, and competitive clean energy sector, companies need clear regulatory frameworks ensuring a strong domestic market for these goods.

The recent experience of the U.S. auto industry provides an instructive case study. While the technology in our cars has advanced significantly in the last two decades, the typical new vehicle today consumes gasoline at about the same rate as one produced in the late 1980s. But with gas prices again rising, consumers are increasingly turning to more fuel-efficient vehicles. Spurred by fuel economy standards enacted in 2007, American automakers have been ready to meet their customers' needs. U.S. automakers reported strong sales and combined profits of nearly $5.9 billion in the first quarter of 2011, and all three cited higher sales of fuel-efficient vehicles as a contributing factor. Last year, the Smart car was the only conventional car available in the United States with a fuel economy rating of 40 miles per gallon or better. Today there are nine, and three of them—the Cruze, Elantra, and Focus—were among the 10 top-selling vehicles last month. All three are made in the United States.

Unfortunately, similar examples in the clean energy field must be found outside the United States. In Germany, for instance, renewable energy policies helped boost jobs in the renewable energy sector from 160,000 in 2004 to 370,000 in 2010. The German government credits this dramatic growth in clean energy jobs as a major factor in its relatively fast recovery from the 2008 recession. Germany's renewable energy sector is projected to employ about 450,000 to 580,000 workers by 2020, and between 500,000 and 600,000 in 2030.

By contrast, U.S. clean energy manufacturers are increasingly finding their biggest growth opportunities overseas. First Solar, Inc., of Arizona, the world's second largest solar manufacturer, plans to build a 2,000-megawatt solar photovoltaic power plant in China—the largest planned project of its kind in the world.

While First Solar will also add new manufacturing jobs at its U.S. facilities, at least 71 percent of its planned growth is outside the United States. U.S. firms remain among the world's top innovators. But if our clean energy firms are to invest and create jobs at home, and compete effectively overseas, we must provide the regulatory certainty that creates strong, sustained demand for their goods here in the United States. Doing so will strengthen our economy while protecting the United States against the risks of climate change.

## Conclusion

Mr. Chairman, U.S. inaction on climate change exposes our nation to real and rising risks. The longer we delay action, the harder it will be to avert the worst consequences of warming, the higher the cost of coping with those that cannot be avoided, and the further we fall behind other countries in the clean energy race. Taking steps now to expand clean energy and reduce greenhouse gas emissions is quite clearly in our strong national interest. As the world's largest economy, leading innovator, and largest cumulative emitter, the United States also has a responsibility to the international community. Thanks to U.S. efforts, the global climate effort now appears headed on a more reasonable course. Our ability to continue to shape that effort in the years ahead depends heavily on a demonstrated commitment to address climate change here at home.

Steven F. Hayward

## → NO

# Climate Change Negotiations: Implausible and Unpromising

I will begin with my contentious conclusion, which is that the international diplomacy of climate change is the most implausible and unpromising initiative since the disarmament talks of the 1930s, and for many of the same reasons; that the Kyoto Protocol and its progeny are the climate diplomacy equivalent of the Kellogg-Briand Pact of 1928 that promised to end war (a treaty that is still on the books, by the way), and finally, that future historians are going to look back on this whole period as the climate policy equivalent of wage and price controls to fight inflation in the 1970s.

The diplomatic approach—the United Nations Framework Convention on Climate Change UNFCCC)—first set in motion formally at the Rio Earth Summit in 1992 has reached a dead end. I think the dead end of what might be called "first generation climate diplomacy" was tacitly on view at the last major climate summit in Cancun a few months ago. It is important to understand the deeper reasons why if we are going to chart a new course on climate that has a better chance of making real progress.

When the issue of climate change came to the fore in the late 1980s, the diplomatic community approached it in a way that seemed eminently sensible on the surface: what diplomatic frameworks have worked before for similar kinds of global problems? In other words, diplomats reached for what was on the shelf. There were basically three models for problems of global reach that had shown varying degrees of success: the arms control and anti-proliferation regimes; the long-running and painstaking trade liberalization process; and third and perhaps most applicable, the Montreal Protocol that facilitated the organized phase out of chlorofluorocarbons. The last two, especially the Montreal Protocol, are the precedents that former Vice President Gore liked to cite as reasons for his support and enthusiasm for the Kyoto Protocol. And on the surface the comparative logic seems plausible: if we can reach a binding and enforceable agreement to phase out chlorofluorocarbons, why not a similarly structured agreement to phase out hydrocarbons?

But once you poke beneath the surface, a number of fundamental asymmetries between these precedents and the problem of climate change become apparent, but whose implications were resisted for the understandable reasons of diplomatic and institutional inertia. I'll confine myself to just a few of the many that came into play.

From U.S. House of Representatives, May 25, 2011.

First, the problem of climate change is orders of magnitude more complex and difficult than the problem of ozone depletion. It is not necessary to embrace the skeptical position about "uncertainty" in climate science to suggest that the same kind of policy dynamic found in the problem of the ozone layer would work equally well for a warming planet. In the case of chlorofluorocarbons and the ozone layer, the scientific evidence was straightforward, the time scale was relatively short, and, most importantly, there were scalable substitutes for CFCs available at a reasonable cost. By contrast, the climate science is much more complex, and even if the complexities wash out, the focus on near-term reductions in greenhouse gas emissions is unlike the near-term reduction in CFCs under the Montreal Protocol for a blindingly simple reason: There are no economically scalable substitutes to fossil fuels available on the global level and in the relatively short time frame contemplated by climate orthodoxy.

The second asymmetry concerns the divide in interests between wealthy nations and poorer developing nations. Poor nations have an overriding interest in affordable energy, which means cheap energy, which means fossil fuel energy. The architects of the Kyoto Protocol recognized this, just as we have recognized this in the trade liberalization process and in the phase out schedules of the Montreal Protocol. But the two-tiered structure of emission limit commitments contemplated in Kyoto came at the very moment that the mid-20th century's conceptual dichotomy between "developed" and "developing" nations was breaking down very rapidly. The hazard of potentially costly emissions limits for wealthy nations was that it would accelerate the globalizing trend of driving manufacturing activity to the developing nations. In fact, the two-tiered architecture of the climate emissions restrictions actually increased the near-term incentives for developing nations to resist emission limits. We should not have been surprised that many developing nations, especially China and India, made it clear that they will not go along with binding emission limits for future iterations of the Kyoto Protocol. In this respect climate diplomacy foundered on the same kind of problems that have made the trade liberalization process so slow and excruciating, even though it is a process that promises to make everyone richer.

A process that entails slowing down economic growth, even marginally, is going to be much more difficult to achieve.

The more recent answer to this problem was climate assistance to developing nations. On the merits this policy is incommensurate with the nature and scale of the problem, and appears more as an attempt simply to bribe developing nations into going along with the preferred agenda of wealthy nations. Many developing nations are happy to go along with the charade if we'll actually send the cash.

One of the problems of the sheer sprawling nature of climate change science and policy is that it became something of an all-purpose issue on which advocates could attach their pet ideas and concerns. The idea of climate adjustment assistance has revived at the UN an old idea from the 1970s—what was called then the "New International Economic Order." The premise of the New International Economic Order, as explained at the time by West Germany's

Chancellor Willy Brandt, was that there needed to be "a large scale transfer of resources to developing countries." This was back in the hey-day of post-colonial Western guilt, and it came to an abrupt end in the 1980s when President Reagan forcefully repudiated it at a UN summit in, coincidentally, Cancun.

But climate assistance has revived the old idea of requiring wealthy nations to indemnify poor nations. The German newspaper *Neue Zürcher Zeitung* observed shortly before the Cancun summit last year: "The next world climate summit in Cancun is actually an economy summit during which the distribution of the world's resources will be negotiated." What prompted this conclusion was a candid admission from a UN official closely involved with the climate negotiations, German economist Ottmar Edenhoffer: "But one must say clearly that we redistribute de facto the world's wealth by climate policy. Obviously, the owners of coal and oil will not be enthusiastic about this. One has to free oneself from the illusion that international climate policy is environmental policy. This has almost nothing to do with environmental policy anymore."

This is the kind of loose and unserious talk that brings discredit to the UN and to international climate diplomacy. But it is very popular with much of the UN's constituency, and America's diplomatic corps indulges this mentality with polite indifference. With only a few exceptions, such as under [U.S. ambassadors to the United Nations] Pat Moynihan in the 1970s and Jeane Kirkpatrick in the 1980s, American diplomats do not call out this kind of redistributionist enthusiasm, or if they have, that fact goes un-advertised to the American public, which quite sensibly hears these kinds of sentiments and forms a low opinion of the UN.

I conclude briefly with two observations. First, the nation that made the largest climate assistance commitment at Cancun—to the tune of $15 billion—was Japan. I don't think there is anyone who thinks Japan should make good on that commitment right now. This suggests how events may rapidly change our perceptions and priorities of risk.

Second, what approach can replace the UN diplomatic track? This is a long subject, but a more likely path to more significant climate outcomes would focus not on emissions limits but an emphasis on cheap decarbonization of energy through innovation, the approach we at AEI [American Enterprise Institute] have recommended in collaboration with the Brookings Institution and the Progressive-leaning Breakthrough Institute in California in a report called "Post-Partisan Power." And the diplomatic framework for this would ignore the UN and start with the leading economies of the OECD [Organization of Economic Cooperation and Development] nations, a process begun tentatively by the Bush Administration, but which now appears to have been embraced by the Obama Administration in the aftermath of the failures of Copenhagen and Cancun.

# EXPLORING THE ISSUE

## Are International Negotiations to Control Global Warming Useful?

## Questions for Critical Thinking and Reflection

1. What has been your perceived experience of global warming?
2. There has been a tendency among Americans, at least, to support restraints on $CO_2$ emissions and other steps to curb global warming but to resist paying the lifestyle or economic price to implement many of the steps, such as higher gasoline taxes to suppress use. How far would you be willing to go to support such steps?
3. How would you feel about the dangers of nuclear energy versus the dangers of global warming?

## Is There Common Ground?

A first international effort to control $CO_2$ emissions was the UN-sponsored treaty called the Kyoto Protocol in 1997. It requires the industrialized countries to significantly cut their $CO_2$ emissions but imposed no limits on developing countries including China and India. Objecting to this, the United States did not ratify the treaty. With the limits set by the Kyoto Protocol extending only through 2012, an international conference gathered in 2009, in Copenhagen, Denmark, to try to establish a few round of reductions. The resulting Copenhagen Accord adopted new limits, but was still adjudged a failure by many analysts because none of the limits was binding and even the nonbinding limits were cuts in projected future levels, not from current levels. It is clear that unless countries get much more serious about reducing $CO_2$ emissions they will continue to grow. Indeed, even if the Copenhagen targets are met, they will only slow down the growth. Between 2000 and 2010, the world growth rate has averaged about 3 percent annually.

Over the last century or so, most of the emissions have come from the United States and Western Europe, and, thus, they arguably have a special burden to curb global warming. But in the past few years, China has become the major source of $CO_2$ emissions. As of 2011, it produced 29 percent of the global total, compared to 16 percent by the United States. From a different perspective, though, U.S. per capita emissions are about twice those of China. The European Union is third (11 percent) in terms of emissions, and India is fourth (6 percent), just ahead of Russia and Japan. For annual reports on emissions, go to the website of PBL—The Netherlands Environmental Assessment Agency—at www.pbl.nl/en/publications/2012/. Some countries use considerable amounts of nuclear energy, and that reduces their $CO_2$ emissions. Nuclear power provides

78 percent of electricity in France compared to 18 percent of Germany's electricity, a difference that helps account for the fact that German's per capita $CO_2$ emissions are about 50 percent higher than those of France. Fears have long held back the development of nuclear power, and those fears were compounded by the March 2011 earthquake and tsunami that severely damaged Japan's Fukushima Dai-ichi nuclear power plant and caused some leaks of radioactivity into the air and surrounding waters. Opponents of nuclear power portray what happened as a warning. Proponents of nuclear power note that the consequences have not been anywhere near as dire as those initially projected and argue that steps can be taken to make nuclear power plants safer. There is also geothermal, wind, and other possible sources of no/low emissions energy, but they currently are both expensive and far from being adequate to power a significant part of the energy needs of an advanced economy. Perhaps a country could develop these resources through a massive effort equivalent to the Manhattan Project used by the United States during World War II to build the atomic bomb. But the need for huge financial resources in a time of a weak economy has made any such project unlikely.

## Additional Resources

More on the issues involved in this debate is found in David G. Victor, *Global Warming Gridlock: Creating More Effective Strategies for Protecting the Planet* (Cambridge University Press, 2011). The political milieu in which domestic and international efforts to limit or reverse global warming exist is covered by Anthony Giddens, *The Politics of Climate Change* (Polity, 2011). The U.S. Environmental Protection Agency has a good site on global warming at http://epa.gov/climatechange/ index.html. Also excellent is the UN's entry site on global warming information at www.un.org/wcm/content/site/climatechange/ gateway. An Internet site that takes a skeptical view of the alarm over global warming can be found at www.globalwarming.org/. Taking the opposite view is the Environmental Defense Fund at www.fightglobalwarming.com/, a site that includes the ability to engage your individual impact on global warming at www.ucsusa.org/.

# Contributors to This Volume

## EDITOR

**JOHN T. ROURKE, PhD,** is a professor emeritus of political science at the University of Connecticut. He has written numerous articles, book chapters, and papers, and is also the author of *Congress, the Executive, and U.S. Foreign Policymaking* (Westview Press, 1985); *International Relations on the World Stage*, 12 editions (McGraw-Hill, 1987–2008); *Making Foreign Policy: United States, Soviet Union, China* (Brooks/Cole, 1990); *Presidential War and American Democracy: Rally Round the Chief* (Paragon House, 1993); and *America's Politics: A Diverse Country in a Globalizing World* (Paradigm, 2011). Professor Rourke is the co-author of *Direct Democracy and International Politics: Deciding International Issues Through Referendums*, with Richard Hiskes and Cyrus E. Zirakzadeh (Lynne Rienner Publisher, 1992); *Making American Foreign Policy*, with Ralph Carter and Mark Boyer, 2 editions (Brown & Benchmark, 1994, 1996); and *International Politics on the World Stage: Brief Edition*, with Mark Boyer, 8 editions (McGraw-Hill, 1996–2009). In addition to this edition of *Taking Sides: Clashing Views in World Politics* (McGraw Hill, 1987–2007), he is the editor of *Taking Sides: Clashing Views on Controversial Issues in American Foreign Policy*, 2 editions (Dushkin 2000, 2002) and *You Decide: Current Debates in American Politics*, 9 editions (Longman, 2004–2012). A long career in both the academic and applied sides of politics has convinced the author that politics impacts everyone and that those who become knowledgeable and get active to promote what they believe in, whether that is based on self-interest or altruism, are the single most important driving force in the ultimate contest: politics.

# AUTHORS

**MAHMOUD ABBAS** is chairman of the Palestine Liberation Organization (PLO) and president of the Palestinian National Authority.

**HOWARD BERMAN** is a Democratic member of the U.S. House of Representatives from California.

**PIETER BOTTELIER** is a nonresident scholar in Carnegie's International Economics Program, and senior adjunct professor of China studies at the School of Advanced International Studies (SAIS) at Johns Hopkins University. He has held numerous positions at the World Bank including senior advisor to the vice president for East Asia, chief of the resident mission in Beijing, and director for Latin America.

**JASON CHAFFETZ** is a Republican member of the U.S. House of Representatives from Utah.

**GORDON G. CHANG** is a Forbes.com columnist specializing in China. He worked as a lawyer in Hong Kong from 1981 to 1991 and in Shanghai from 1996 to 2001 and is the author of *The Coming Collapse of China* (Random House, 2001) and *Nuclear Showdown: North Korea Takes on the World* (Random House, 2006).

**DEAN CHENG** is a research fellow for Chinese political and security affairs at The Heritage Foundation.

**HILLARY RODHAM CLINTON** is the U.S. Secretary of State. She formerly served as a U.S. senator from New York and holds a JD degree from Yale University.

**ARIEL COHEN** is a senior research fellow for Russian and Eurasian Studies and International Energy Policy at The Heritage Foundation. He is the author of numerous articles and book chapters and *Russian Imperialism: Development and Crisis* (Greenwood/Praeger, 1996) and the editor of *Eurasia in Balance* (Ashgate Publishing, 2005). He hold a PhD from the Fletcher School of Law and Diplomacy at Tufts University.

**URI DADUSH** is a senior associate in and the director of the International Economics Program at the Carnegie Endowment of International Peace. His former posts at the World Bank have included director of international trade and director of economic policy. He holds a PhD in business economics from Harvard University.

**ELLIOT DIRINGER** is vice president of international strategies at the Pew Center on Global Climate Change (the Center for Climate and Energy Solutions). He is a former reporter and editor at the *San Francisco Chronicle*, served from 1997 to 2000 as director of communications and senior policy advisor at the White House Council on Environmental Quality and deputy assistant to the president and deputy White House press secretary (2000–2001). He has a BA degree in environmental studies from Haverford College and was a Nieman fellow studying environmental law and policy at Harvard University.

**JONATHAN F. FANTON** is president of the John D. and Catherine T. MacArthur Foundation. He has also served as president of the New School for Social

Research and vice president for Planning at the University of Chicago. He has a PhD in American history from Yale University.

**STEVEN GROVES** is Bernard and Barbara Lomas fellow in the Margaret Thatcher Center for Freedom, a division of the Kathryn and Shelby Cullom Davis Institute for International Studies, The Heritage Foundation. He has served as senior counsel to the U.S. Senate Permanent Subcommittee on Investigations and as an assistant attorney general for the state of Florida. Groves received his law degree from Ohio Northern University.

**STEVEN F. HAYWARD** is the F. K. Weyerhaeuser fellow at the American Enterprise Institute. He served as contributing editor of the journal *Reason* (1990–2001) and is the author of several books including a two-volume biography of Ronald Reagan, *The Age of Reagan, 1964–1980: The Fall of the Old Liberal Order* (2001) and *The Age of Reagan: The Conservative Counterrevolution: 1980–1989* (2009). He has a PhD from Claremont Graduate School.

**HU JINTAO** serves as a general secretary of the Communist Party of China, president of the People's Republic of China, and chairman of the Central Military Commission.

**SIMON JOHNSON** is the Ronald Kurtz Professor of Entrepreneurship, MIT Sloan School of Management, and a senior fellow at the Peterson Institute for International Economics. He is also co-founder of http://BaselineScenario. com; a member of the Congressional Budge Office's Panel of Economic Advisers; and a member of the Federal Deposit Insurance Corporation's Systemic Resolution Advisory Committee.

**WALTER B. JONES** is a Democratic member of the U.S. House of Representatives from North Carolina.

**DENNIS KUCINICH** is a Democratic member of the U.S. House of Representatives from Ohio.

**BARBARA LEE** is a Democratic member of the U.S. House of Representatives from California.

**MICHAEL W. LEWIS** is a professor of law at Ohio Northern University's Pettit College of Law, where he teaches and writes in the fields of international law and the law of armed conflict. He has served as a U.S. Navy fighter pilot and holds a JD from Harvard University.

**ANDREW C. McCARTHY** is a columnist for the *National Review*. He is a former assistant U.S. attorney for the Southern District of New York and during that time led the 1995 terrorism prosecution of Sheik Omar Abdel Rahman and eleven others for their roles in the 1993 bomb attack on World Trade Center in New York City. He has a JD from New York University's law school.

**BUCK McKEON** is a Democratic member of the U.S. House of Representatives from California.

**BENJAMIN NETANYAHU** is the prime minister of Israel and chairman of the Likud political party. He earlier served as Israel's minister of finance (2003–2005) and minister of foreign affairs (2002–2003). He was born in Israel, but live extensively in the United States, earning his high school degree there and bachelor's and master's degrees from the Massachusetts Institute of Technology.

**MARY ELLEN O'CONNELL** is the research professor of international dispute resolution at the Kroc Institute for International Peace Studies, the University of Notre Dame, and also the Robert and Marion Short Professor of Law at the university's law school. Among her publications is *The Power and Purpose of International Law* (Ohio State University Press, 2008). She earned her JD from Columbia University.

**RON PAUL** is a Republican member of the U.S. House of Representatives from Texas.

**PEACE PLEDGE UNION** is the oldest secular pacifist organization in Great Britain. Since 1934 it has been campaigning for a warless world.

**STEVEN PIFER** is the director of the Brookings Arms Control Initiative and a senior fellow in the Center on the United States and Europe. He is a former U.S. ambassador to Ukraine and served as Deputy Assistant Secretary of State (2001–2004) and as special assistant to the president and senior director for Russia, Ukraine, and Eurasia, National Security Council (1996–1997).

**PAUL R. PILLAR** teaches in the Security Studies Program at Georgetown University and was the national intelligence officer for the Near East and South Asia at the Central Intelligence Agency from 2000 to 2005. He has a PhD from Princeton University.

**NORMAN PODHORETZ** is the editor-at-large of *Commentary* and widely acknowledged as one of the most influential conservative thinkers of his time. He was awarded the Presidential Medal of Freedom by George W. Bush in 2004.

**RAVINDER RENA** is an associate professor of economics at the Eritrea Institute of Technology. He earned a PhD in economics at Osmania University, India.

**SUSAN E. RICE** is the U.S. permanent representative to the United Nations. During the presidency of Bill Clinton, she served in a range of high level posts including assistant secretary of state for African affairs (1997–2001). Rice also has been a Rhodes Scholar at Oxford University, and earned a doctorate there.

**ILEANA ROS-LEHTINEN** is a Republican member of the U.S. House of Representatives from Florida and chair of the Committee on Foreign Affairs.

**OTTO J. REICH** is the president of Otto Reich Associates, LLC, an international consulting firm, and a former U.S. assistant secretary of state for the Western Hemisphere (2002–2004). He has also served as the president's special envoy for the Western Hemisphere, as U.S. Ambassador to Venezuela, and as assistant administrator of the U.S. Agency for International Development.

**BRETT SCHAEFER** is the Jay Kingham fellow in international regulatory affairs at The Heritage Foundation. He has an MA degree in international development economics from the School of International Service at

American University. He has published an edited book, *ConUNdrum: The Limits of the United Nations and the Search for Alternatives* (Rowman & Littlefield, 2009).

**ADAM SMITH** is a Democratic member of the U.S. House of Representatives from Washington.

**BAKER SPRING** is F. M. Kirby Research Fellow in National Security Policy in the Douglas and Sarah Allison Center for Foreign Policy Studies at The Heritage Foundation. He served as a defense and foreign policy expert on the staffs of U.S. Senators Paula Hawkins (R-FL) and David Karnes (R-NE). He received his master's degree in national security studies from Georgetown University.

**ELLEN TAUSCHER** is the U.S. Under Secretary of State for Arms Control and International Security. She has served in the U.S. House of Representatives representing the Tenth Congressional District of California. She has been an investment banker and a member and officer of the New York Stock Exchange. Tauscher holds a BS degree from Seton Hall University.

**BRUCE S. THORNTON** is a research fellow at the Hoover Institution and a professor of classics and humanities at California State University in Fresno, California. He received a PhD degree in comparative literature from the University of California at Los Angeles. His most recent book is *The Wages of Appeasement: Ancient Athens, Munich, and Obama's America* (Encounter Books, 2011).

**ARTURO A. VALENZUELA** is the assistant secretary of state for the Bureau of Western Hemisphere Affairs, U.S. Department of State. During the Bill Clinton presidency, Valenzuela served as deputy assistant secretary of state for Inter-American Affairs and as special assistant to the president and senior director for inter-American affairs at the National Security Council. His academic posts have included professor of government and director of the Center for Latin American Studies in the Edmund A. Walsh School of Foreign Service at Georgetown University and professor of political science and director of the Council on Latin American Studies at Duke University. He holds a PhD in political science from Columbia University.

**PETER VAN UHM** is a general in the Royal Netherlands Army and Chief of the Netherlands' Defense Staff (the equivalent of the U.S. Joint Chiefs of Staff).

**MELANNE VERVEER** is ambassador-at-large, Office of Global Women's Issues, U.S. Department of State. She earlier served the former chief of staff for first lady Hillary Rodham Clinton and was chairman of the board of the Vital Voices Global Partnership, an international private organization supporting global women's leadership. She has an MA from Georgetown University.

**GUIDO WESTERWELLE** is Germany's Foreign Minister. He has served in the Germany's Parliament since 1966 and was vice chancellor of Germany from 2009 to 2011. He was also the chairman of the Free Democratic Party of Germany from 2001 to 2011.